0   1   2-5   6-10   11-20   21-40   40+

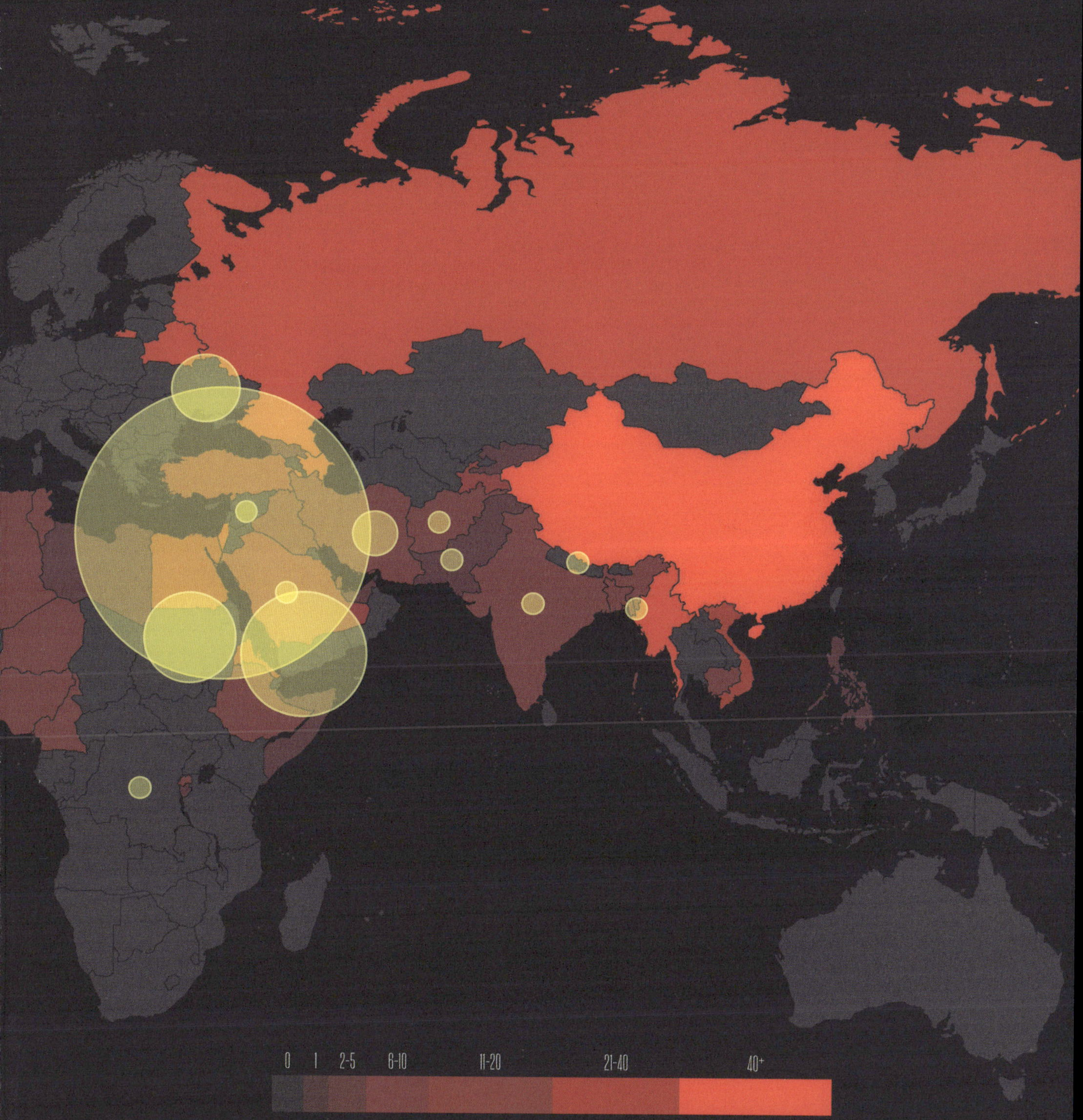

JOURNALISTS IN STATE CUSTODY AS OF 1 DECEMBER 2025

ABBAS
AL-DAILAMI
Yemen

ABDO TAHER
MUSLEH AL-SAADI
Yemen

ABDUL
GHAFOR ABED
Afghanistan

ABDULAZIZ
AL-SHEIKH
Yemen

ABDULLAH
AL-HARAZI
Yemen

ABDULLAH MAHDI
ABDULLAH AL-BAHRI
Yemen

ABDULQAWI
MOHAMMED SALEH
AL-ASFOUR
Yemen

ABDULRAHMAN
MOHAMMED
MOHAMMED JAMAN*
Yemen

ADAM
ABU HARBID
Palestine

AHMAD
QALAJA*
Palestine

AHMED ABU
AL-ROUS*
Palestine

AHMED
ABU AZIZ
Palestine

AHMED
ABU EISHA
Palestine

AHMED
AL SHAYYAH
Palestine

AHMED
AL-HELOU
Palestine

AHMED
MANSOUR
Palestine

AL-SHYKH AL-SAMANY
SAADALDYN MOUSA
ABDULLA 'SHEIKHO'*
Sudan

ALNOR
SULEIMAN ALNOR
Sudan

AMAL MOHAMMED
GHALEB AL-MANAKHI
Yemen

ANAS
AL-SHARIF
Palestine

ANTONI
LALLICAN*
Ukraine

AREEJ
SHAHEEN*
Palestine

ASADUZZAMAN
TUHIN
Bangladesh

AYMAN
HANIYEH
Palestine

BASHIR HUSSEIN
AHSAN DABLAN
Yemen

FARIS ABDO ALI
AL-RUMAISA
Yemen

FAROUK
AL-ZAHIR
Sudan

FATMA
HASSONA*
Palestine

FISTON
WILONDJA*
Democratic
Republic of Congo

GASTÓN
MEDINA
Peru

HASSAN
ABU WARDA
Palestine

HASSAN
AL-QISHAWI*
Palestine

HASSAN
DOUHAN
Palestine

HASSAN FADL
AL-MAWLA MOUSA
Sudan

HASSAN
SAMOUR
Palestine

HILMI
AL-FAQAAWI
Palestine

HOSSAM
SHABAT
Palestine

HUSSAM
AL-MASRI
Palestine

IBRAHIM
HAJJAJ*
Palestine

IBRAHIM
MUDAWI
Sudan

IBRAHIM
ZAHER
Palestine

IMTIAZ
MIR
Pakistan

ISLAM
ABED
Palestine

ISLAM
AL-KOMI
Palestine

ISMAIL
ABU HATAB*
Palestine

ISMAIL
BADDAH*
Palestine

JAMAL
AL-ADHI
Yemen

JAVIER
HÉRCULES
Honduras

LUTF AHMED
NASSER HADIYAN
Yemen

MAGDY ABDEL
RAHMAN
Sudan

MAHMOUD
ISLIM AL-BASOS*
Palestine

MAHMOUD ISSA
ABU SHIRBY
Palestine

MAHMOUD
WADI*
Palestine

MARIAM
ABU DAGGA*
Palestine

MOAMEN
ABU ALOUF*
Palestine

MOAMEN
ALIWA
Palestine

MOAZ
ABU TAHA*
Palestine

MOHAMMED
AL DAYA
Palestine

MOHAMMED AL
KUAIFI*
Palestine

MOHAMMAD
AL-KHALDI
Palestine

MOHAMMED
AL-OMEISI
Yemen

MOHAMMED
AL-TALMAS
Palestine

MOHAMMED ALAA
AL-SAWALHI*
Palestine

MOHAMMED ALI
HAMOUD AL-DAWI
Yemen

MOHAMMED
IMAD AL-SULTAN
Palestine

MOHAMMED
MANSOUR
Palestine

MOHAMMED
NOUFAL
Palestine

MOHAMMED
QREIQEH
Palestine

MOHAMMED
SALAMA
Palestine

MUKESH
CHANDRAKAR
India

MURAD HALBOUB
AL-FAQIH
Yemen

MUSAB
AL-HATTAMI
Yemen

NIMA
RAJABPOUR
Iran

NOUREDDINE
ABDO
Palestine

OLENA
HRAMOVA
Ukraine

OMAR
AL DIRAWI*
Palestine

OSAMA
BALOUSHA*
Palestine

QAIS ABDO
AHMED AL-NAQEEB
Yemen

RASMI
JIHAD SALEM
Palestine

SAED ABU
NABHAN*
Palestine

SALEH
ALJAFARAWI
Palestine

SALEH
BAYRAMI
Iran

SAMI MOHAMMED
HUSSEIN AL-ZAIDI
Yemen

SARI MAJID
AL-SHOUFI*
Syria

SULEIMAN
HAJJAJ
Palestine

SURESH
RAJAK
Nepal

TAJ AL-SIR
AHMED SULEIMAN
Sudan

TETYANA
KULYK
Ukraine

TURKI
AL-JASSER
Saudi Arabia

YAHIA
BARZAQ*
Palestine

YAHYA
SOBEIH
Palestine

YEVHEN
KARMAZIN
Ukraine

YOUSSEF SHAMS
AL-DIN AL-BAHRI
Yemen

IN 2025, 93 JOURNALISTS WERE KILLED CARRYING OUT THEIR WORK

Journalists face an increasingly hostile environment worldwide. At least 93 journalists were killed while carrying out their work across 15 countries in 2025. More than half of those deaths occurred in Palestine, and the Committee to Protect Journalists (CPJ) states that Israel has committed more targeted killings of journalists than any other government's military since records began, threatening free reporting almost to extinction. Worldwide, people working to supply reliable information are attacked, kidnapped, or imprisoned. Together with the flood of misinformation and a death-squeeze on revenue for the independent press, these threats endanger freedom and democracy.

Names marked with an asterisk (*) were photojournalists. The country listed is where the journalist was killed, with a confirmed motive. *See disclaimer in the colophon.*

WORLD PRESS PHOTO 2026

World Press Photo connects the world to the stories that matter by presenting outstanding work by photojournalists and documentary photographers from around the globe.

In 2026, an independent jury awarded 42 of the entries submitted by 3,747 photographers worldwide.

Decisions were made based on visual quality, storytelling approach, and commitment to diversity; and celebrated local voices, dedication, and a range of styles. Stories covered the global overstep of power, the climate crisis, and conflict, but also resistance, rebuilding, recovery, and the dignities of resilience.

JOUMANA EL ZEIN KHOURY
EXECUTIVE DIRECTOR, WORLD PRESS PHOTO

FOREWORD

Around the world, press freedom is under pressure. In some places it is being eroded slowly, through legislation and intimidation. In others, it is attacked openly, through censorship, violence, or the strategic flooding of public space with misinformation. In such a climate, the very existence, and necessity, of the press is in jeopardy.

As part of an organization that carries the word Press in its name, I find myself returning again and again to fundamental questions: What is the press today? What does it mean in different parts of the world? Who defines it, who protects it, and who challenges it? And, for an organization whose core is photojournalism, the question that inevitably follows is: Is photojournalism still relevant? Will it survive?

Over the past year, as part of our continued efforts to set standards and to understand the field, I have had conversations with photo editors from news organizations across continents. At one point, I asked them: In a world as polarized and complicated as ours, how do you balance stories and narratives? How do you continue to show that you are not there to take sides, but to tell stories as they are? How do you navigate the daily turbulence that comes with being a vehicle for storytelling?

Their answer was both simple and profound: We do the best we can. We stand by our ethics, our commitment to truth-telling, and our values. And if we get something wrong one day, we correct it the next.

That is when a realization struck me. As World Press Photo, we only get to do it once.

It may sound obvious, but when you are immersed in the intensity of your work, some truths reveal themselves slowly. A newspaper publishes daily. We award stories annually. Our selection becomes a record of the year, a reference point. There is no "tomorrow's edition" to rebalance or reframe.

That realization deepened my respect for the process behind every awarded story.

The selection is made by an independent jury that undertakes a rigorous and conscientious review. The debates are thoughtful, nuanced, and at times difficult. And yet, what stands out most is the intentionality behind each decision. Especially this year.

Intentionality in upholding technical excellence without compromise. Intentionality in representing people and communities with dignity and humanity. Intentionality in embracing a diversity of visual styles and voices across regions. Intentionality in balancing heavy stories with hopeful and resilient ones. And above all, intentionality in recognizing the local, regional, and international importance of each story.

This year's awarded stories embody that intentionality.

There is intentionality in awarding an image of a panda, not because it is cute, but because it provides evidence that pandas still exist in the wild. In a time of environmental fragility, proof matters.

There is intentionality in awarding the Photo of the Year: a heart-wrenching moment outside a courthouse in New York City, where a man awaiting a hearing about his immigration status is pulled away from his daughters by ICE agents. The image may resemble others we have seen over the years, but the jury recognized it as a defining moment, a ground zero of a broader migration crisis. It was not awarded only because it took place in the United States, nor only because of the political climate surrounding

President Trump's second term, but because it centers the human being at the heart of policy. Because it reminds us that the consequences of decisions made in one country ripple across the world.

Across the awarded stories, I sensed something more: a thread that binds them together.

Poetry.

Not in the romantic sense, but in the careful composition, in the patience of observation, in the respect given to subjects. A quiet poetry rooted in humanity, and above all, in dignity.

Dignity in the portrait of Doña Paulina, a survivor of sexual violence in Guatemala, who 40 years later won a court case recognizing her and 35 other women as survivors. Dignity in an image from Gaza, where a family sits around a table in the rubble of their city and their destroyed apartment, insisting on setting out chairs, laying a tablecloth, and breaking their Ramadan fast together despite everything they have lost.

These are not images of despair alone. They are images of resilience. They show us not only what humanity endures, but how humanity persists.

So, is photojournalism still relevant?

If relevance means helping us see clearly in moments of confusion, then yes. If relevance means holding power to account while preserving the dignity of those most affected, then yes.

If relevance means creating a shared space where global audiences can pause, look, feel, and think, then yes.

In a world saturated with images, trustworthy visual storytelling is not obsolete. It is essential.

And if you take the time to truly look at these images, to sit with them, to question them, to allow them to move you, I hope you might arrive at the same conclusion I have:

How could it not be?

AFRICA

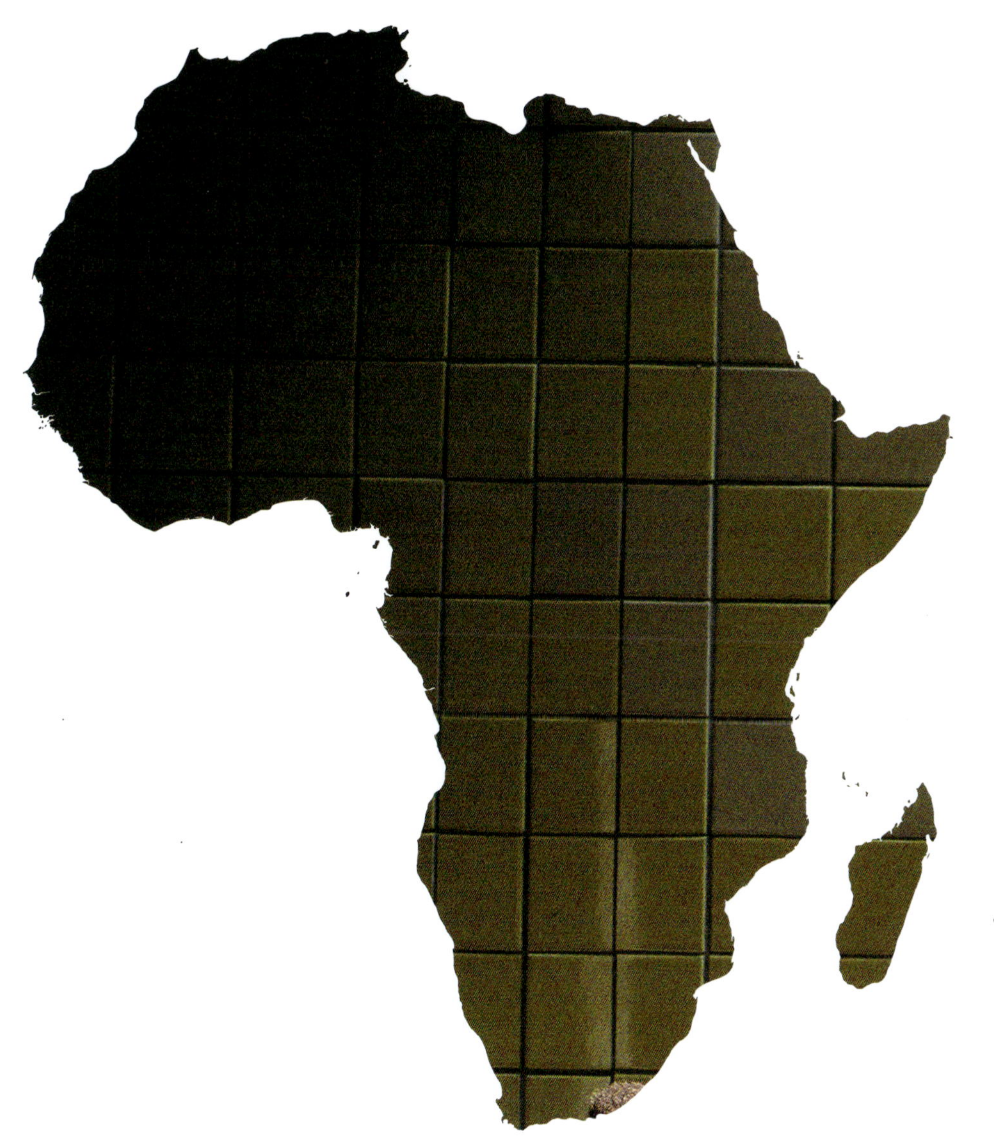

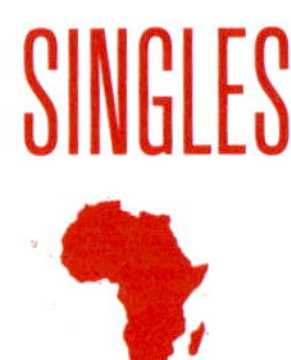

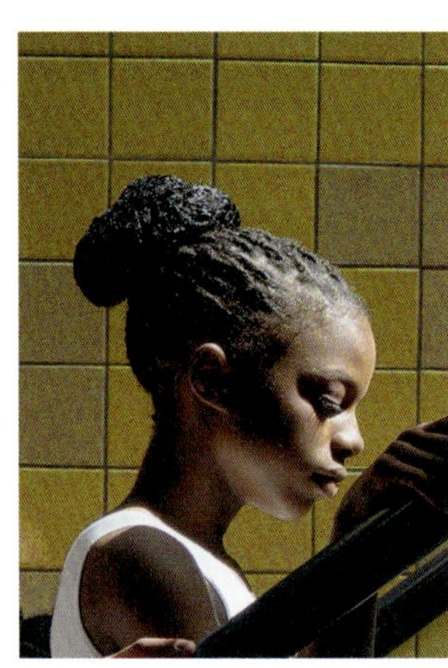

IHSAAN HAFFEJEE

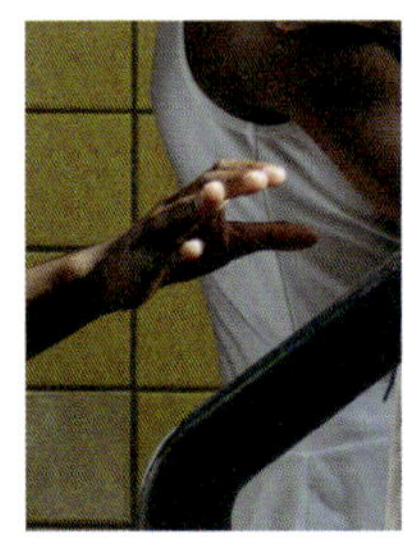

In apartheid South Africa, ballet was the preserve of white culture, inaccessible to people of color. Today, the Joburg Ballet School offers subsidized training to children from historically disadvantaged backgrounds, with locations in Soweto, Alexandra, and Braamfontein. Parents describe seeing their children learn ballet as something they never thought possible.

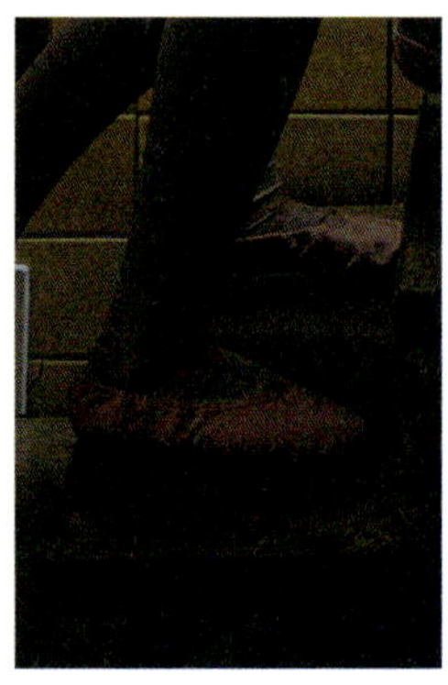

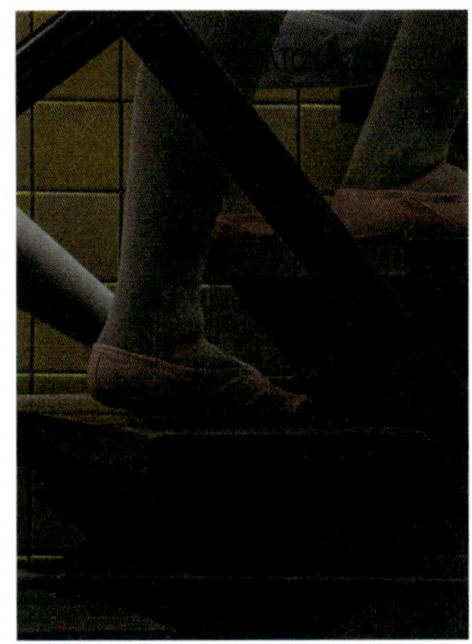

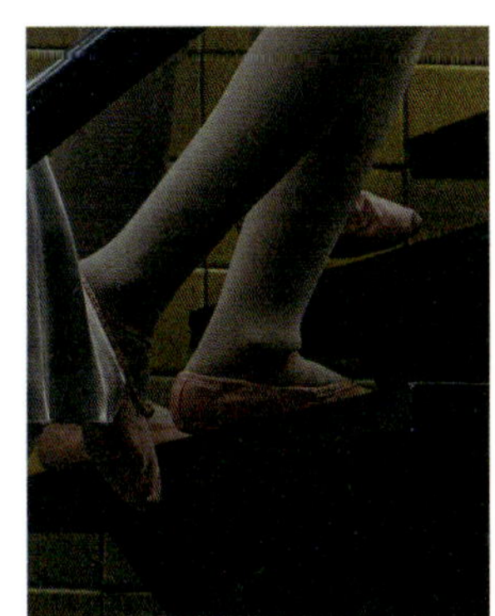

JOBURG BALLET SCHOOL

Young dancers from the Joburg Ballet School backstage at the Soweto Theatre during their year-end performance.
Soweto, South Africa, 7 December 2025 / Ihsaan Haffejee, for GroundUp

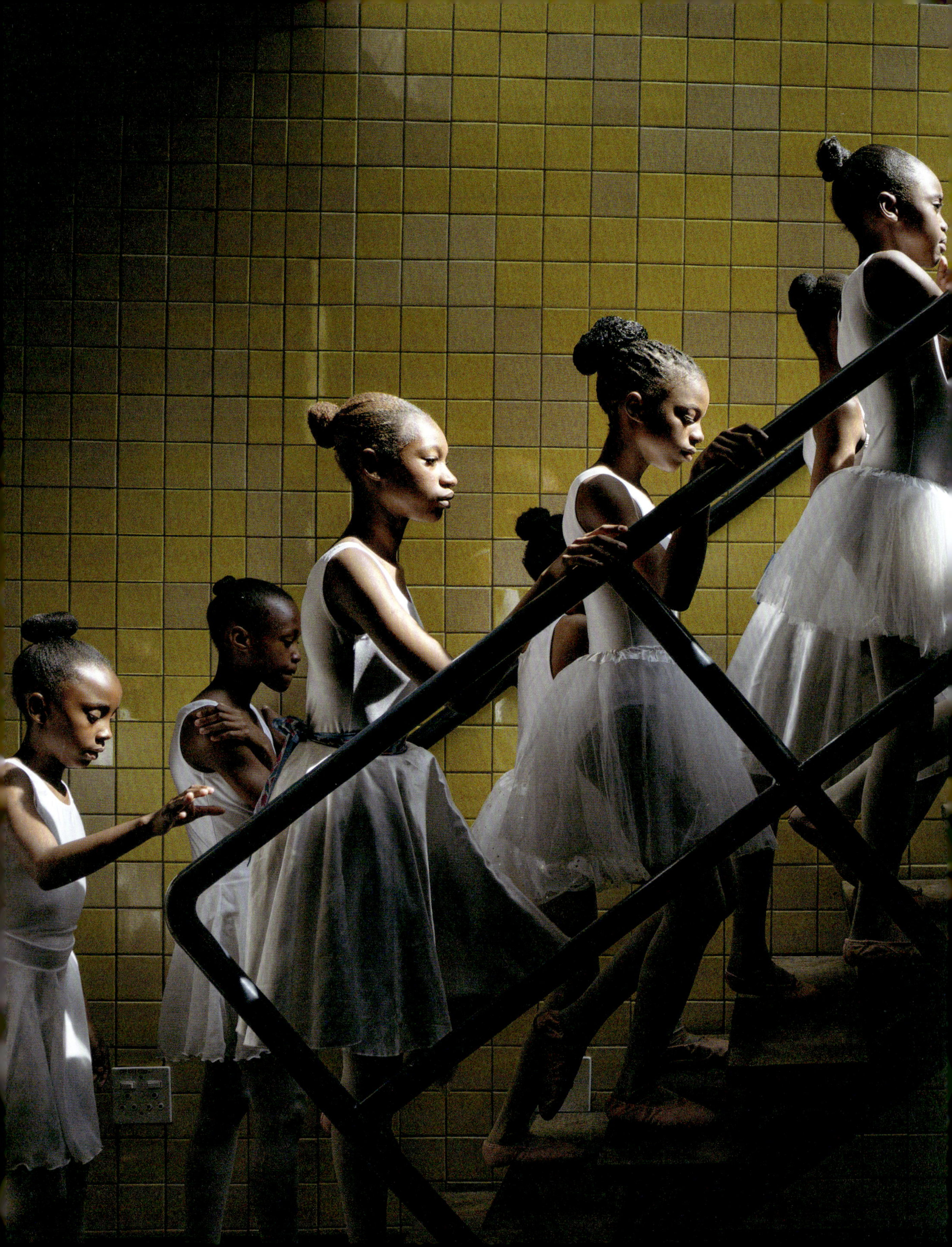

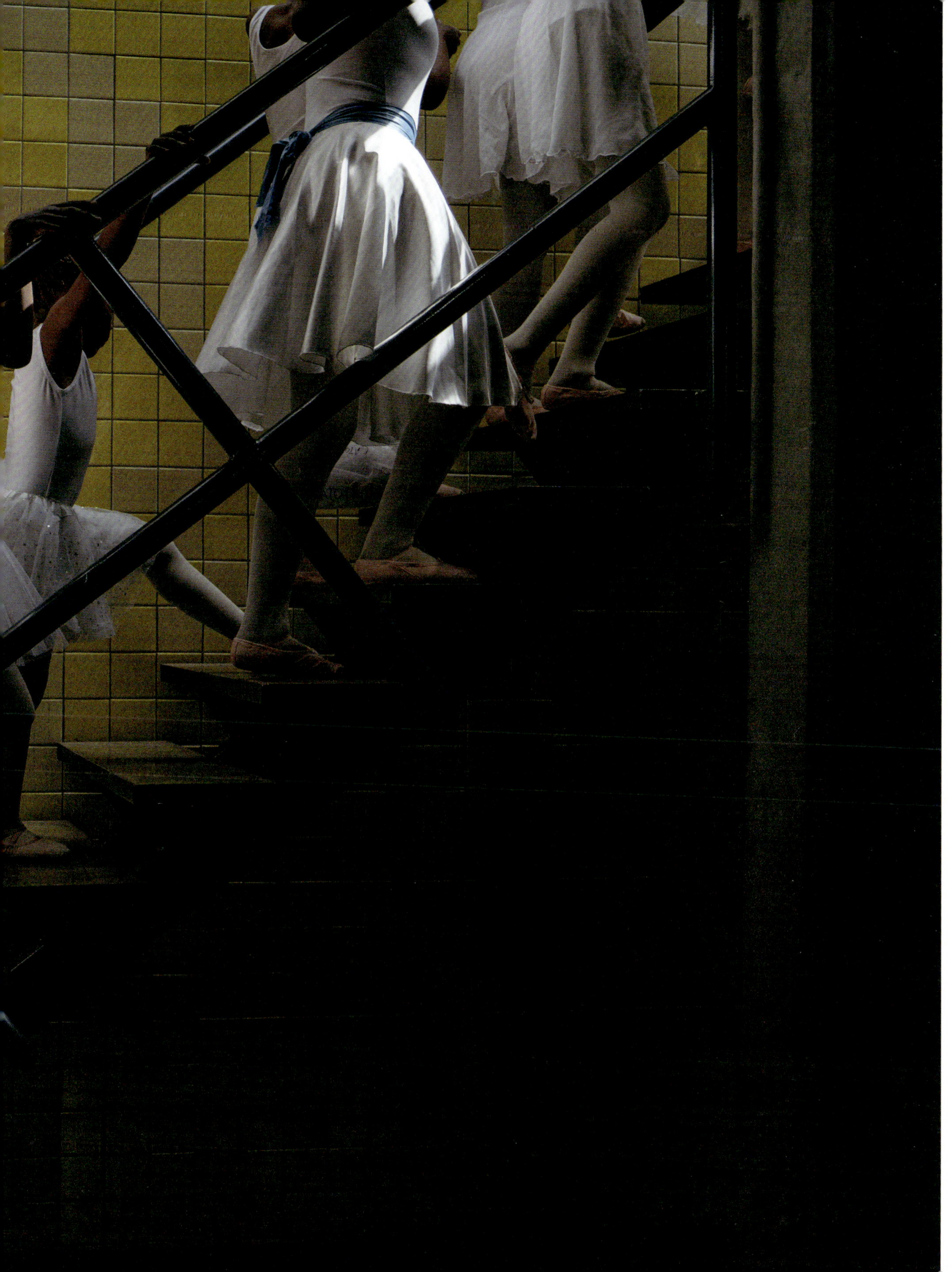

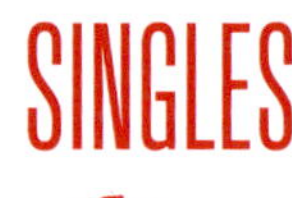
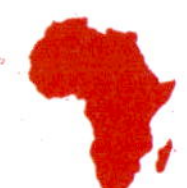

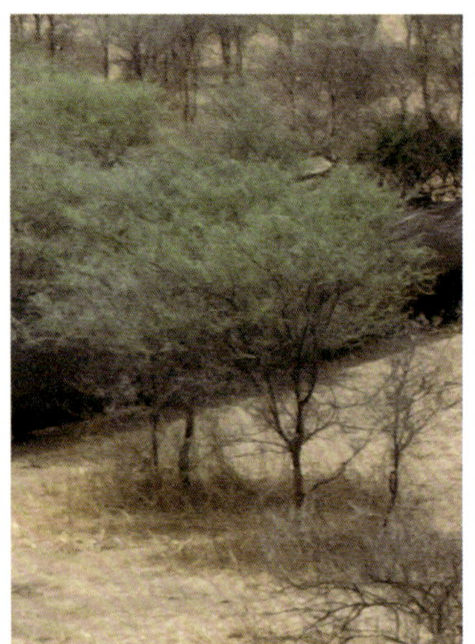

WHEN GIANTS FALL

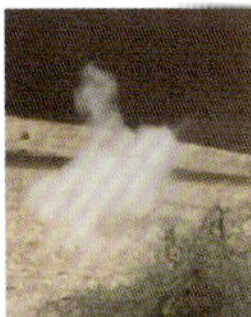

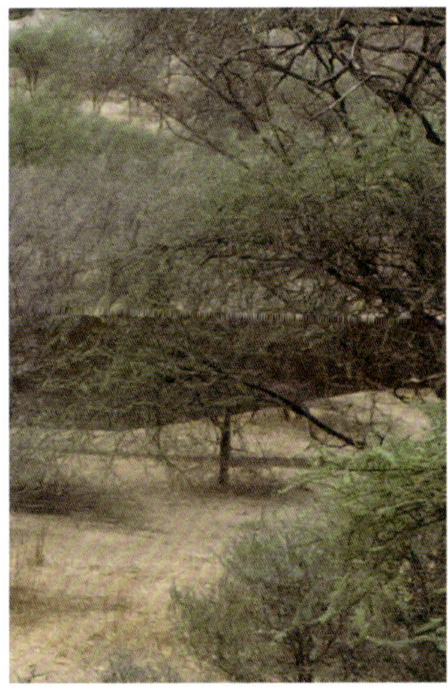

In 2025, the government of Zimbabwe authorized the culling (killing for the purpose of population control) of 50 elephants in the Savé Valley Conservancy. This decision followed a 2024 cull of 200. Authorities say the growing population has surpassed what the land can sustain, worsening human-wildlife conflict as drought drives elephants searching for food and water into closer contact with people. Wildlife organizations dispute claims of overpopulation and condemn culling. They have raised concerns including the fracturing of elephant social structures, and the trauma inflicted on surviving animals, which could increase aggression toward humans.

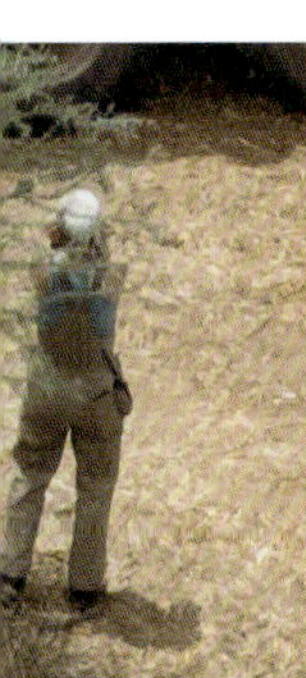

HALDEN KROG

Professional hunters shoot a family of elephants identified for culling. Sango Wildlife Conservancy, Savé Valley Conservancy, Zimbabwe, 23 October 2025 / Halden Krog, for *Daily Mail*

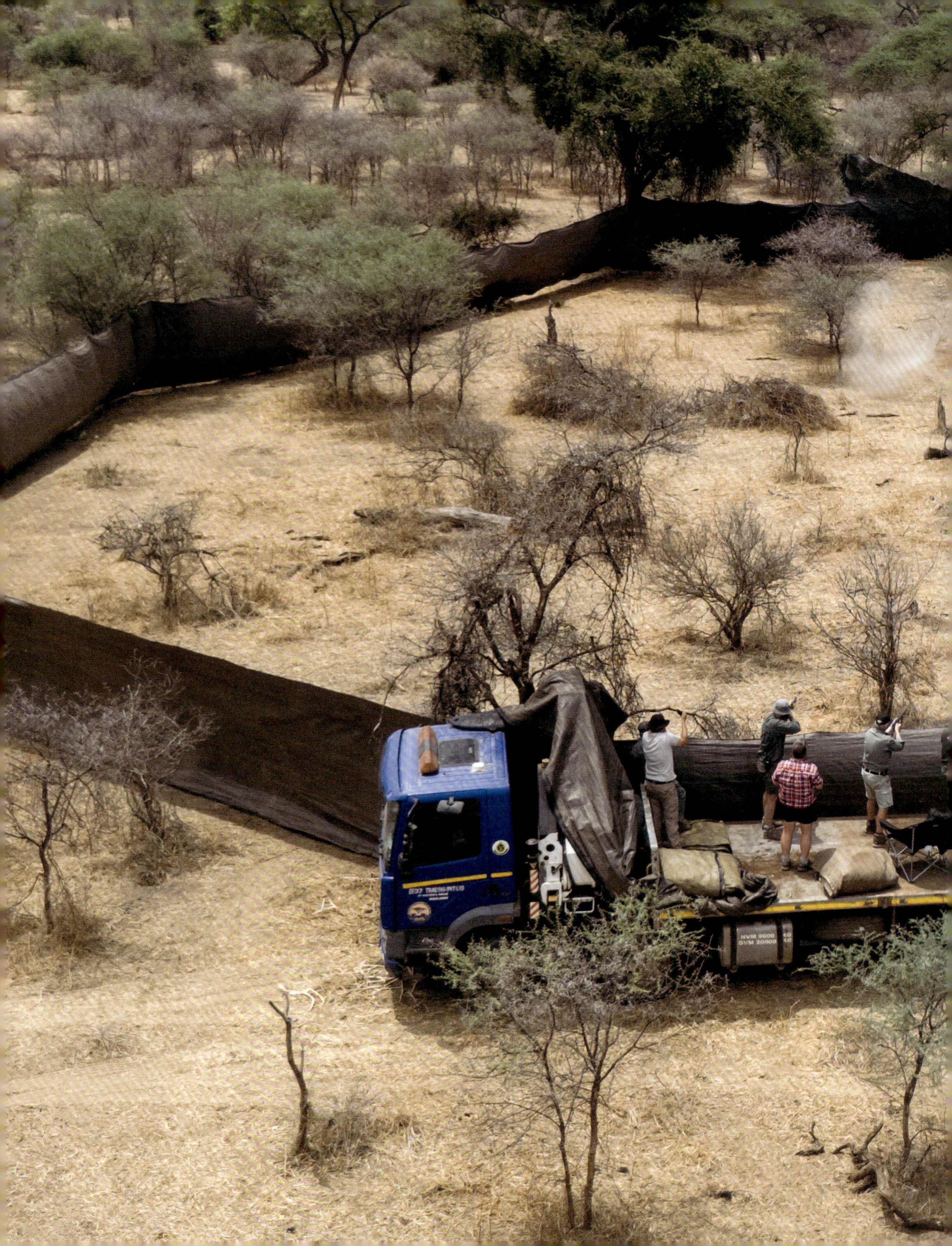

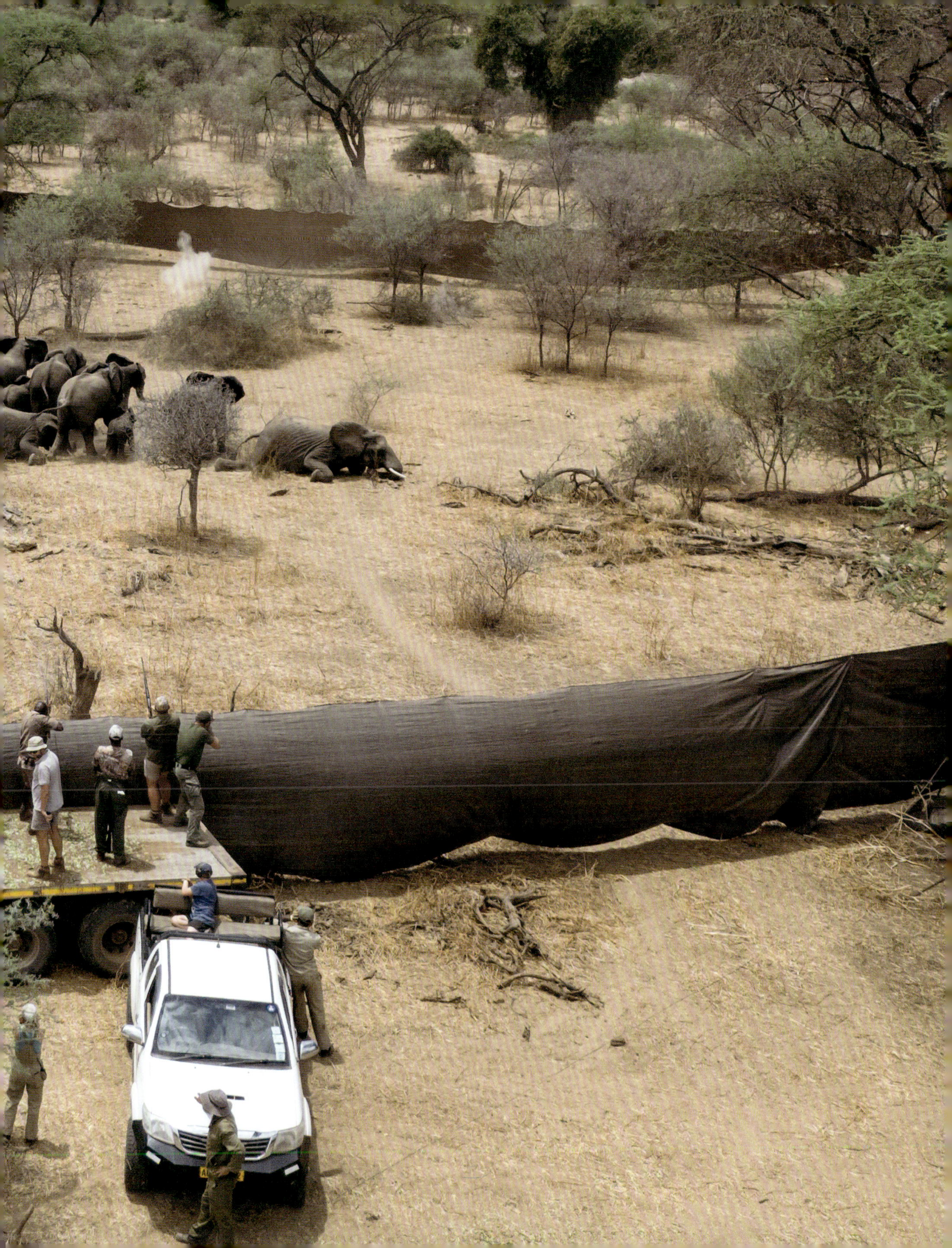

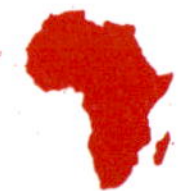

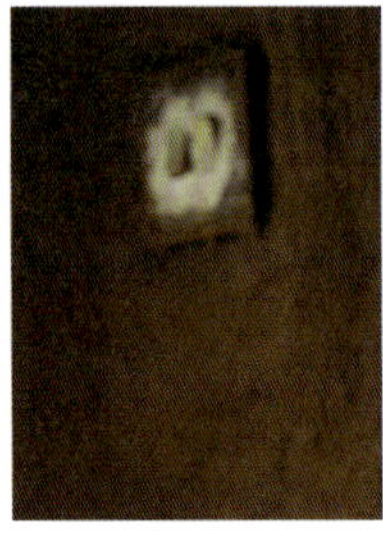

Tens of thousands of Kenyan women migrate to Saudi Arabia for domestic work, where many endure abusive conditions, including passport confiscation and withheld wages. While working there, Edith Magomere Ingasiani hid her pregnancy; unmarried women who give birth risk arrest. She delivered her daughter Blessings alone in January 2016, raising her in the shadows for years. When Edith tried to return home to Kenya, Blessings' lack of documents trapped them in bureaucratic limbo. In 2024, they finally made it back. "Home is always the answer," she says. "It took eight years to get there."

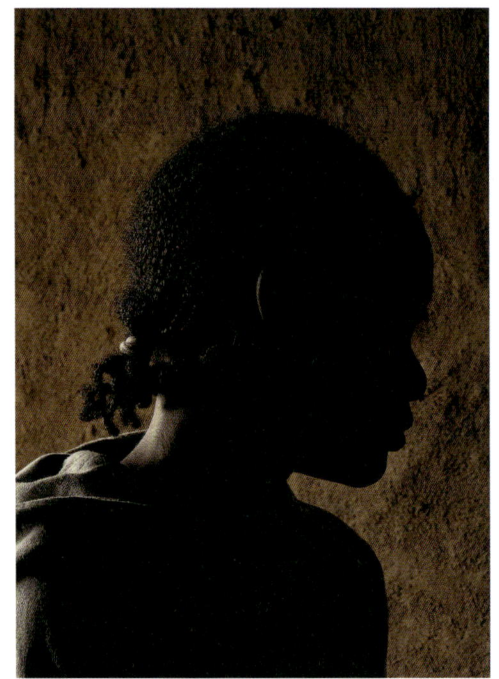

CHI
DO

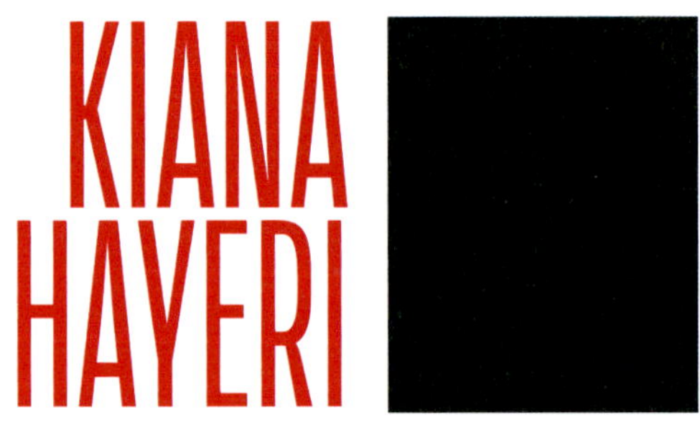

KIANA
HAYERI

...LDREN WHO
...NOT EXIST

Edith Magomere Ingasiani and her daughter Blessings Iminza (9), at their home. Blessings was born in Saudi Arabia without a birth certificate. Vihiga County, Kenya, 30 August 2025 / Kiana Hayeri, for *The New York Times*

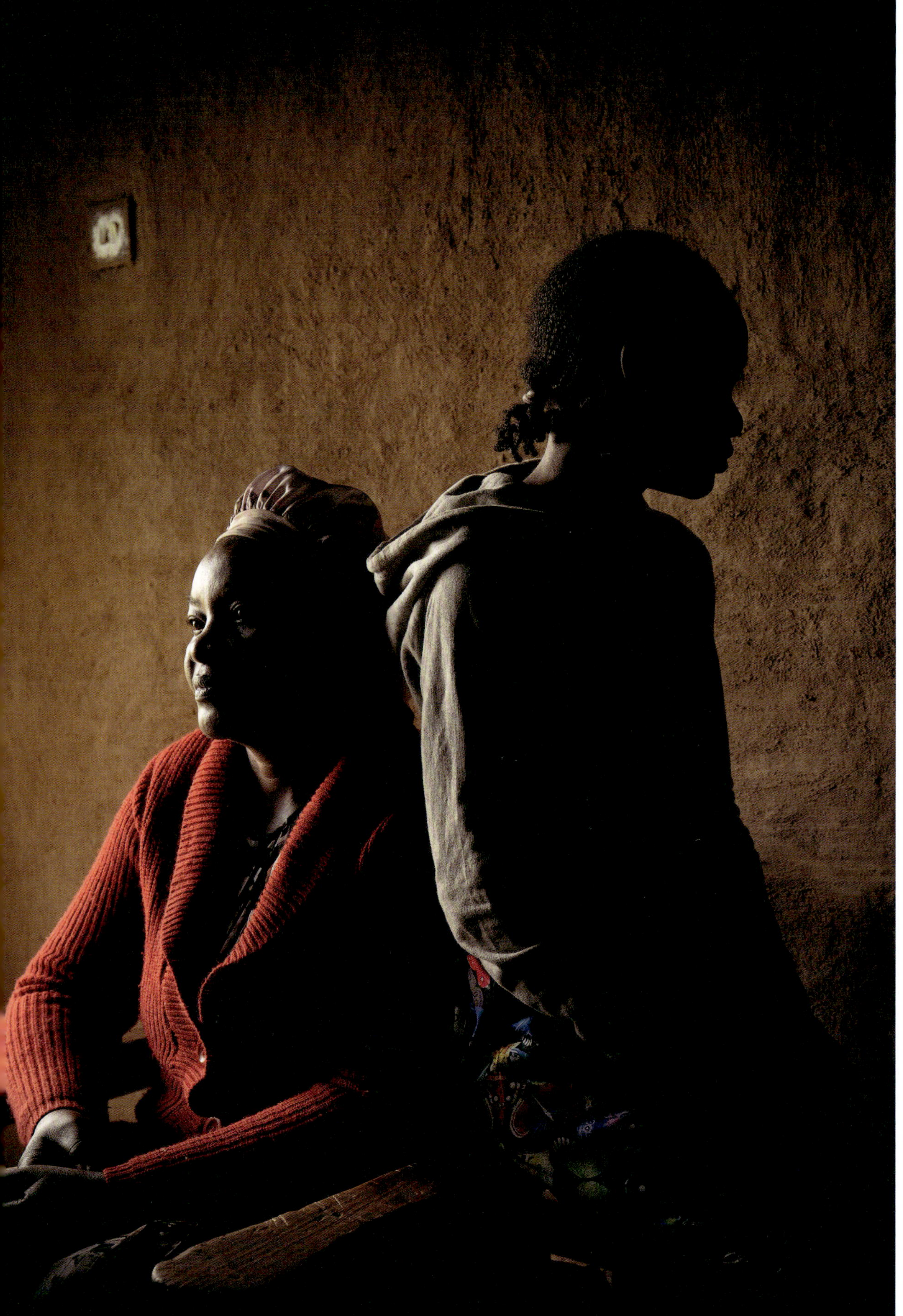

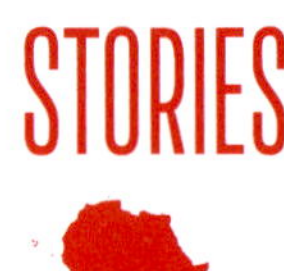

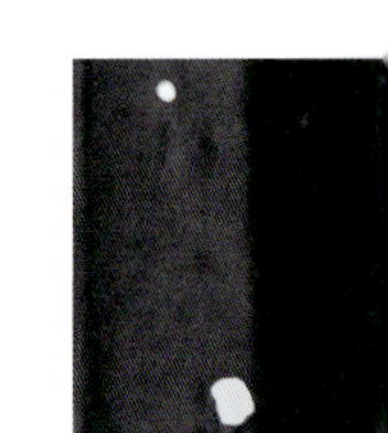

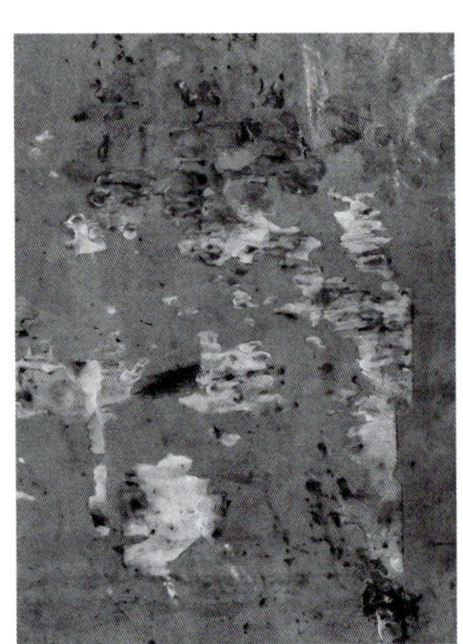

SUDAN'S WAR: A NATION TRAPPED

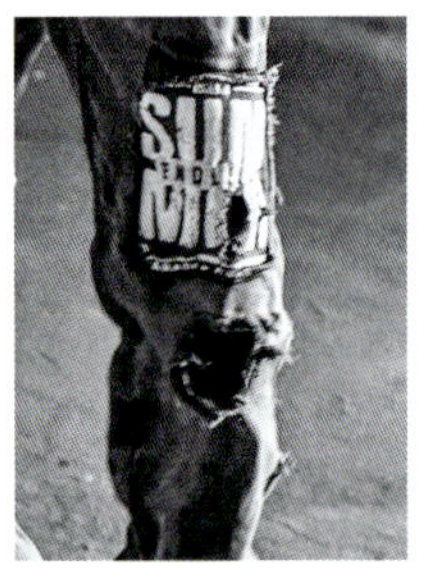

ABDULMONAM EASSA

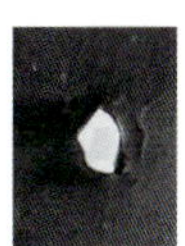

After a 2019 revolution overthrew decades of dictatorship, Sudan's democratic hopes were crushed by a military coup in 2021. Two years later, the army and paramilitary forces turned on each other, beginning a war that has spiraled into one of the world's worst humanitarian crises. As famine spreads and essential services collapse, foreign powers continue to fuel the conflict with weapons. Over 13 million people have been displaced, and at least 150,000 killed. The UN reports that civilian killings more than doubled in 2025 compared with the previous year.

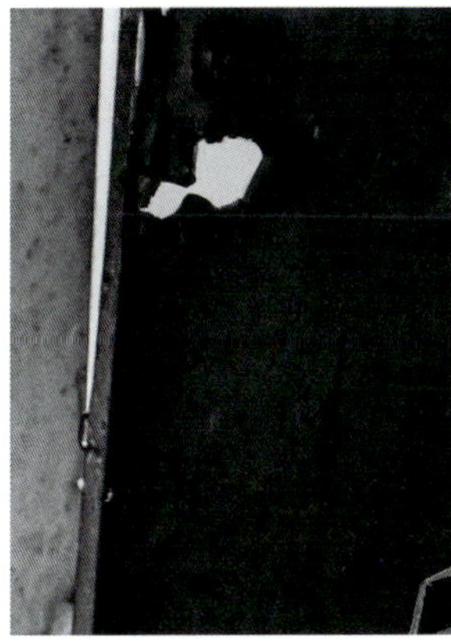

Haneen, whose parents were killed during the war, lives at the Al-Mahaba social center, which shelters orphaned children. Omdurman, Sudan, 6 December 2025 / Abdulmonam Eassa, for *Le Monde*

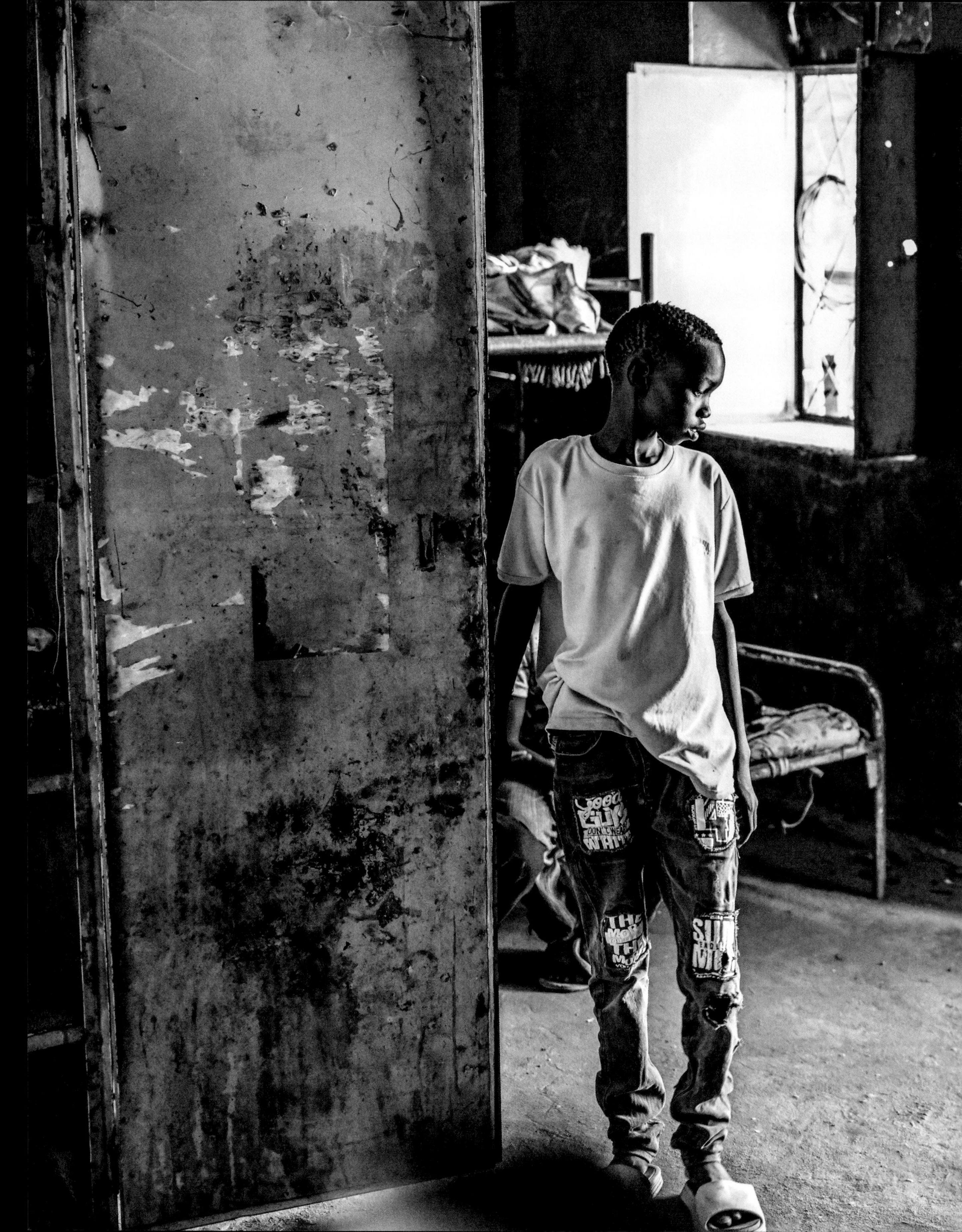

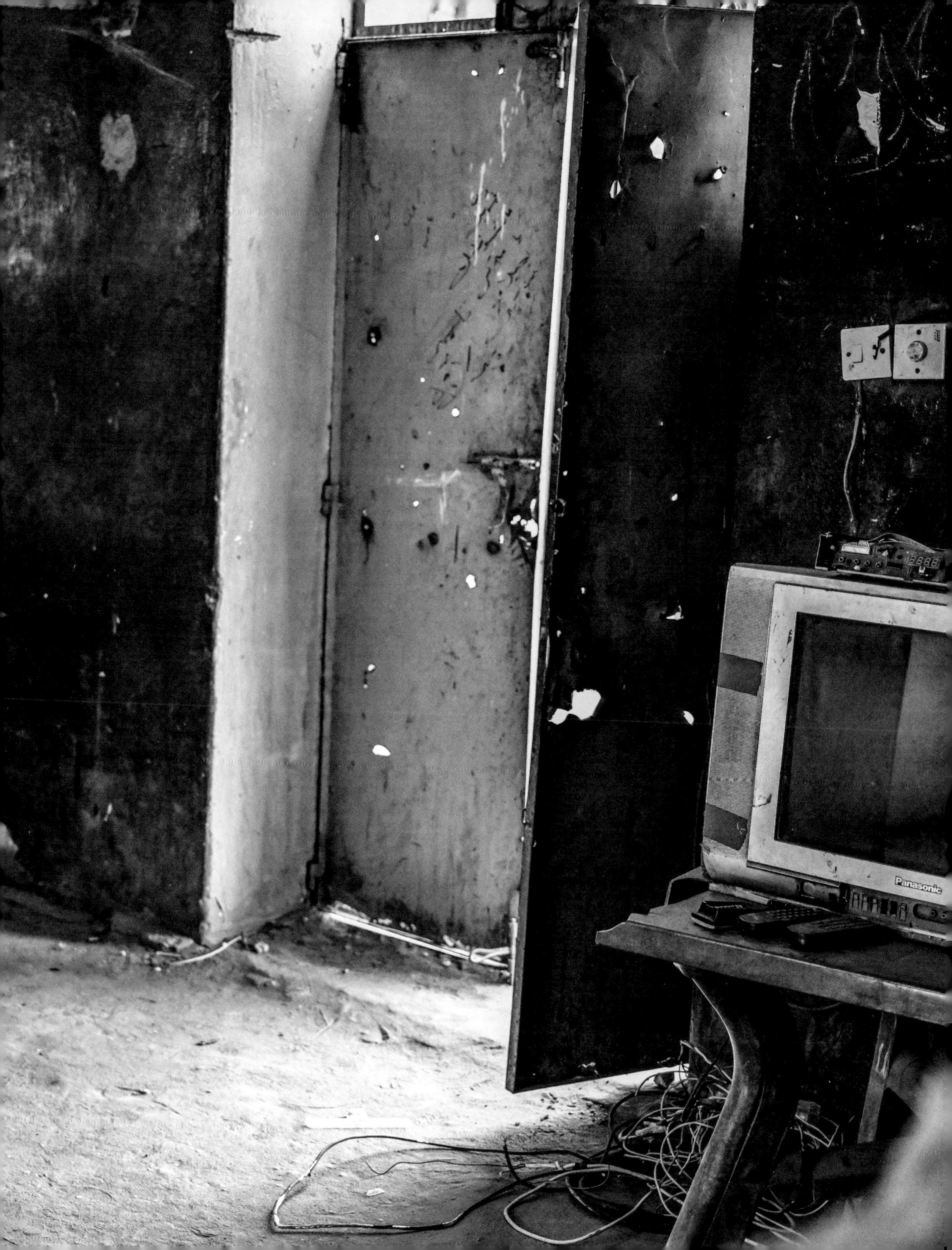

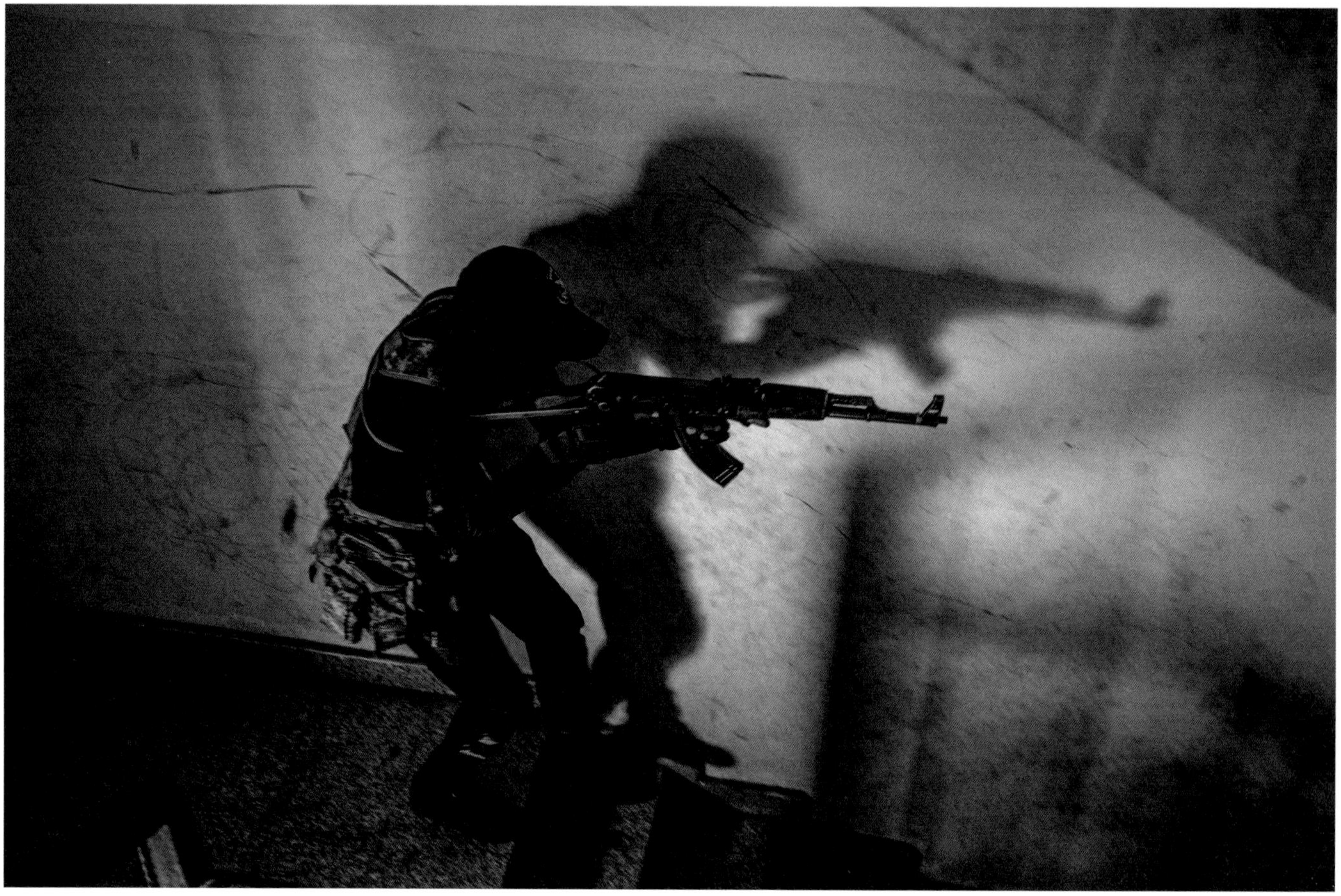

A soldier descends from a building as fighting continues. Frontline images like this are rare,
due to heavily restricted access for journalists. Omdurman, Sudan, 1 November 2024

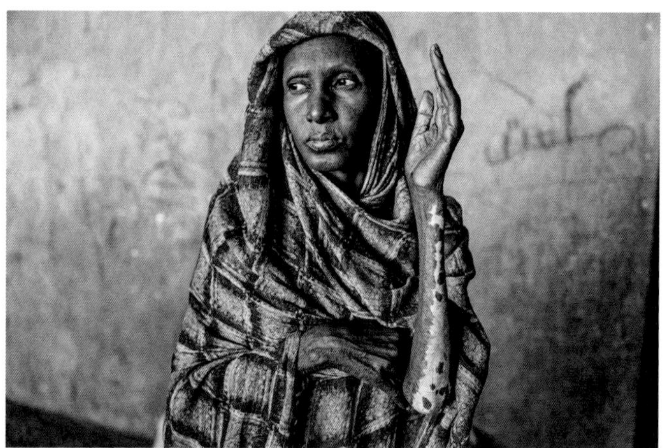

Alhaja Abdallah, a displaced woman from Bara, shows her scars from a fire
at Al-Mohad camp. Paramilitary forces have set multiple displacement
camps ablaze. El-Obeid, Sudan, 10 December 2025

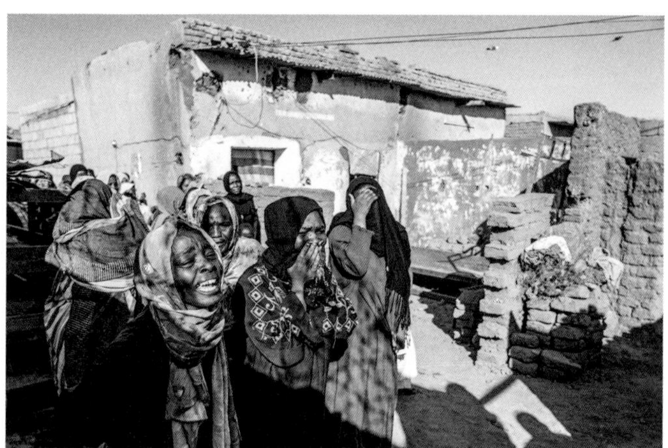

Malak Ahmad mourns her husband, Abobakr Jaber, who was killed by
a mortar shell that struck the school where their family was sheltering.
Omdurman, Sudan, 26 October 2024

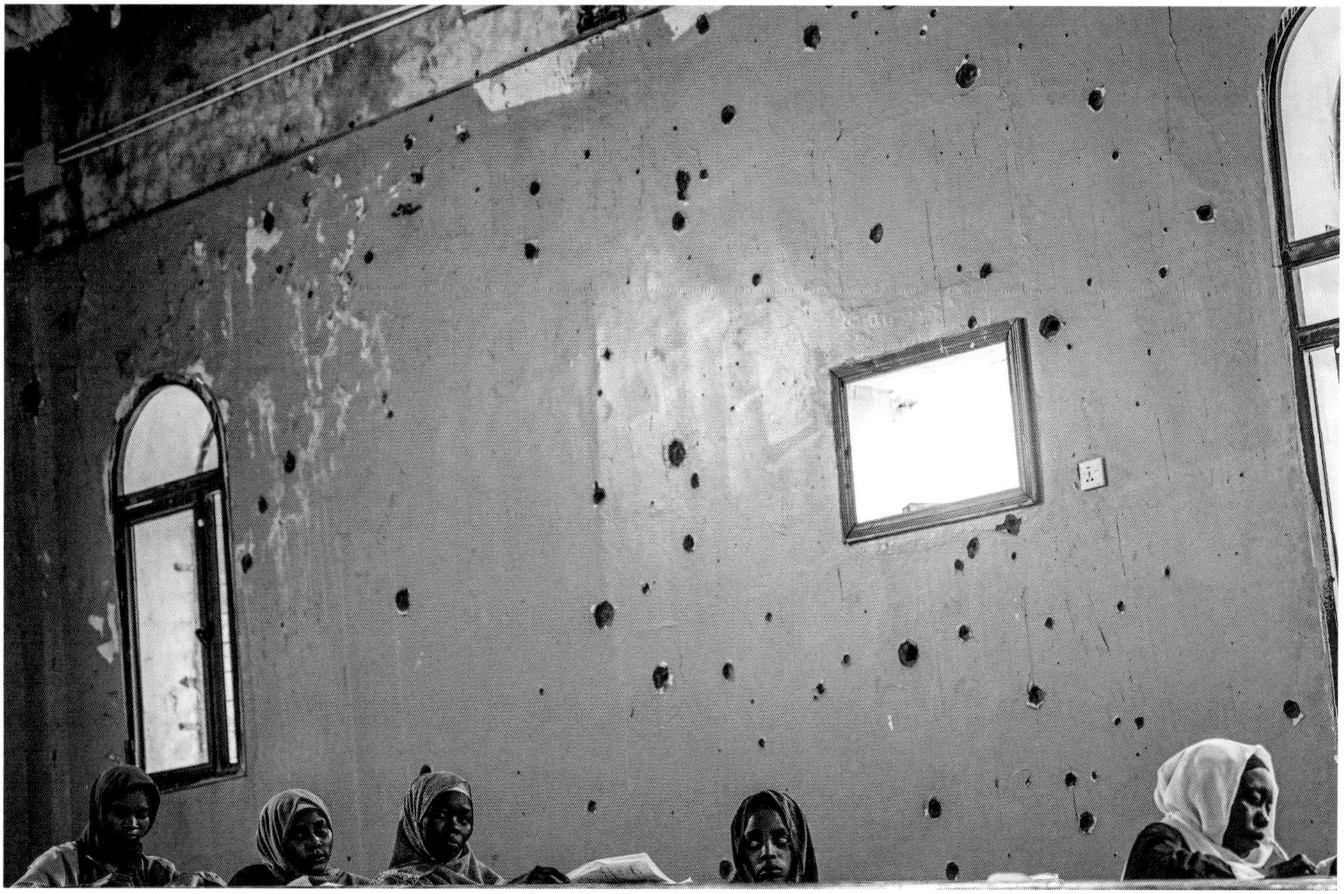

Students take exams at the war-damaged Omdurman Islamic University. Schools and universities have been attacked and mostly closed since fighting began. Omdurman, Sudan, 4 December 2025

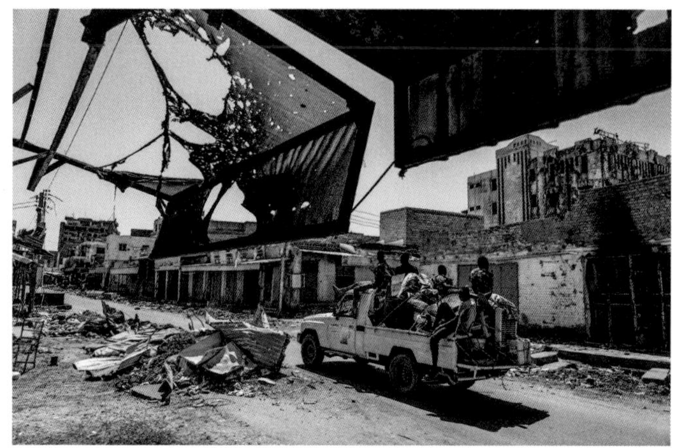

A group of soldiers passes through a damaged market in Sudan's second most populous city, a site of continuous fighting since April 2023. Omdurman, Sudan, 25 October 2024

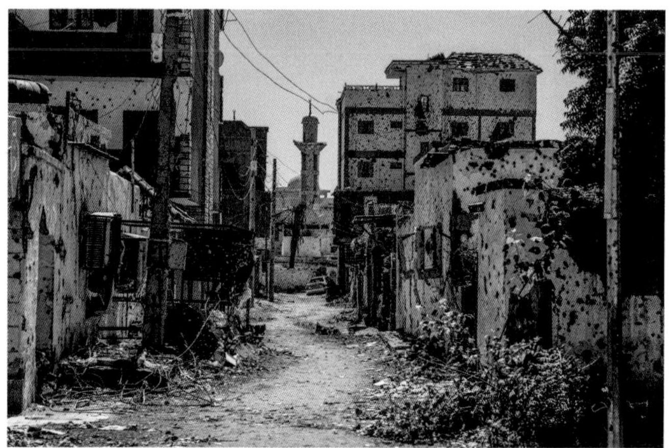

Damaged houses and the Sheikh GaribAllah Mosque in Wad Nubawi. Religious and cultural sites have been attacked across the country. Omdurman, Sudan, 30 October 2024

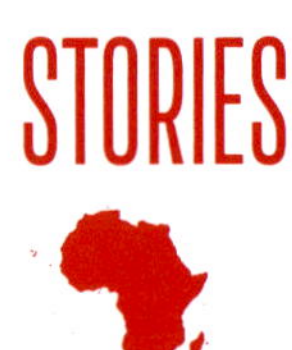

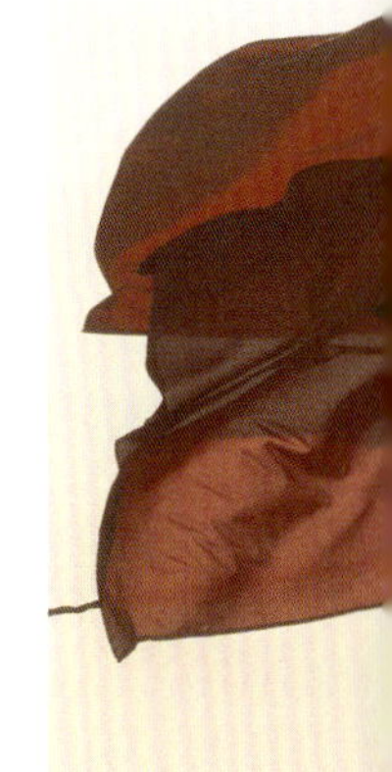

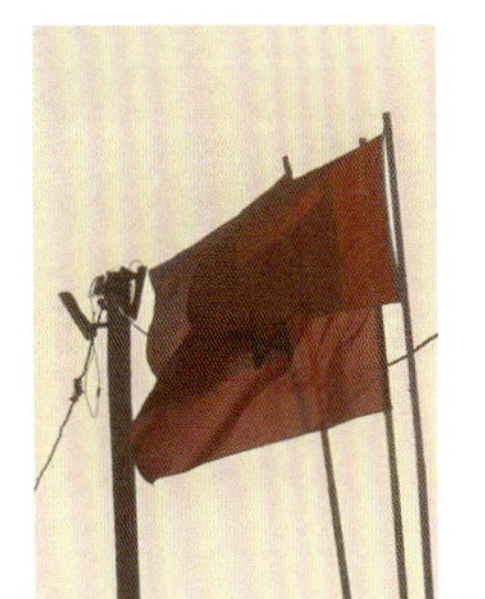

CHANTAL
PINZI

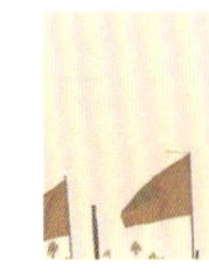

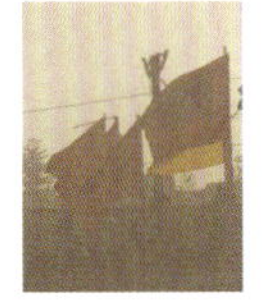

FARĪSĀT: GUNPOWDER'S DAUGHTERS

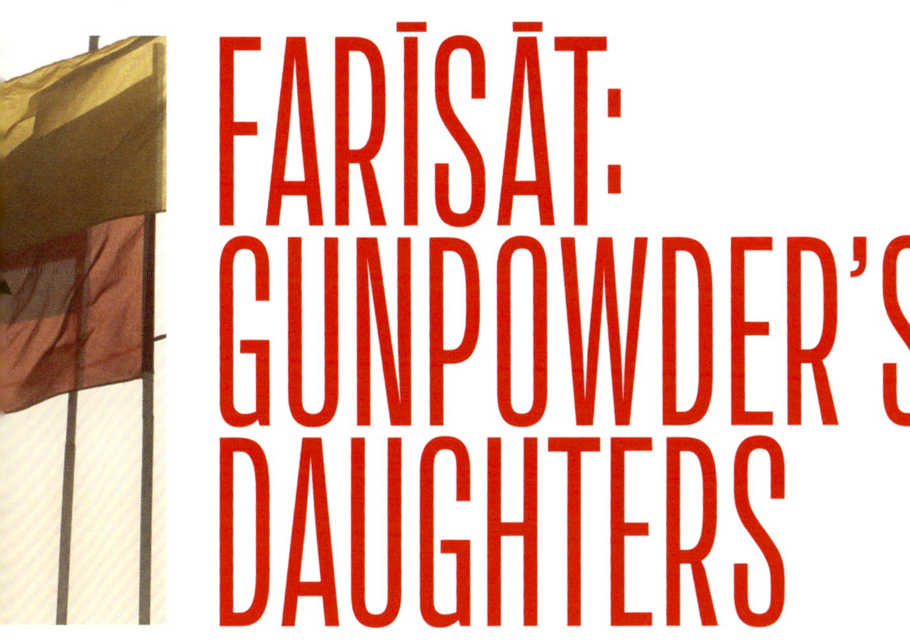

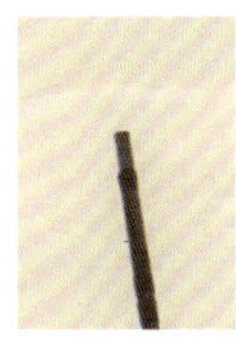

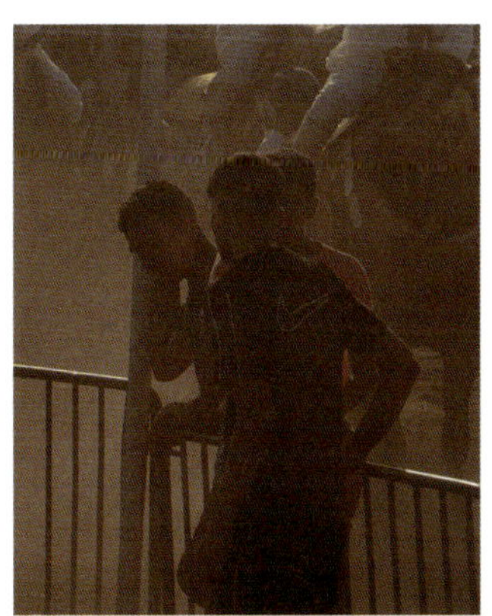

Tbourida is a UNESCO-recognized Moroccan equestrian tradition dating back to the 16th century. Troupes gallop in unison, firing rifles in a choreographed performance of cavalry warfare. Historically excluded, female riders have fought for inclusion since Morocco's 2004 family code reforms strengthened women's legal rights. Today, seven all-female troupes now ride among some 300. These *farīsāt* (horsewomen) bear significant personal costs, funding their own horses, costumes, and gunpowder permits. Their perseverance stands as a powerful claim to women's rightful place in Moroccan cultural heritage.

A Tbourida festival where only one of the performing troupes was made up of women. Sidi Rahal, Morocco, 8 August 2025 / Chantal Pinzi, Panos Pictures

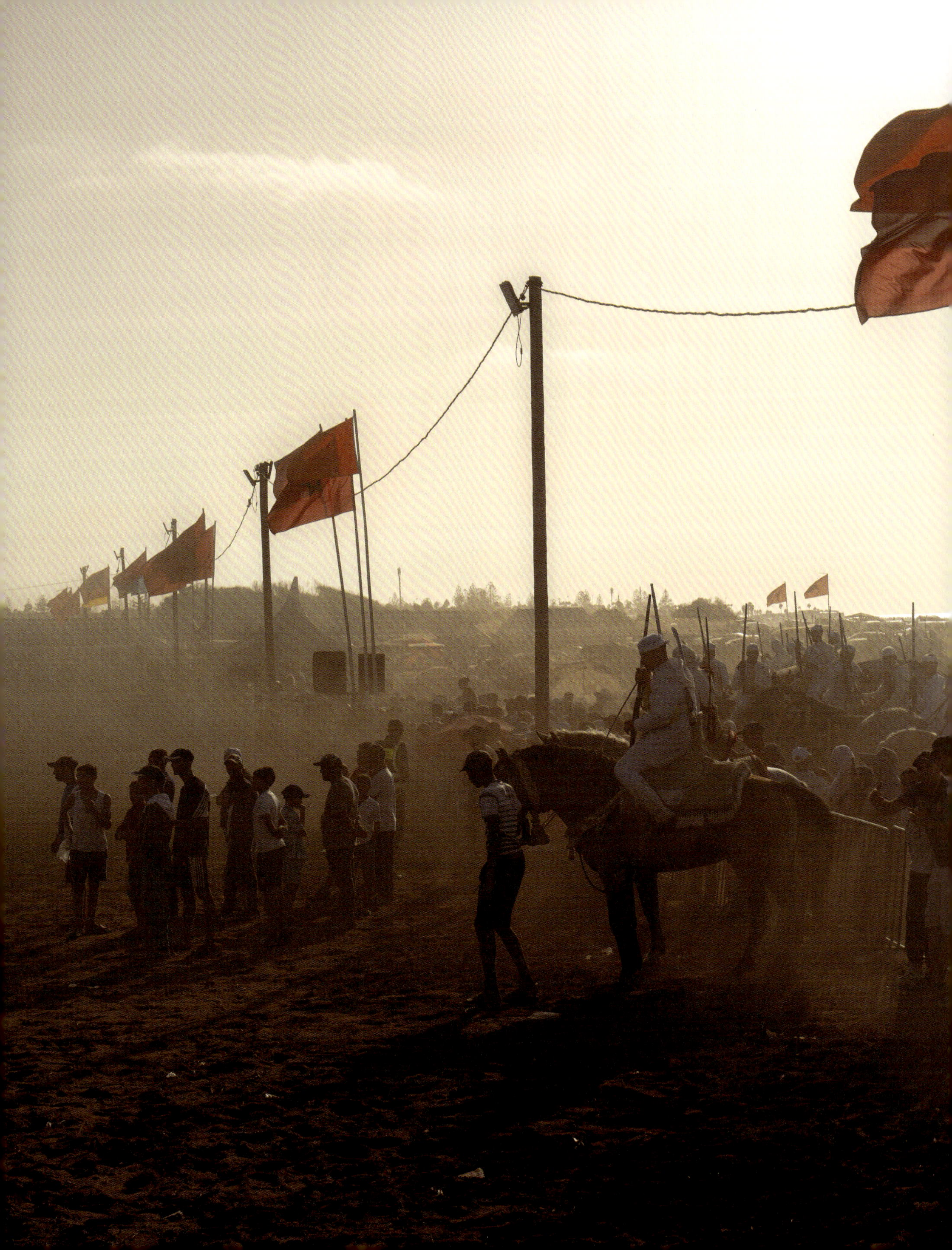

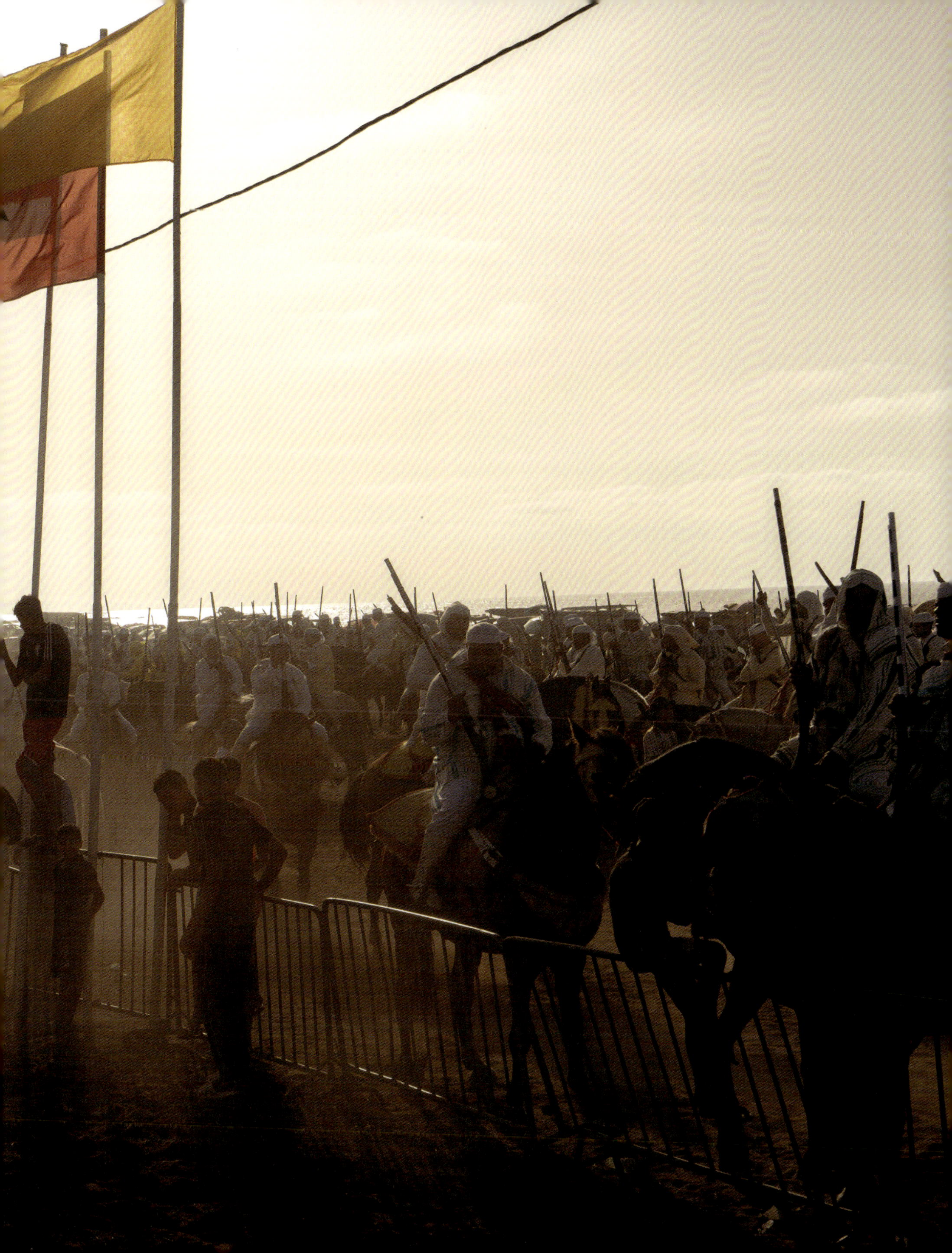

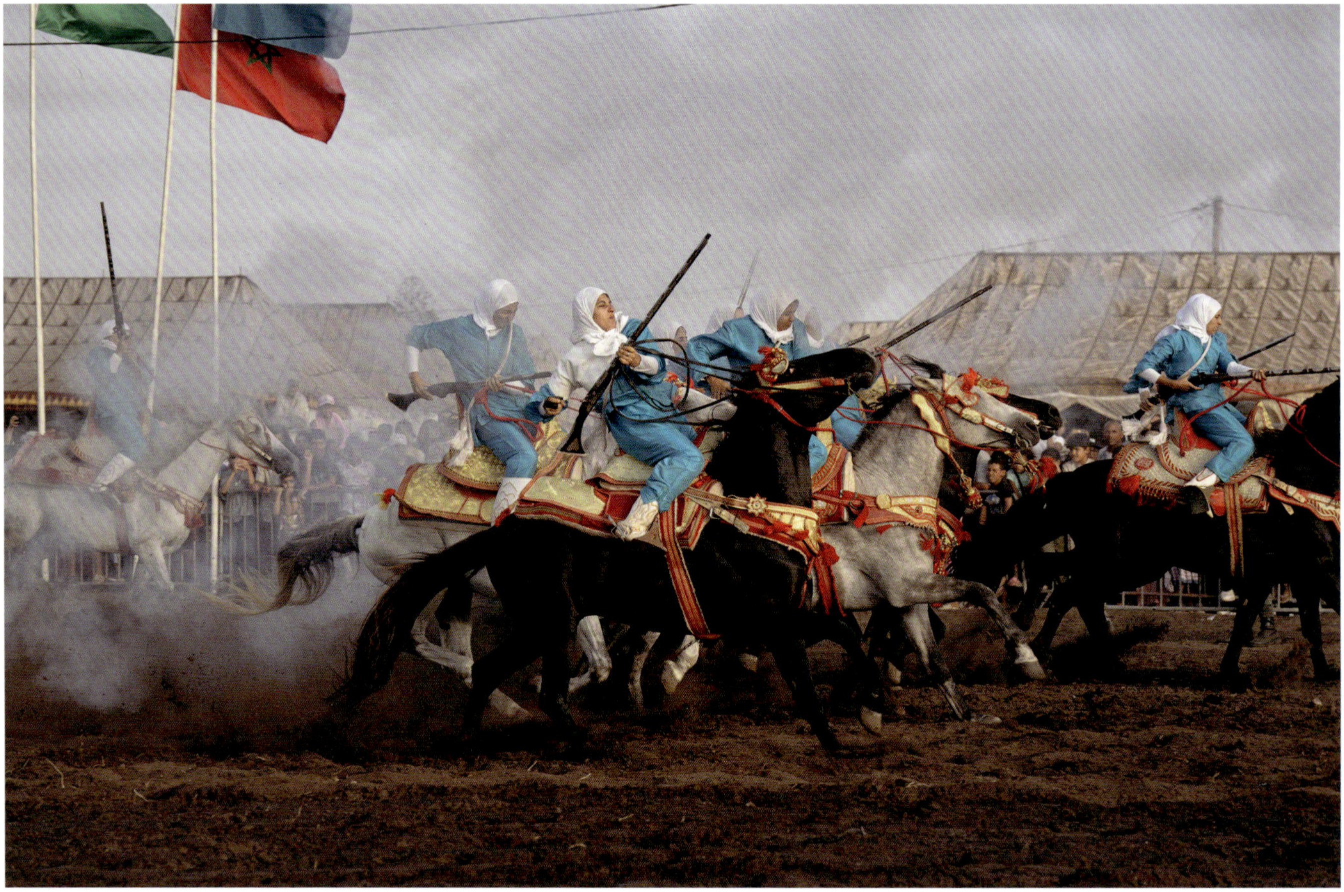

Noura attempts to control her horse after firing, the most dangerous part of the performance.
Riders risk injury from gunpowder or falling and being trampled. Sidi Rahal, Morocco, 8 August 2025

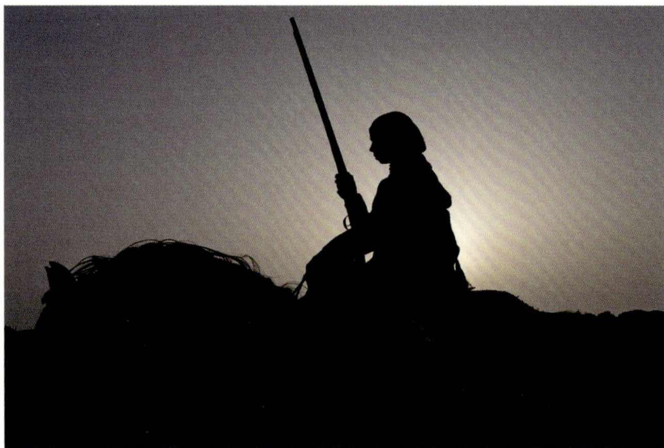

Ilhad Talid during a training session. Tbourida demands years of practice; riders must gallop in unison while loading and firing a rifle, requiring exceptional balance, coordination, and horsemanship. Marrakesh, Morocco, 1 August 2025

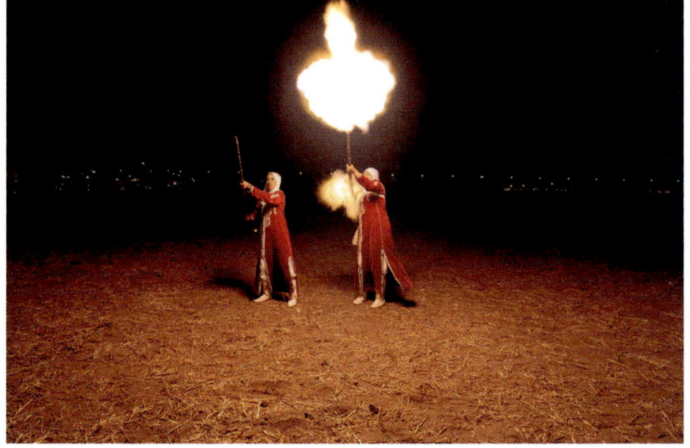

Two riders unload rifles that failed during the performance, a necessary safety measure to ensure no gunpowder remains inside. Sidi Rahal, Morocco, 7 August 2025

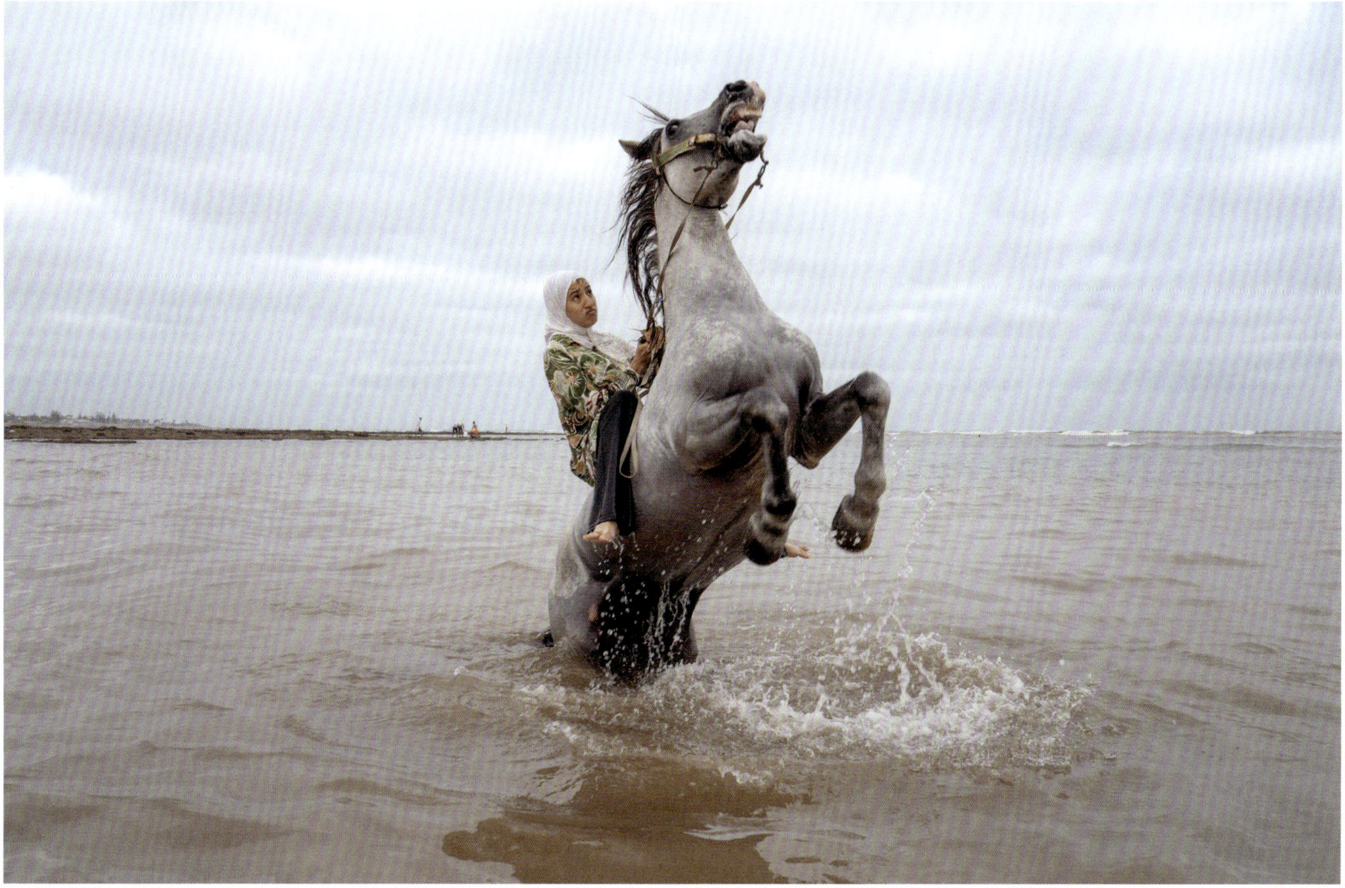

Ghita Jhiate manages her unruly stallion. Long forbidden by her father to participate in Tbourida, she finally realized her dream of riding alongside pioneer Zahia Aboulait in 2025. Sidi Rahal, Morocco, 6 August 2025

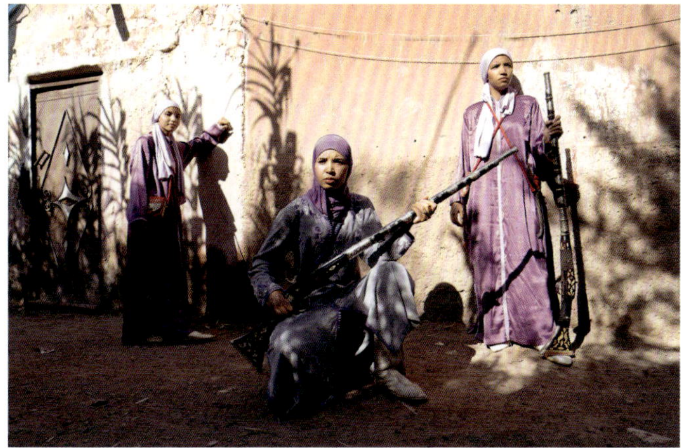

Hanane Talid and her sisters in traditional Tbourida garments, echoing the warriors who used the performance to intimidate invaders. Marrakesh, Morocco, 31 July 2025

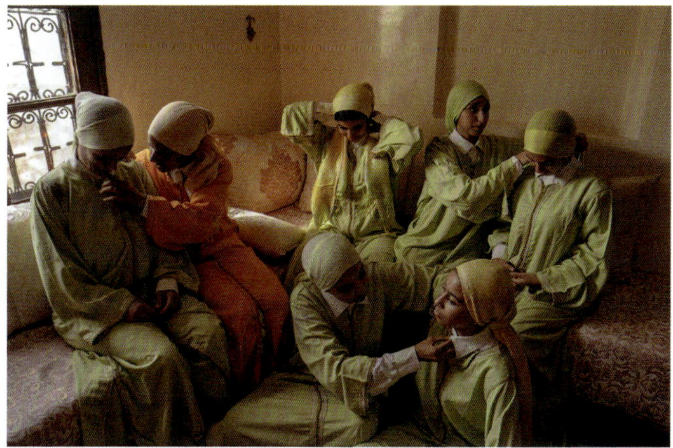

The troupe of Bouchra Nabata, one of the first women to take part in Tbourida in Morocco, dresses in traditional clothing. Rabat, Morocco, 13 August 2025

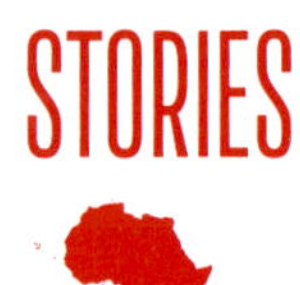

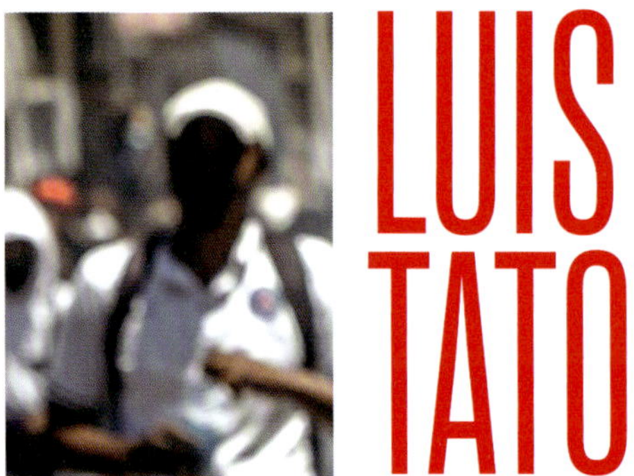

LUIS TATO

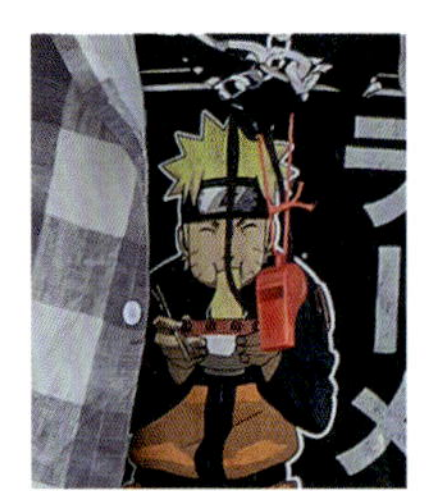

MADAGASCAR'S GEN Z PROTESTS

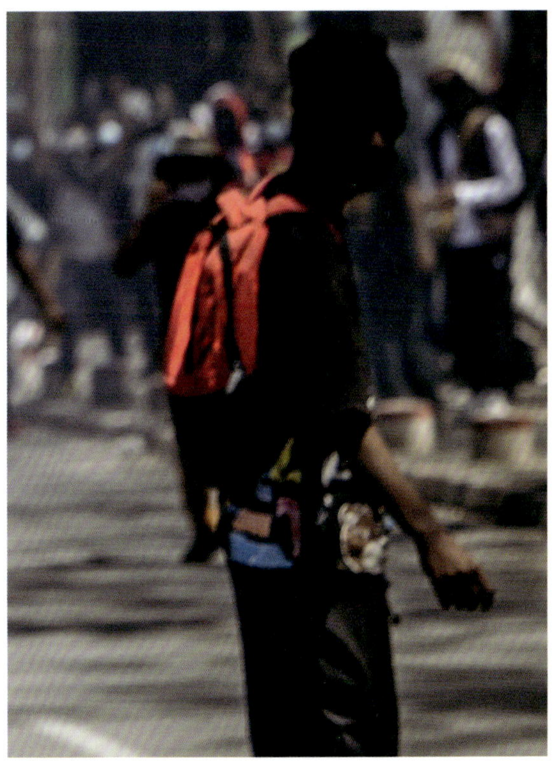

In September 2025, students began protesting across Madagascar over failing public services, corruption, and economic hardship. When President Andry Rajoelina dissolved his government but refused to resign, demonstrations intensified. On 11 October, the CAPSAT military unit defected to join the protesters, the same force that had installed Rajoelina in a 2009 coup. Days later, the military seized power, promising elections within two years. In a pattern seen across Gen Z uprisings in Bangladesh, Nepal, and Bulgaria, Madagascar's youth forced regime change, but were excluded from shaping the political transition that followed.

A student holds the flag adopted by Gen Z protesters globally. The symbol comes from the Japanese manga One Piece, in which pirates stand up to corrupt rulers. 9 October 2025
All photos taken in Antananarivo, Madagascar / Luis Tato, Agence France-Presse

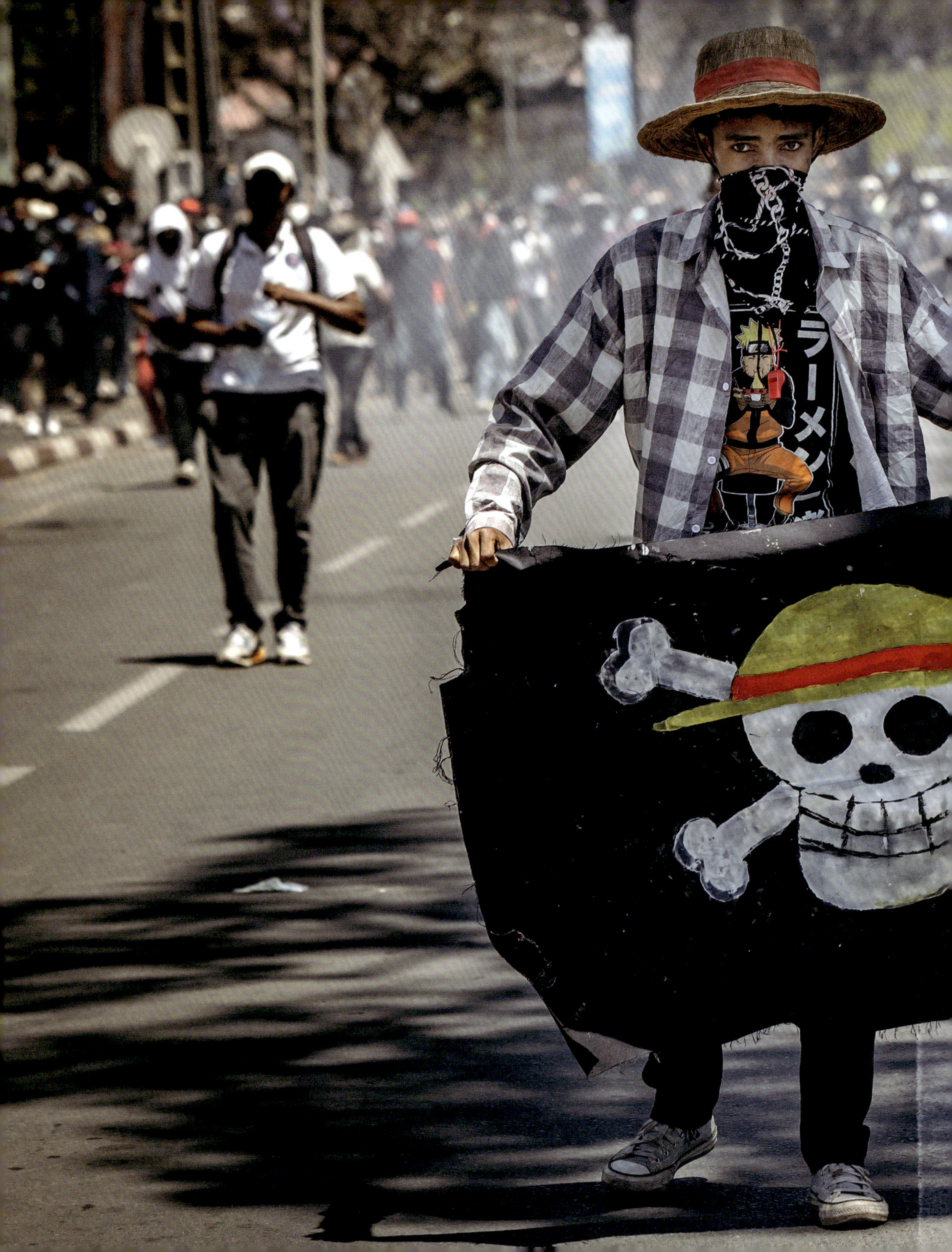

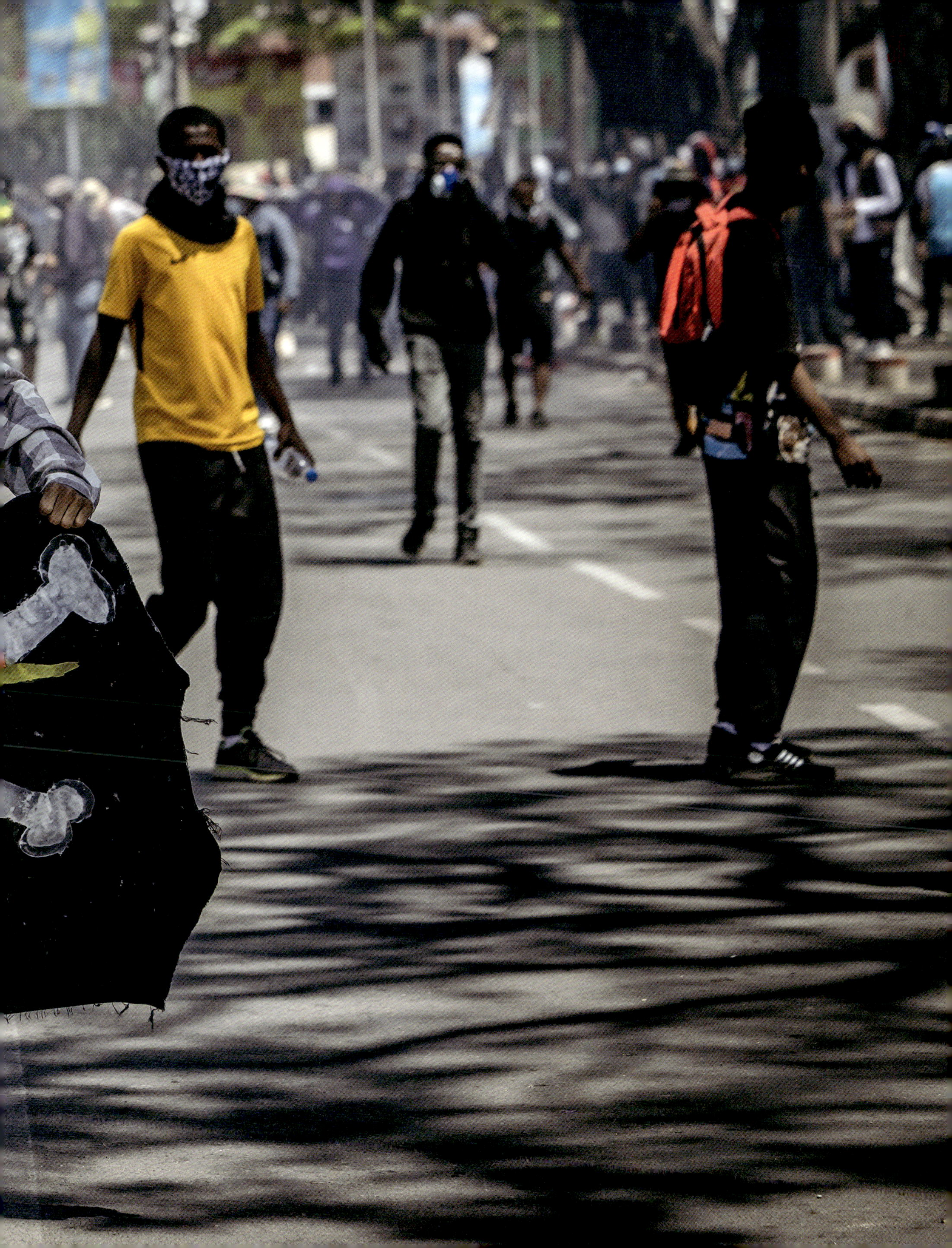

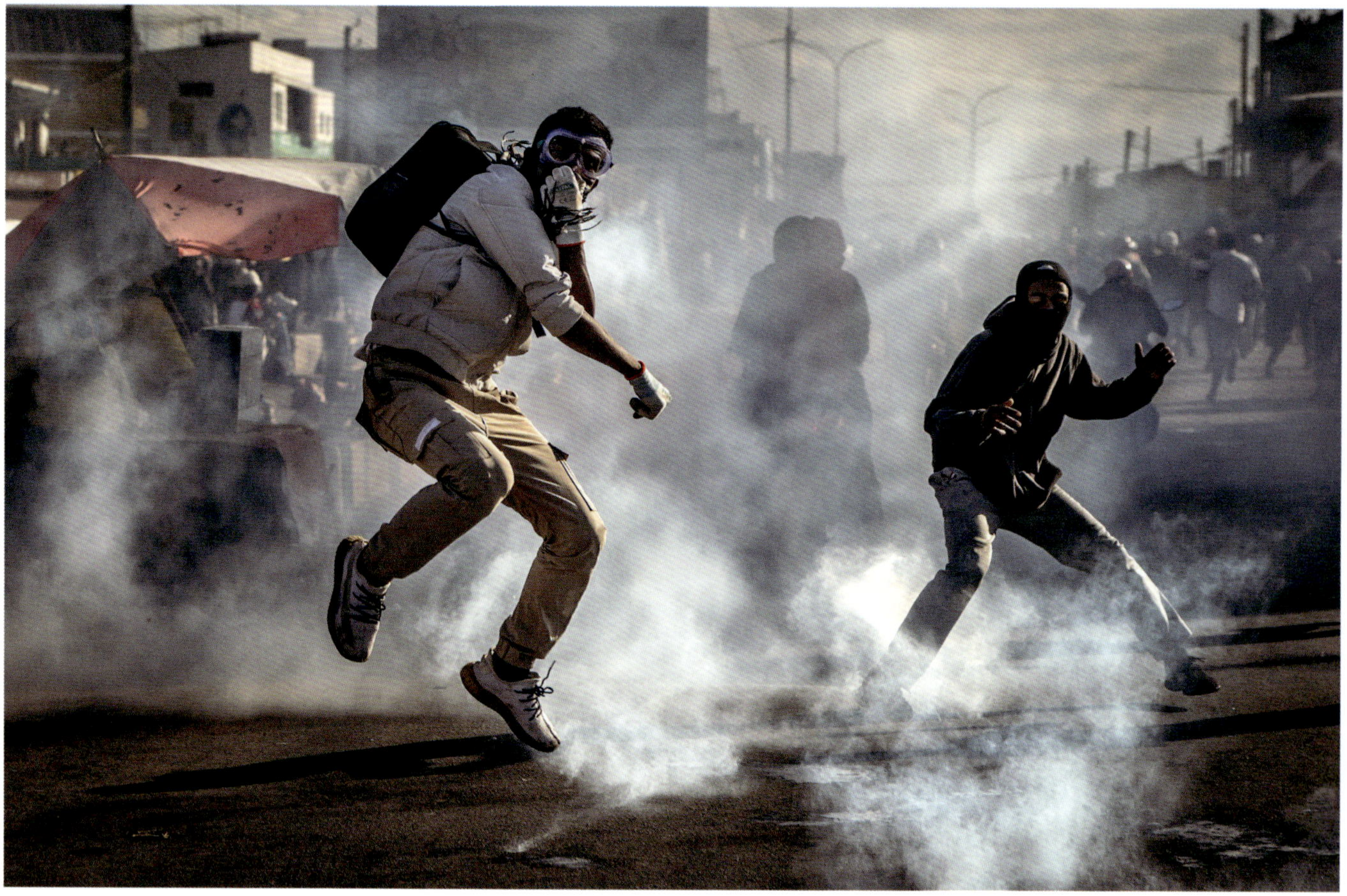

A protester jumps to avoid a tear gas canister during clashes with Malagasy security forces at a demonstration calling for the resignation of President Andry Rajoelina. 6 October 2025

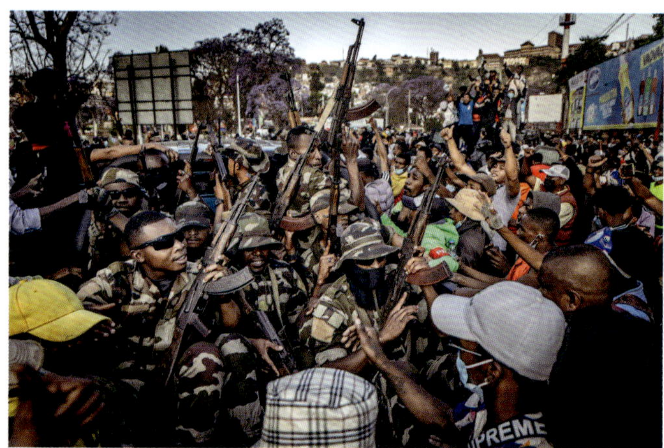

Members of the CAPSAT military unit ride a pickup truck as protesters celebrate their arrival, following clashes between demonstrators and security forces. 11 October 2025

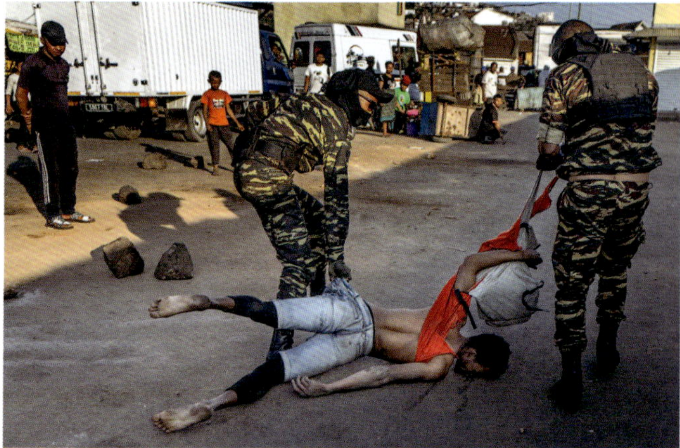

Members of the Malagasy Gendarmerie drag a severely beaten protester during clashes that killed at least 22 people and injured more than 100 others. 9 October 2025

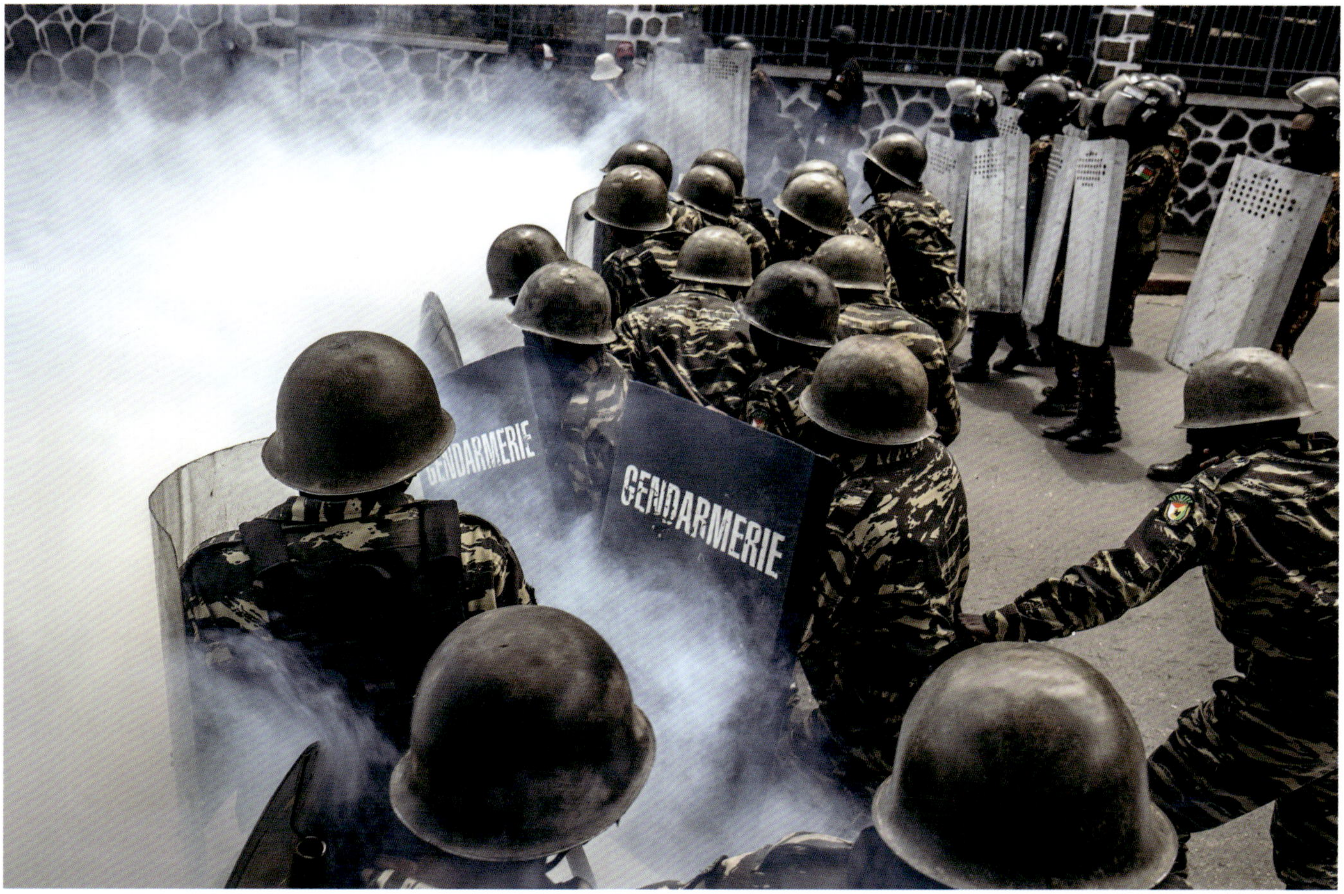

Members of the Malagasy Gendarmerie take cover behind their shields amid tear gas during clashes between demonstrators and security forces. 11 October 2025

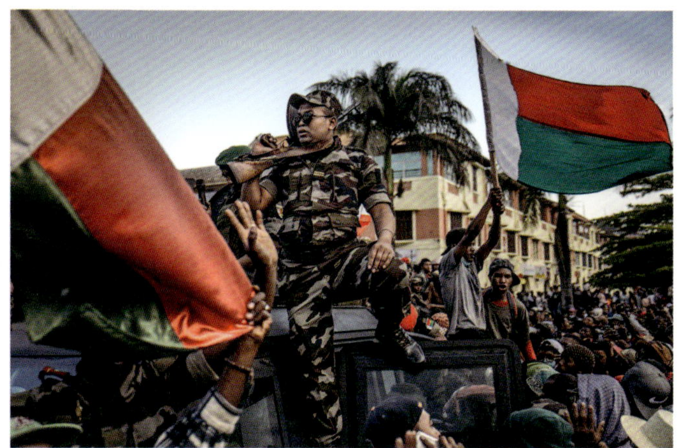

Protesters cheer and wave flags outside City Hall as members of the CAPSAT military unit ride on an armored vehicle. 11 October 2025

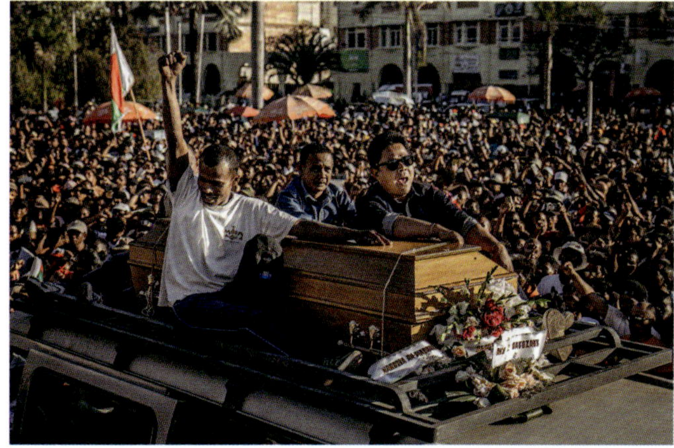

Family members of Safidy Rakotoarisoa, a protester allegedly killed during demonstrations, carry his coffin atop a van and sing the national anthem. 13 October 2025

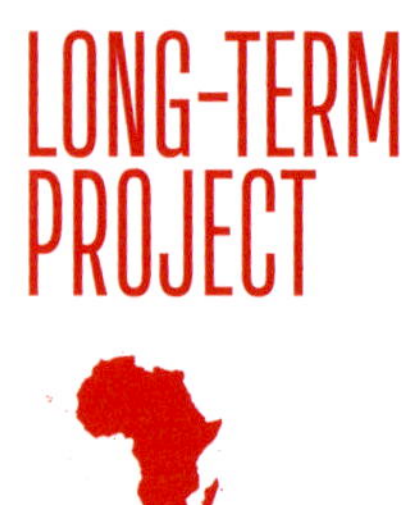

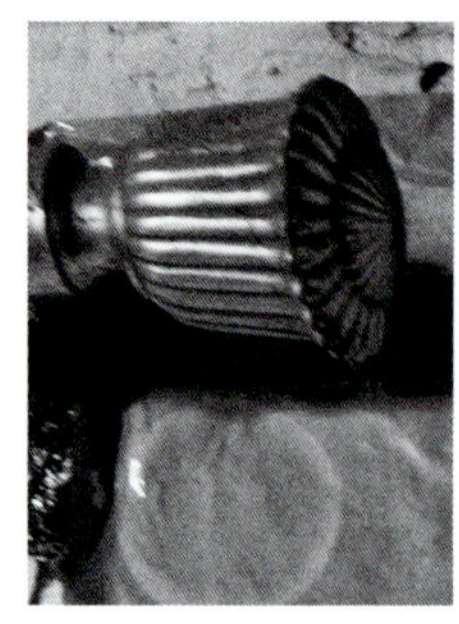

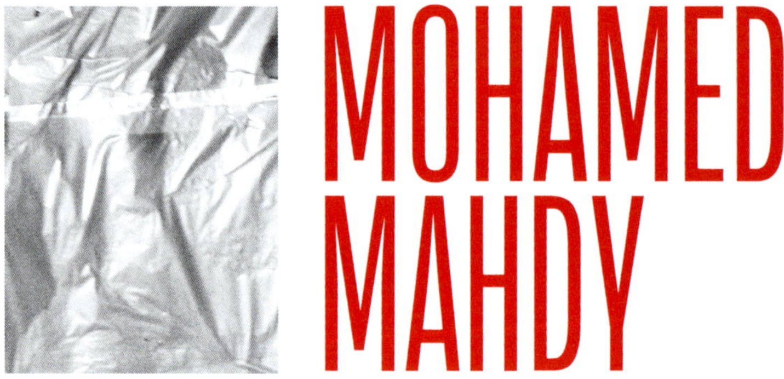

MOHAMED MAHDY

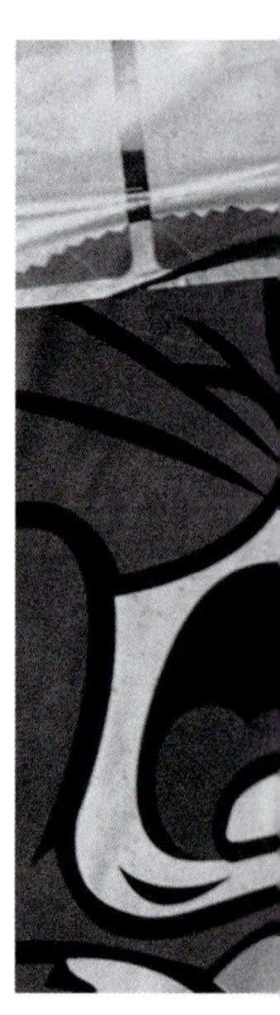

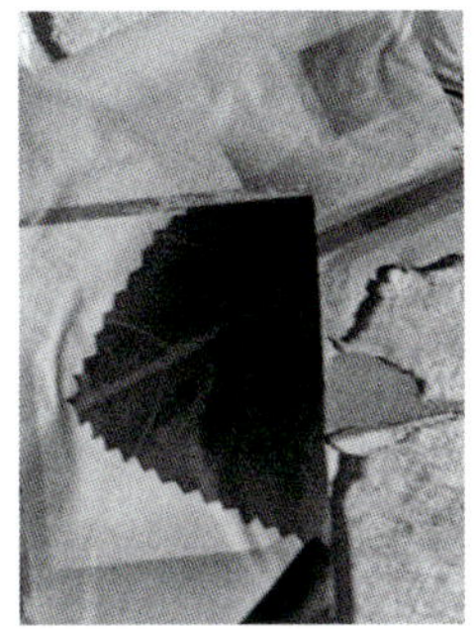

More than 30,000 residents of Wadi El-Qamar, also known as Moon Valley, in western Alexandria, Egypt, live less than 15 meters from a cement factory that fills their homes with toxic dust. Children are born with asthma. Families suffer from lung disease and irreversible respiratory damage. In 2016, the photographer – who lives nearby and has asthma himself – began documenting their stories and ongoing legal battles. This project has helped secure medical and legal aid for families while revealing how industrial practices that fuel the climate crisis devastate the most vulnerable communities first.

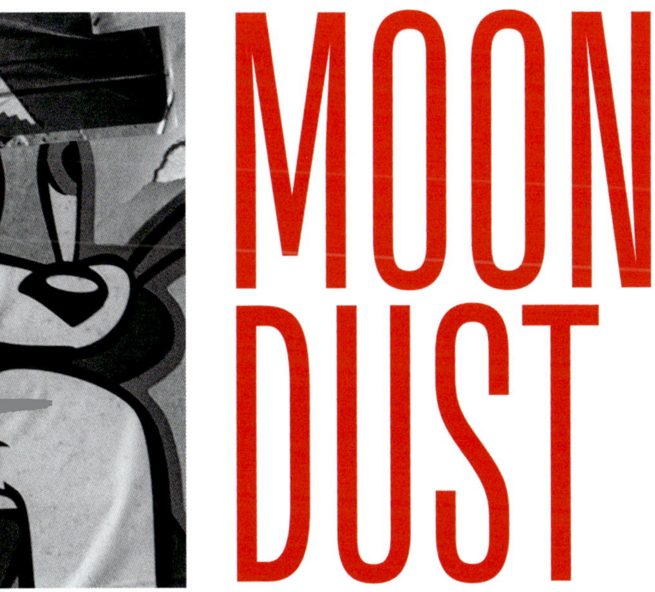

MOON DUST

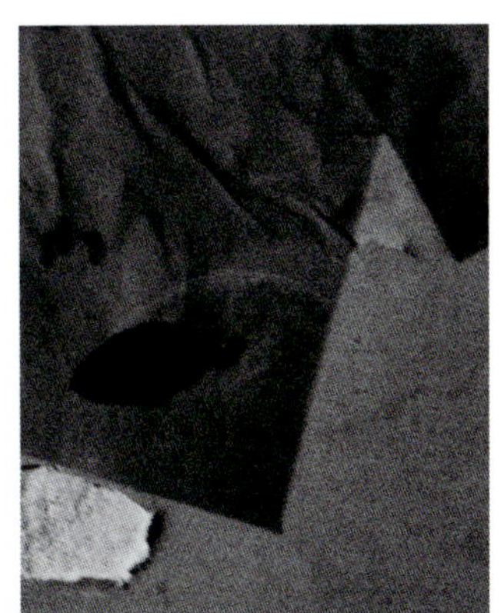

Vibrations from the Titan cement factory damage the walls of nearby houses and cause roofs to give way. Ola, who lives directly opposite, patches cracks with stickers and tape. 18 March 2018
All photos taken in Alexandria, Egypt / Mohamed Mahdy, Arab Documentary Photography Program

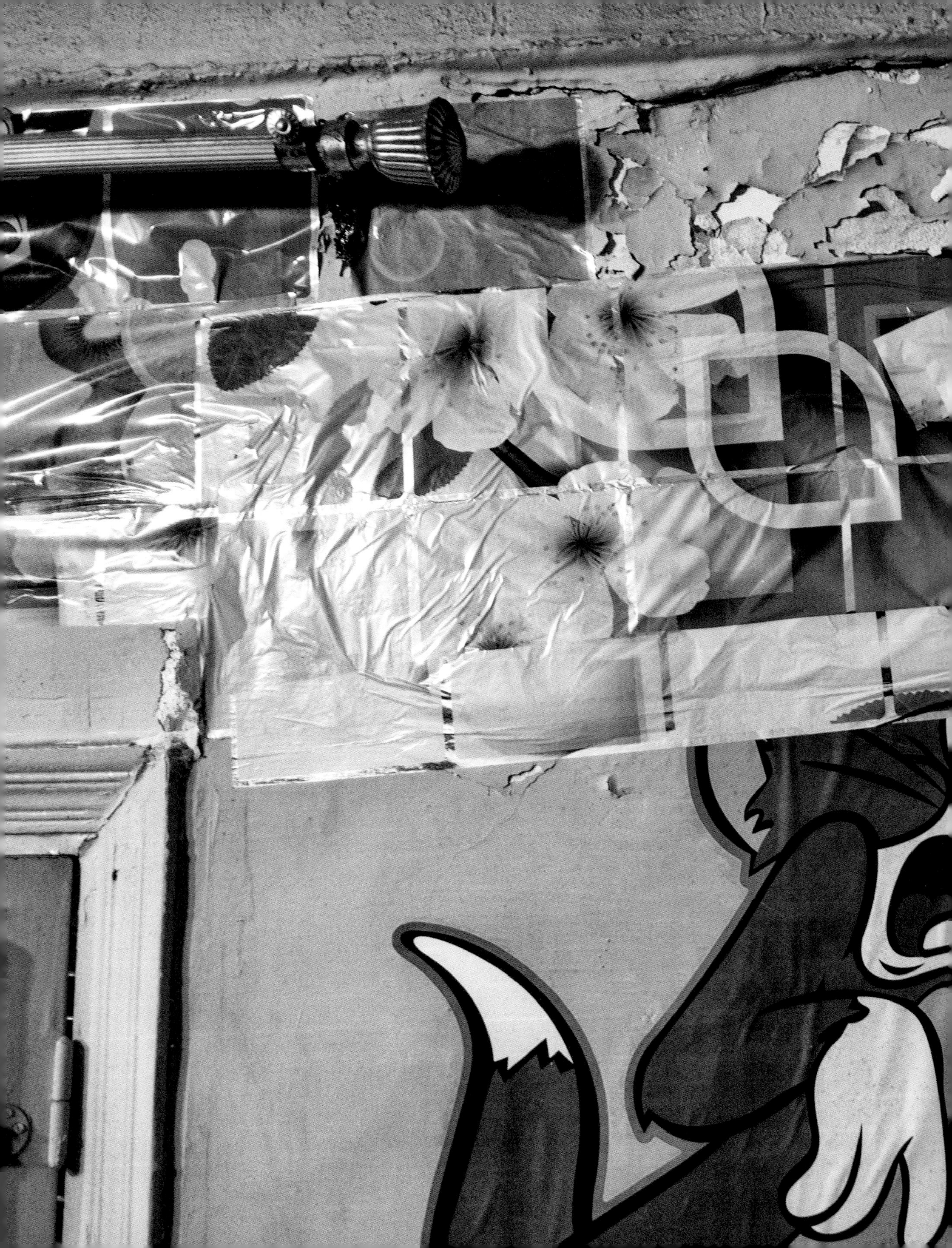

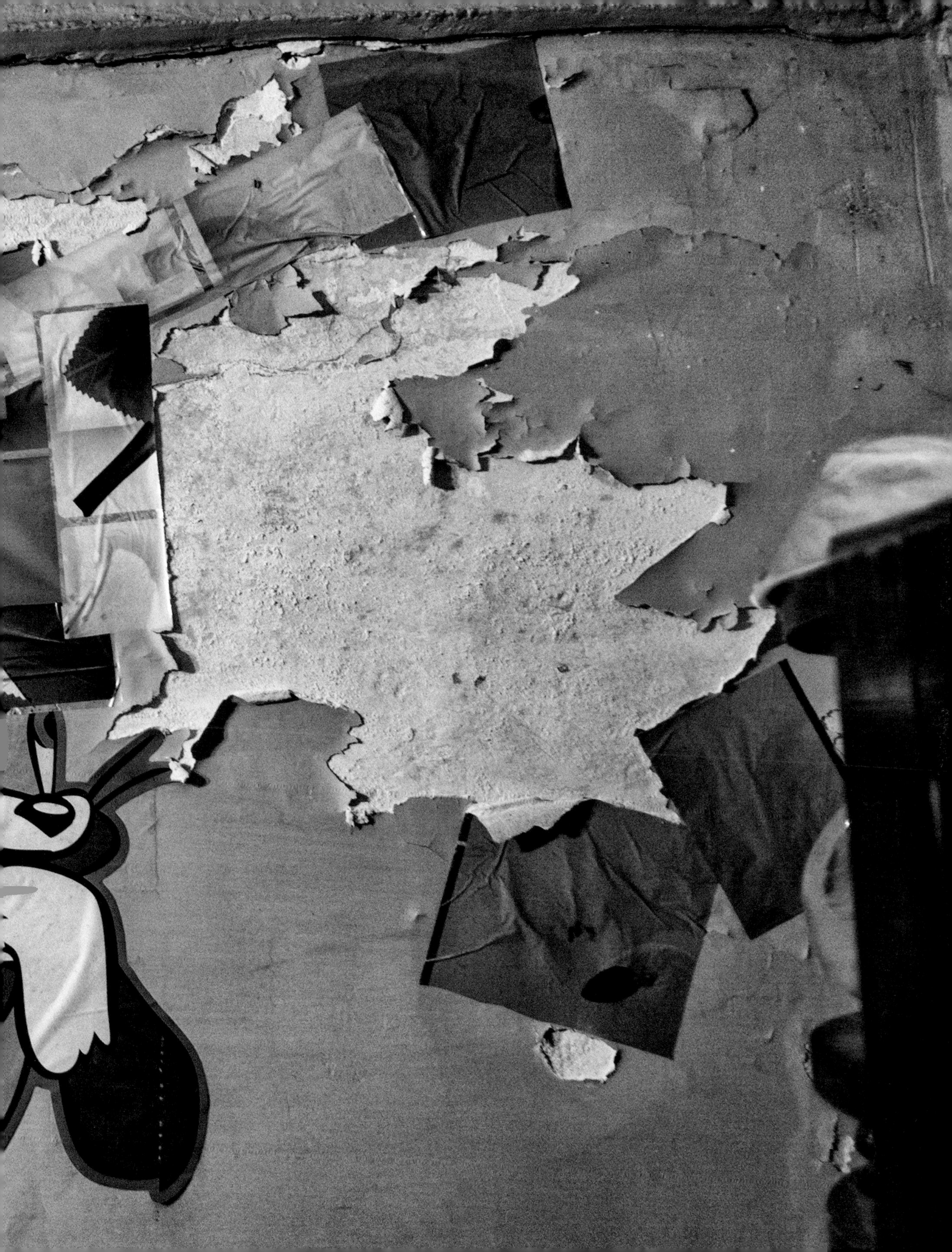

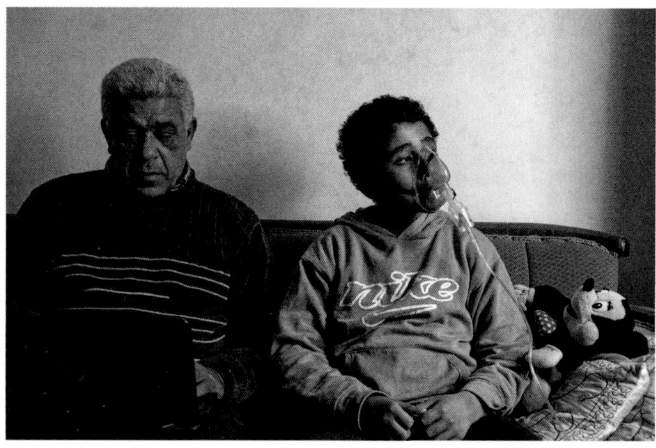

Ahmed (11), photographed with his father Saeed, was born with asthma and uses a ventilator three times a day. He plays goalkeeper in football as it requires less physical strain. 31 January 2017

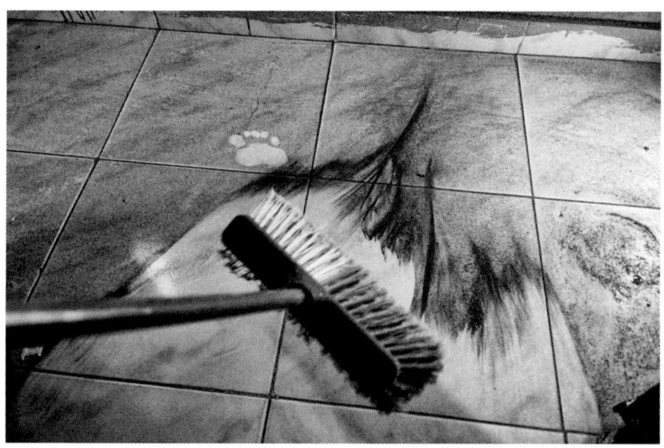

Dust on the floor of a Moon Valley home. If windows are left open for just half an hour, nearly one centimeter of dust accumulates. 18 March 2018

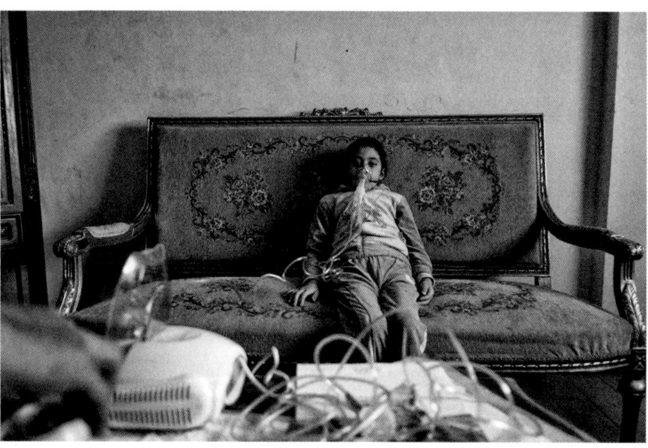

Amal (11) uses a breathing ventilator, which she has relied on since developing asthma as a toddler. 31 January 2018

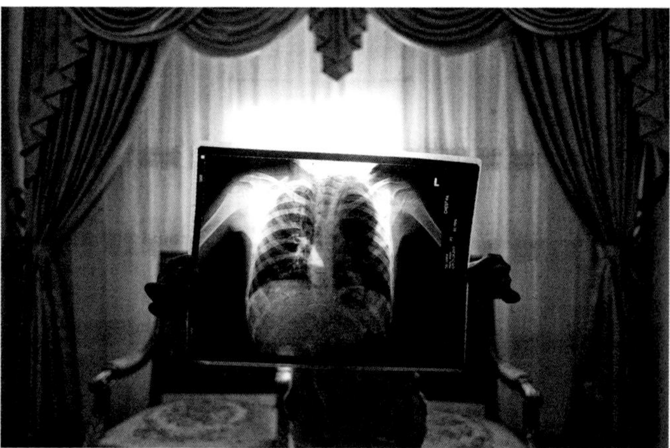

Amal holds an X-ray of her lungs. She moved to Moon Valley at three years old and developed asthma within months. 31 January 2018

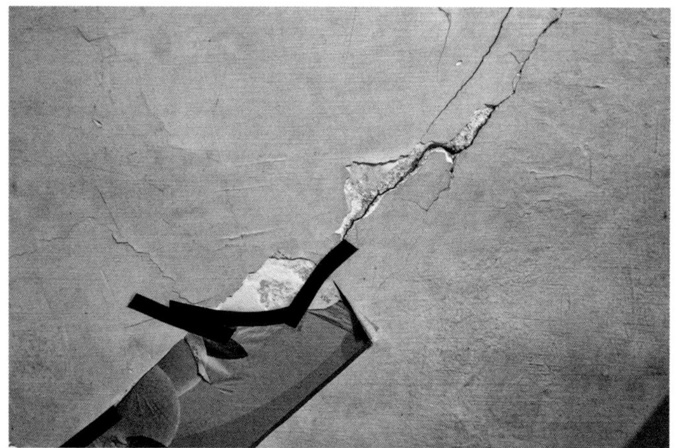

Tape covers a crack caused by factory vibrations. "Now we're supposed to buy the cement they're killing us with to repair the house," says Ola, who lives opposite the factory. 18 March 2018

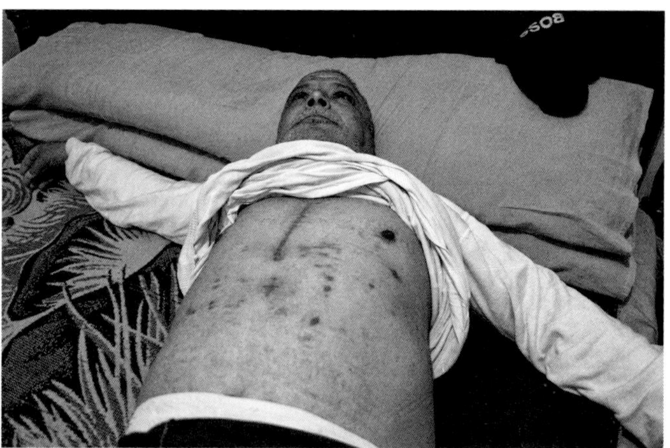

Ahmed Aniny filed a lawsuit but waited ten years without a ruling. After multiple surgeries, he insisted on this photograph: "I want everyone to see what happened." He has since passed away. 29 December 2017

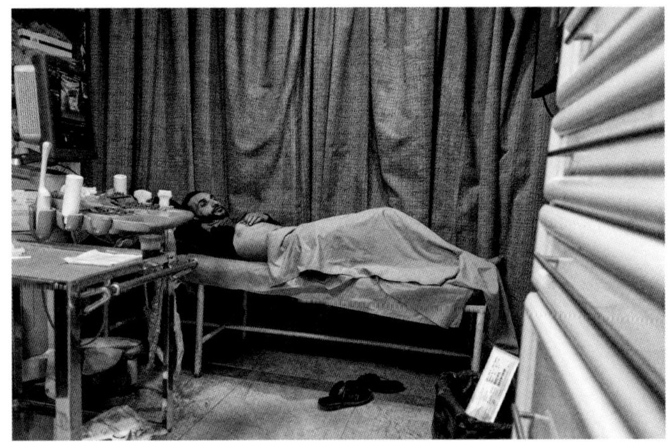

Abdelrahman prepares to have fluid removed from his lungs. Funds for his treatment were raised through this project. 9 January 2018

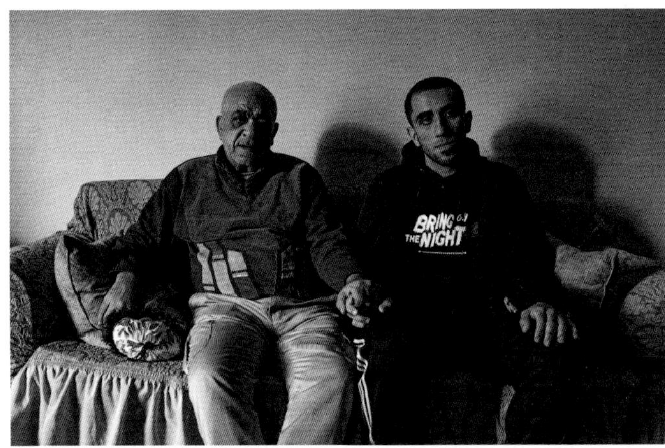

Ahmed (now 20) and Saeed. They won their lawsuit after years of legal battles – a rare victory and the first environmental case won in Egyptian courts. 13 December 2025

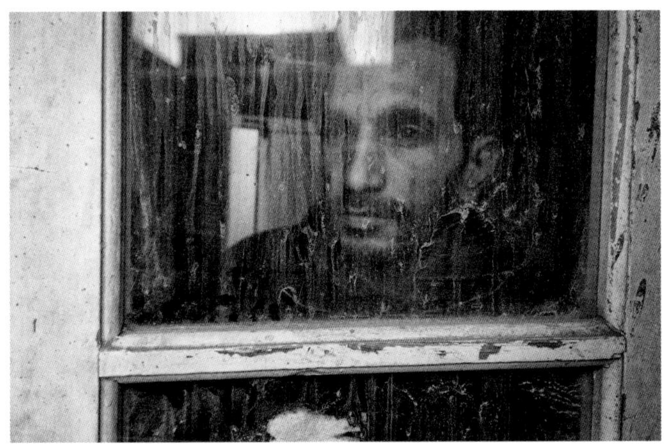

Abdelrahman, who spent everything he had on treatment, uses only 20% of his lung capacity due to silicosis. His fiancée left him, as he had no money or energy left for marriage. 14 February 2018

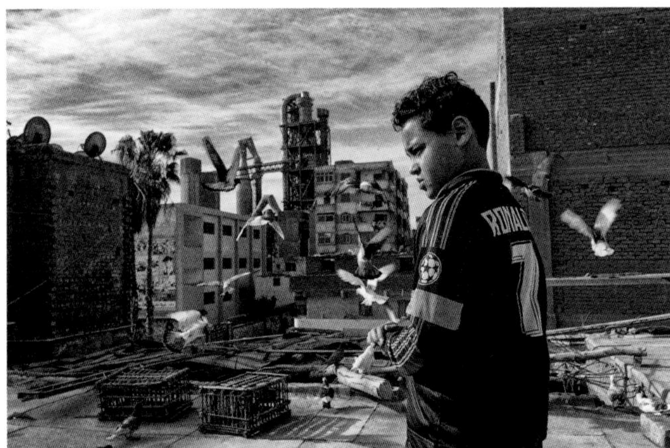

Awady, who was born with asthma, raises pigeons as a hobby. "Every day, I am afraid I won't be able to play football again," he says. 14 February 2018

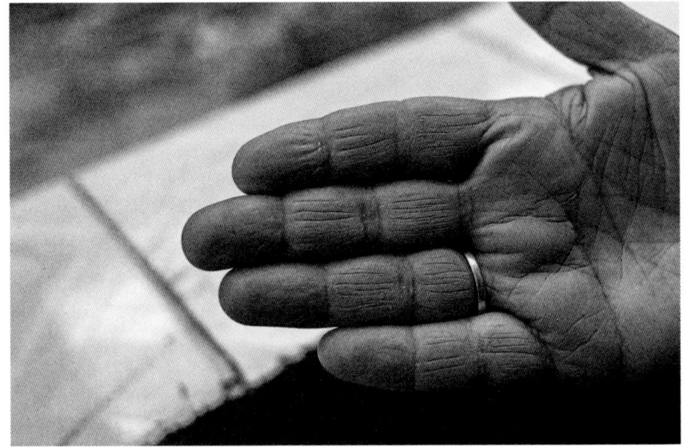

"We've grown up with the dust; it is our companion," Ola says. "You eat it as you walk, and find it in your beds and closets, almost everywhere." 9 October 2017

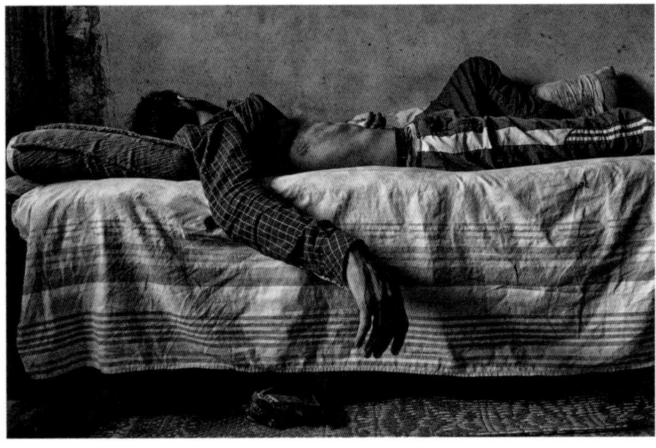

Abdelrahman (33) rests in his room. "The doctor told me I might not survive six months, but here I am, just sleeping," he says. 20 October 2017

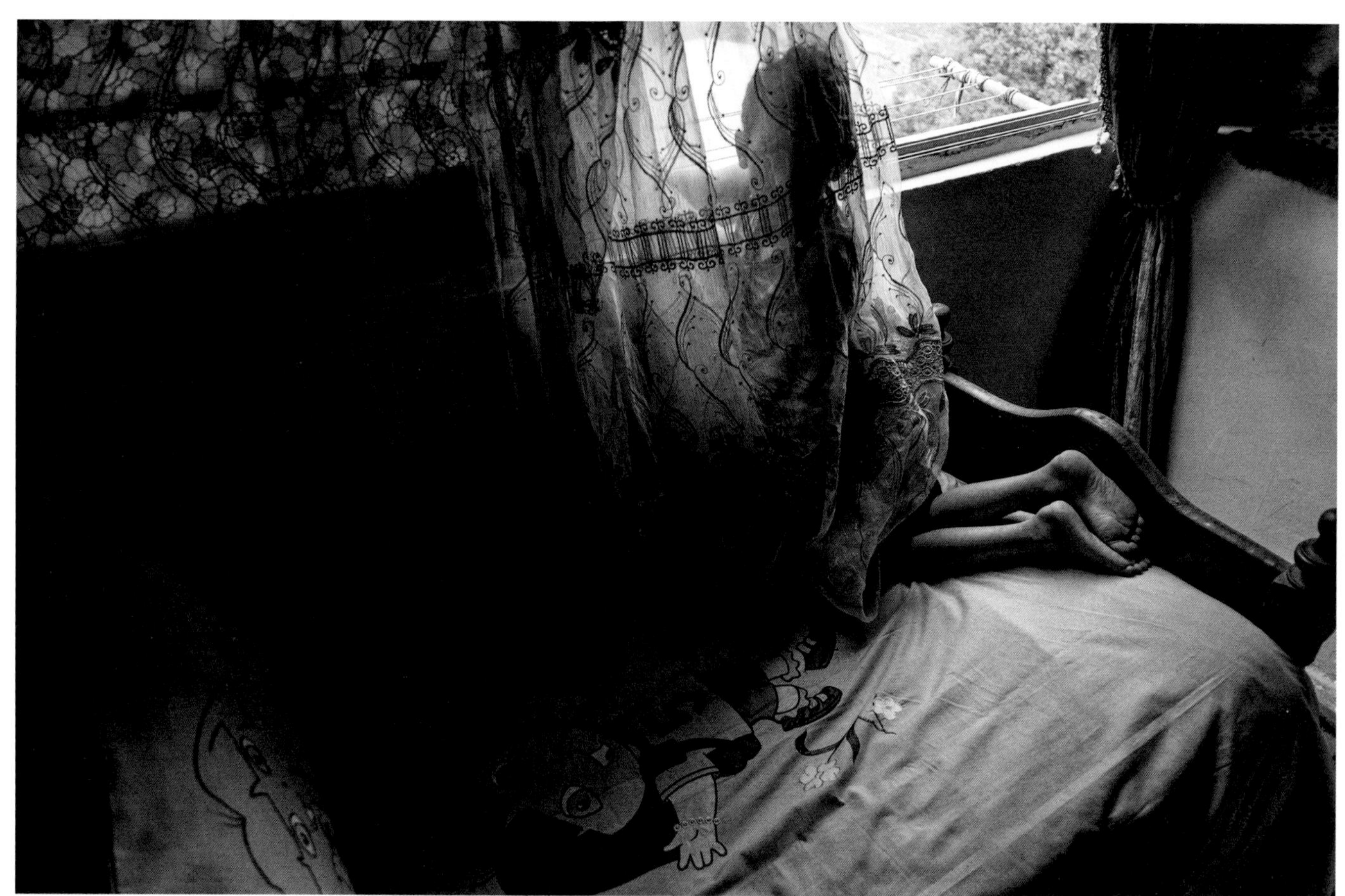

Yousef, who has asthma, rarely leaves his home. Like many children in Moon Valley, his condition keeps him isolated, affecting his mental and emotional well-being. 9 October 2017

—

HOW CAN PHOTOJOURNALISM HAVE IMPACT?

When made with compassion and dignity, images turn witness into action – compelling policymakers and the public alike to respond.

—

Kira Pollack,
Global jury chair

Photojournalism creates impact when it becomes a relationship. Real impact comes from listening, returning, and allowing ourselves to change – so stories grow with communities, challenge power structures, and reflect people with dignity.

—

Karla Gachet Vega,
South America jury

When seeing no longer guarantees believing, photojournalism has impact by capturing authentic moments.

—

Wang Hui Fen,
Asia-Pacific and Oceania jury

Photographs move and compel people from one corner of the world to feel connected to another person somewhere else in a way words can never do.

—

Sima Diab,
West, Central, and South Asia jury

Photojournalism has impact by providing evidence and becoming a bridge between the ground and the audience.

—

Maheder Haileselassie,
Africa jury

By documenting events truthfully, photojournalism creates a lasting record of our time. Newsrooms and media consumers share a responsibility to support and protect this craft.

—

Solana Cain,
North and Central America jury

Photojournalists create impact by addressing topics of local and global relevance with depth and rigor, sharing information, data, and images that deepen our understanding of the world and its challenges.

—

Silvia Omedes,
Europe jury

ASIA-PACIFIC AND OCEANIA

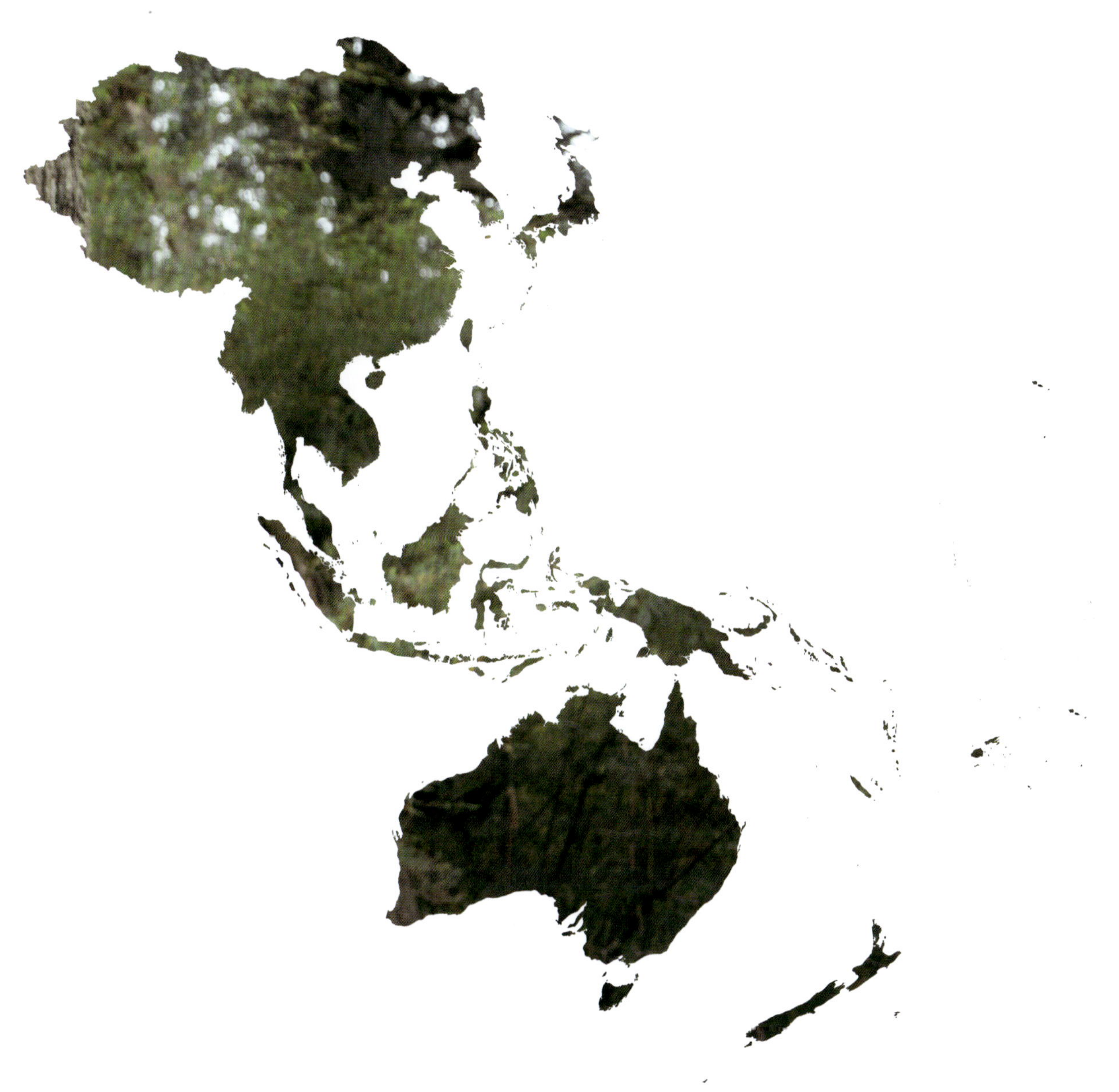

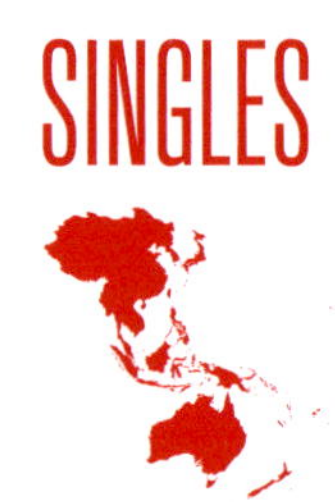

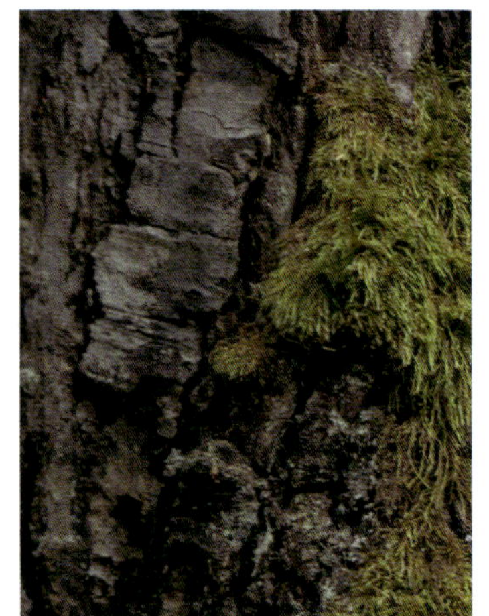

MOUNTAIN RESIDENT OF WANGLANG

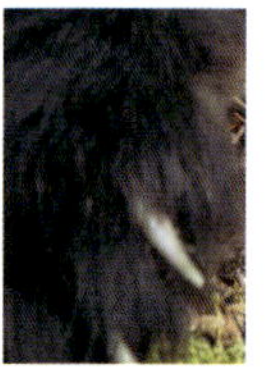

Recent population estimates suggest that fewer than 2,000 pandas remain in the wild, and only a few dozen individuals live within Wanglang National Nature Reserve's 323-square-kilometer territory. This rare sighting was made possible through a pilot exchange program between the National Geographic Society and wildlife biologists, aimed at supporting wildlife monitoring efforts and fostering cross-cultural cooperation in conservation. Established in 1965, Wanglang is one of China's oldest wild panda nature reserves and today serves as a key site for education and scientific research collaboration within the larger Giant Panda National Park system.

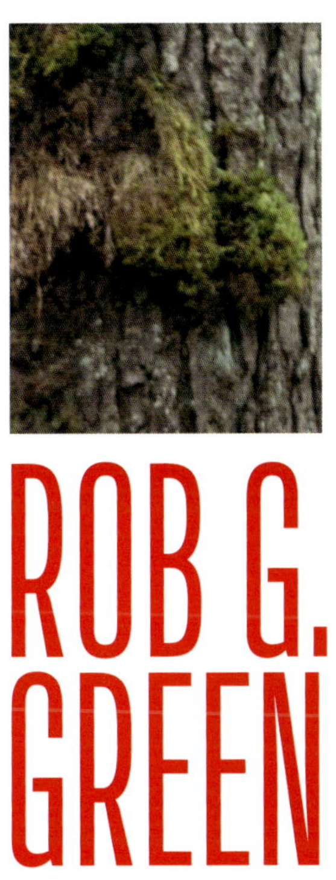

ROB G. GREEN

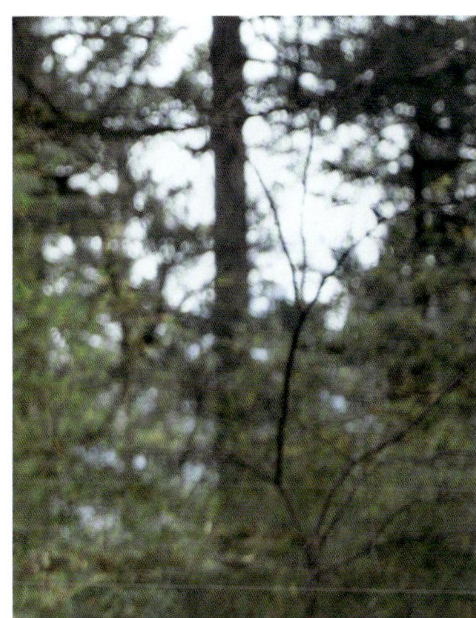

A wild giant panda is captured by a camera trap in the Wanglang National Nature Reserve. Sichuan, China, 11 November 2025 / Rob G. Green, National Geographic Society, Henry Luce Foundation

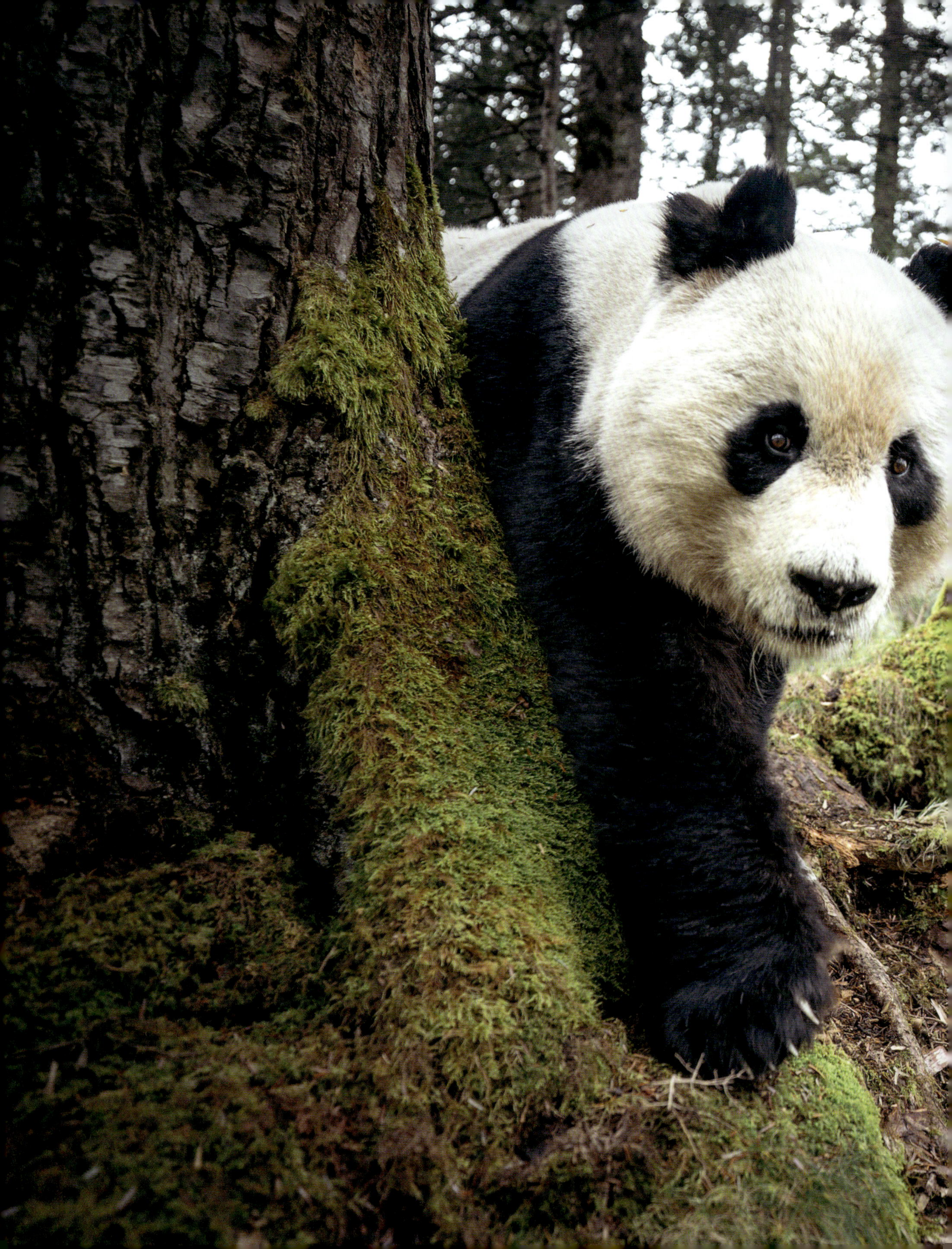

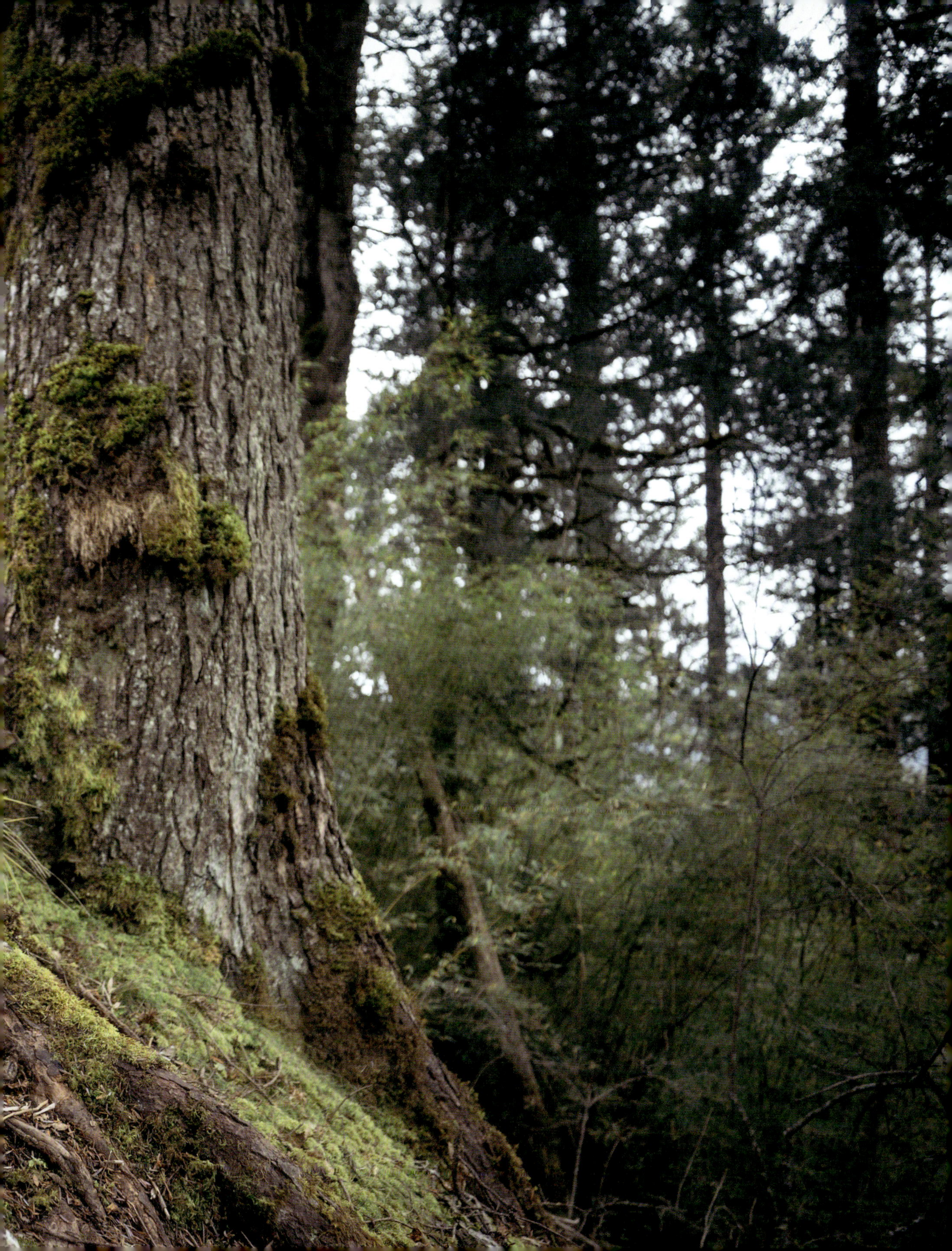

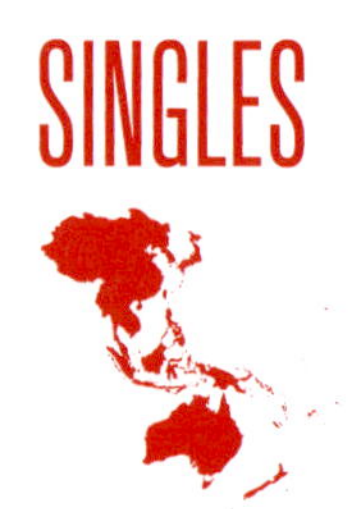

TYRONE SIU

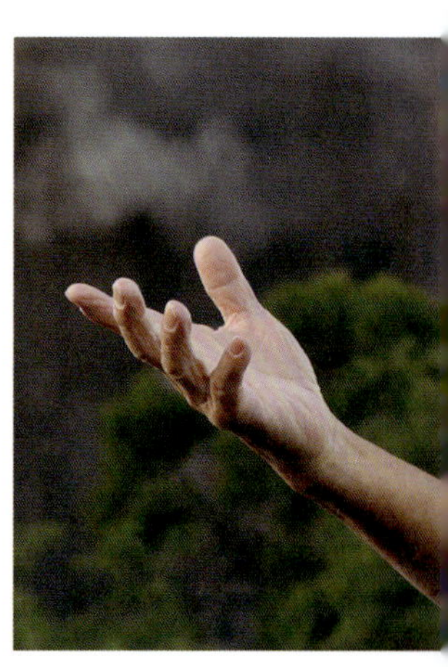

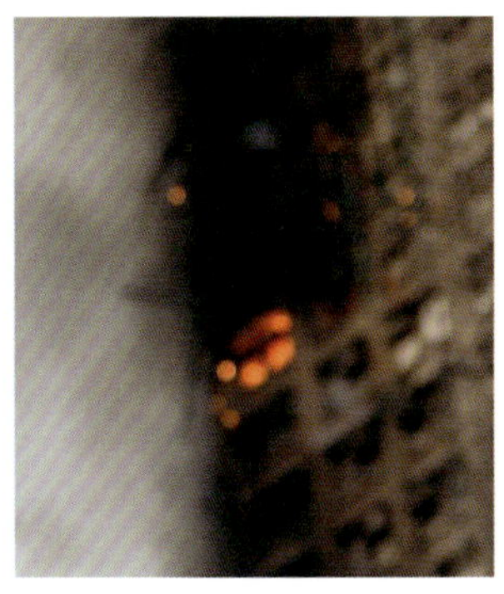

A massive fire at the Wang Fuk Court housing complex in Tai Po claimed 168 lives, becoming Hong Kong's deadliest fire since 1948. While no official cause has been reported, investigations by Hong Kong authorities found that bamboo scaffolding, construction netting, and flammable Styrofoam boards on windows acted as accelerants for the fire, trapping residents inside. More than 2,000 firefighters were involved in rescue efforts, killing one and injuring twelve.

A DESPERATE PLEA

Mr Wong cries out in anguish as fire engulfs the Tai Po housing complex he calls home. Moments earlier, he phoned his wife, who was trapped in the building, and they exchanged what would be their final words.
Hong Kong, 26 November 2025 / Tyrone Siu, Reuters

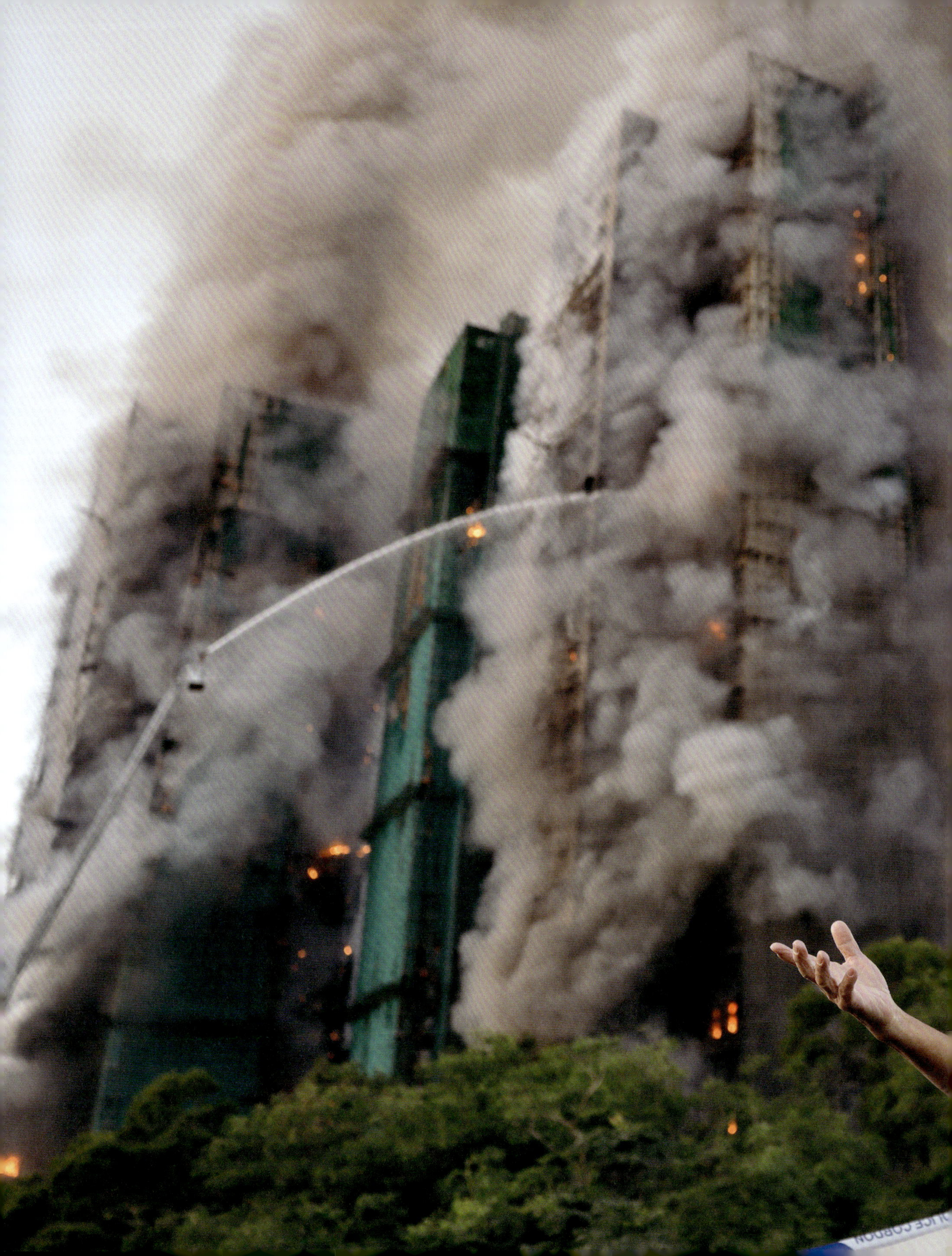

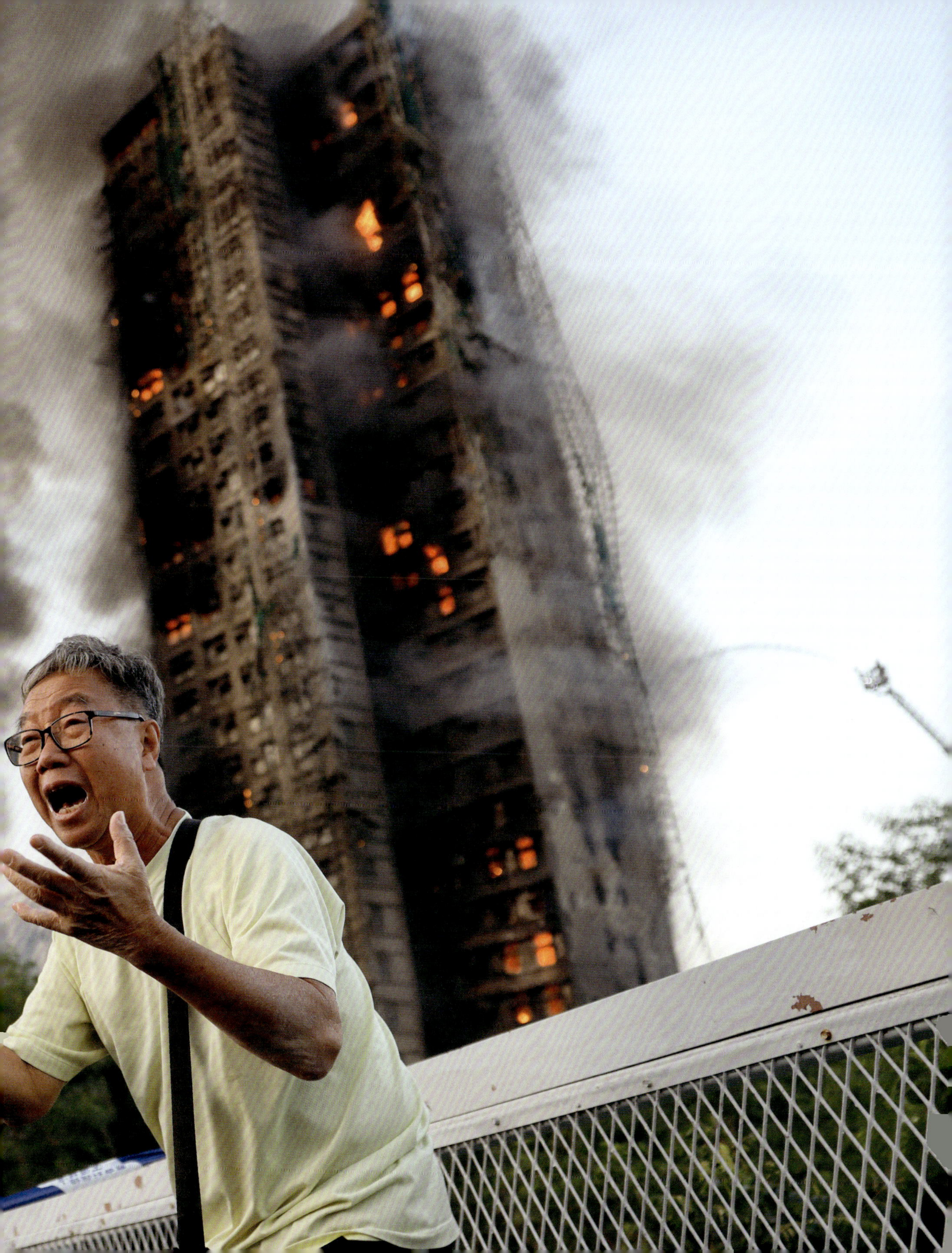

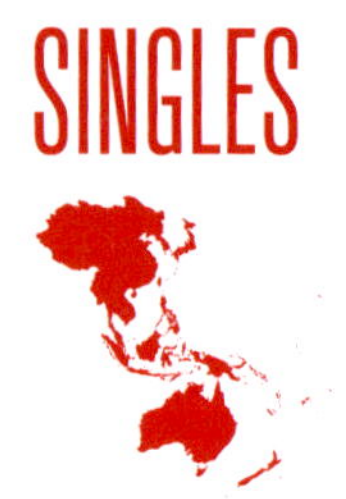

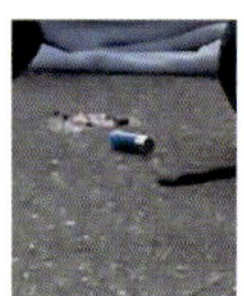

During Bondi Beach's "Chanukah by the Sea," a community event celebrating the Jewish holiday, two armed men motivated by ISIS ideology attacked participants, killing 15 people. The victims included 10-year-old Matilda and 87-year-old Ukrainian Holocaust survivor Alexander Kleytman. Prime Minister Anthony Albanese called the mass shooting an antisemitic attack and the deadliest terrorist incident on Australian soil ever. The shooting has prompted a significant re-evaluation of public security and religious freedom protections in Australia.

EDWINA PICKLES

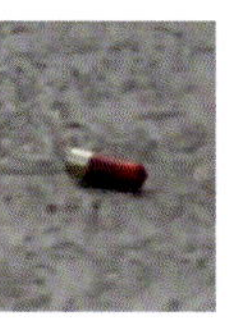

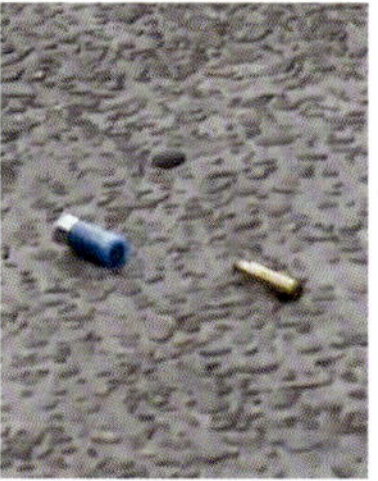

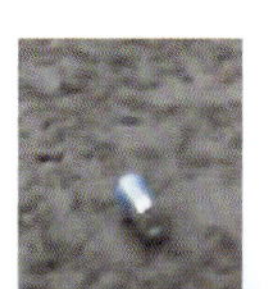

BONDI BEACH TERROR ATTACK

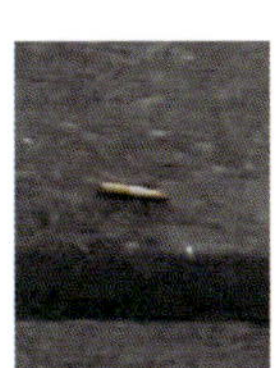

An overwhelmed police officer leans over near the bodies of Boris (69) and Sofia (61) Gurman. During the Bondi Beach Terror Attack, the couple were killed while attempting to disarm one of the shooters. Sydney, Australia, 14 December 2025 / Edwina Pickles, *The Sydney Morning Herald*

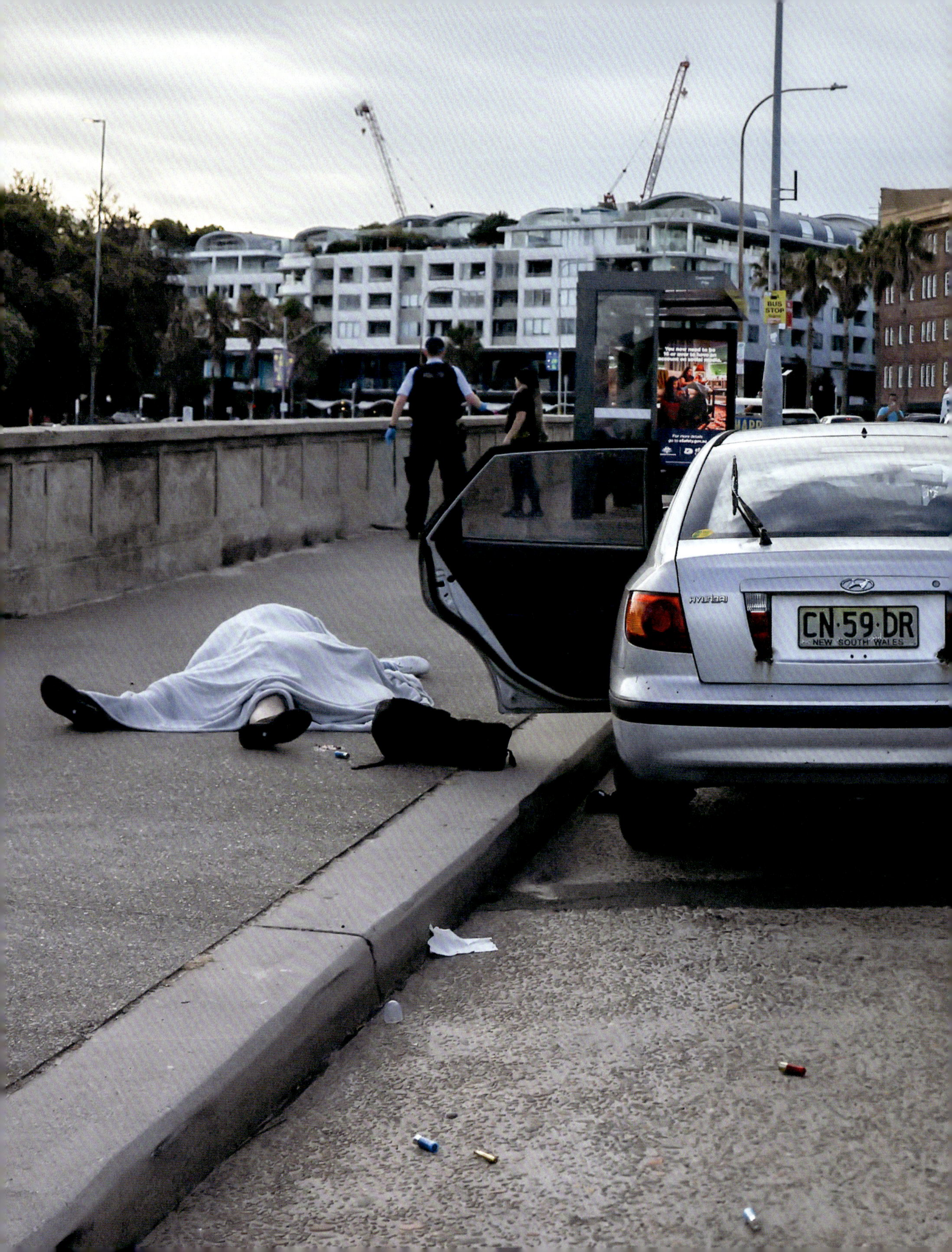

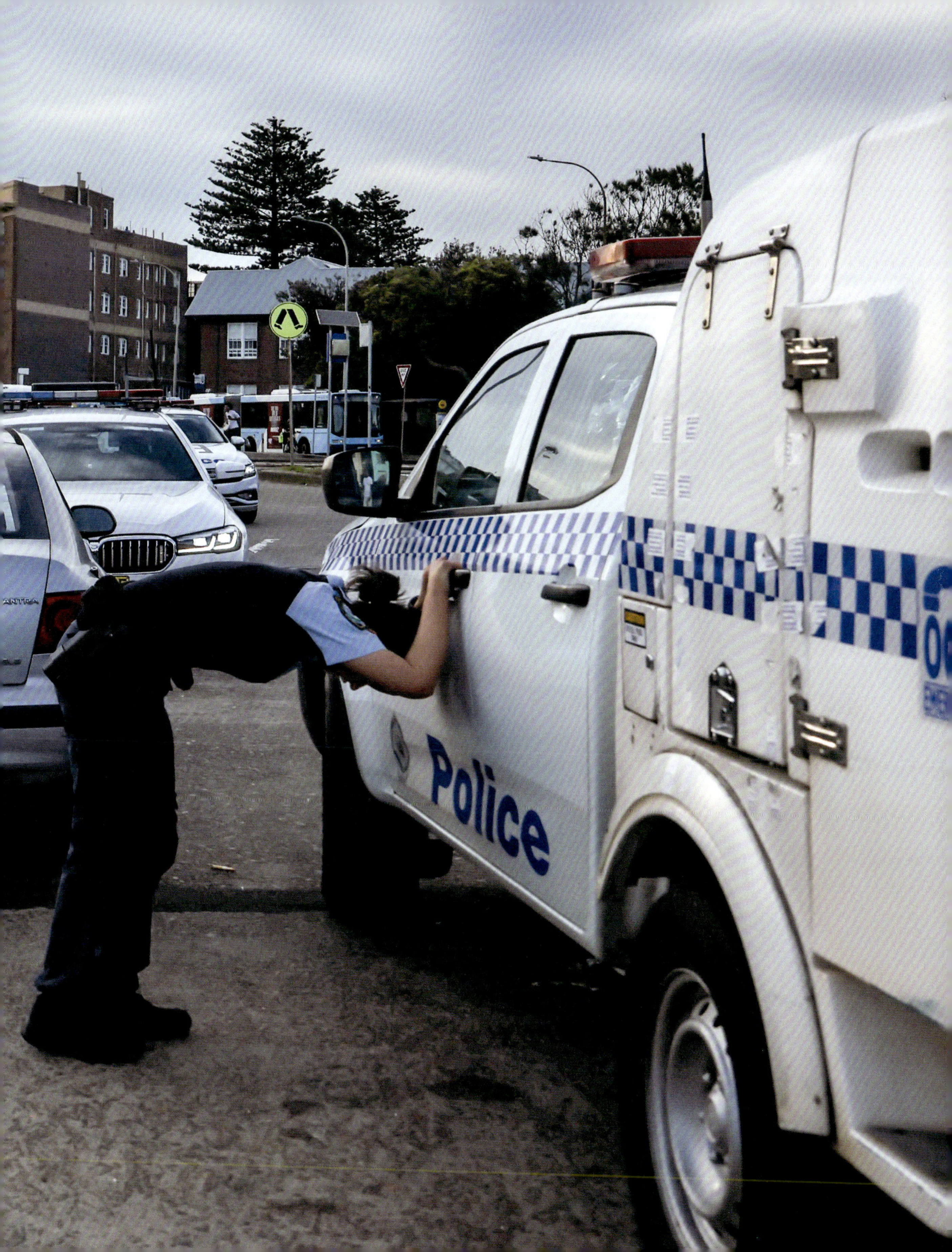

Police

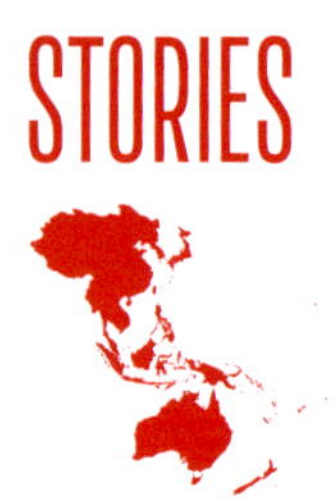

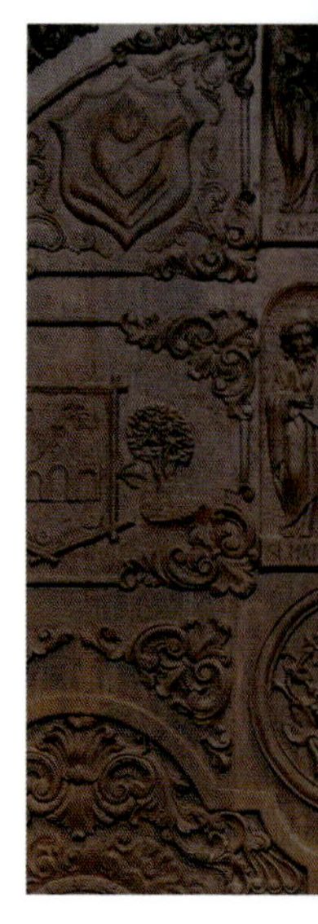

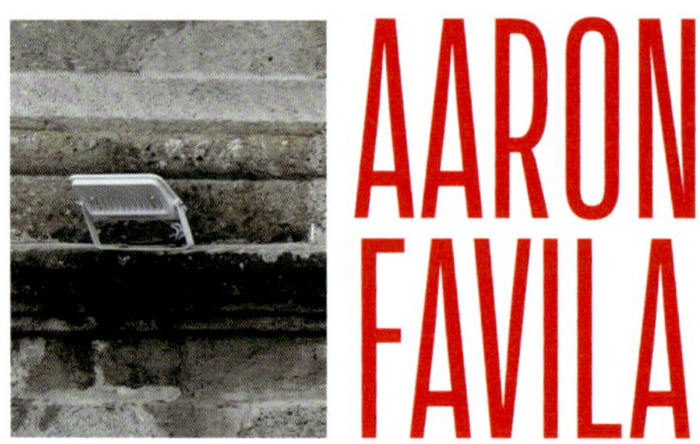

AARON FAVILA

When Typhoon Wipha hit the Philippines and flooded Barasoain Church, Jade Rick Verdillo and Jamaica Aguilar faced a difficult decision: should they cancel their wedding or proceed with the marriage? The couple carried on despite high waters, a testament to love and resilience in the face of severe weather. Located on a delta, Bulacan province is vulnerable to more frequent and extreme floods caused by aging drainage systems, dredging projects, overextraction of groundwater, and climate change.

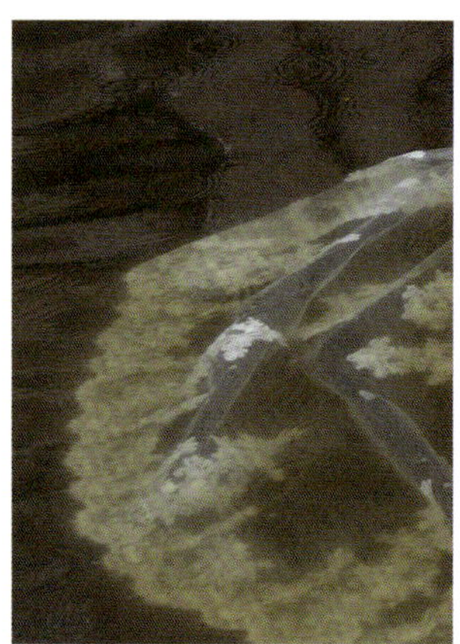

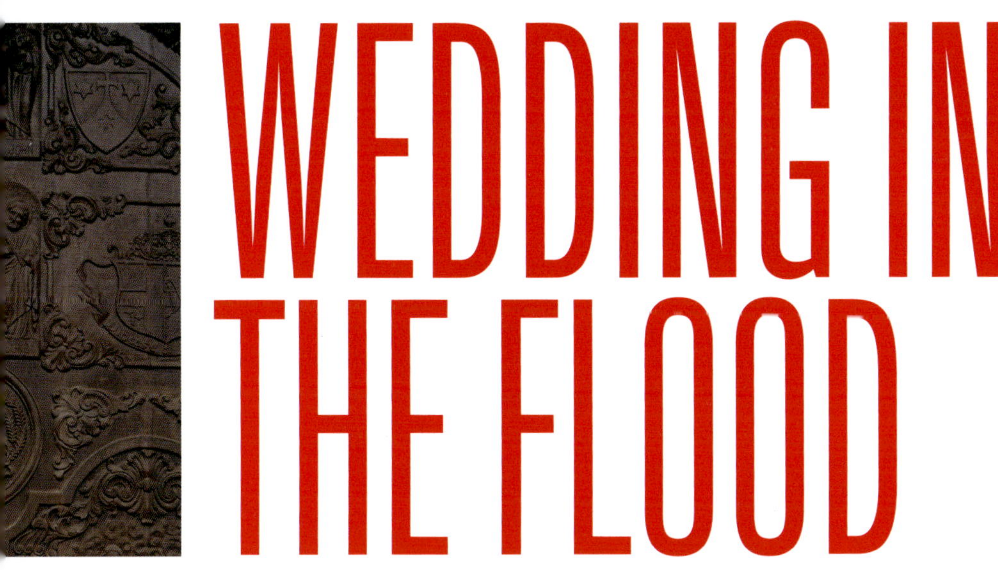

WEDDING IN THE FLOOD

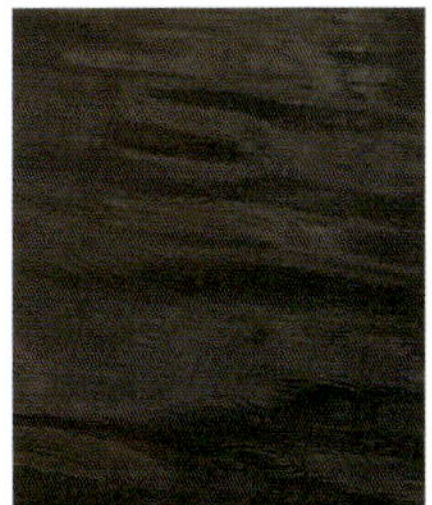

Bride Jamaica Aguilar prepares to enter the flooded Barasoain Church for her wedding. The Barasoain Church, a national landmark, is situated in a region where nearly 75% of the population is exposed to flooding hazards. All photos taken in Malolos, Bulacan province, Philippines on 22 July 2025 / Aaron Favila, Associated Press

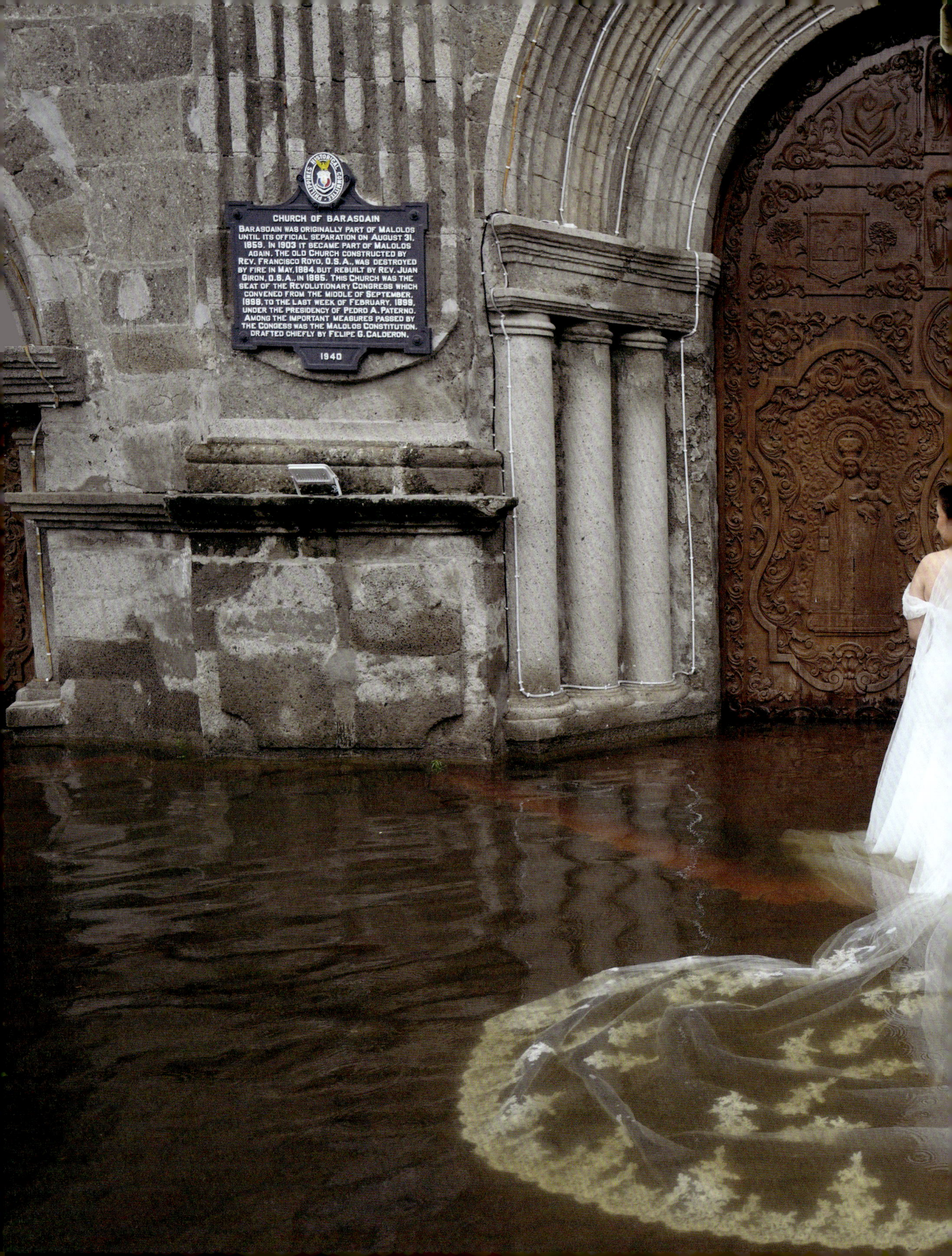
PHILIPPINES HISTORICAL COMMITTEE

CHURCH OF BARASOAIN
BARASOAIN WAS ORIGINALLY PART OF MALOLOS
UNTIL ITS OFFICIAL SEPARATION ON AUGUST 31,
1859. IN 1903 IT BECAME PART OF MALOLOS
AGAIN. THE OLD CHURCH CONSTRUCTED BY
REV. FRANCISCO ROYO, O.S.A., WAS DESTROYED
BY FIRE IN MAY, 1884, BUT REBUILT BY REV. JUAN
GIRON, O.S.A., IN 1885. THIS CHURCH WAS THE
SEAT OF THE REVOLUTIONARY CONGRESS WHICH
CONVENED FROM THE MIDDLE OF SEPTEMBER,
1898, TO THE LAST WEEK OF FEBRUARY, 1899,
UNDER THE PRESIDENCY OF PEDRO A. PATERNO.
AMONG THE IMPORTANT MEASURES PASSED BY
THE CONGESS WAS THE MALOLOS CONSTITUTION,
DRAFTED CHIEFLY BY FELIPE G. CALDERON.

1940

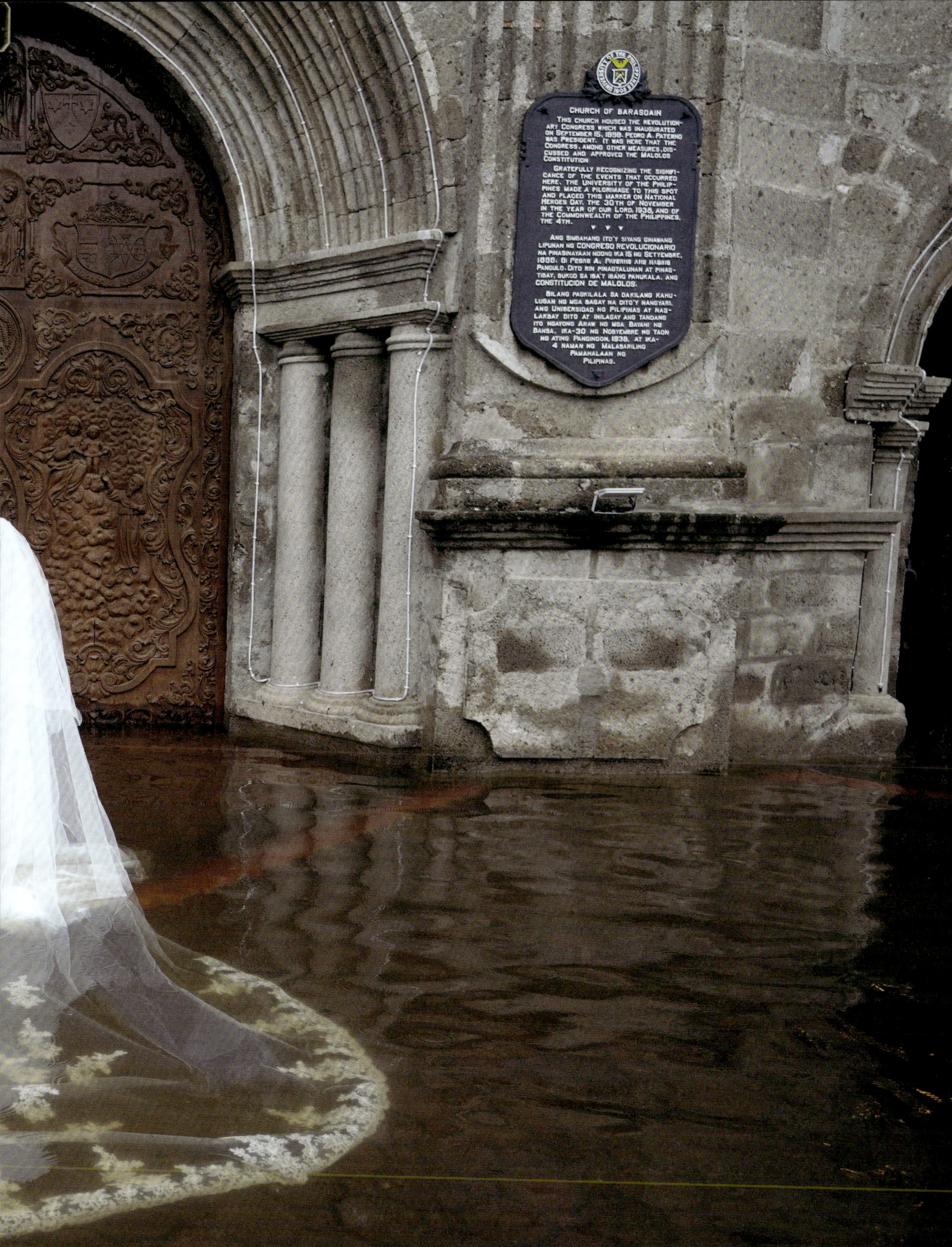

CHURCH OF BARASOAIN
THIS CHURCH HOUSED THE REVOLUTIONARY CONGRESS WHICH WAS INAUGURATED ON SEPTEMBER 15, 1898. PEDRO A. PATERNO WAS PRESIDENT. IT WAS HERE THAT THE CONGRESS, AMONG OTHER MEASURES, DISCUSSED AND APPROVED THE MALOLOS CONSTITUTION
GRATEFULLY RECOGNIZING THE SIGNIFICANCE OF THE EVENTS THAT OCCURRED HERE, THE UNIVERSITY OF THE PHILIPPINES MADE A PILGRIMAGE TO THIS SPOT AND PLACED THIS MARKER ON NATIONAL HEROES DAY, THE 30TH OF NOVEMBER IN THE YEAR OF OUR LORD, 1938, AND OF THE COMMONWEALTH OF THE PHILIPPINES, THE 4TH.
ANG SIMBAHANG ITO'Y SIYANG GINAWANG LIPUNAN NG CONGRESO REVOLUCIONARIO NA PINASINAYAAN NOONG IKA 15 NG SETYEMBRE, 1898. SI PEDRO A. PATERNO ANG NAGING PANGULO. DITO RIN PINAGTALUNAN AT PINAGTIBAY, BUKOD SA IBA'T IBANG PANUKALA, ANG CONSTITUCION DE MALOLOS.
BILANG PAGKILALA SA DAKILANG KAHULUGAN NG MGA BAGAY NA DITO'Y NANGYARI, ANG UNIBERSIDAD NG PILIPINAS AY NAGLAKBAY DITO AT INILAGAY ANG TANDANG ITO NGAYONG ARAW NG MGA BAYANI NG BANSA, IKA-30 NG NOBYEMBRE NG TAON NG ATING PANGINOON, 1938, AT IKA-4 NAMAN NG MALASARILING PAMAHALAAN NG PILIPINAS.

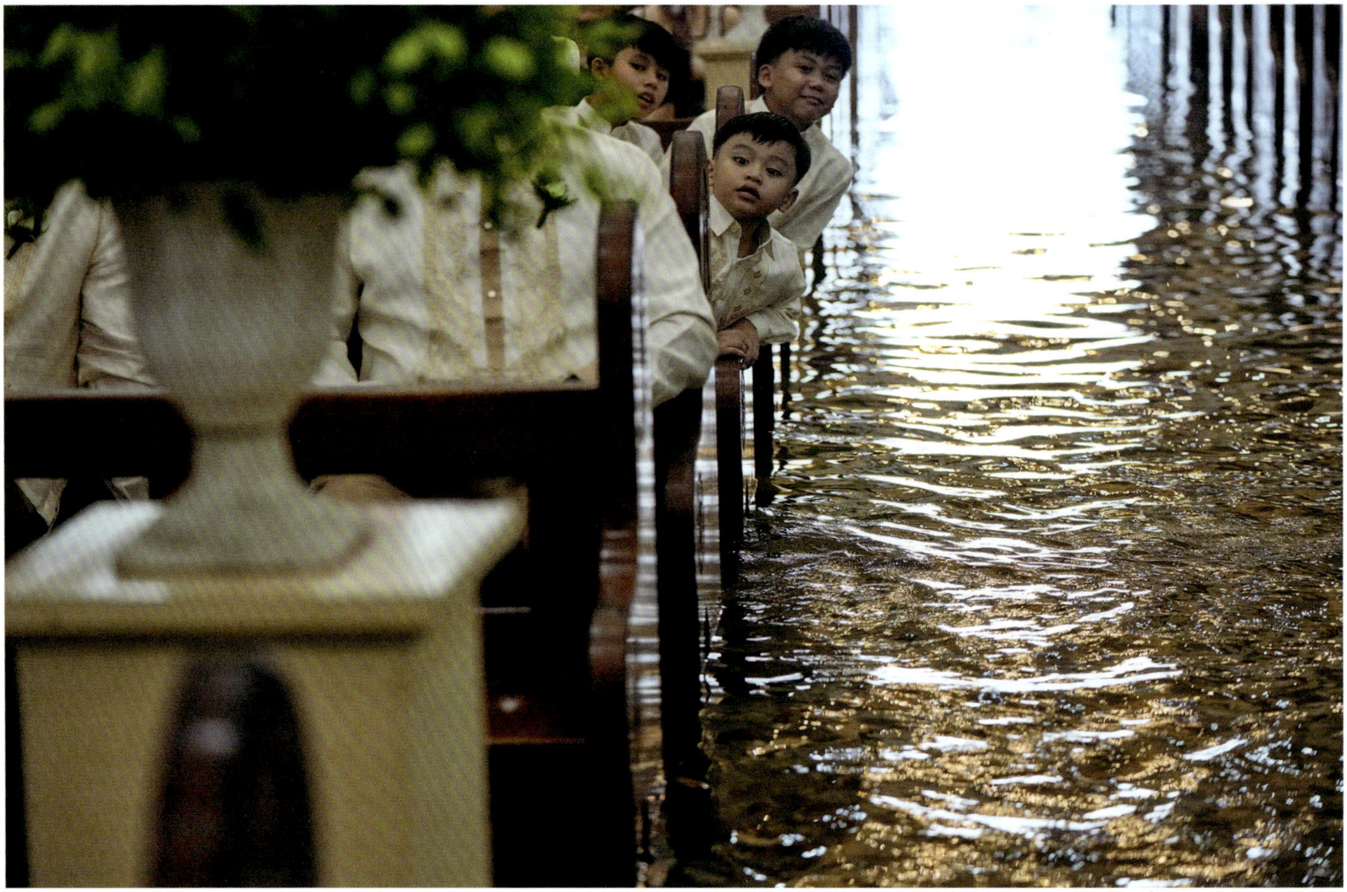

Inside the church, young guests look on attentively. The intensity of tropical cyclones and associated rainfall that has hit the Philippines has significantly increased since 2012.

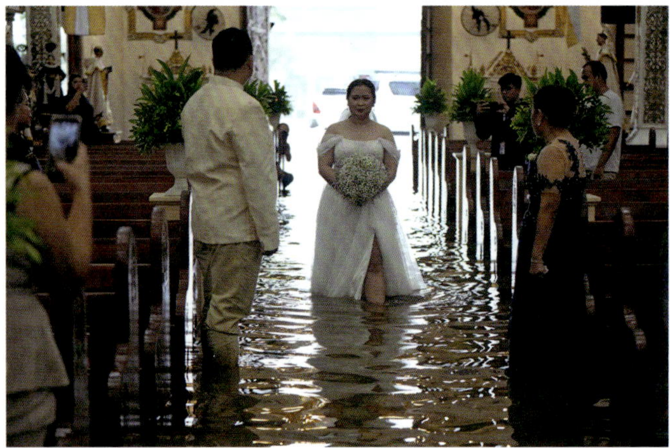

Jamaica Aguilar walks down the flooded aisle of the Barasoain Church. She considered canceling the ceremony the night before when her wedding planners warned her that the flooding could get worse.

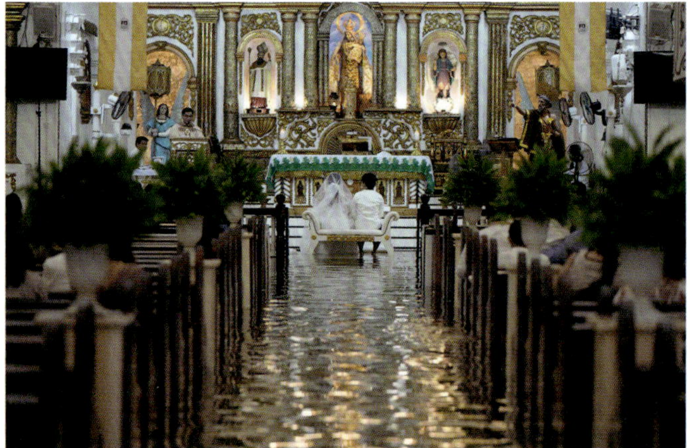

Jade Rick Verdillo and Jamaica Aguilar sit before the altar. After a ten-year courtship, the couple embraced the flood as one of the challenges to navigate in a relationship.

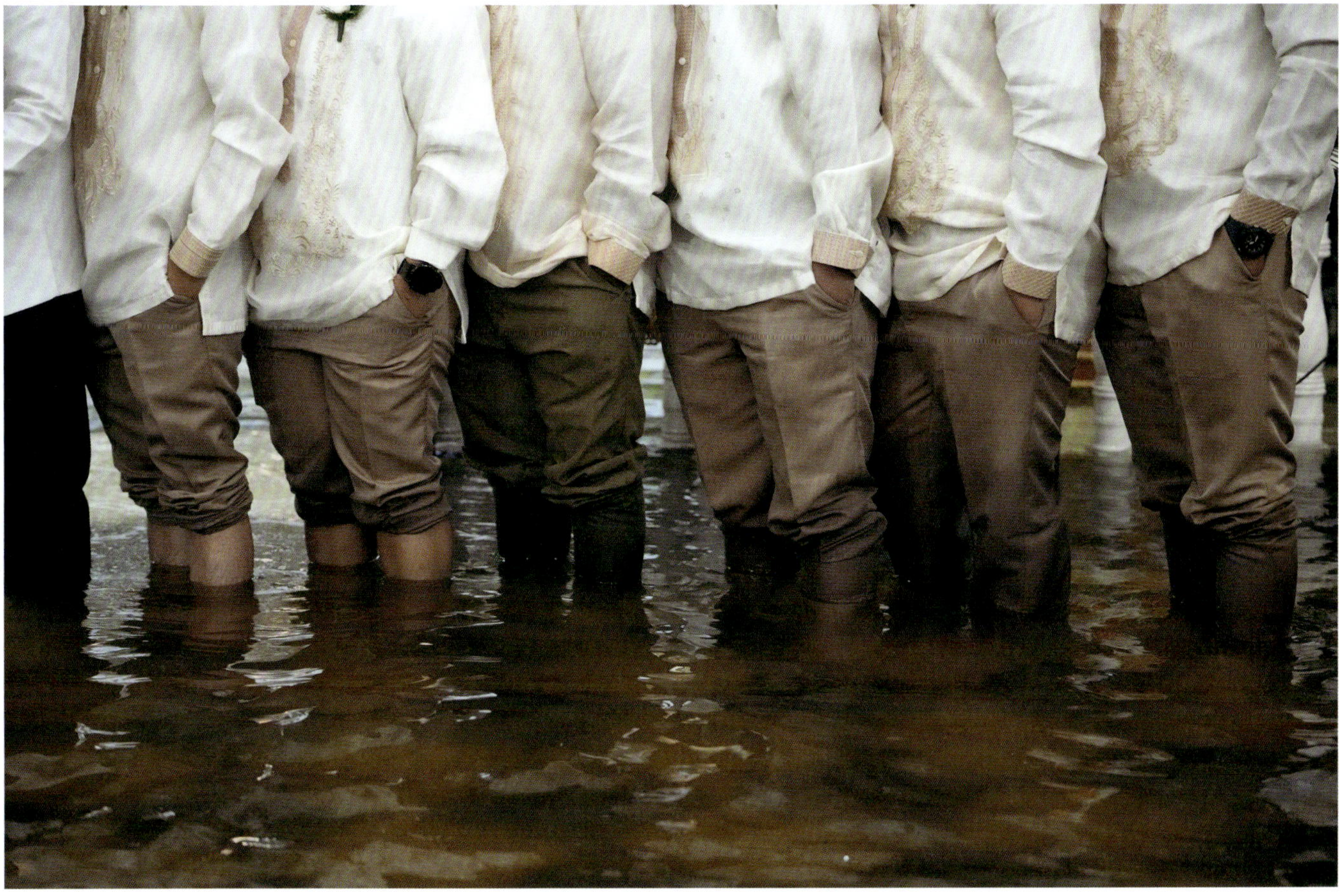

Groomsmen and guests wearing *barong tagalog*, the national dress of the Philippines, stand knee-deep in floodwaters. Local advocates increasingly link flooding to systemic failures in infrastructure and resource management.

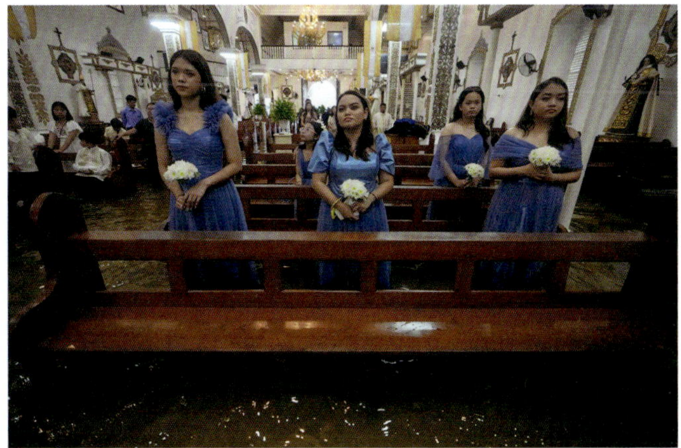

Bridesmaids stand in the flooded Barasoain Church. Known as the "Cradle of Democracy in the East," the church was the site of the 1898 congress that ratified the first Philippine Constitution.

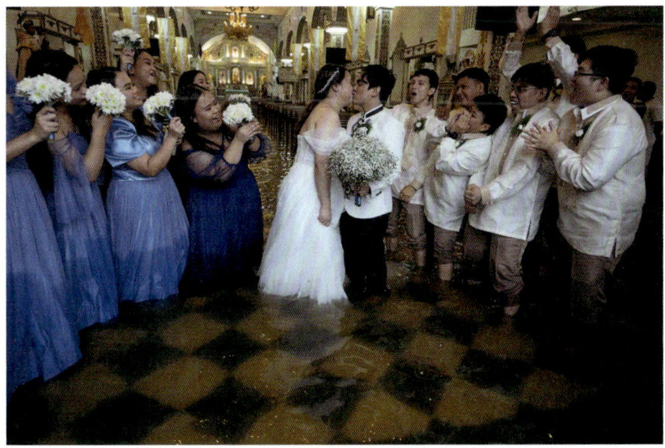

The newlyweds share a kiss as guests cheer. The couple have been together for ten years. According to Verdillo, "This is just one of the struggles that we've overcome."

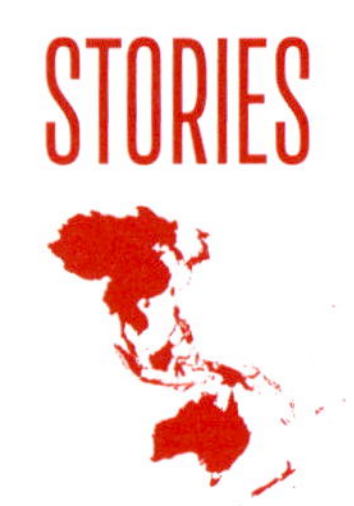

JES AZNAR

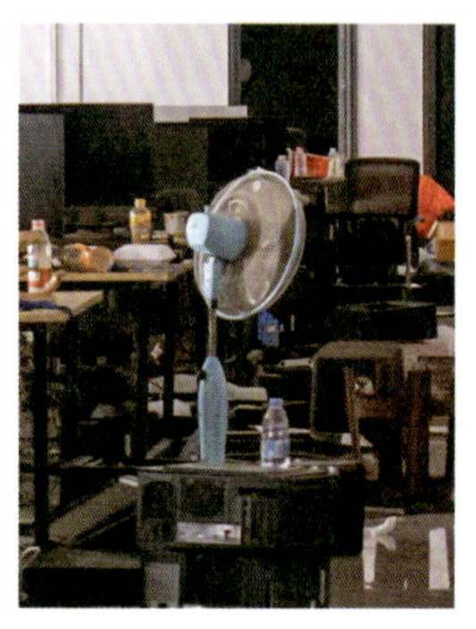

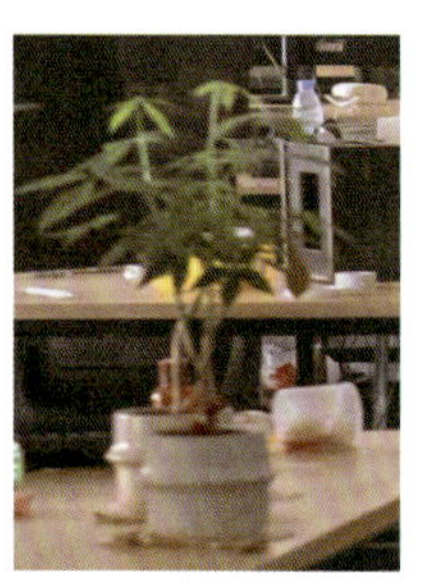

SCAM HUB UNDER SIEGE

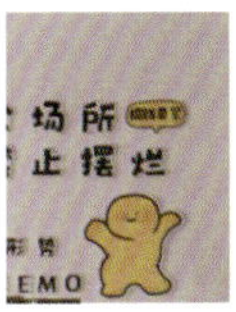

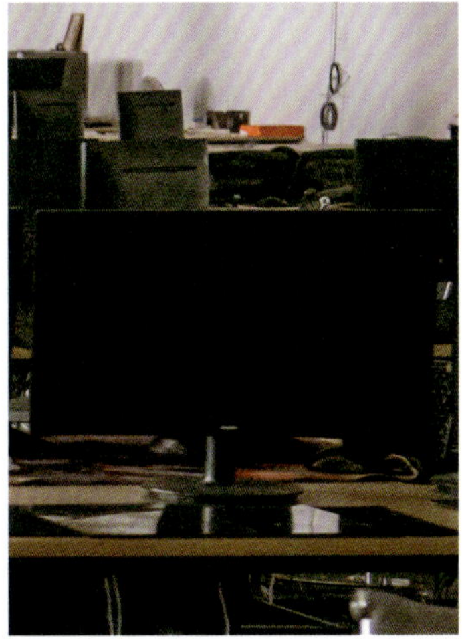

On 21 November 2025, the Karen
National Liberation Army captured
Shunda Park, a massive cyber-scam
compound in Myanmar's Karen State.
As the country's civil war intensifies,
lawless border regions have become
hubs for a lucrative online scam industry.
Hundreds of thousands of people from
around the world have been trafficked
into Southeast Asia and forced into
labor for these illegal enterprises.
When rebel forces ousted the
junta-allied militia guarding the park,
thousands of workers from 30 nations
were stranded in Myanmar.

Offices in Shunda Park were left in disarray after a surge of fighting between the Myanmar military and the opposition militia nearby.
Some parts of the complex resembled professional executive suites; others trapped workers in a "Sisyphean loop" of 12-hour shifts.
All photos taken in Min Let Pan, Myanmar on 5 December 2025 / Jes Aznar, for *The New York Times*

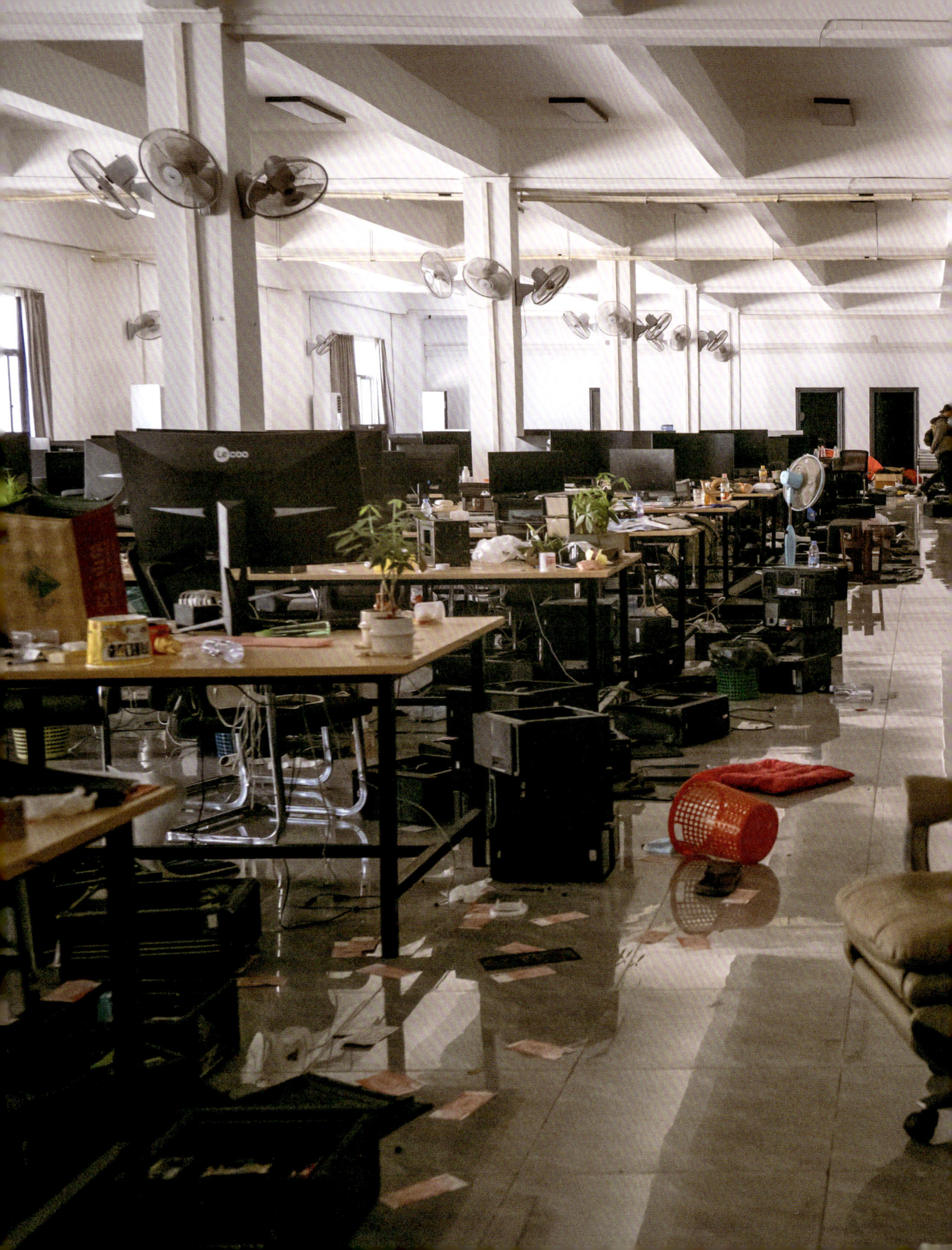

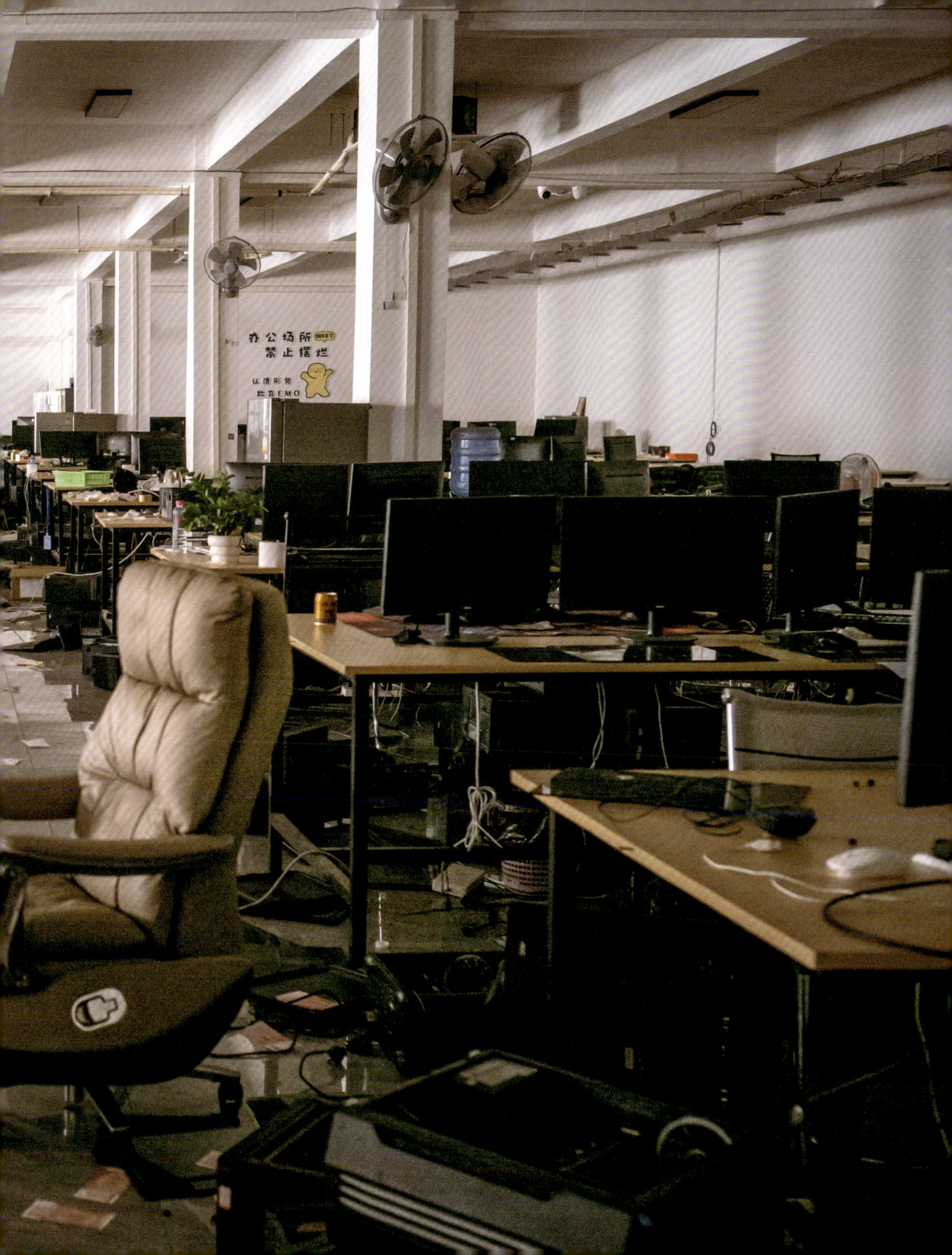
办公场所
禁止摆烂
认清形势
放弃EMO

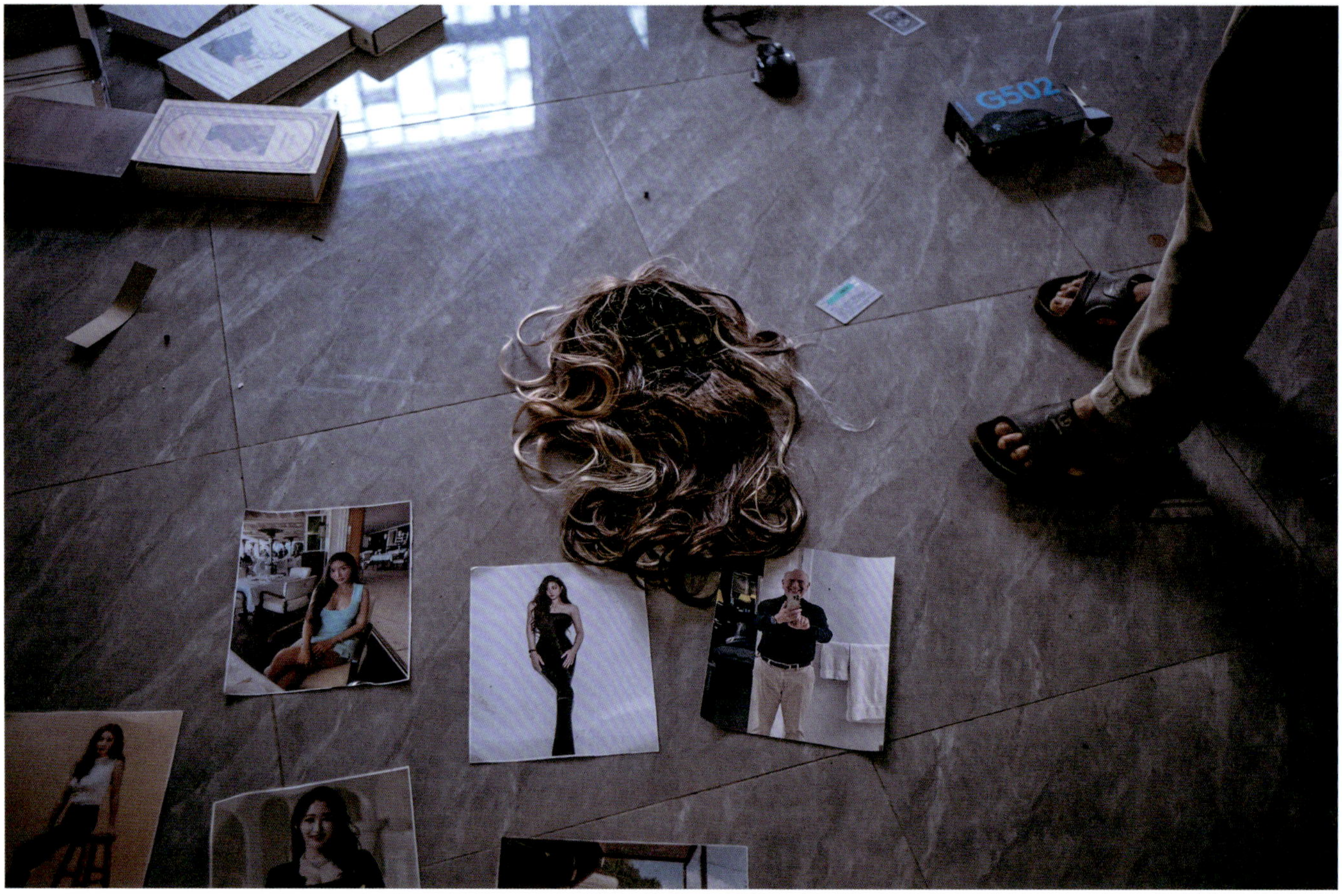

Photographs and props used to fake online personas and build relationships with victims.

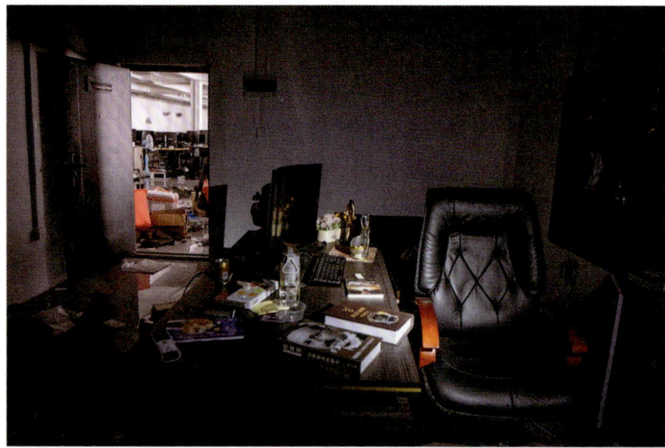

Fake books and other props furnish an abandoned streaming room decorated to appear on camera as an executive office.

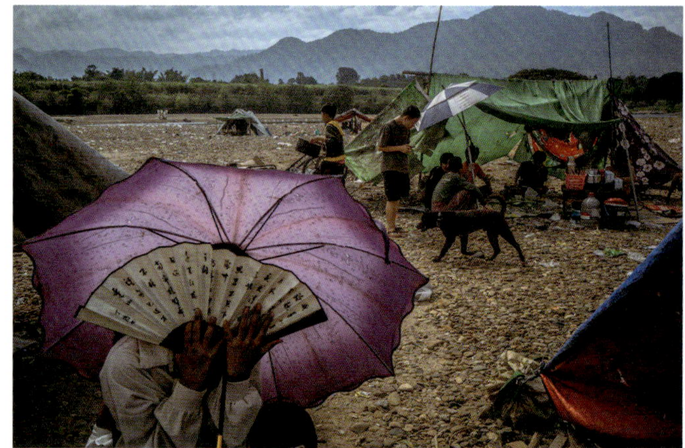

Stranded workers at a makeshift shelter near the Moei River. Many workers had their documents and passports seized by the scam center bosses and could not cross the border into Thailand.

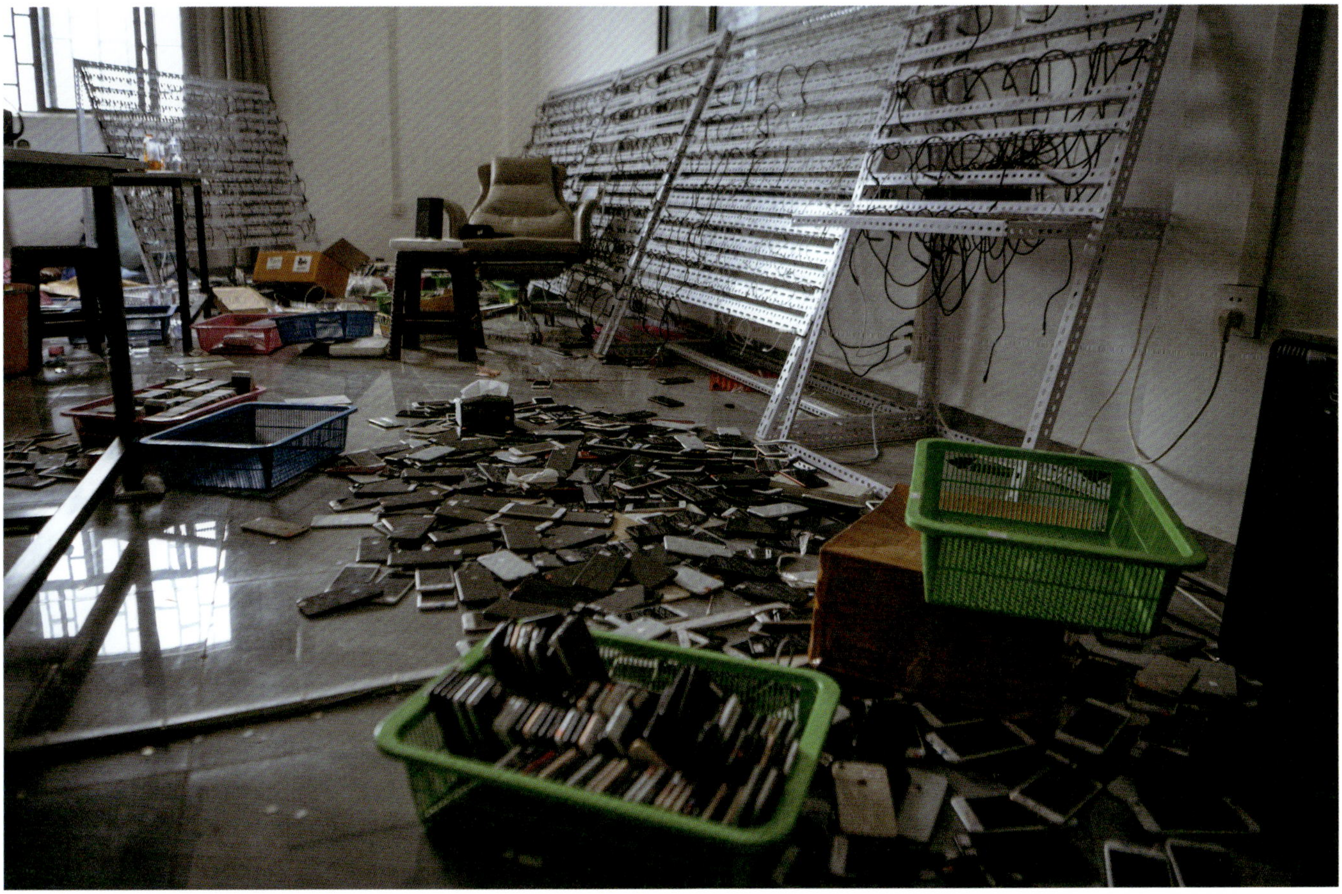

Discarded cellphones litter the Shunda Park complex after its capture. The scammers used generative intelligence, deepfake videos, fraudulent businesses, websites, and financial apps to reel in victims from around the world.

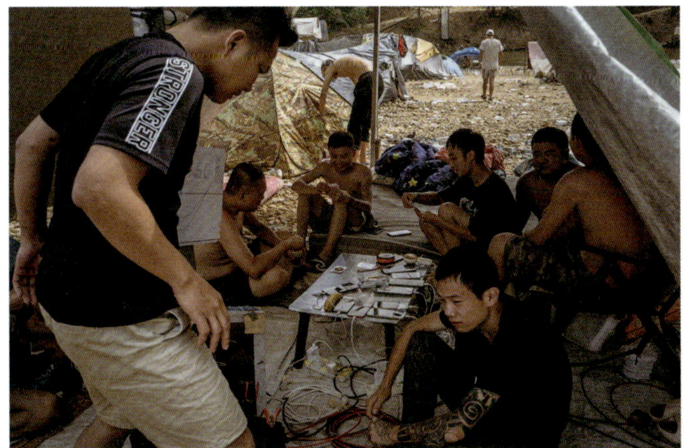

Former workers at the scam center pass time at a makeshift shelter near the Moei River. Among the stranded are Chinese nationals reluctant to return to China for fear of prosecution.

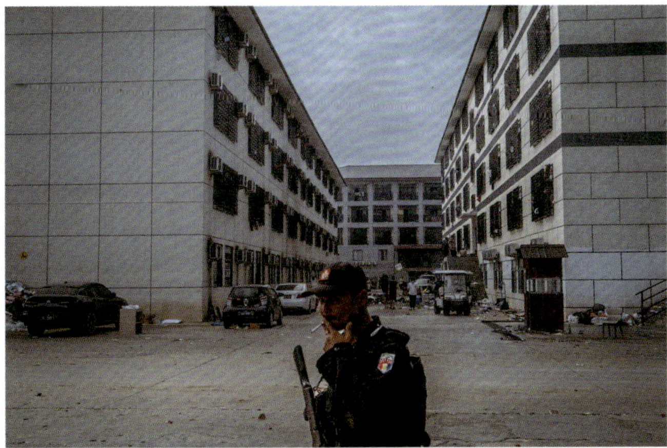

A Karen National Liberation Army soldier patrols the Shunda Park compound. Approximately 900 Chinese employees remained barricaded here for weeks after the raid, fearing that repatriation could lead to immediate arrest by Chinese authorities.

STORIES

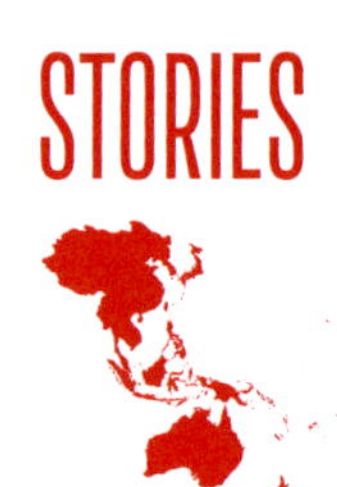

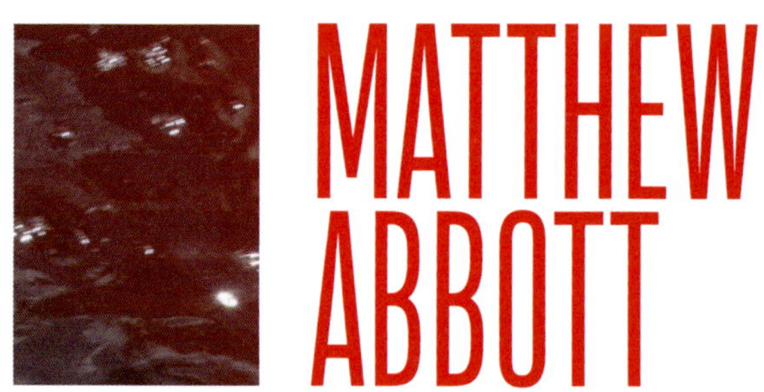

MATTHEW ABBOTT

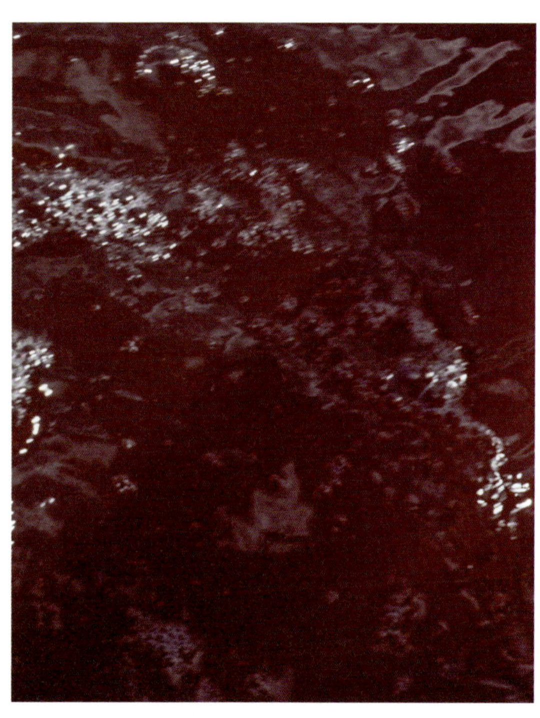

THE LAST DOLPHIN HUNTERS

Fanalei, a low-lying island in the Solomon Islands, stands at a crossroads between contested tradition and a changing economy. For generations, dolphin hunting provided food and income, with dolphin teeth used as ritual currency for bride-price and other forms of local exchange. Today, as rising sea levels displace the community and threaten its future, seaweed farming is providing an economic alternative to the seasonal hunt. As seaweed farming expands, fewer people are available for the collective efforts upon which dolphin hunting depends. This story captures a community reshaped by environmental pressure and shifting traditions.

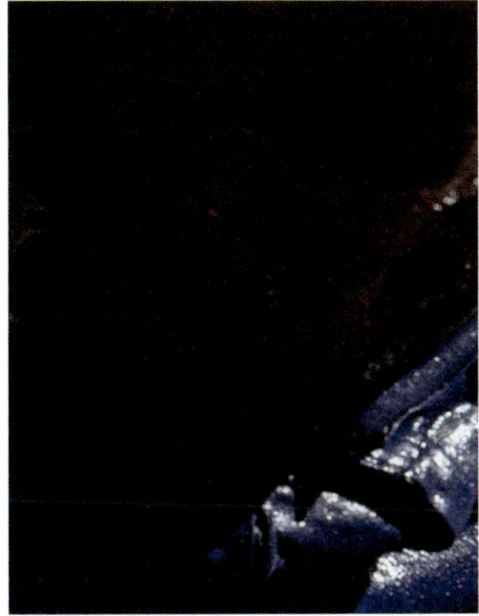

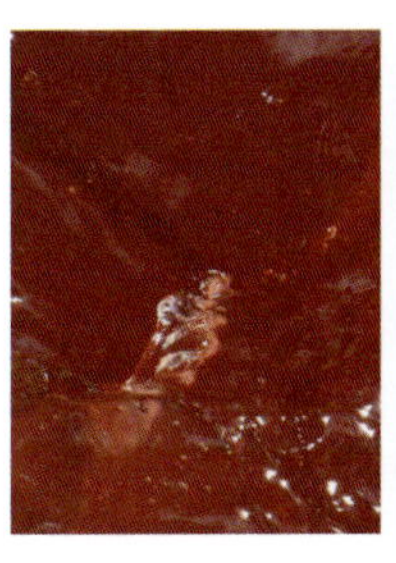

A young man drags a dolphin toward the shore in Walande. While Fanalei struggled this season, the larger sister community of Walande successfully landed a catch to share across the Surodo Lagoon. Maramasike Island, 11 February 2025
All photos taken in South Malaita, Solomon Islands / Matthew Abbott, Oculi, for *The New York Times*

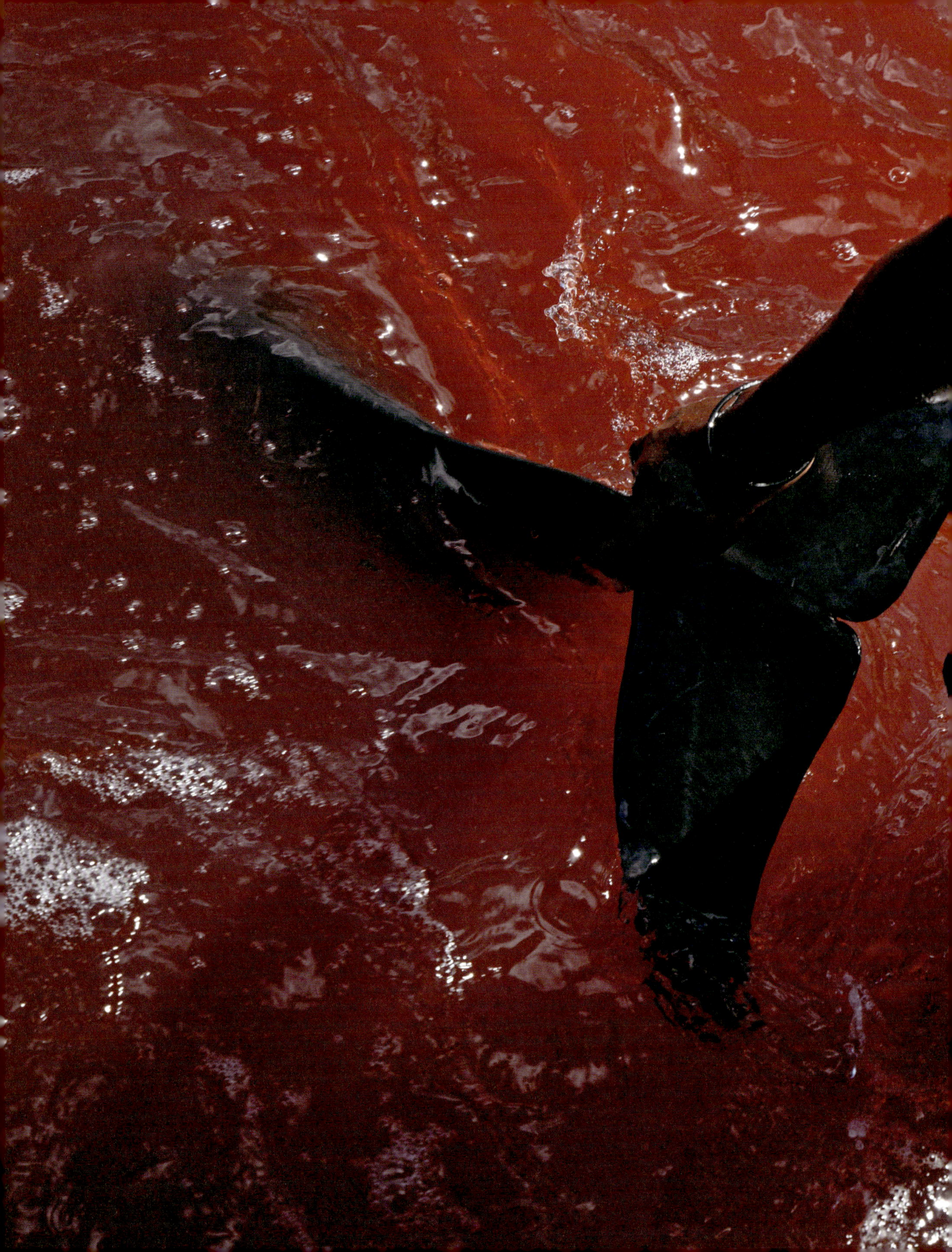

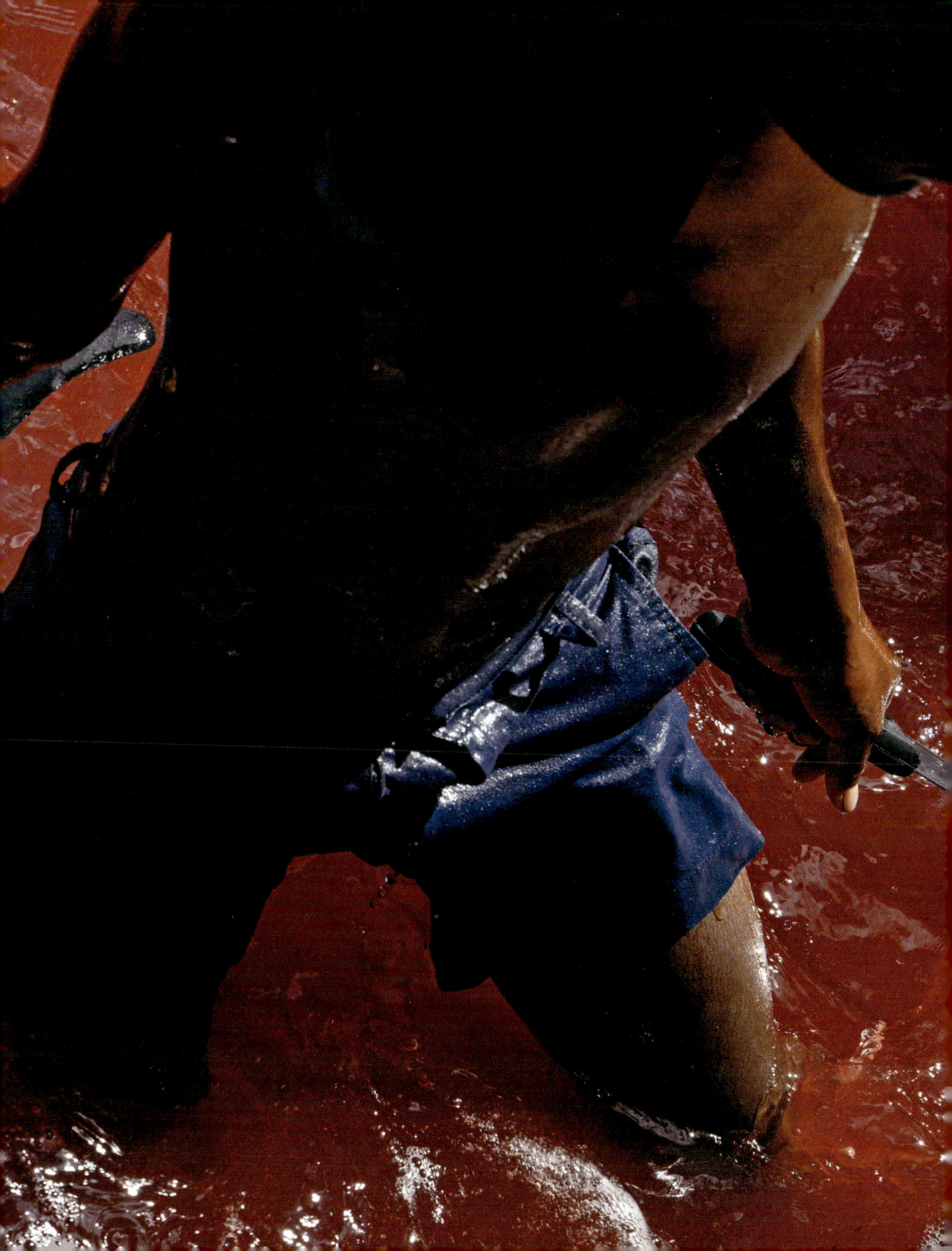

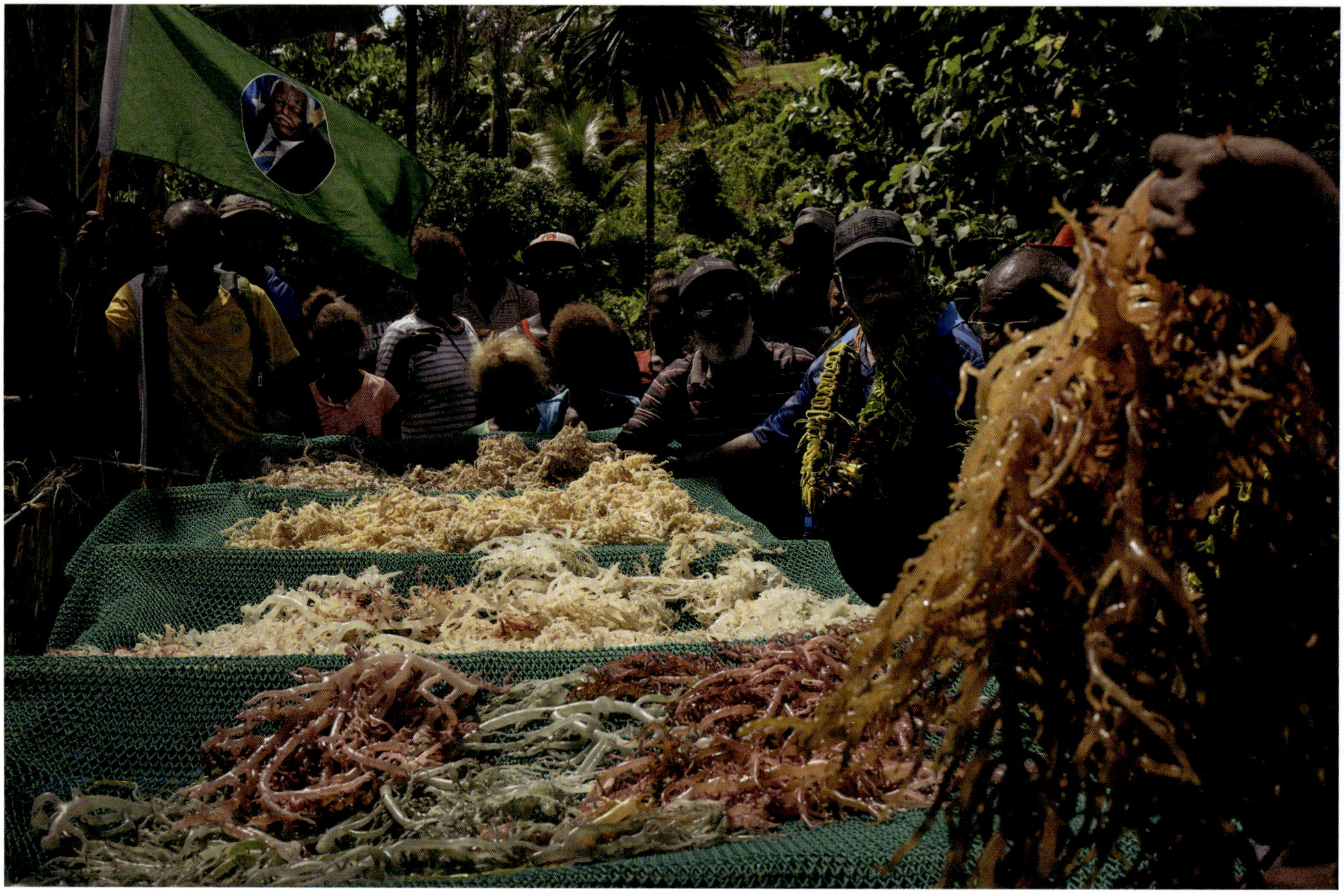

Crowds in Fouele discuss seaweed farming with MP Rick Houenipwela. This new source of income offers a path away from the traditional but controversial dolphin hunt, providing families with a more reliable means of supporting themselves. Fouele Village, Maramasike Island, 12 February 2025

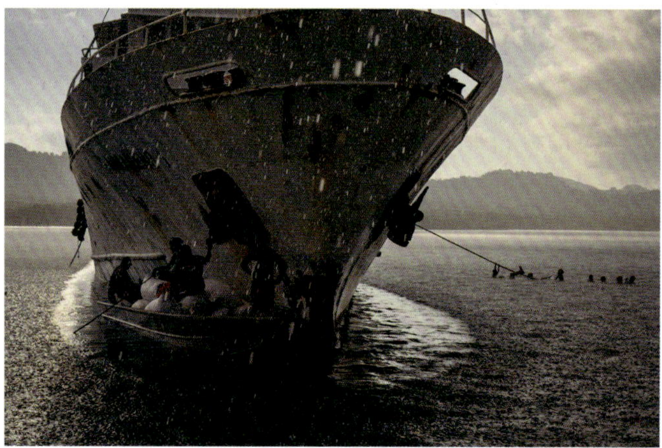

A boat shelters beneath a supply vessel, protecting bags of dried seaweed from a storm. This new export links the remote island to global markets. Fanalei Island, 16 February 2025

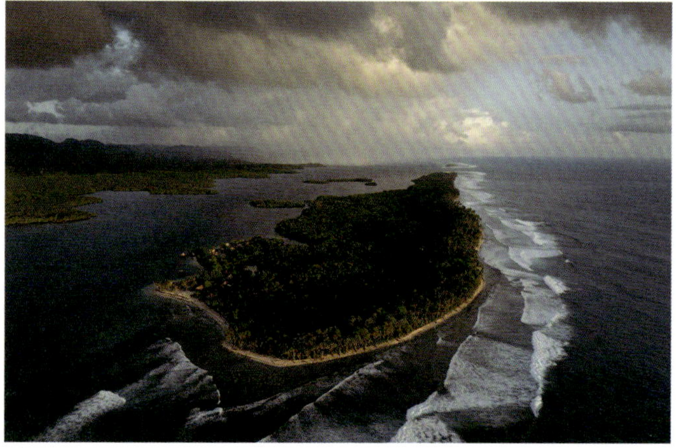

Fanalei Island has been reduced to a narrow strip of sand and coral by rising seas. Residents believe the settlement, once home to dozens of families, will become uninhabitable in the near future. 6 February 2025

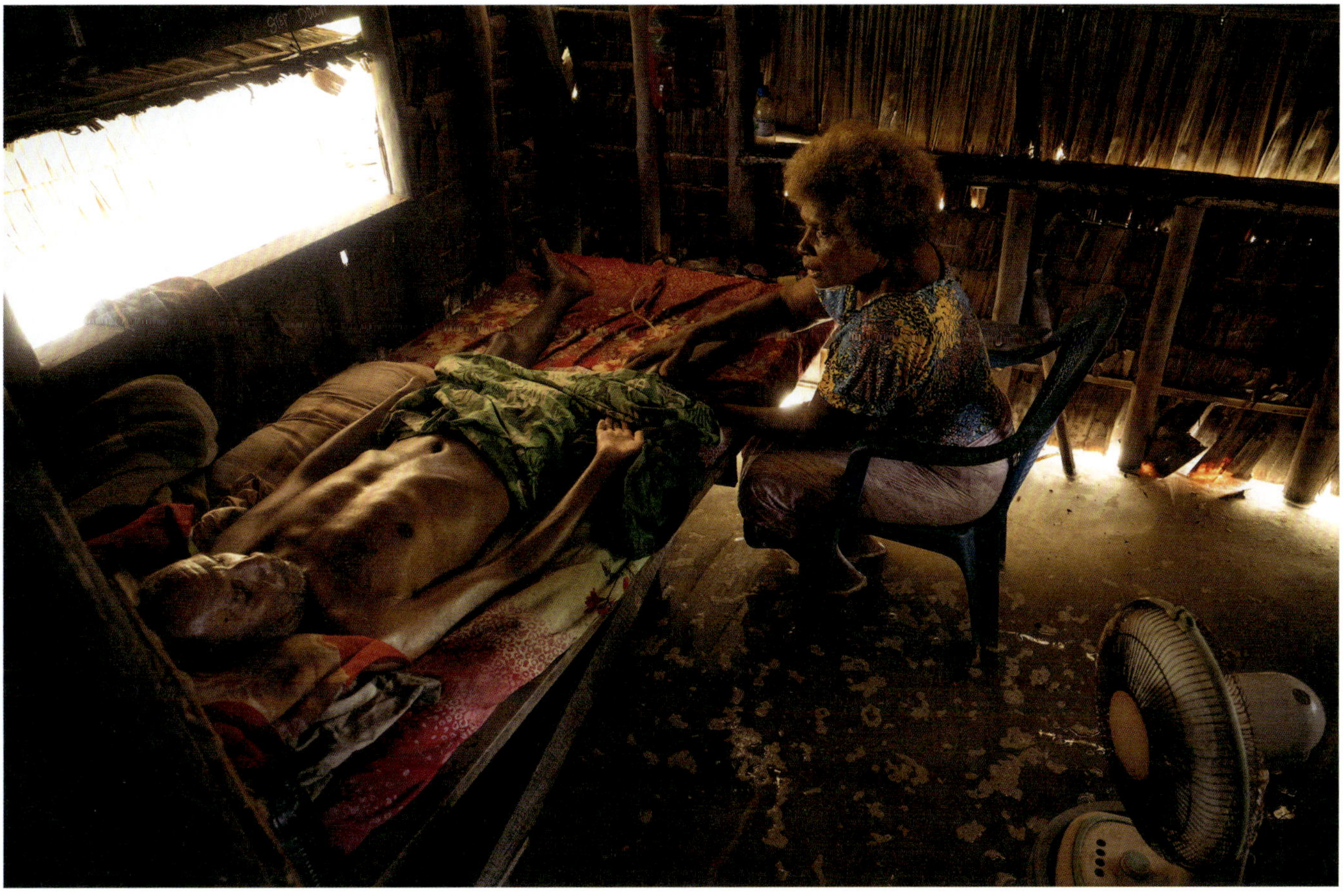

Paralyzed for the past two years, Eddie Sua is confined to a hut that floods during high tides. He notes that without food and income from dolphin teeth, the community would starve. Fanalei Village, Fanalei Island, 16 February 2025

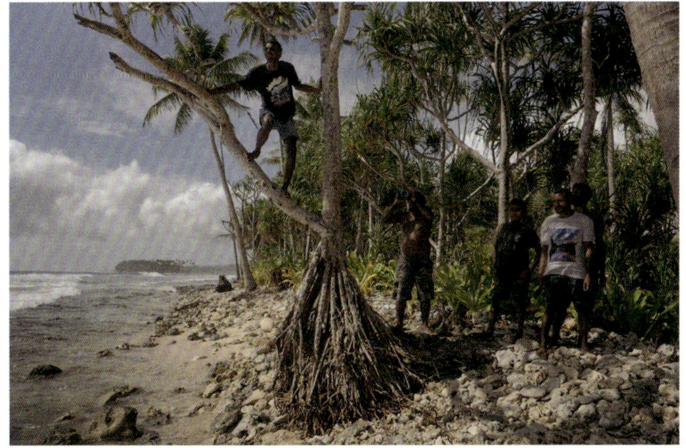

Young men climb palms to scan the lagoon for returning dolphin hunters. Throughout the 2025 hunting season, the men of Fanalei made repeated attempts but did not land a single catch. Fanalei Island, 7 February 2025

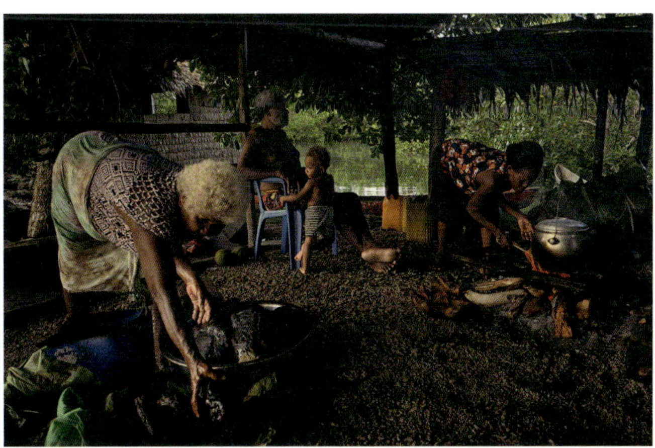

Smoke rises as families cook dolphin meat gifted by neighbors. After an unsuccessful season, Fanalei's residents rely on customary sharing across the Surodo Lagoon. Fanalei Island, 12 February 2025

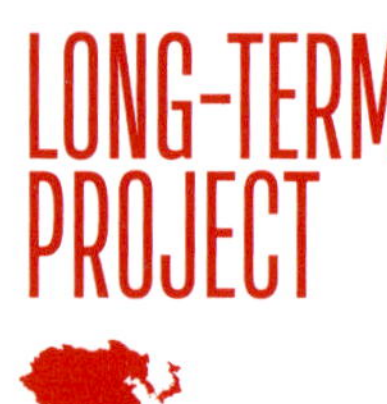

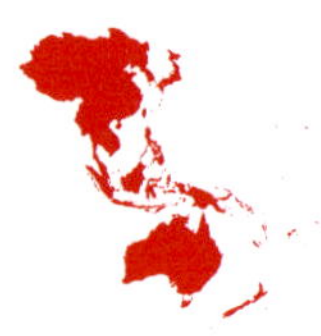

MOTHERHOOD AT 60

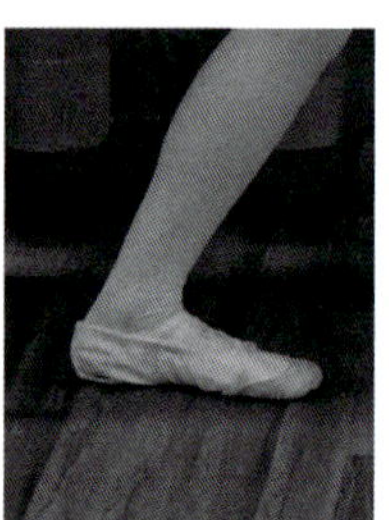

WU FANG

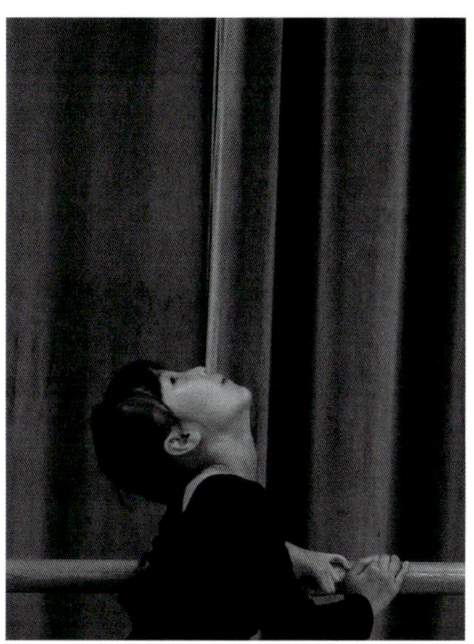

After the death of her only child, retired doctor Sheng Hailin sought in vitro fertilization treatment (IVF) and gave birth to twin girls named Zhizhi and Huihui at the age of 60. This story follows Sheng Hailin's family over 15 years, offering a portrait that is both extraordinary and mundane, but always filled with enduring love. In China, Sheng Hailin is only one of many *shīdú*, parents who have lost their only child born during China's one-child policy era.

Zhizhi and Huihui attend dance training. The cost of the girls' education and extracurricular activities placed a significant financial burden on the aging family. 23 May 2021
All photos taken in Hefei, Anhui Province, China / Wu Fang

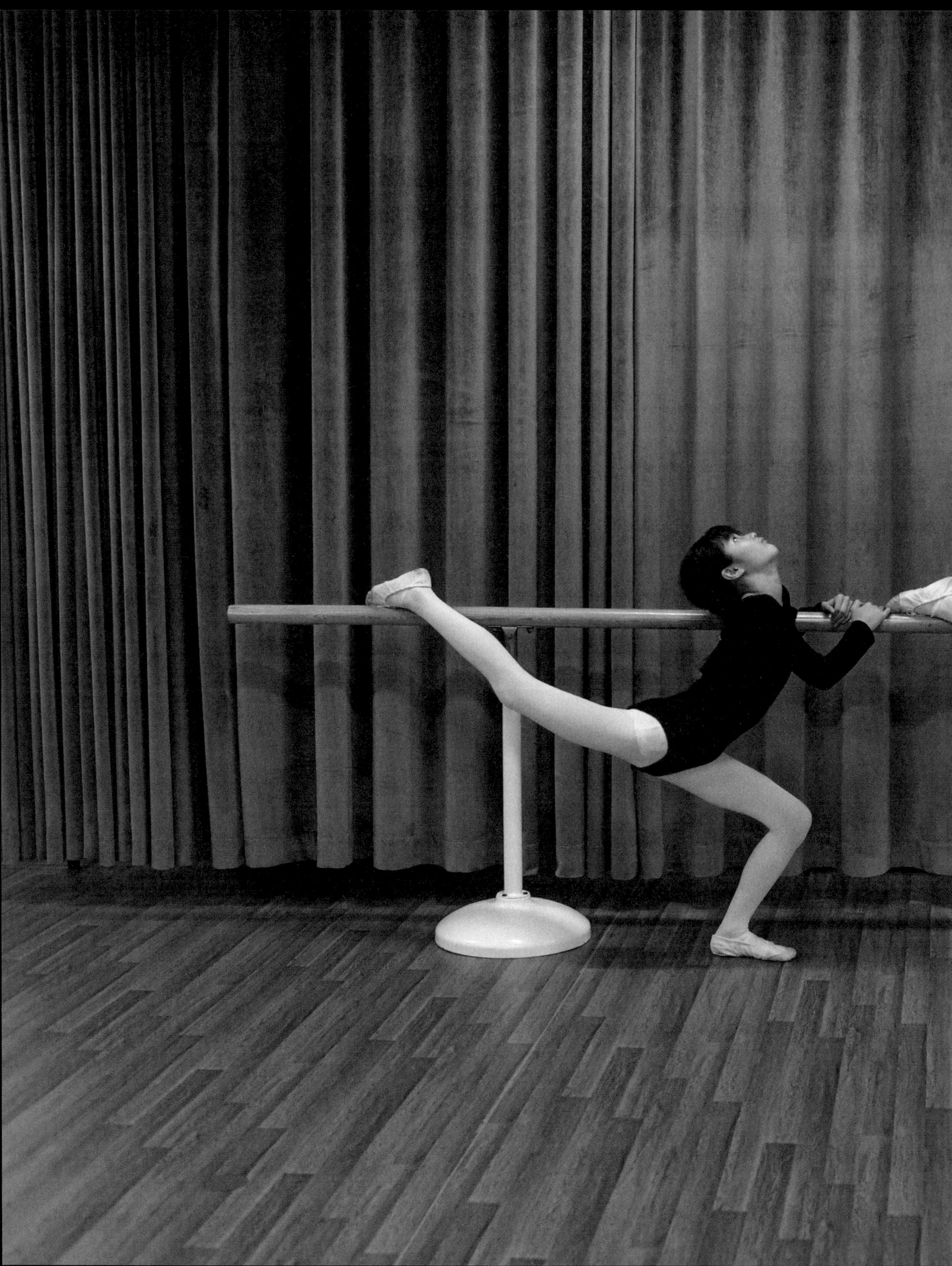

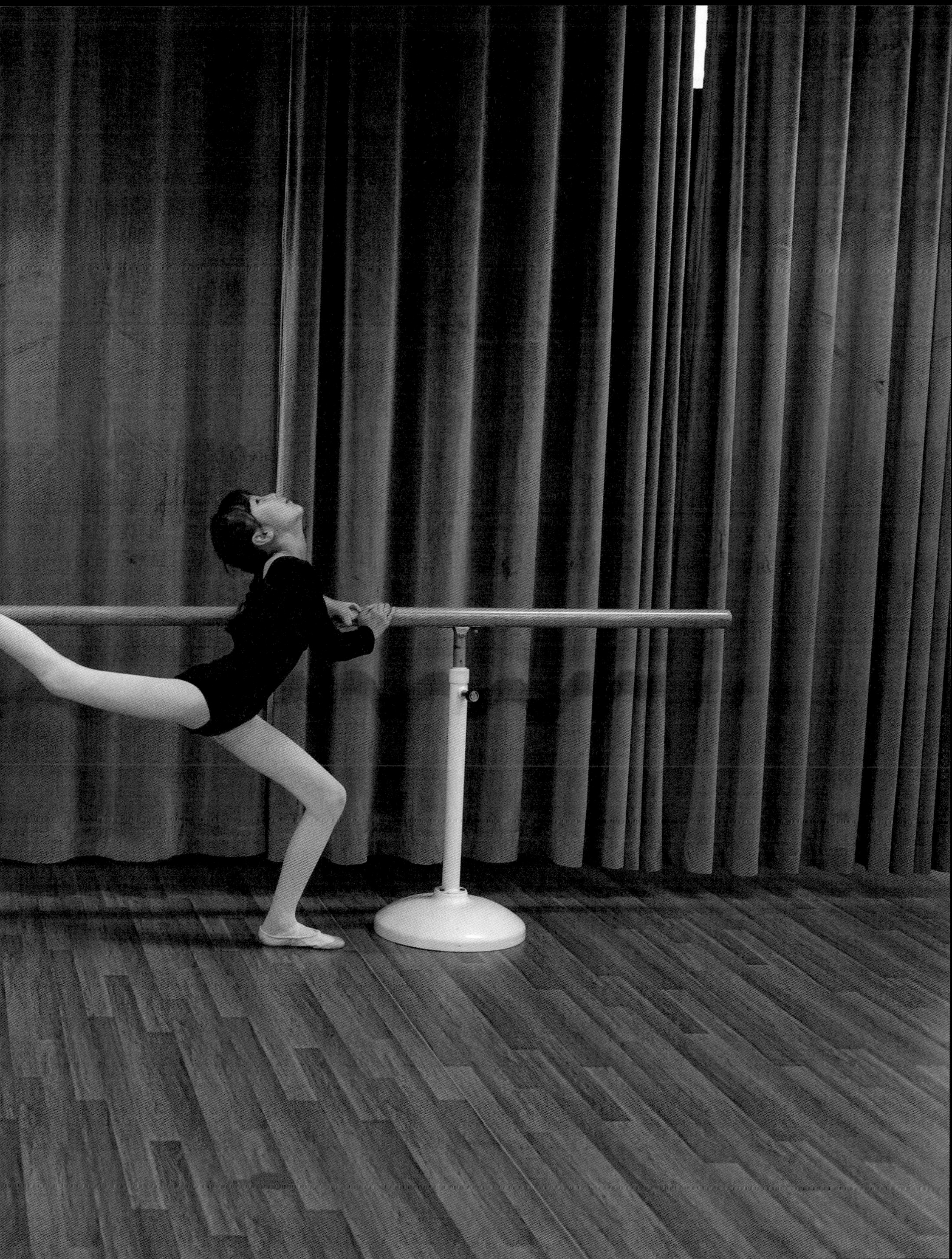

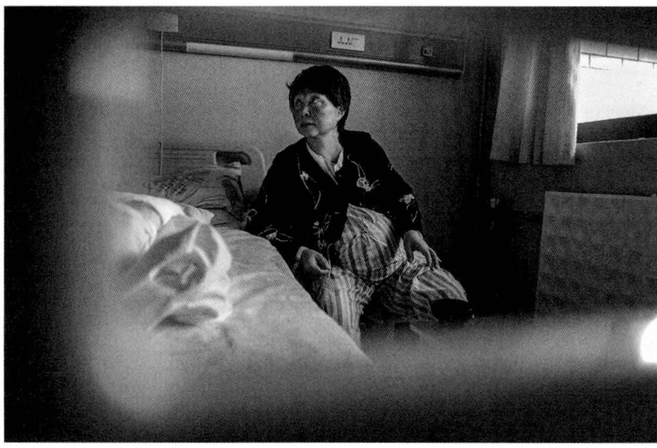

Sheng Hailin prepares for delivery at a hospital in Hefei. At 60 years old and over seven months pregnant, she faced pain, hemorrhaging, and other physical hardships to bring her twin daughters into the world. 25 May 2010

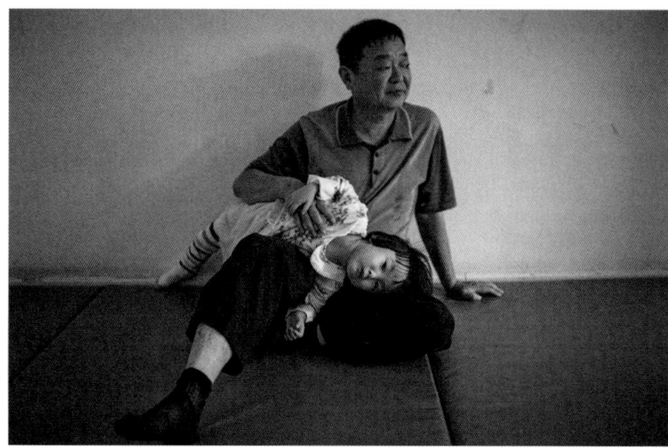

Zhizhi with her father, Wu Jingzhou, at kindergarten. The couple's decision to have children in their 60s sparked debates online over the ethics and responsibilities of elderly parenthood. 7 September 2013

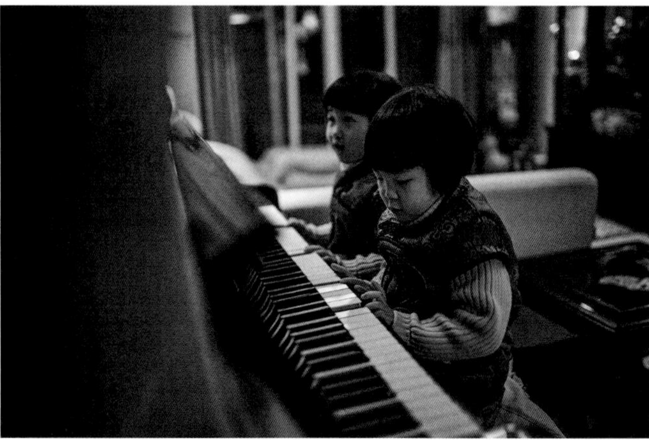

Zhizhi and Huihui practice the piano at home. Dancing, piano, and other educational expenses could not be covered by Sheng Hailin's pension, so she returned to the workforce. 2 December 2013

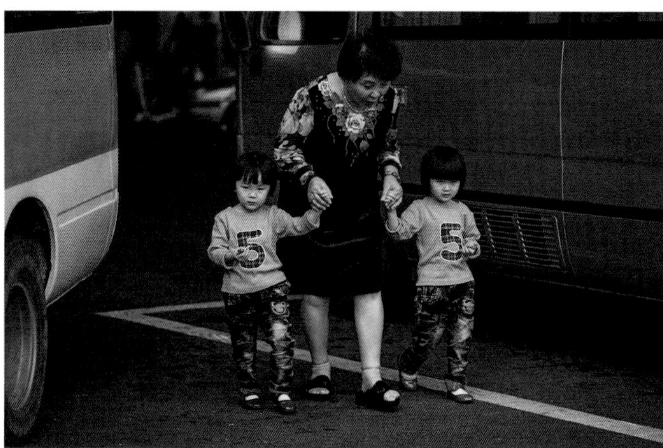

Sheng Hailin reunites with her daughters at the airport. Sheng Hailin had been away on a 20-day lecture trip in the city of Kunming in Yunnan Province. 8 September 2013

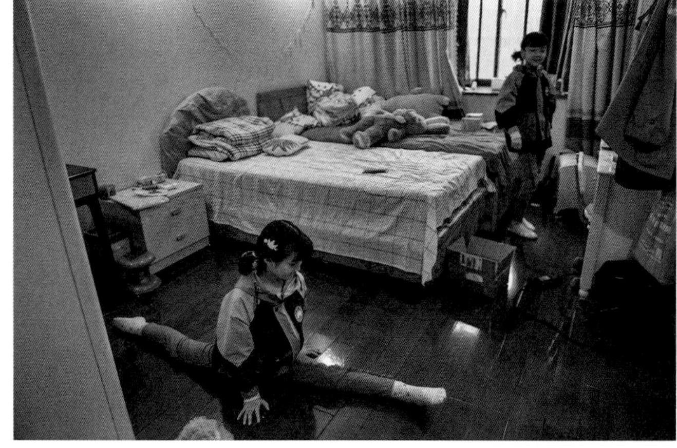

Zhizhi and Huihui play at home. Like many parents around the world during COVID-19 lockdowns, Sheng Hailin felt at a loss over what to do with her children. 23 April 2020

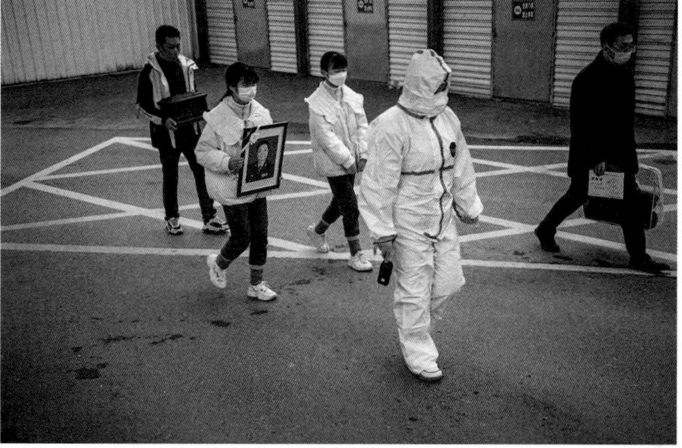

Zhizhi and Huihui carry their father's portrait during his funeral procession. Wu Jingzhou passed away in late 2022, leaving the 72-year-old Sheng Hailin to raise their teenage daughters alone. 8 December 2022

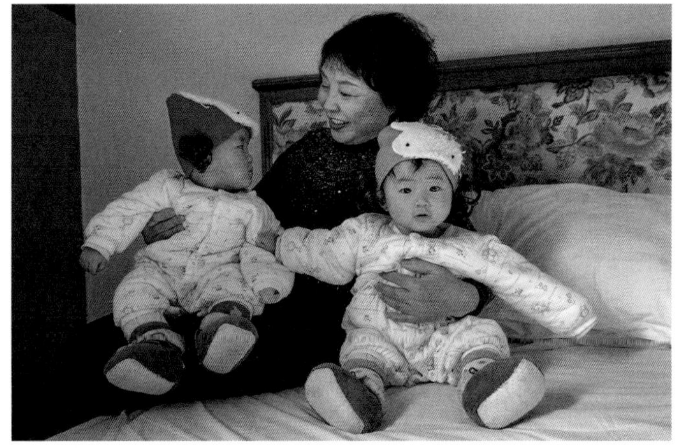

Sheng Hailin at home with Zhizhi and Huihui. The twins are wearing new hats for their first Spring Festival. 30 January 2011

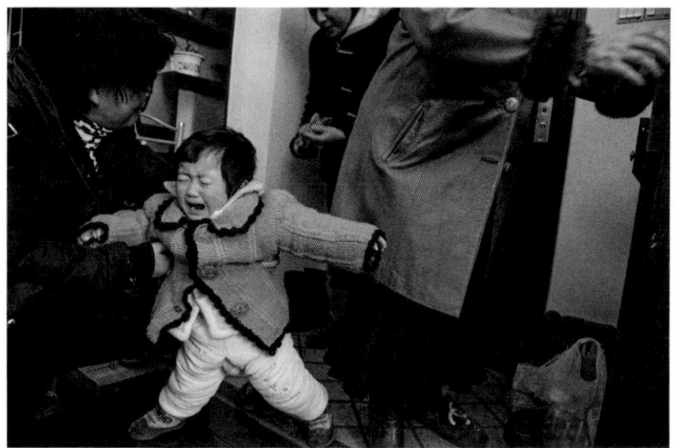

Returning from a work trip, Sheng Hailin is greeted by her daughter, Huihui. To support her young family, the retired doctor went back to work, traveling across China giving lectures on health. 5 March 2012

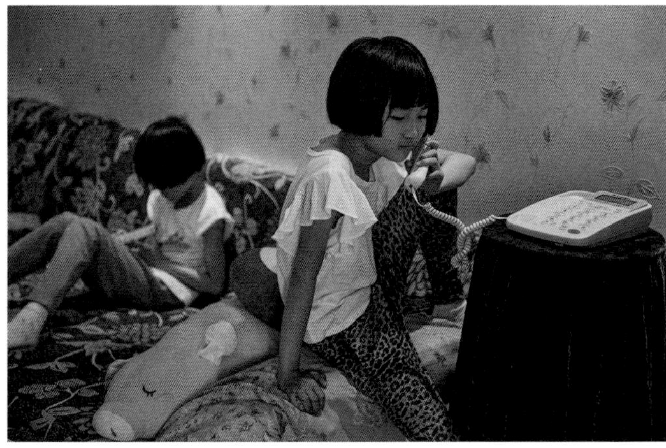

Huihui (8) calls her mother, asking when she will be home from her business trip. Although many of her peers had retired, Sheng Hailin continued to work to support her daughters. 12 May 2018

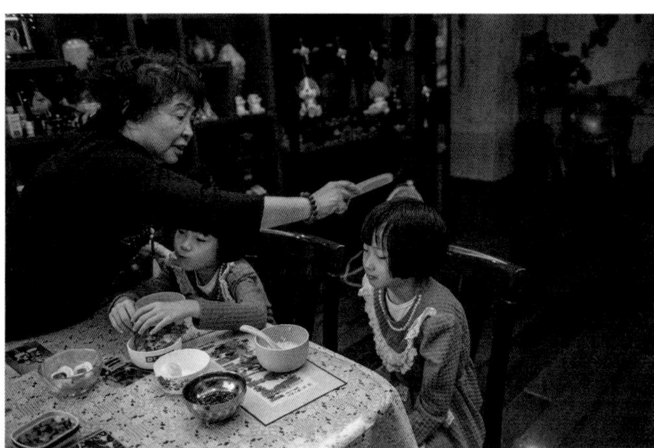

Sheng Hailin combs her daughters' hair before school. As the girls grew, Sheng Hailin faced the increasing challenge of managing their daily needs while navigating her own diminishing physical capabilities. 21 May 2018

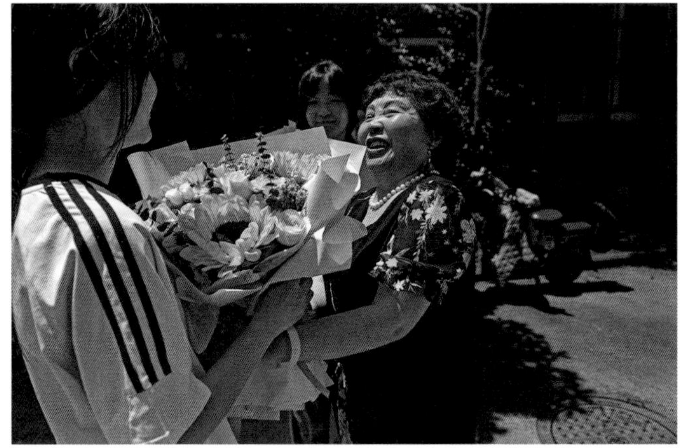

Sheng Hailin presents her daughters with flowers after completing their high school entrance exams. At 75, Sheng Hailin continues to document her life online to support her family's future. 16 June 2025

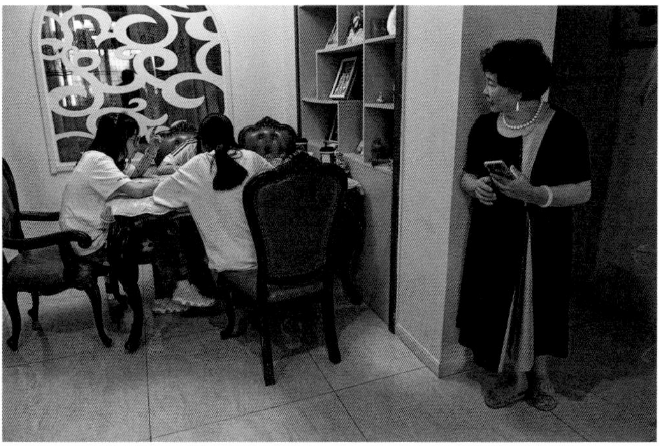

Sheng Hailin oversees a tutoring session at home. As her daughters approached their high school entrance examinations, Sheng Hailin prioritized their education to ensure their future success. 12 June 2025

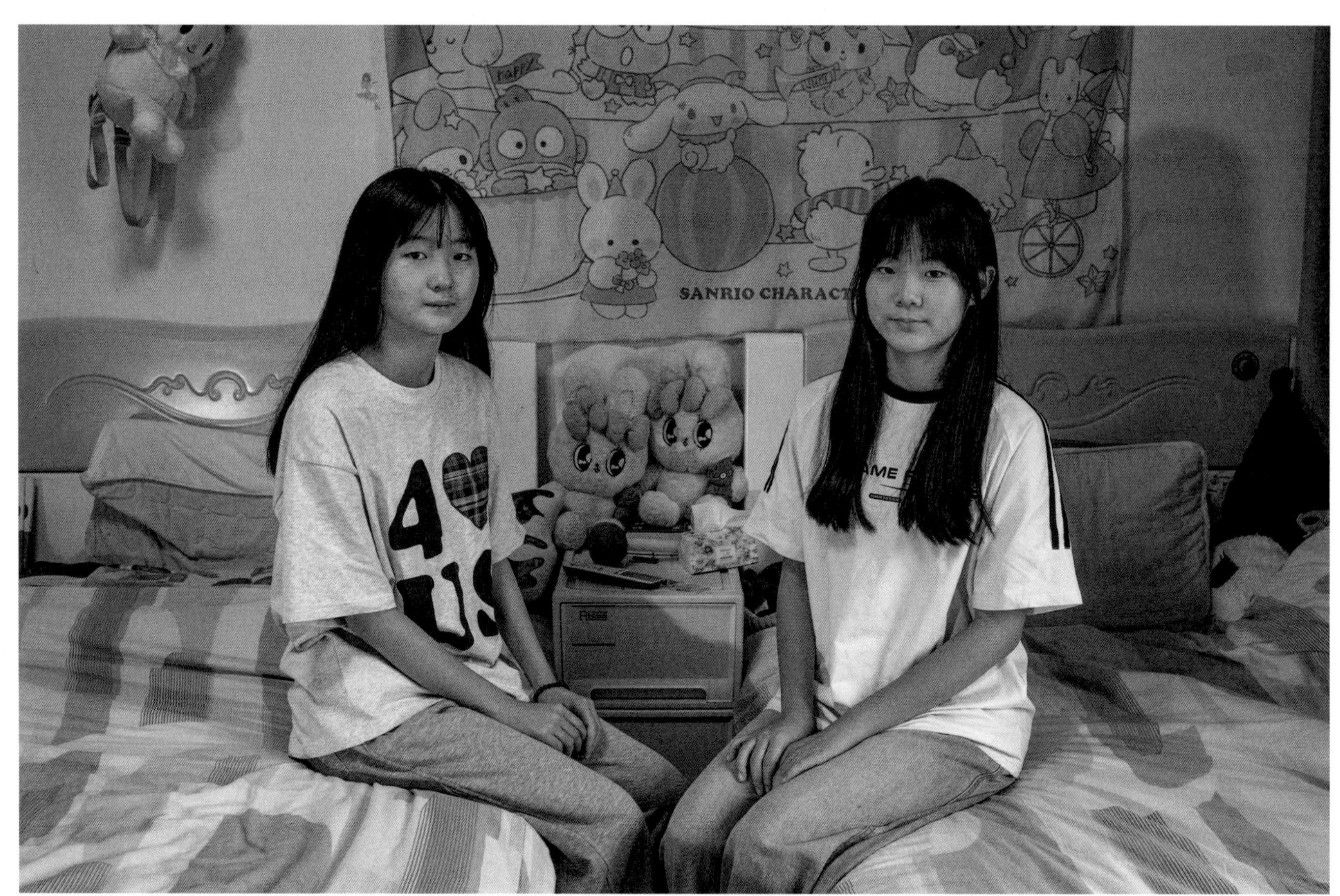

Zhizhi and Huihui celebrate their 15th birthday. 12 June 2025

—

WHY DO WE NEED STORIES OF RESILIENCE, HOPE, AND POSITIVE CHANGE?

Stories of resilience, hope, and positive change inspire and connect us. They remind us of human strength, showing that even in hardship, people can overcome, grow, and create meaningful transformation.

—

Alfred Yaghobzadeh,
West, Central, and South Asia jury

In a world that feels increasingly fractured, stories of resilience and hope are essential – not as a counterweight to tragedy, but as evidence of what's possible.

—

Kira Pollack,
Global jury chair

In a world saturated with trauma and negativity, stories of resilience offer balance, restore perspective, and remind audiences of human strength, dignity, and the possibility of progress.

—

Tsvangirayi Mukwazhi,
Africa jury

We need access to all kinds of stories. Photojournalism also magnifies intimate, local realities, amplifying voices of resilience and resistance. What affects us personally moves us to act – the personal is universal.

—

Silvia Omedes,
Europe jury

Stories of resilience, hope and change help us fight against compassion fatigue in a tired and weary world.

—

Vivek Prakash,
Asia-Pacific and Oceania jury

Many people today feel apathetic toward the news. Sharing stories of joy and resilience is essential, as narratives of positive change restore balance, sustain hope and engagement, foster connection, and better reflect the world's complexity.

—

Solana Cain,
North and Central America jury

People and communities are more than trauma. Stories of resilience and hope restore dignity and agency, revealing how people resist, care, and imagine futures beyond crisis, even within systems shaped by inequality and violence.

—

Karla Gachet Vega,
South America jury

EUROPE

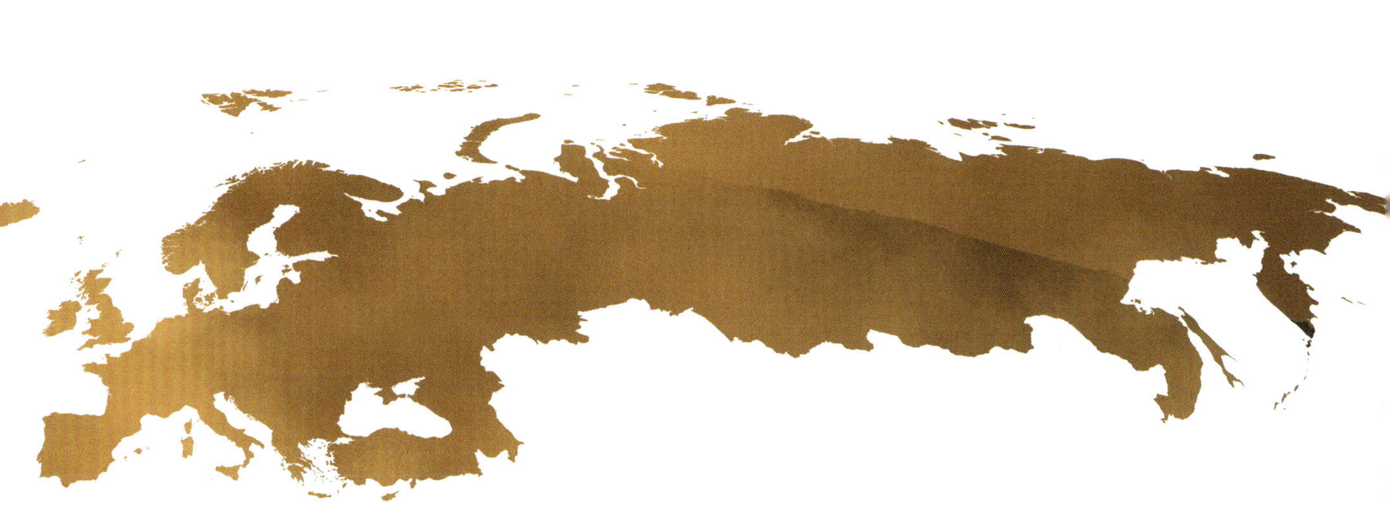

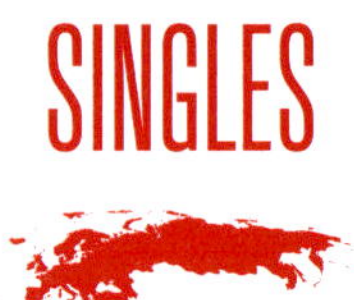

ROIE GALITZ

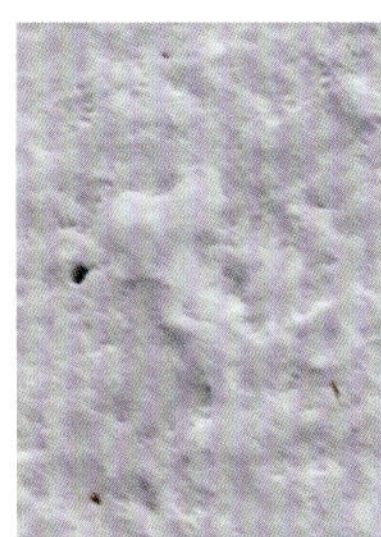

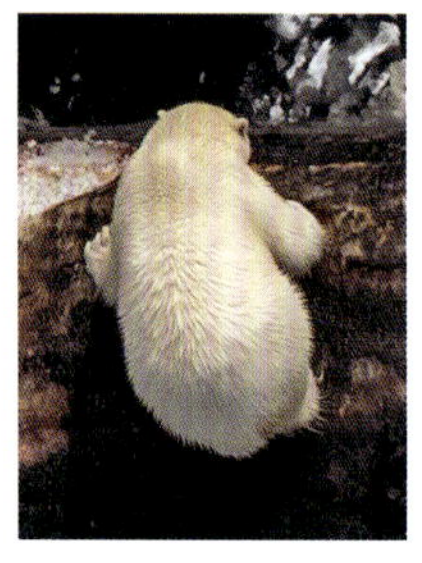

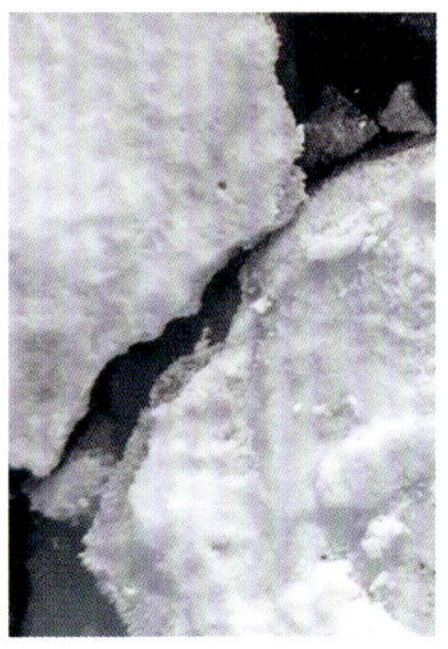

Polar bears are primarily seal predators, but as ice retreats in the summer and hunting becomes harder, they increasingly rely on opportunistic scavenging. Near Svalbard, the ice-free season has lengthened by 20 weeks in the last 30 years. Sperm whales typically avoid ice-covered polar waters, so this carcass was a rare sight. Scientists speculate that after dying, the male sperm whale drifted north, carried by winds and currents. The photographer spent two days observing the scene from a small boat, capturing it by drone to reveal a scale difficult to grasp from sea level.

POLAR BEAR ON SPERM WHALE

A female polar bear feeds on a sperm whale carcass in the polar pack ice north of the Norwegian archipelago, Svalbard. 82º North, International Waters, 8 July 2025 / Roie Galitz

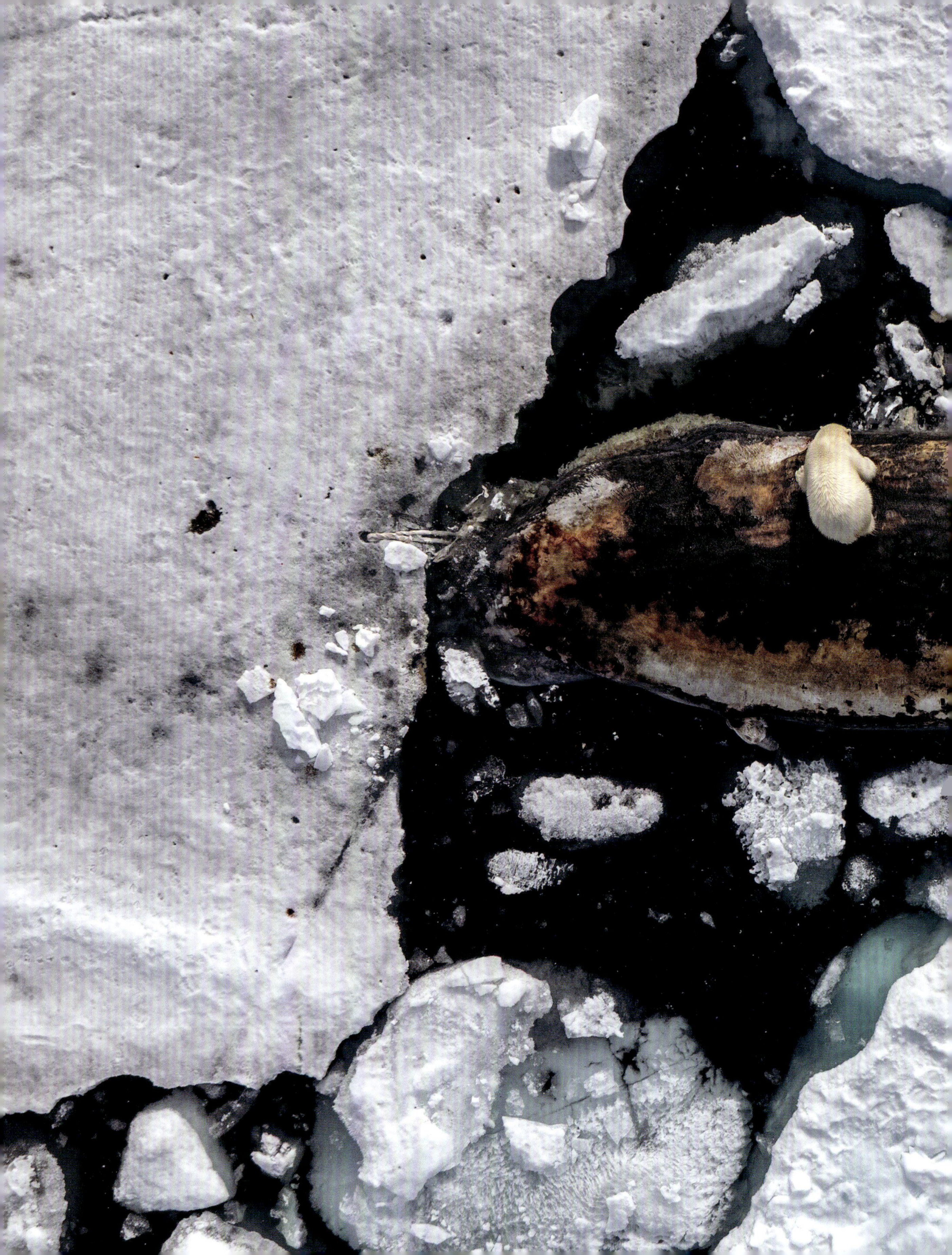

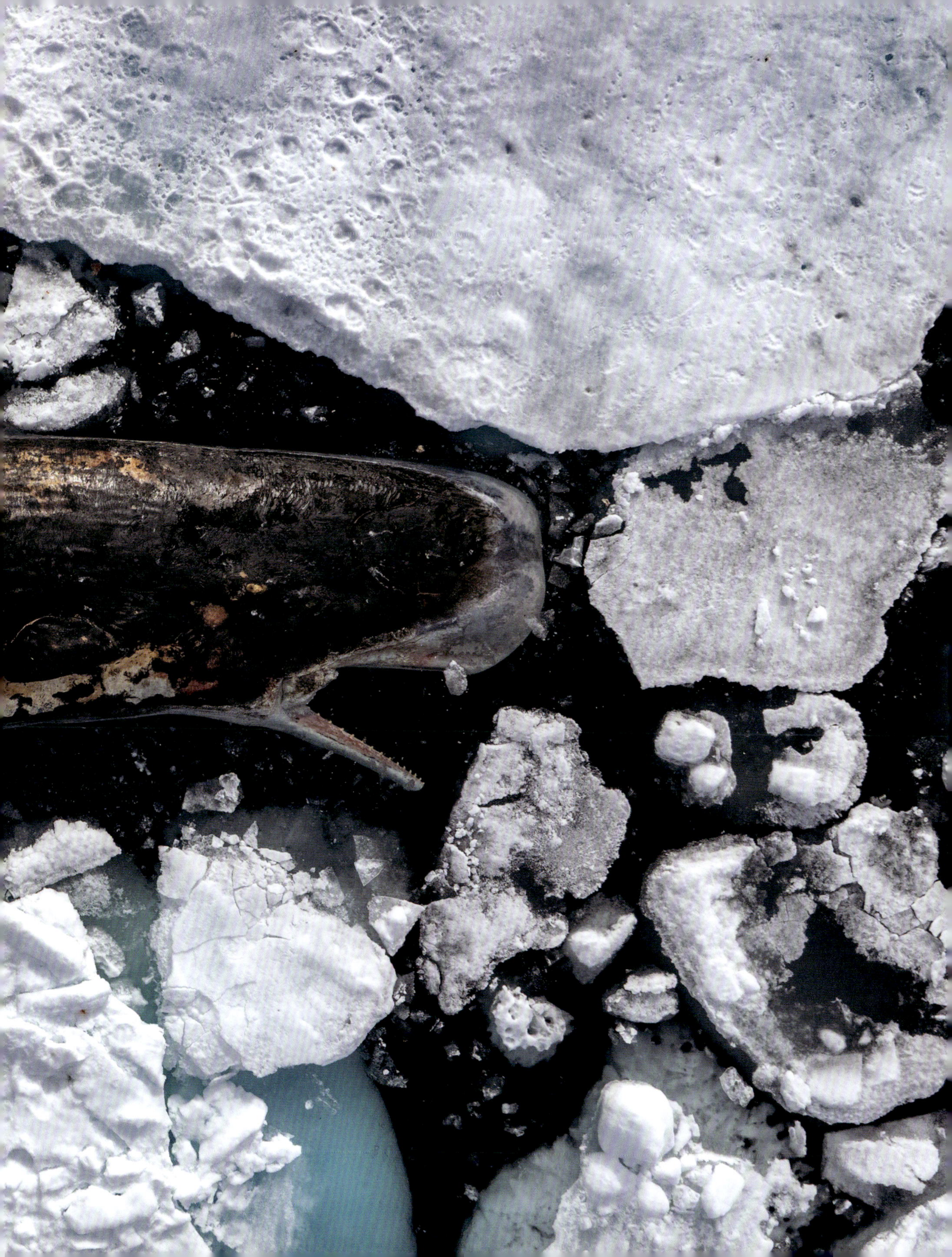

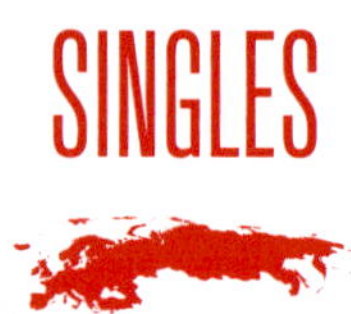

EMMA THE SOCIAL ROBOT

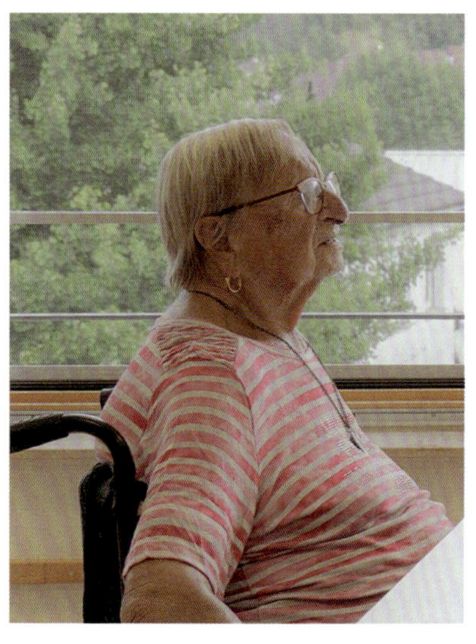

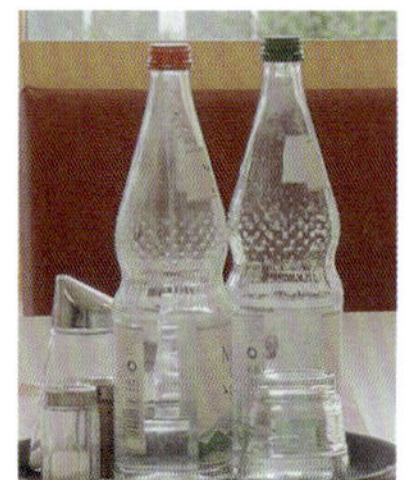

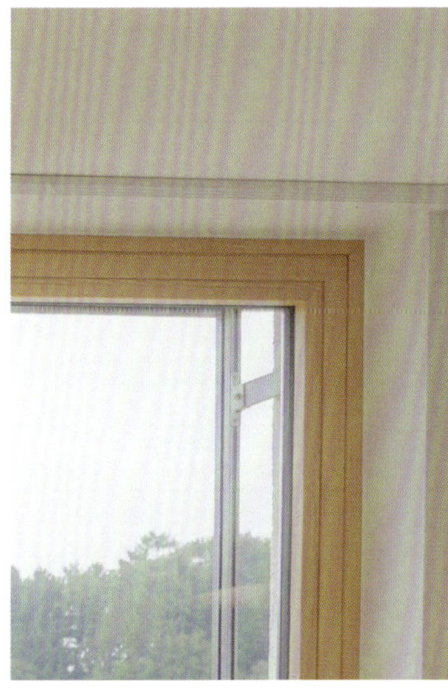

Germany's care homes are facing two crises: staff shortages and loneliness. A 2023 study found that one in five residents aged 80 and older describe themselves as "severely lonely." This reality has prompted trials of social robots like Emma, developed by a Munich-based startup. Waltraud, a resident of Haus im Wiesengrund in Albershausen, had her doubts but over time formed a bond with Emma. "When she tells her jokes, that's really good. That's my kind of humor," says Waltraud, though she emphasizes that human contact is always preferable.

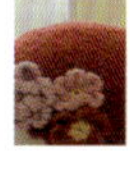

PAULA HORNICKEL

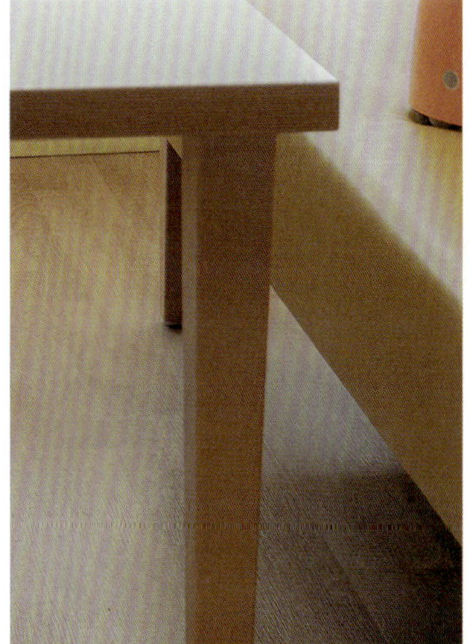

Waltraud talks with Emma, a social robot that recognizes faces and remembers past conversations. Though skeptical at first, Waltraud says she felt connected to Emma over time. Albershausen, Germany, 3 July 2025 / Paula Hornickel

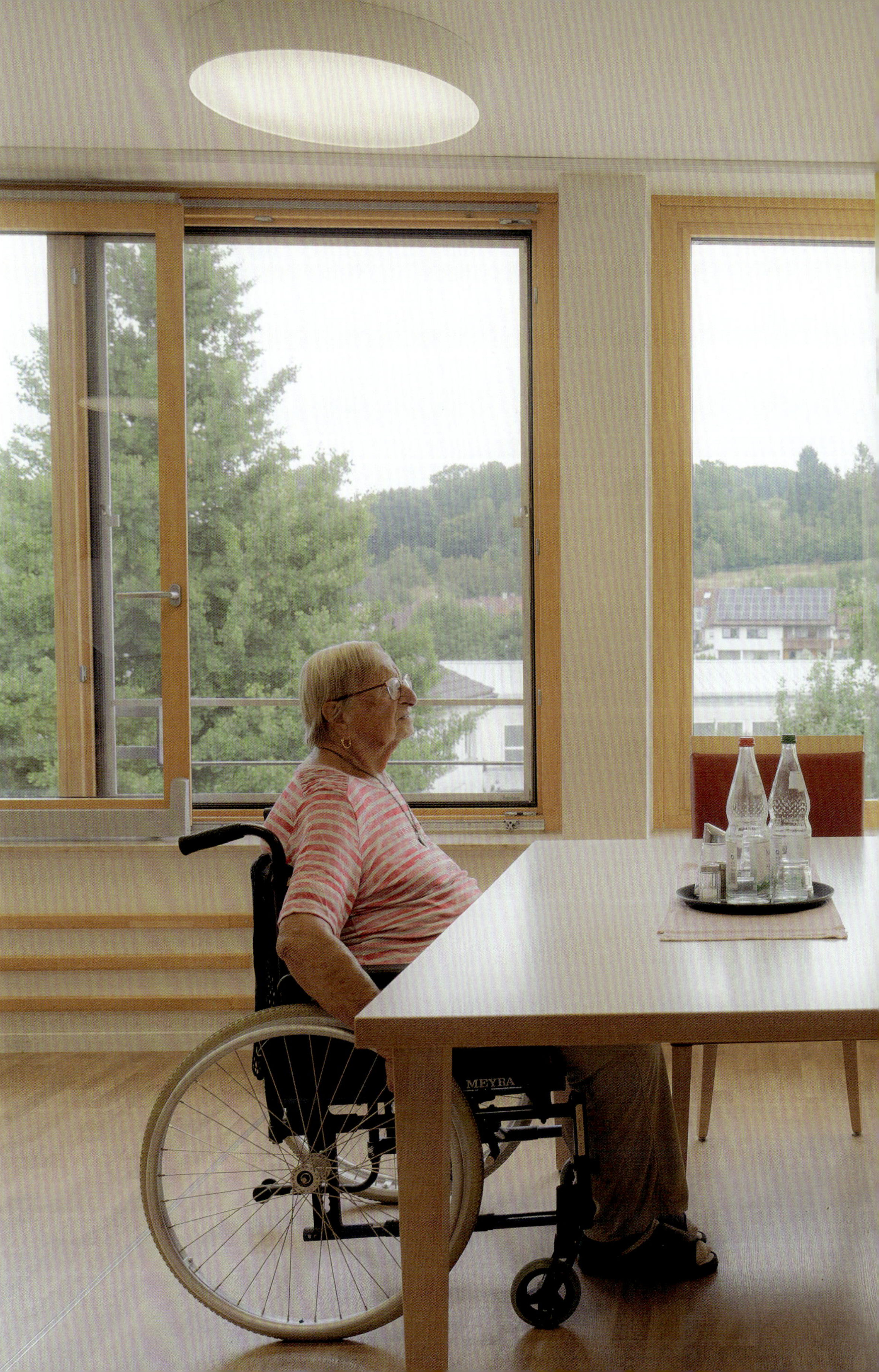

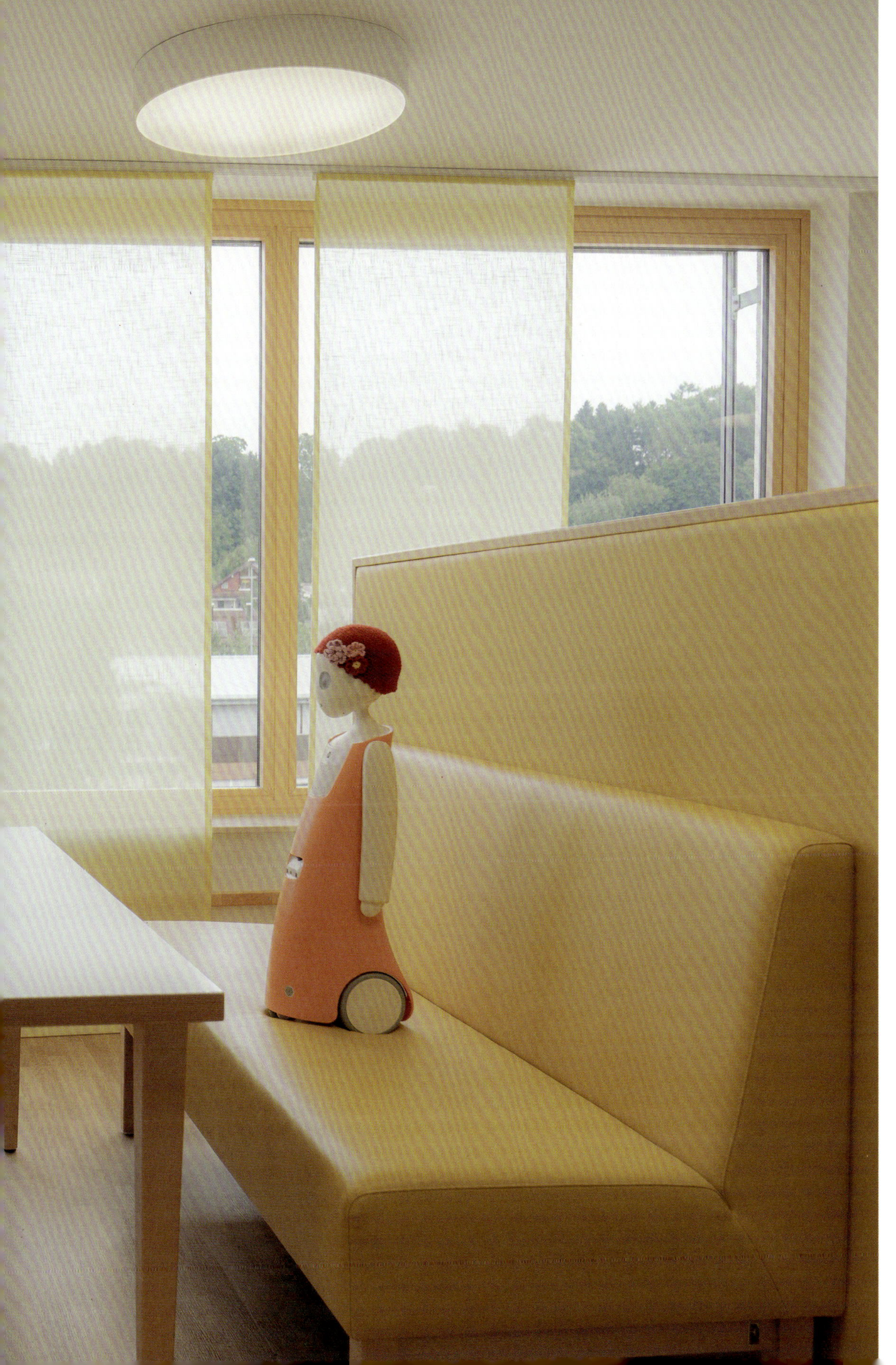

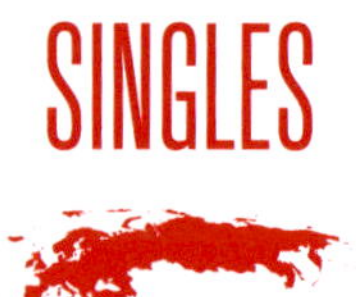

On 24 April 2025, Russia launched one of the deadliest attacks on Kyiv since the start of its full-scale invasion of Ukraine in 2022. Hours after international peace negotiations stalled again, missiles and drones struck at least five residential neighborhoods, killing 13 people and wounding 90. Russia's intensifying air campaign continues to devastate life across the country, systematically targeting infrastructure, hospitals, and educational institutions. By December 2025, at least 14,775 civilians had been killed since the invasion began. April 2025 was the worst month for child casualties in nearly three years.

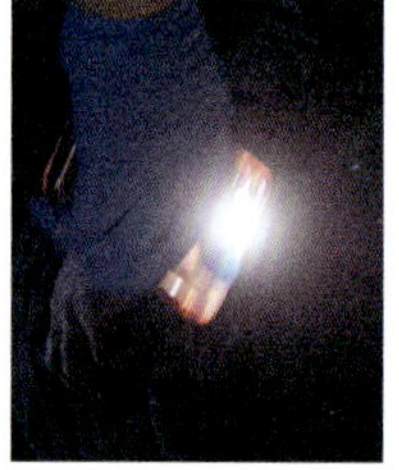

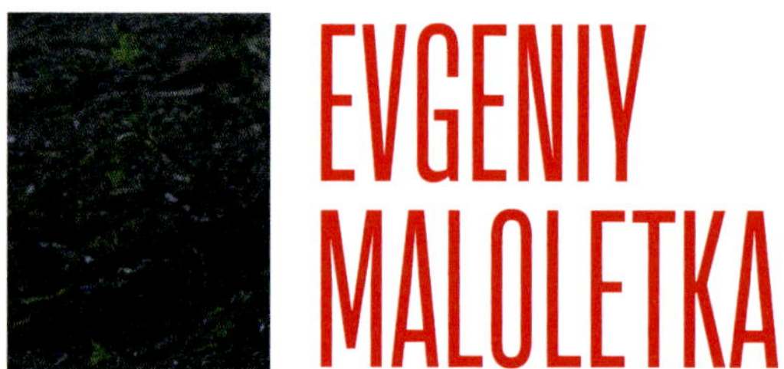

EVGENIY MALOLETKA

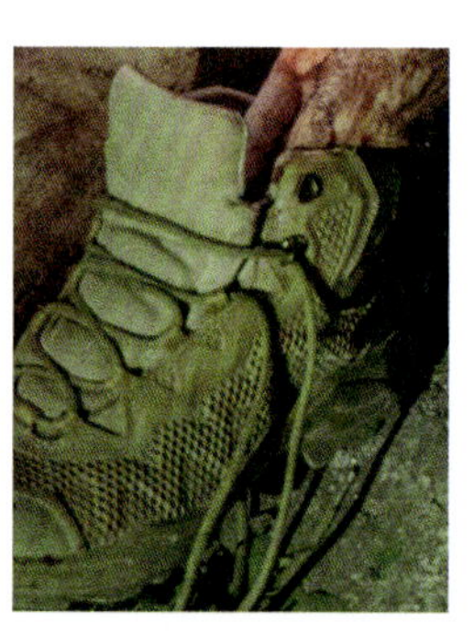

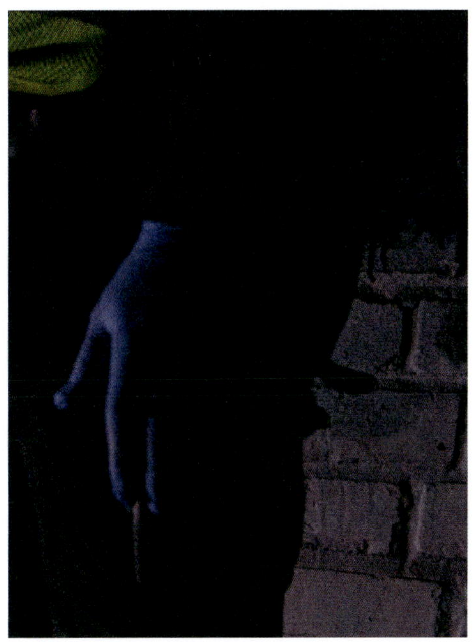

RUSSIAN ATTACK ON KYIV

Valeria Syniuk (65) sits near her badly damaged home.
She was asleep when a Russian missile destroyed the building opposite hers.
Kyiv, Ukraine, 24 April 2025 / Evgeniy Maloletka, Associated Press

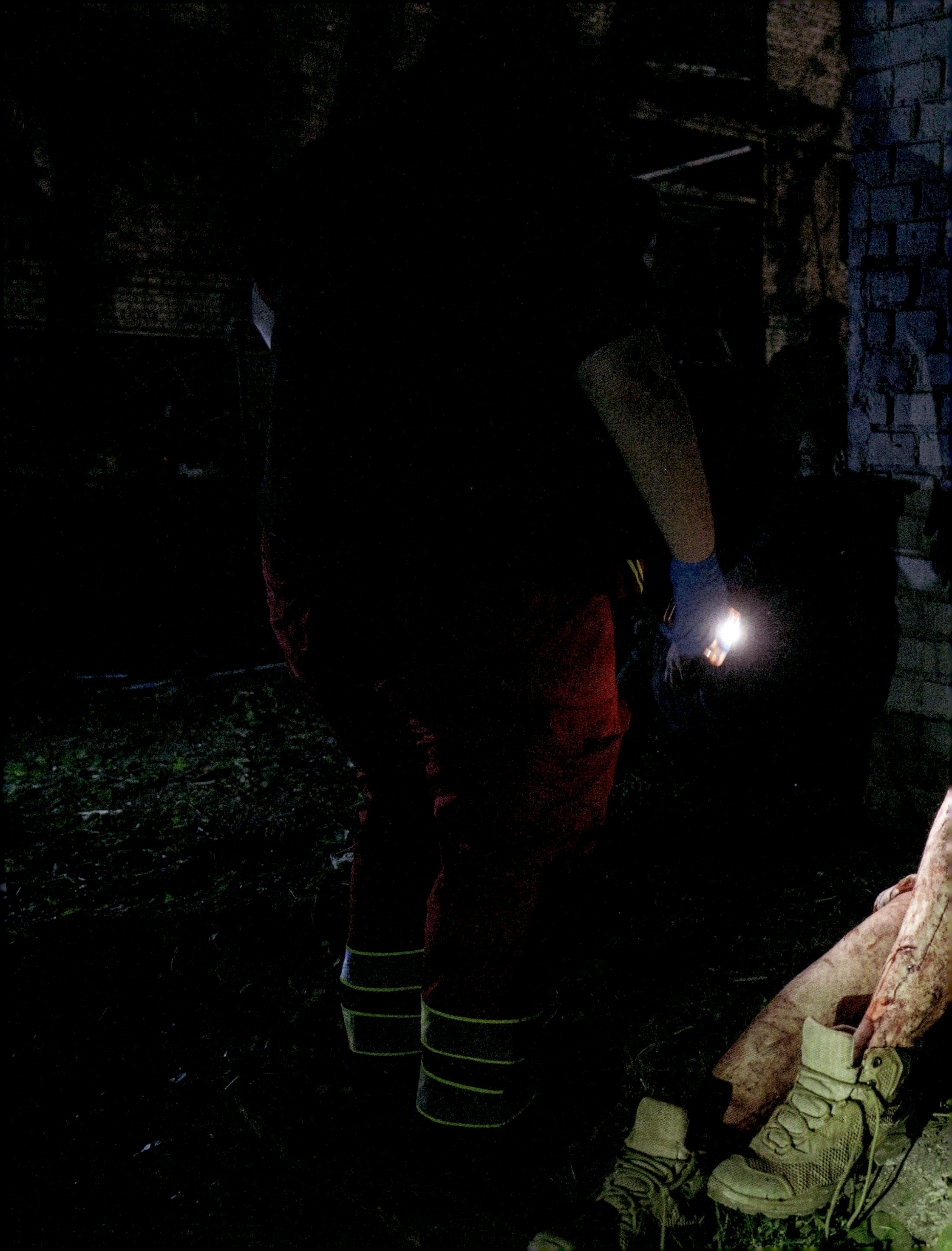

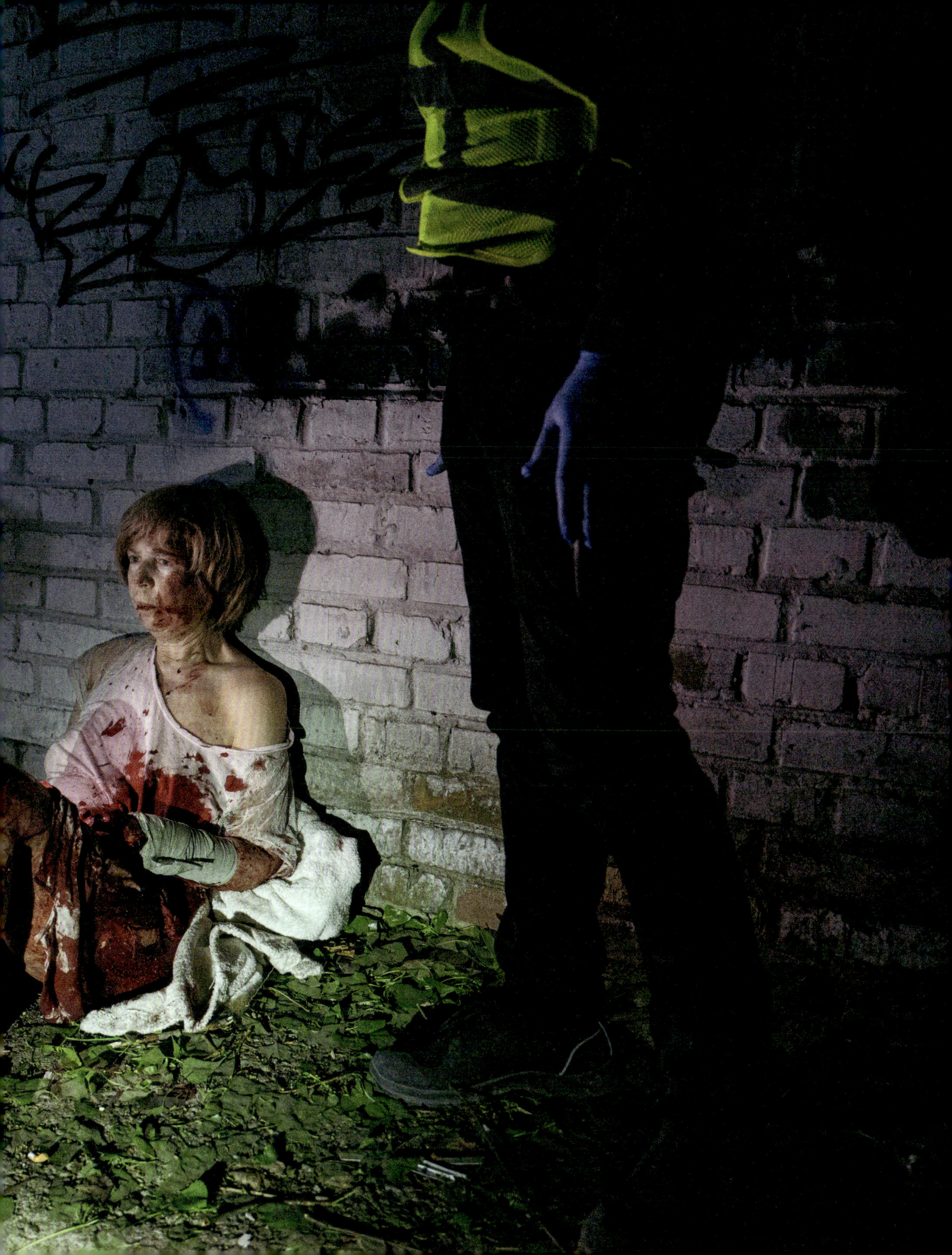

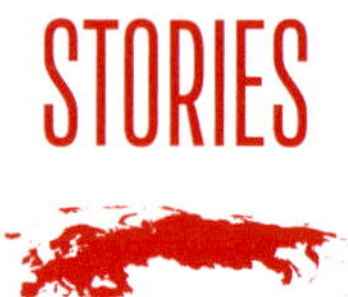

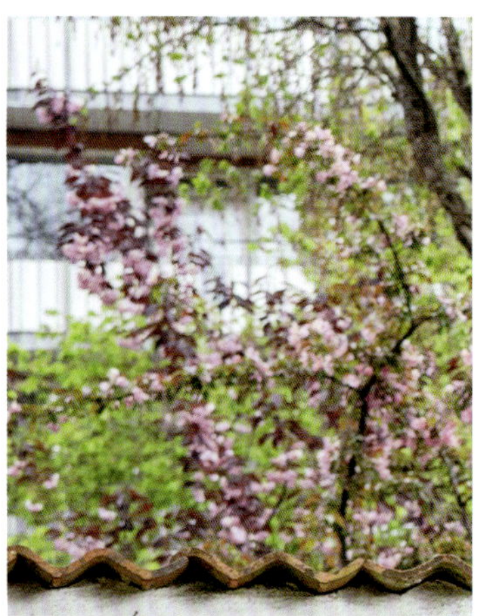

Engla Louise, a former dancer, has lived with severe anorexia nervosa since she was ten years old. At 46, she weighs less than 25 kilograms and has been tube-fed since 2019. Researchers increasingly describe anorexia as a disease of both body and mind. Its causes – not fully understood – are thought to involve neurobiological, genetic, and environmental factors. After decades of treatment, Engla Louise is now considered therapy-resistant and receives palliative care at home. This project aims to broaden the discussion about care for people living with severe eating disorders.

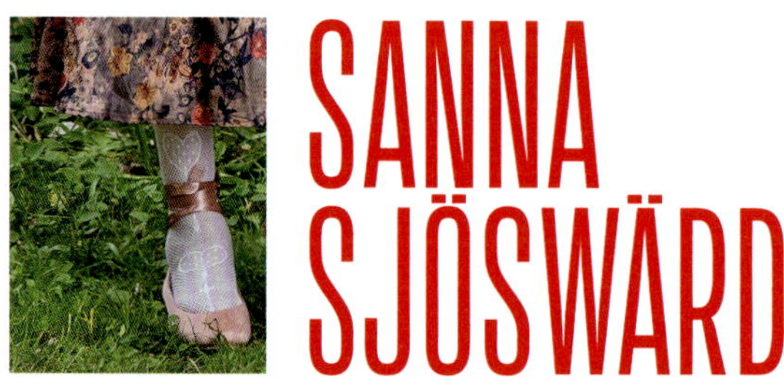

SANNA SJÖSWÄRD

ENGLA LOUISE

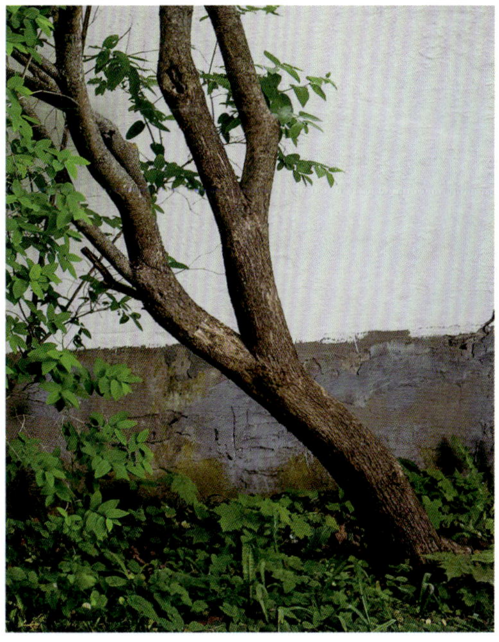

Engla Louise gathers lilacs from the Linköping Garden Society park beside her home. Being surrounded by beauty is important to her. Linköping, Sweden, 14 May 2025 / Sanna Sjöswärd, for *Corren*

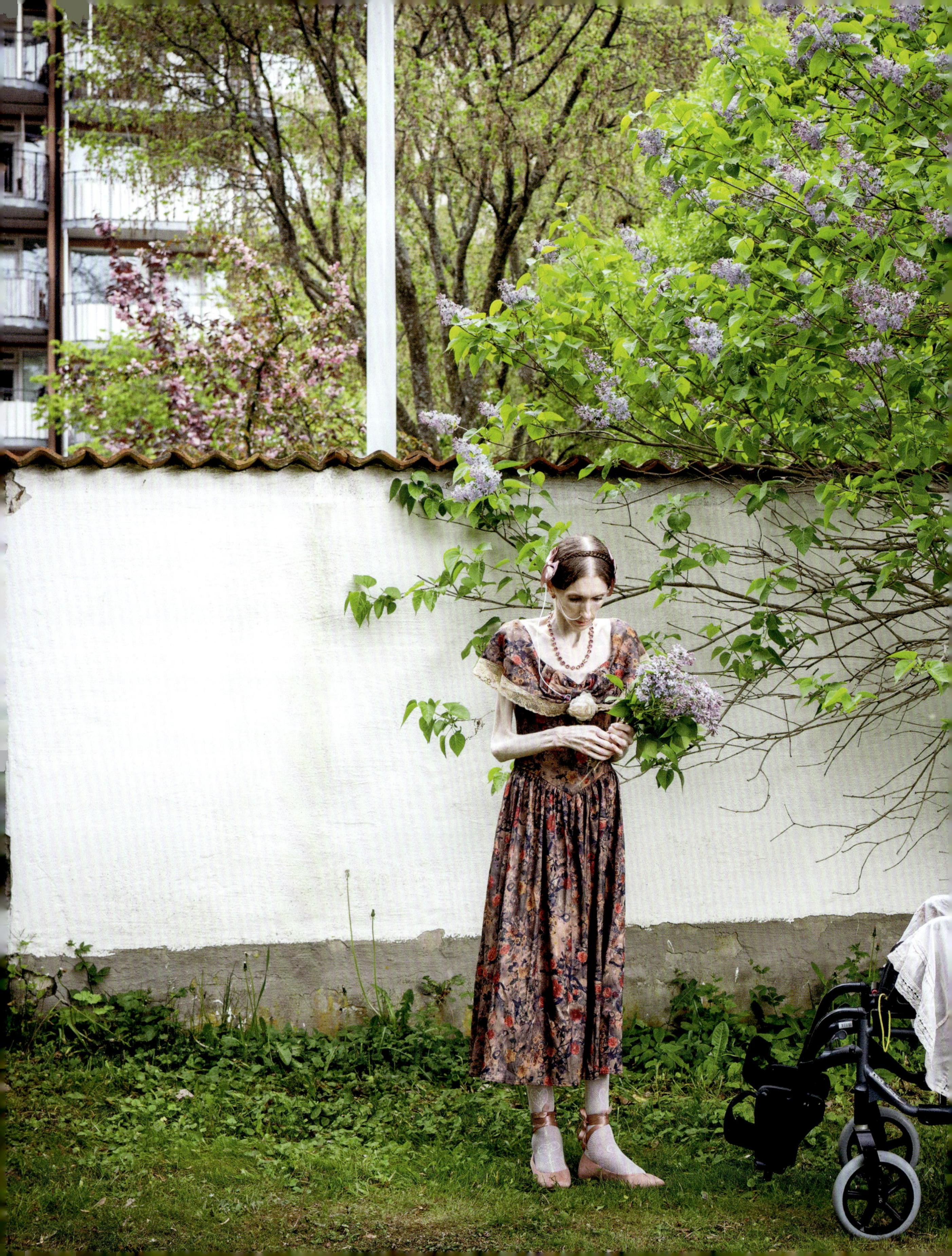

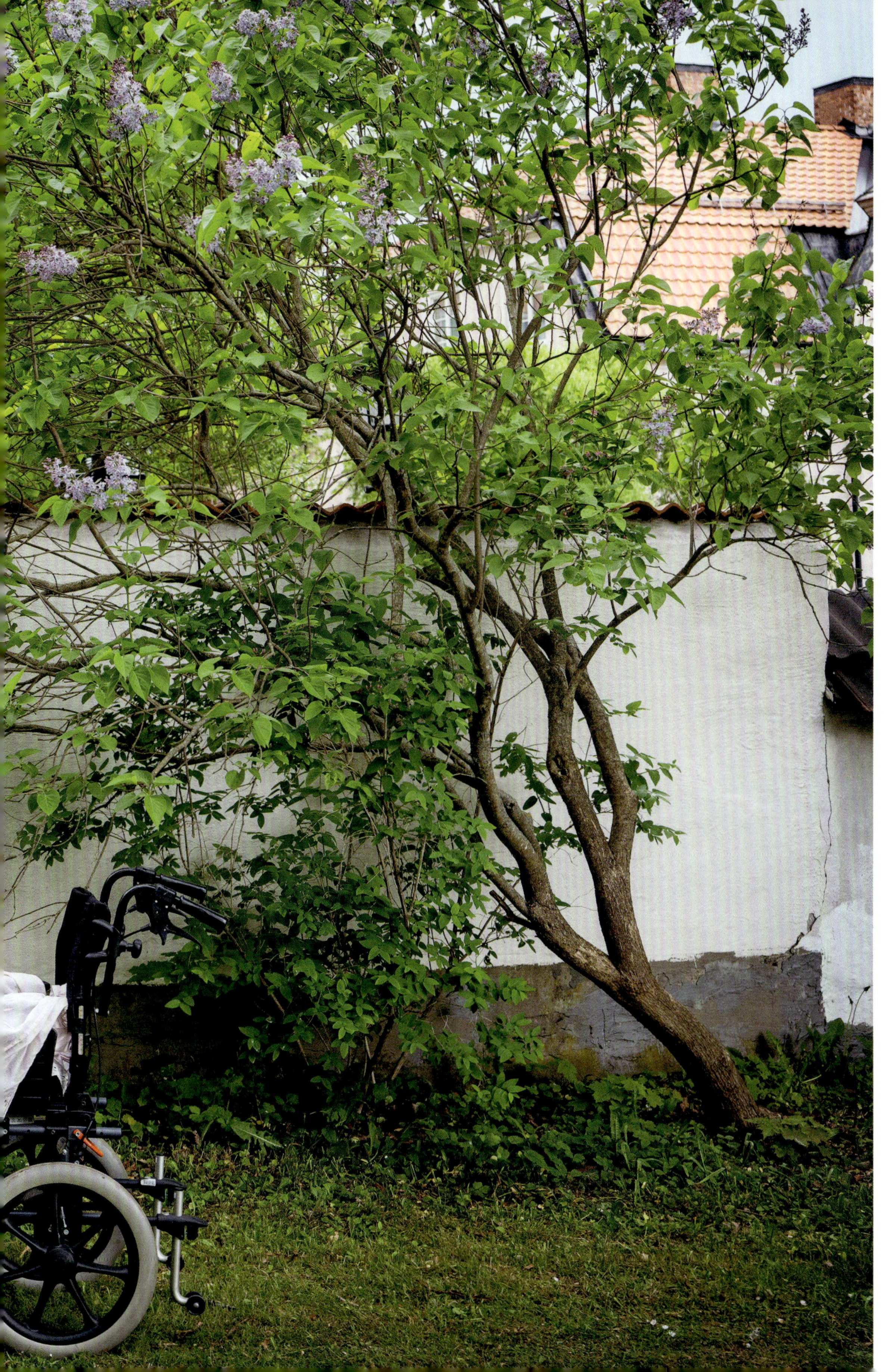

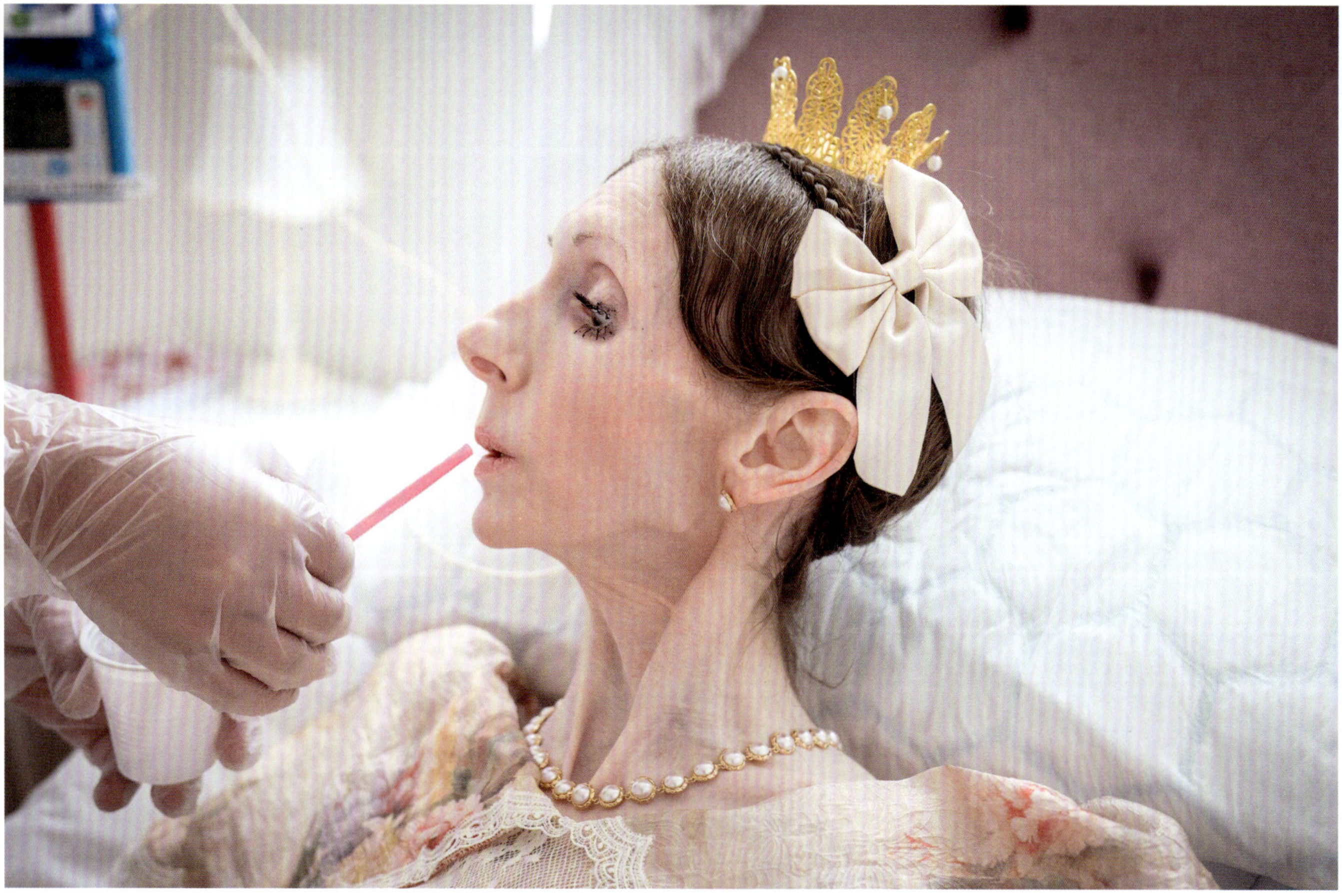

An assistant helps Engla Louise drink through a straw. She previously had daily visits from nurses; now her care relies on a special arrangement involving healthcare services and the municipality. Linköping, Sweden, 2 May 2025

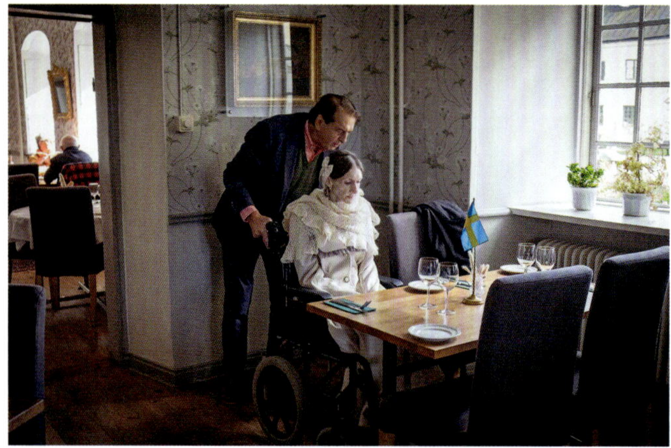

Engla Louise celebrates her 46th birthday on a day trip to Löfstad Castle with her father, Hans Ericsson. "Severely ill anorexia patients do not receive proper care in Sweden," he says. Norrköping, Sweden, 28 September 2025

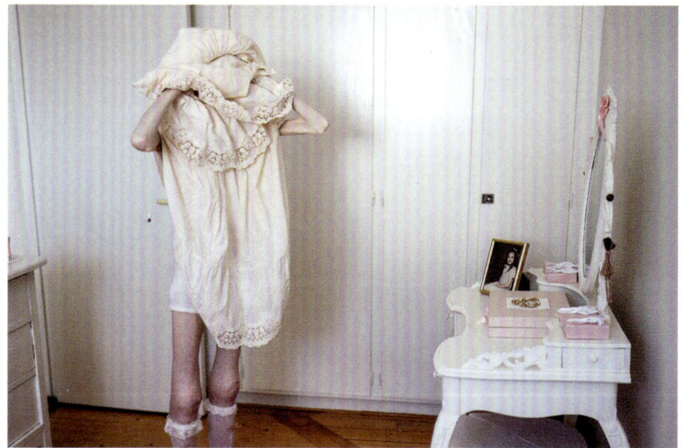

Swelling around Engla Louise's knees reveals severe edema, a sign of organ deterioration. On her dresser is a photograph of her as a young girl, taken before the illness took hold. Linköping, Sweden, 9 August 2025

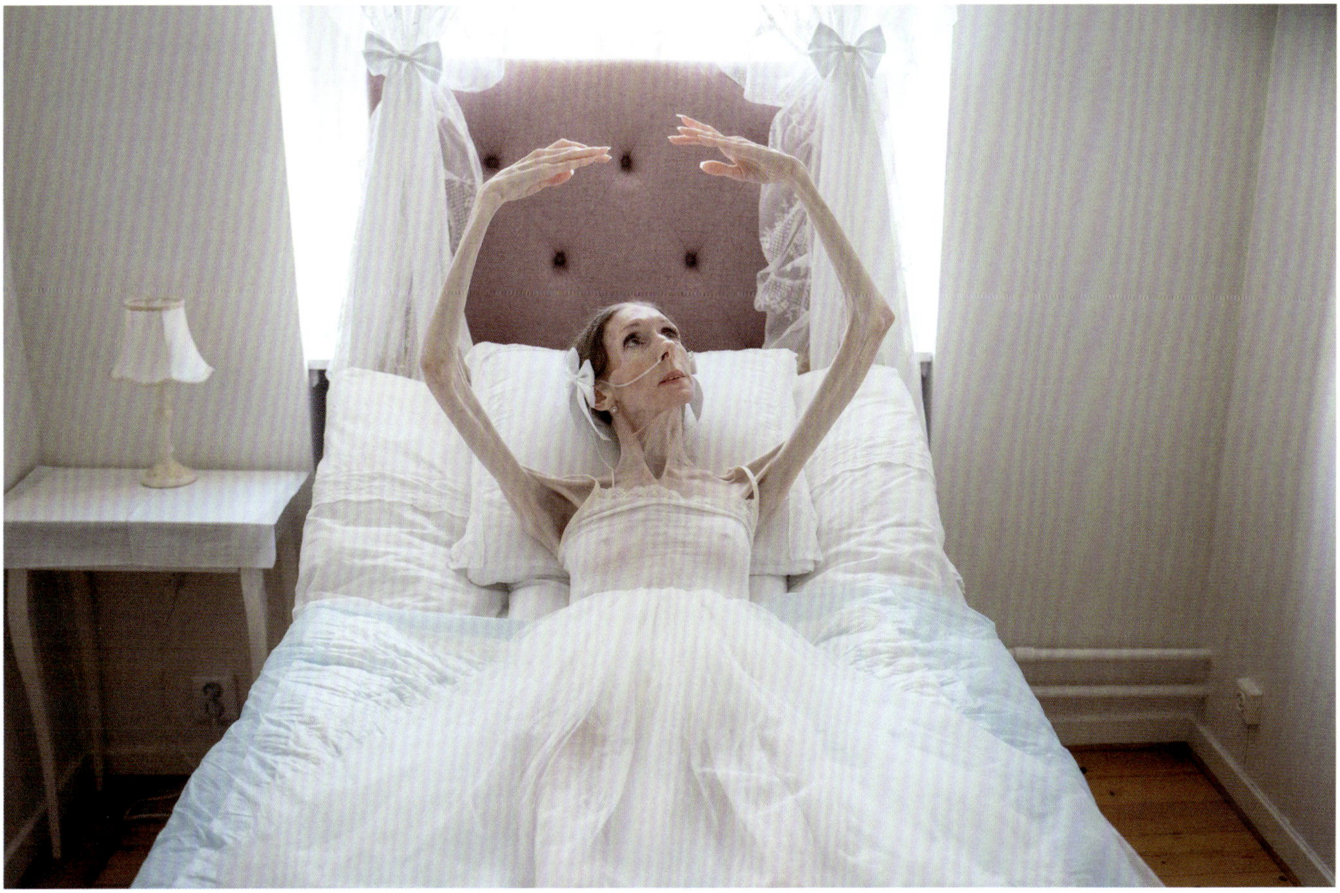

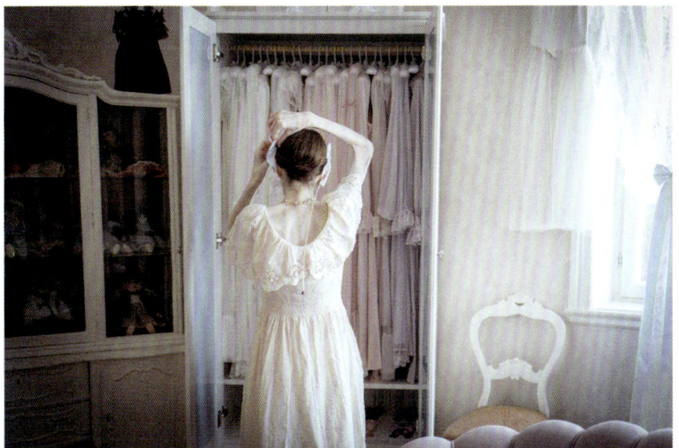

Engla Louise's "bed ballet" – movements performed lying down – keeps her connection to dance alive. Every day at a specific time, she watches ballet on her iPad. Linköping, Sweden, 22 December 2025

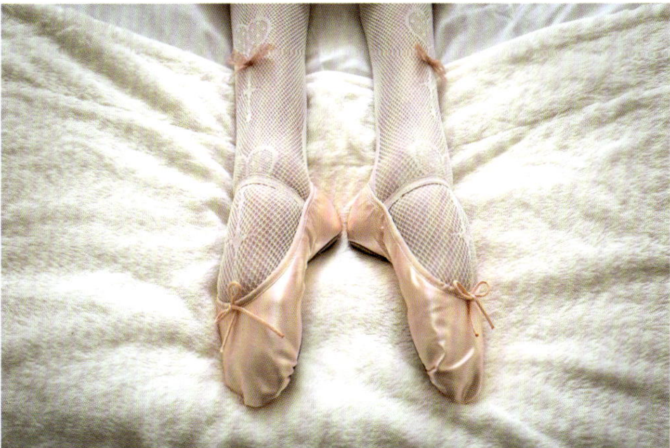

Engla Louise dresses in elaborate 19th-century gowns with lace, full skirts, and pearls. "I want to live and become a ballet dancer. That is my greatest dream," she says. Linköping, Sweden, 9 August 2025

Engla Louise lies in her bed at home. She began ballet at three, developed anorexia at ten, and was not diagnosed until 14. As a teenager, she worked as a professional dancer in Uppsala. Linköping, Sweden, 30 April 2025

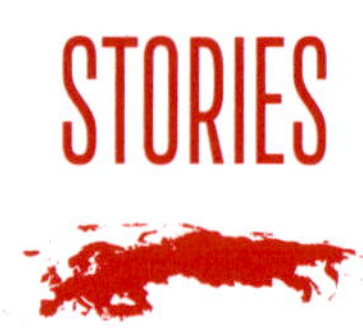

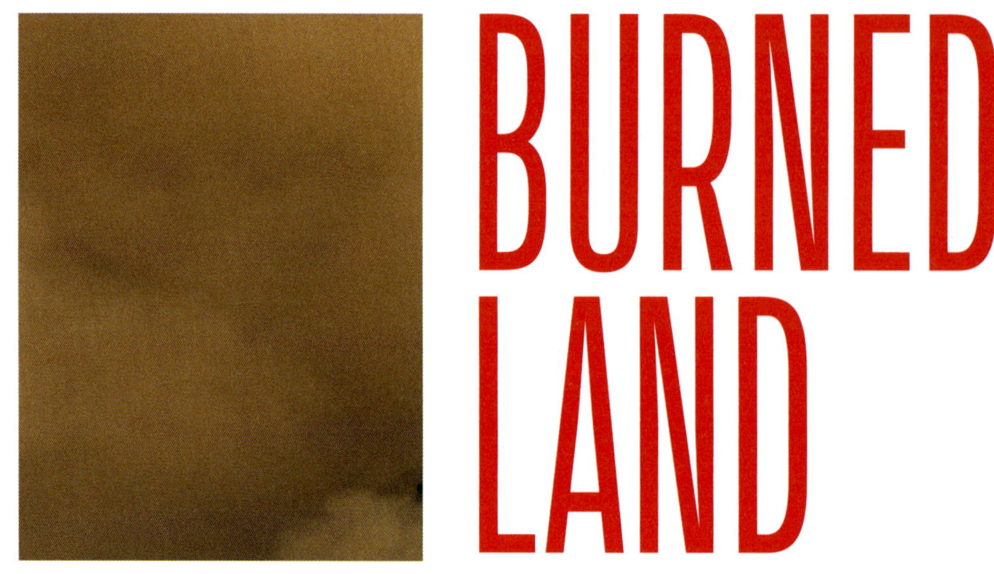

BURNED LAND

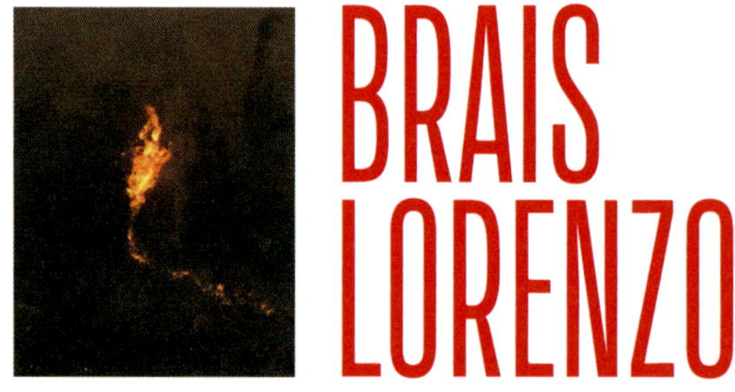

BRAIS LORENZO

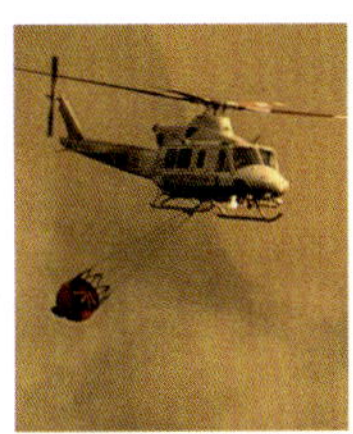

2025 was a record year for wildfires in Europe. More than 200,000 hectares burned across Galicia during Spain's worst fire season in about three decades. The increasingly severe fires in this region are attributed to drought and heat intensified by climate change, rural depopulation, and shortsighted forest management policies, including the widespread planting of highly flammable non-native species. Born in Ourense, the photographer grew up with the smell of smoke every summer and has documented Galician wildfires since 2011.

A wildfire burns at the summit of Peña Trevinca near Casaio, Galicia's highest peak at over 2,000 meters. Ourense, Galicia, Spain, 23 August 2025 / Brais Lorenzo, EFE, Revista 5W, *El País*

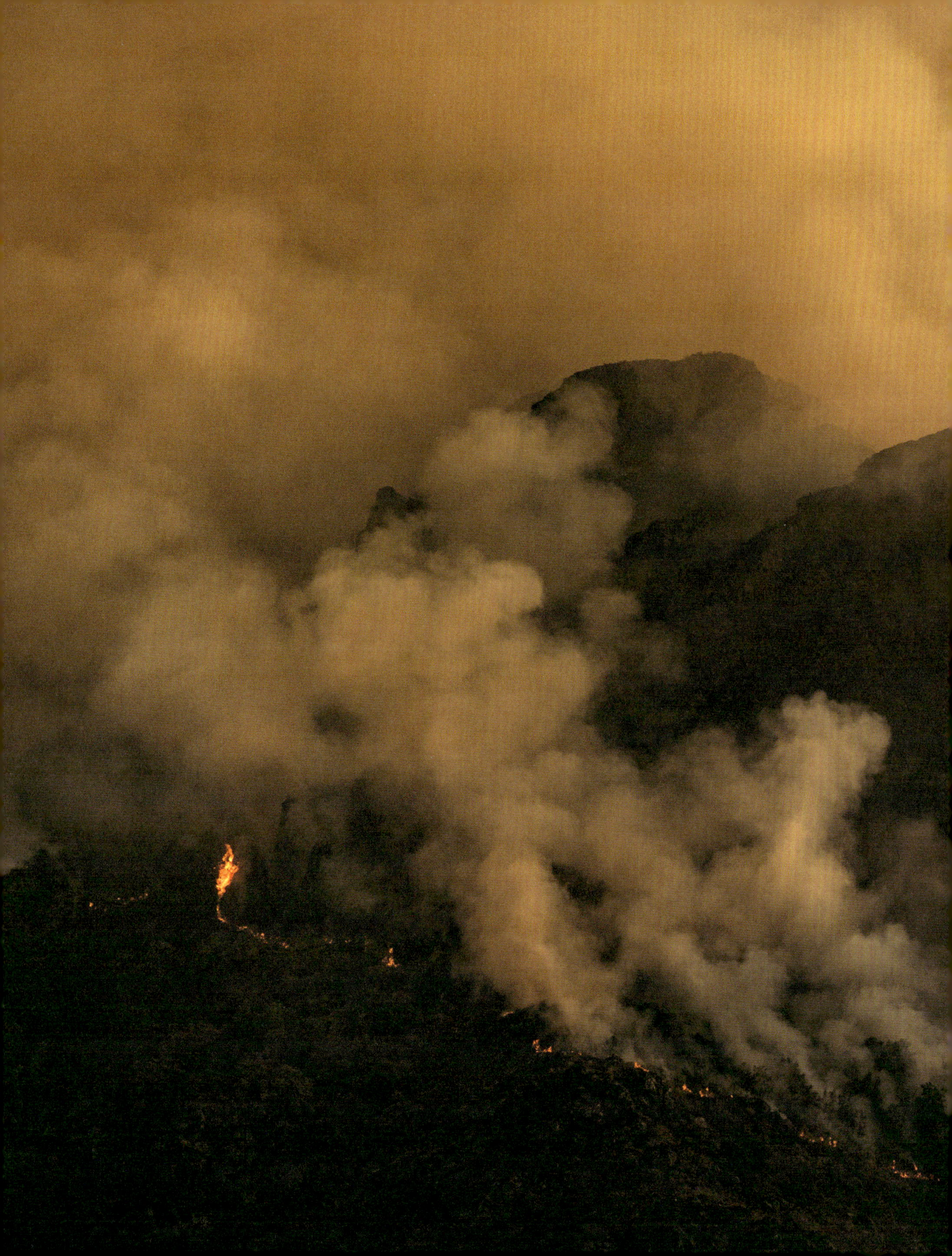

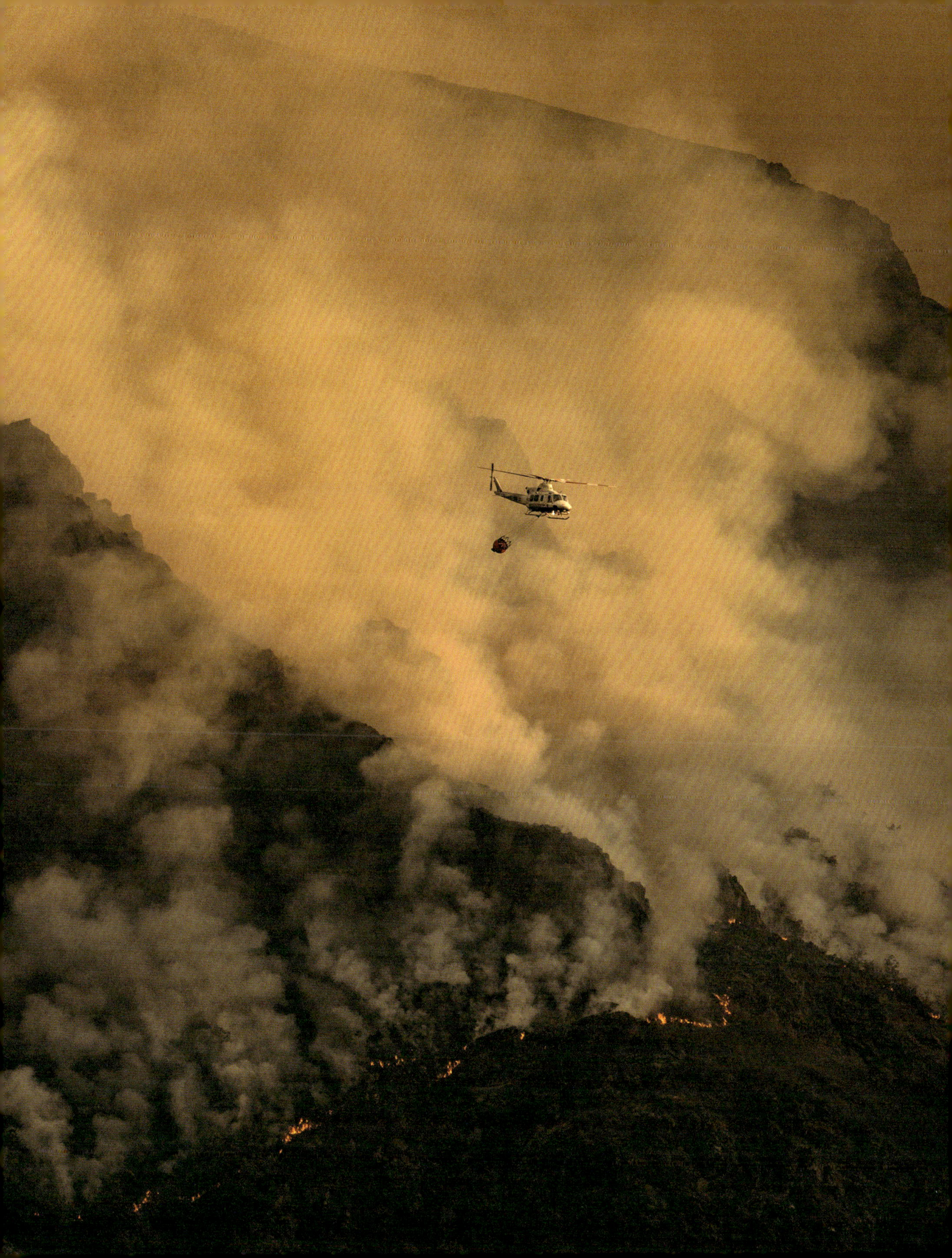

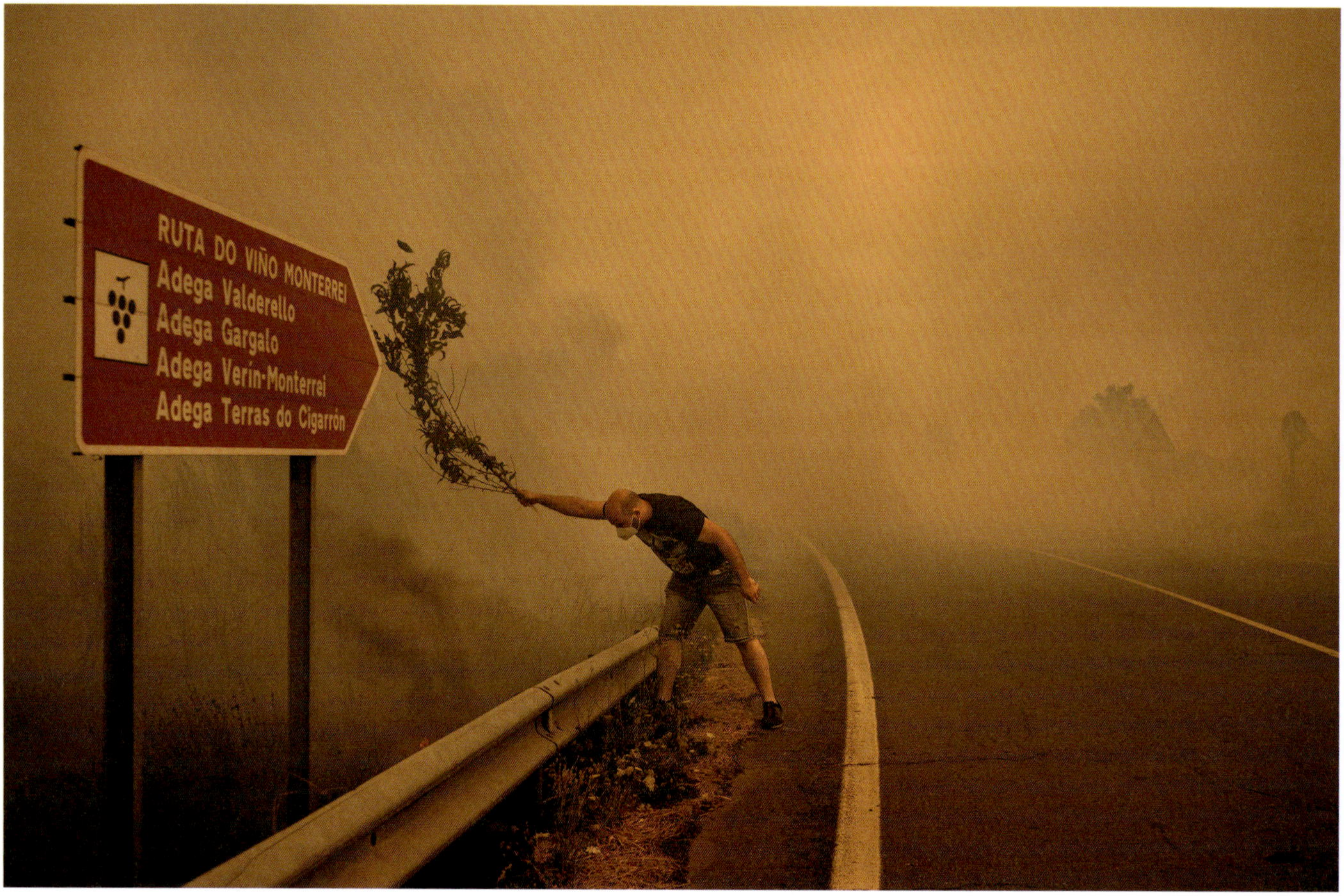

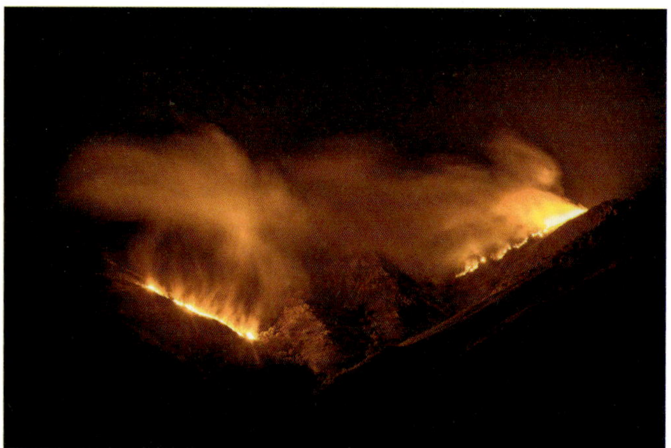

A man fights a wildfire with a branch in Cualedro. When resources are stretched, residents use whatever is available to extinguish flames, including branches, farming tools, and water hoses. Ourense, Galicia, Spain, 15 August 2025

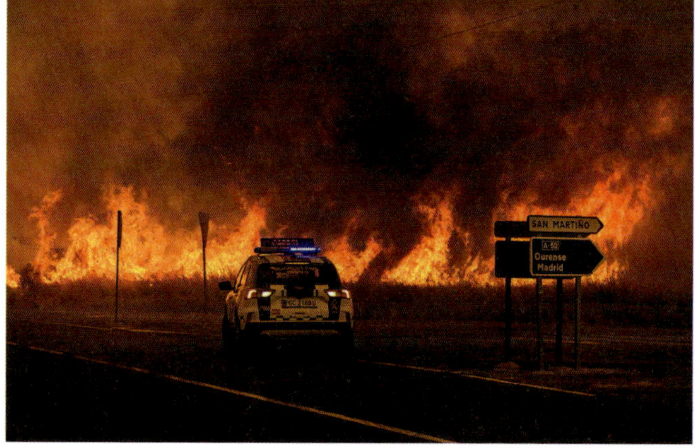

The Larouco wildfire, the worst in Galicia's recorded history, burns through the night as flames reach O Courel – a mountain range of great biodiversity. Sierra de O Courel, Galicia, Spain, 19 August 2025

A Spanish Civil Guard vehicle reverses away from advancing flames at the access road to the Ourense–Madrid Highway in Cualedro, as wildfires cut off roads across the region. Ourense, Galicia, Spain, 15 August 2025

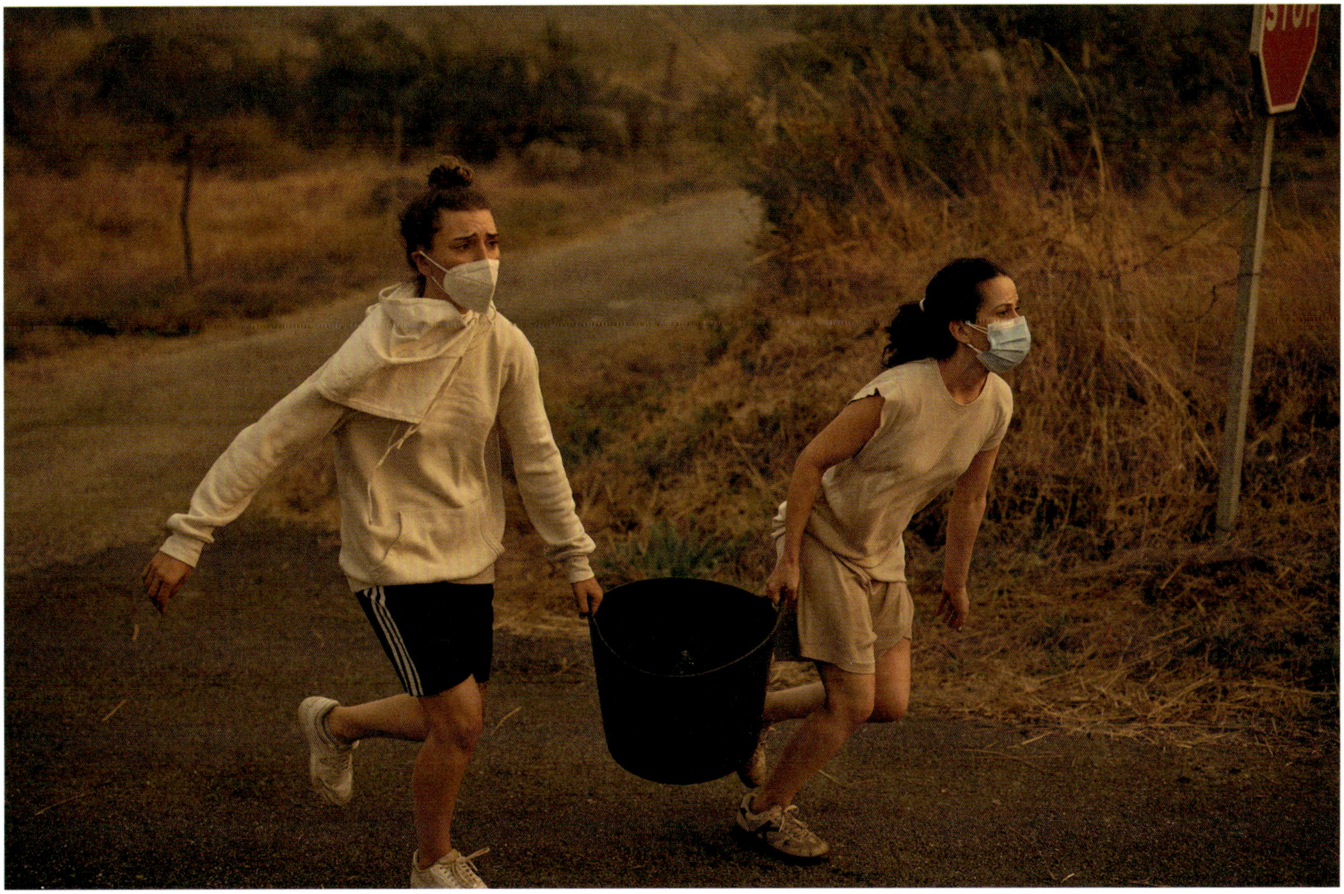

Two women run with a bucket of water to help fight a wildfire in Carballeda de Avia. Ourense, Galicia, Spain, 17 August 2025

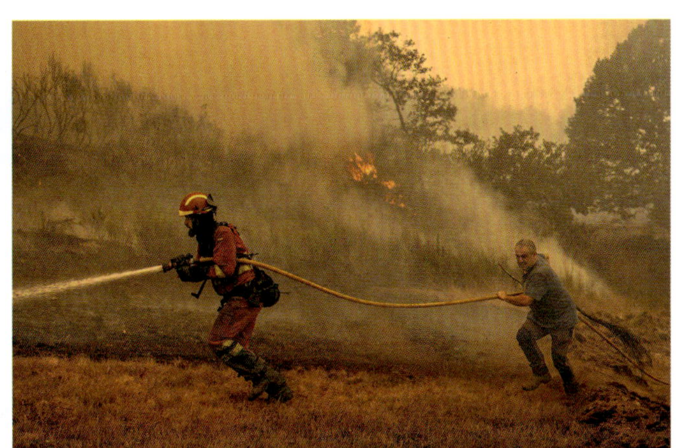

A member of Spain's Military Emergency Unit (UME) and a local resident fight a wildfire in Chandrexa de Queixa. Ourense, Galicia, Spain, 12 August 2025

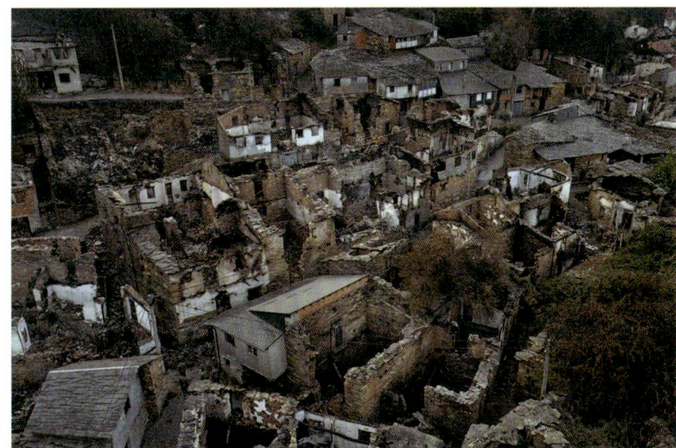

Aerial view of San Vicente de Leira, one of the areas most severely affected by the Larouco wildfire, the worst in Galicia's recorded history. Ourense, Galicia, Spain, 21 August 2025

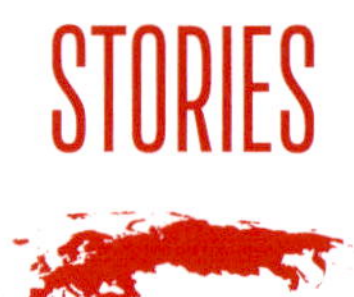

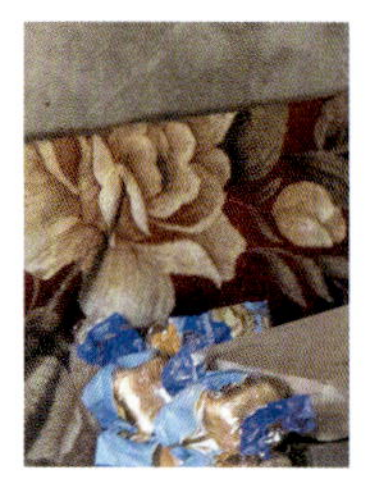

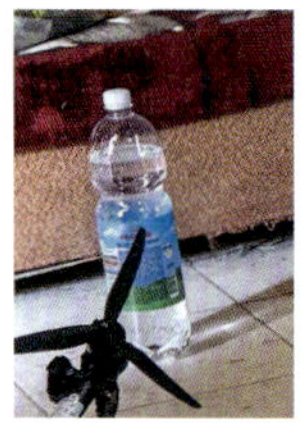

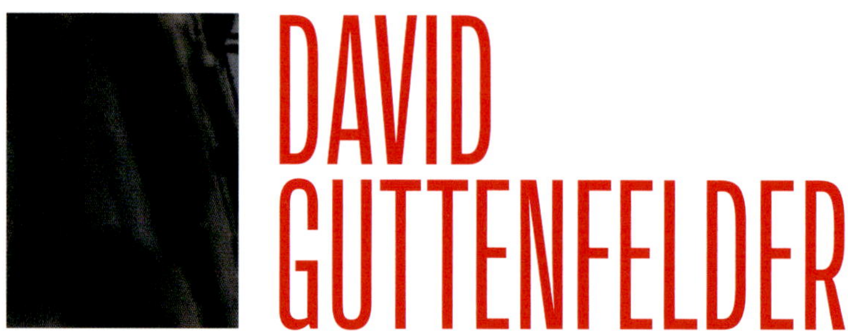

DAVID
GUTTENFELDER

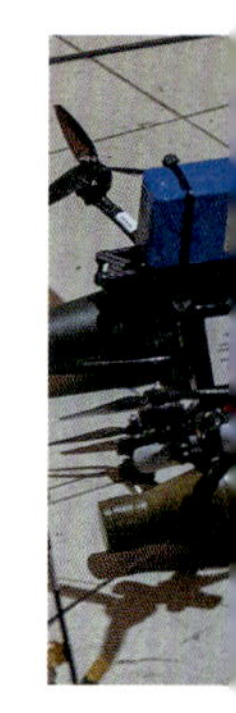

Ukraine's battle against the Russian invasion is reshaping modern combat. Hobby drones are being repurposed into remote-controlled weapons, and mass-produced first-person-view (FPV) drones are piloted from kilometers away with deadly precision. These developments have triggered an unrelenting drone arms race and turned vast areas of Ukraine into "kill zones". Civilians are targeted and displaced, and soldiers spend most of their time in underground bunkers or basements, unable to be resupplied or casualty-evacuated. This story documents Ukraine's efforts to advance its drone capabilities, and the impact of Russian drone attacks on civilians.

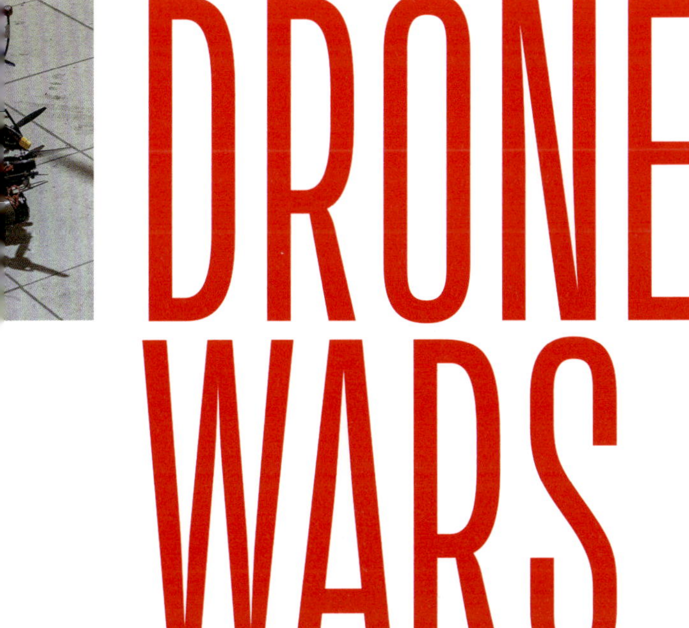

DRONE WARS

A Ukrainian soldier, code-named "Trader," of the Achilles drone strike battalion, prepares FPV drones for attack missions on Russian positions. Kharkiv region, Ukraine, 24 August 2024 / David Guttenfelder, *The New York Times*

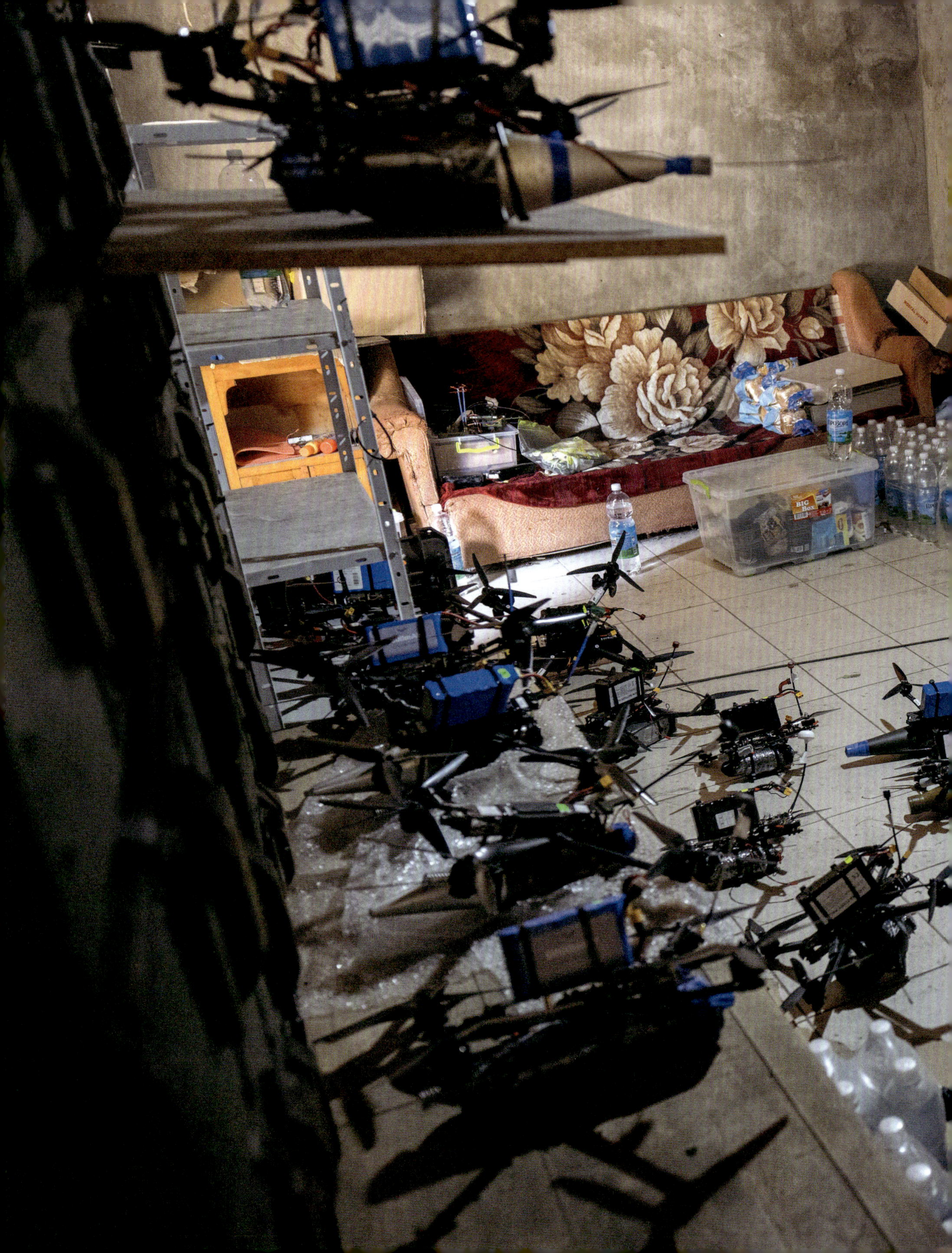

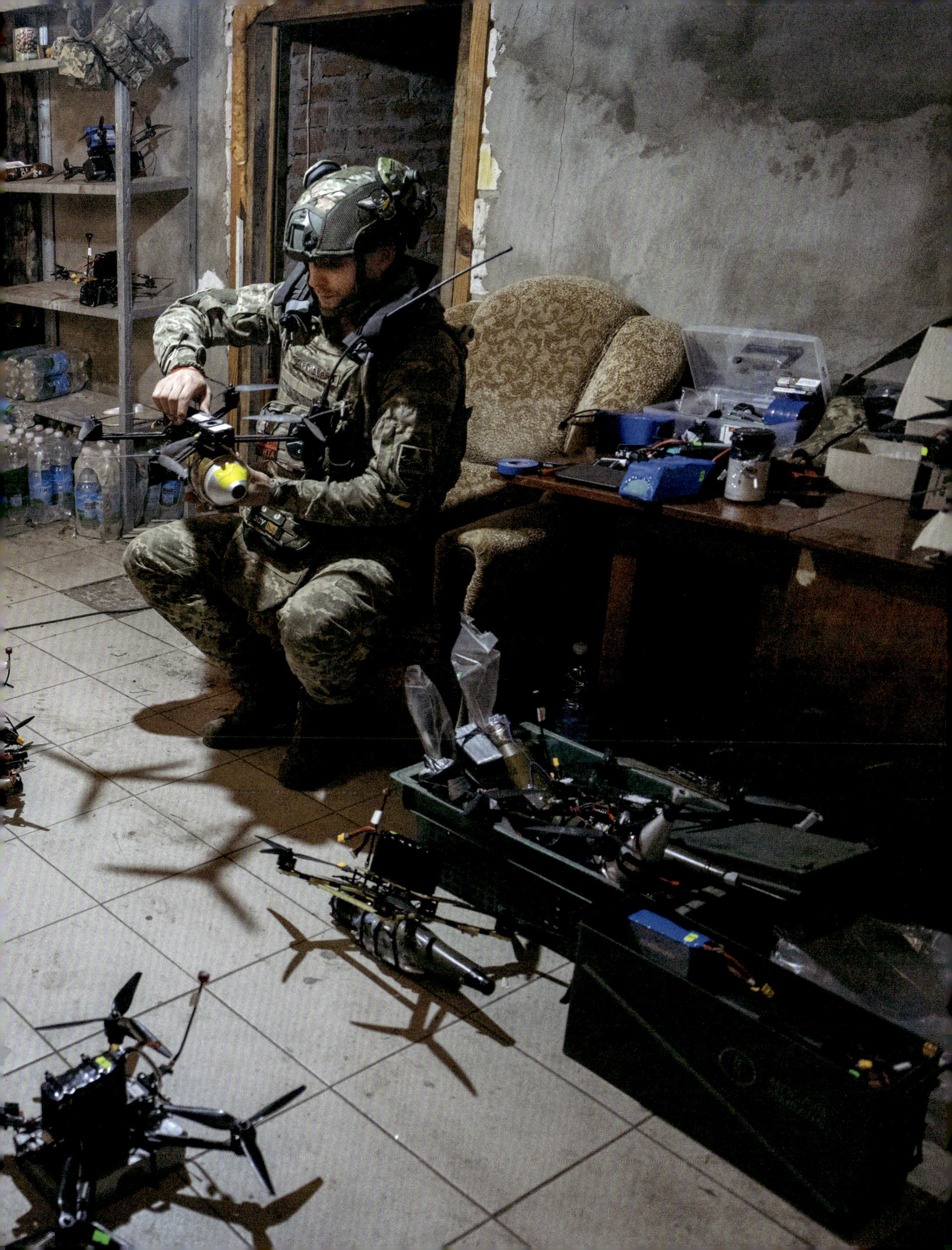

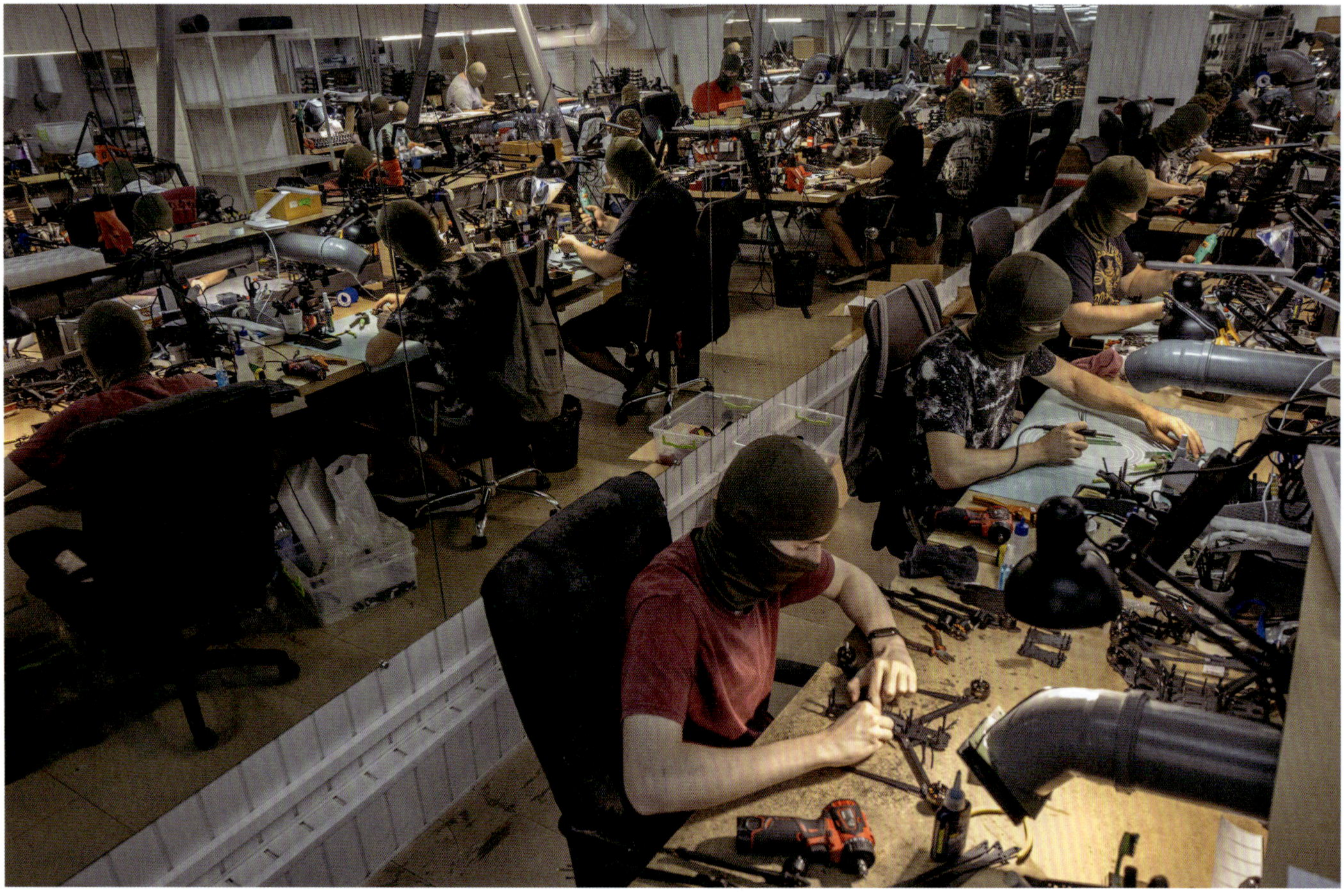

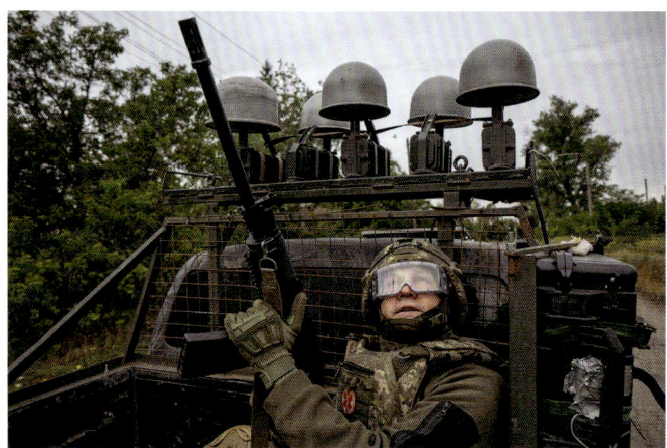

Ukrainian civilians, their identities concealed behind masks, assemble FPV drones in a basement factory. Both Ukraine and Russia now manufacture millions of battlefield drones a year. Central Ukraine, 6 September 2024

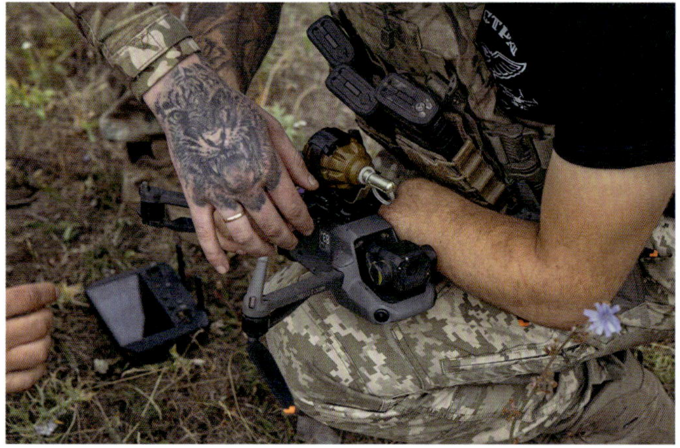

A soldier from Ukraine's 93rd Brigade scans for Russian FPV drones while speeding through Kostyantynivka, a strategic gateway to Ukraine's last major defensive belt in Donetsk. Kostyantynivka, Ukraine, 19 June 2025

A Ukrainian soldier, known by the call sign "Ara," uses his partially amputated arm to steady a drone being fitted with a grenade. Wounded in 2022, he now trains recruits in drone operations. Donetsk region, Ukraine, 5 August 2024

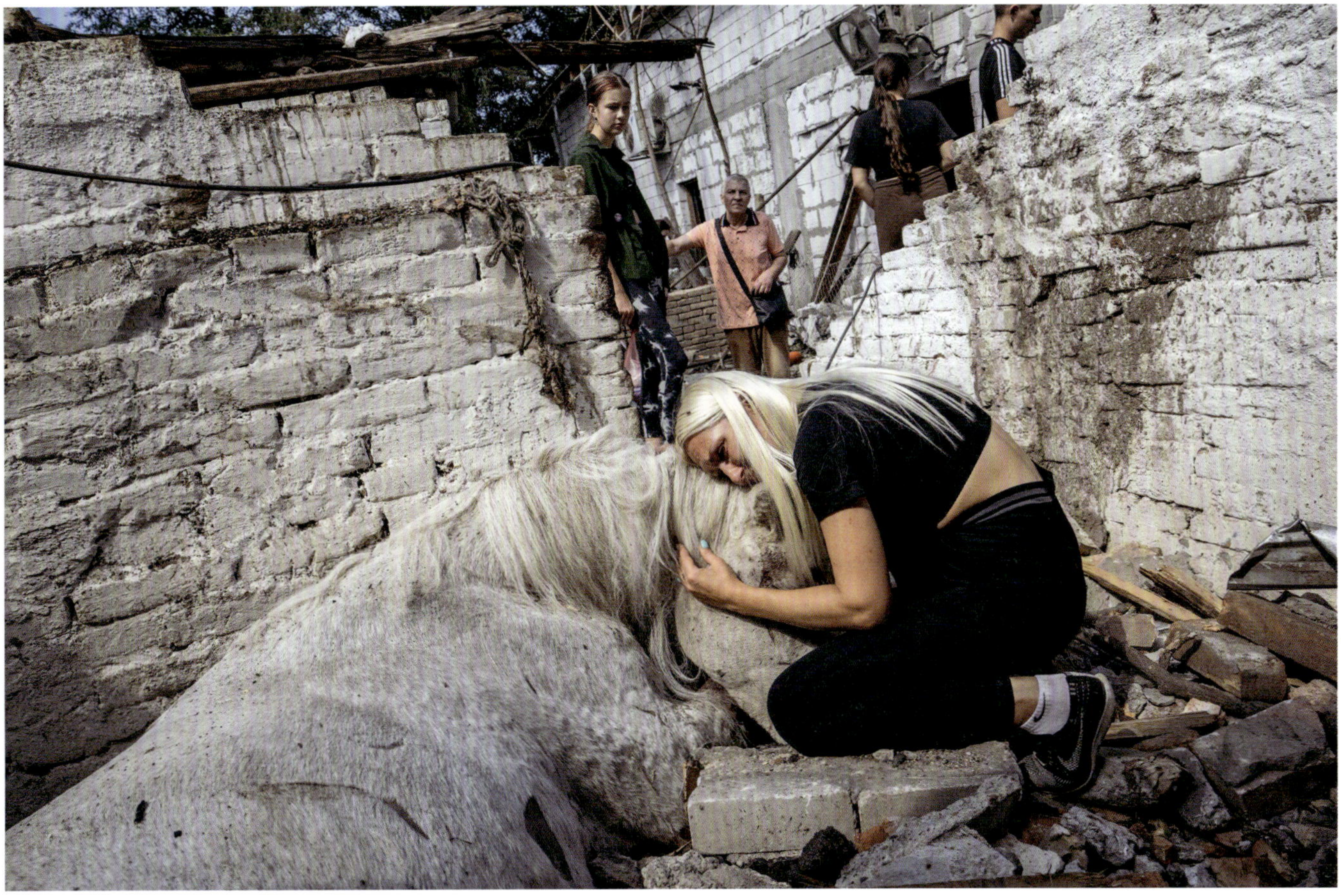

Yulia Vasiakina embraces Kamelia, her 20-year-old horse, killed when Russian long-range drones struck their neighborhood and destroyed most of the surrounding city block. Odesa, Ukraine, 11 July 2025

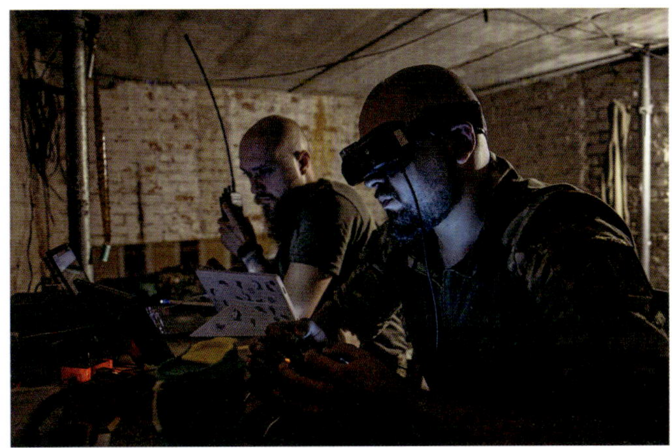

Ukrainian soldiers "Prorok," right, and "Buryi" conduct an FPV drone attack mission on Russian positions from a basement, navigating through live video feeds. Kharkiv region, Ukraine, 24 August 2024

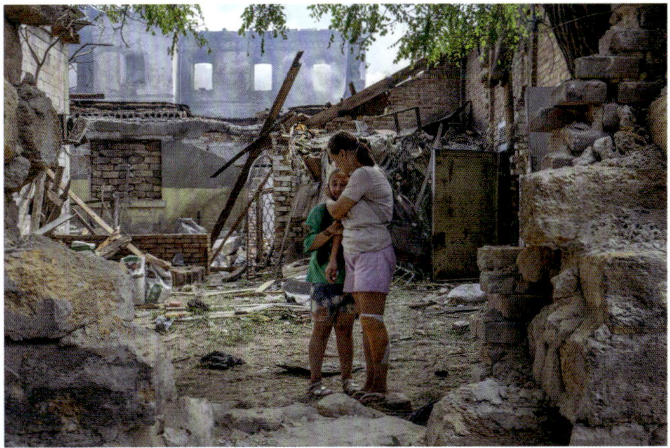

Natalia Harbuznia comforts her daughter Victoria after a swarm of Russian long-range drones attacked their neighborhood, injuring at least 11 people including Natalia. Odesa, Ukraine, 11 July 2025

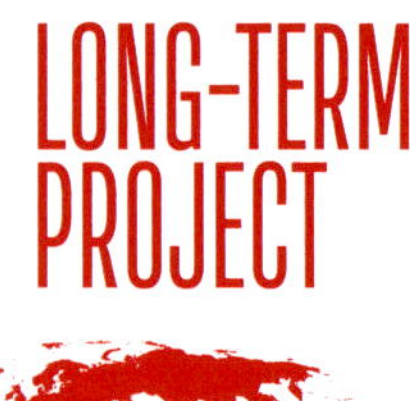

In the peripheral neighborhoods of France's *banlieues*, migrant families navigate postcolonial legacies, higher rates of unemployment, and structural inequality. France's integration system requires migrants to culturally assimilate while prejudice persists, leaving communities caught between exclusion and belonging. Yet these communities are also spaces of creativity and resilience that shape contemporary French culture. Documenting his friends and family, the photographer – born to Cambodian refugees – portrays lives in which community and solidarity are the clearest markers of identity.

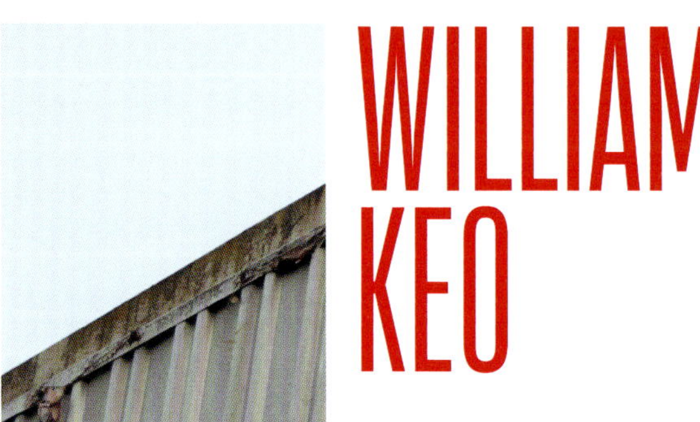

WILLIAM KEO

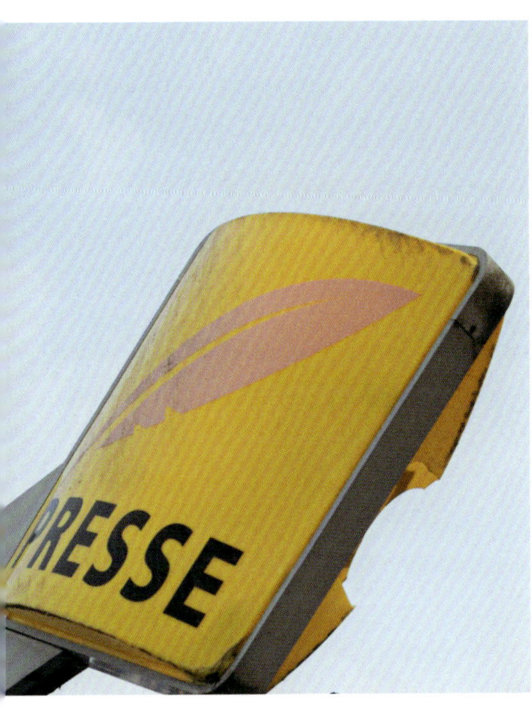

EXTRAMUROS

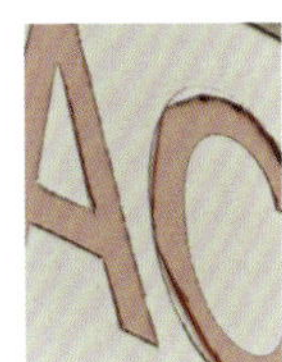

Young men gather on a rooftop in the Briques Rouges, one of Verneuil-sur-Seine's largest social housing projects. France, 21 July 2023 / William Keo, La Bibliothèque Nationale de France, *Die Zeit*

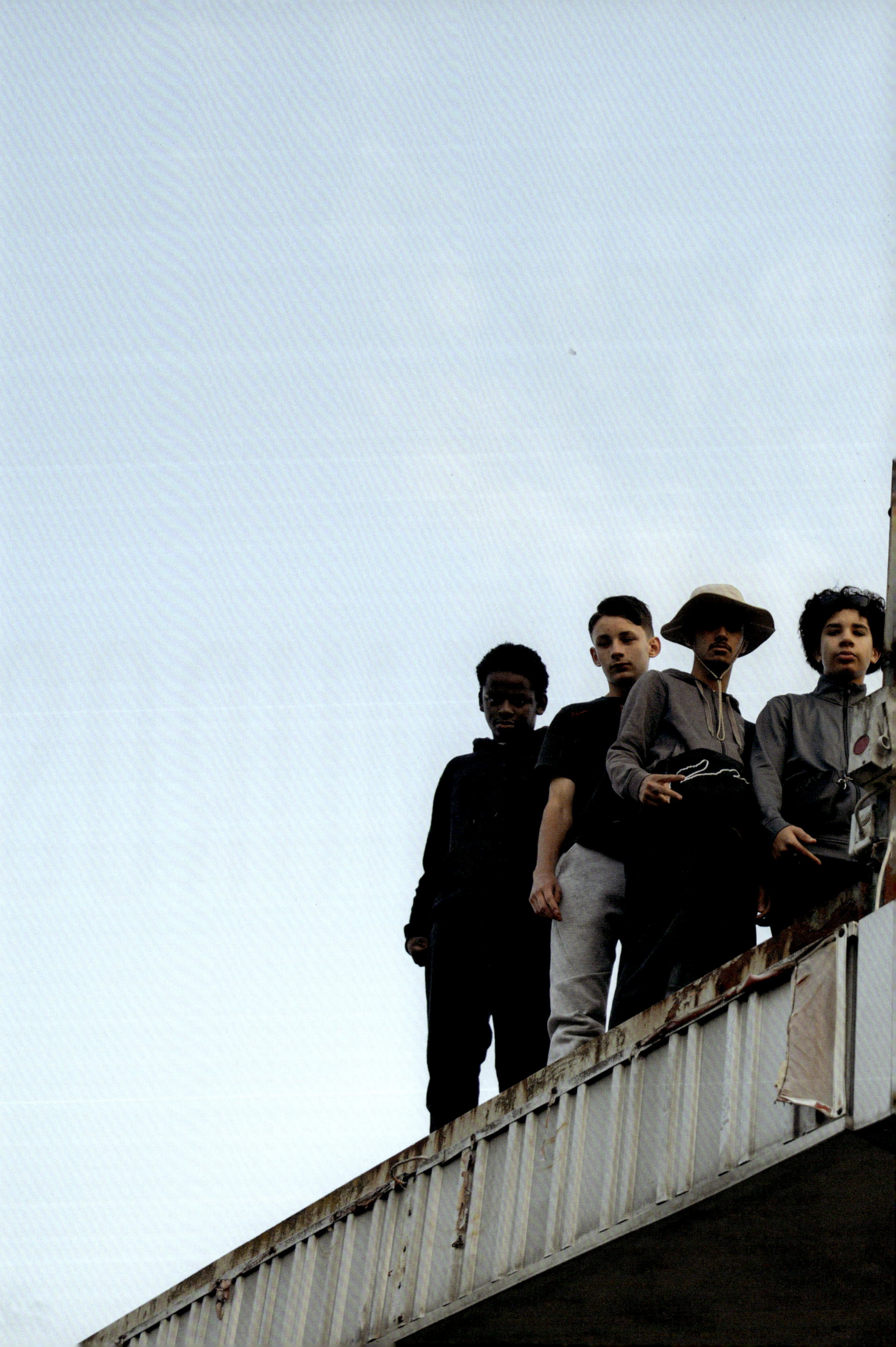

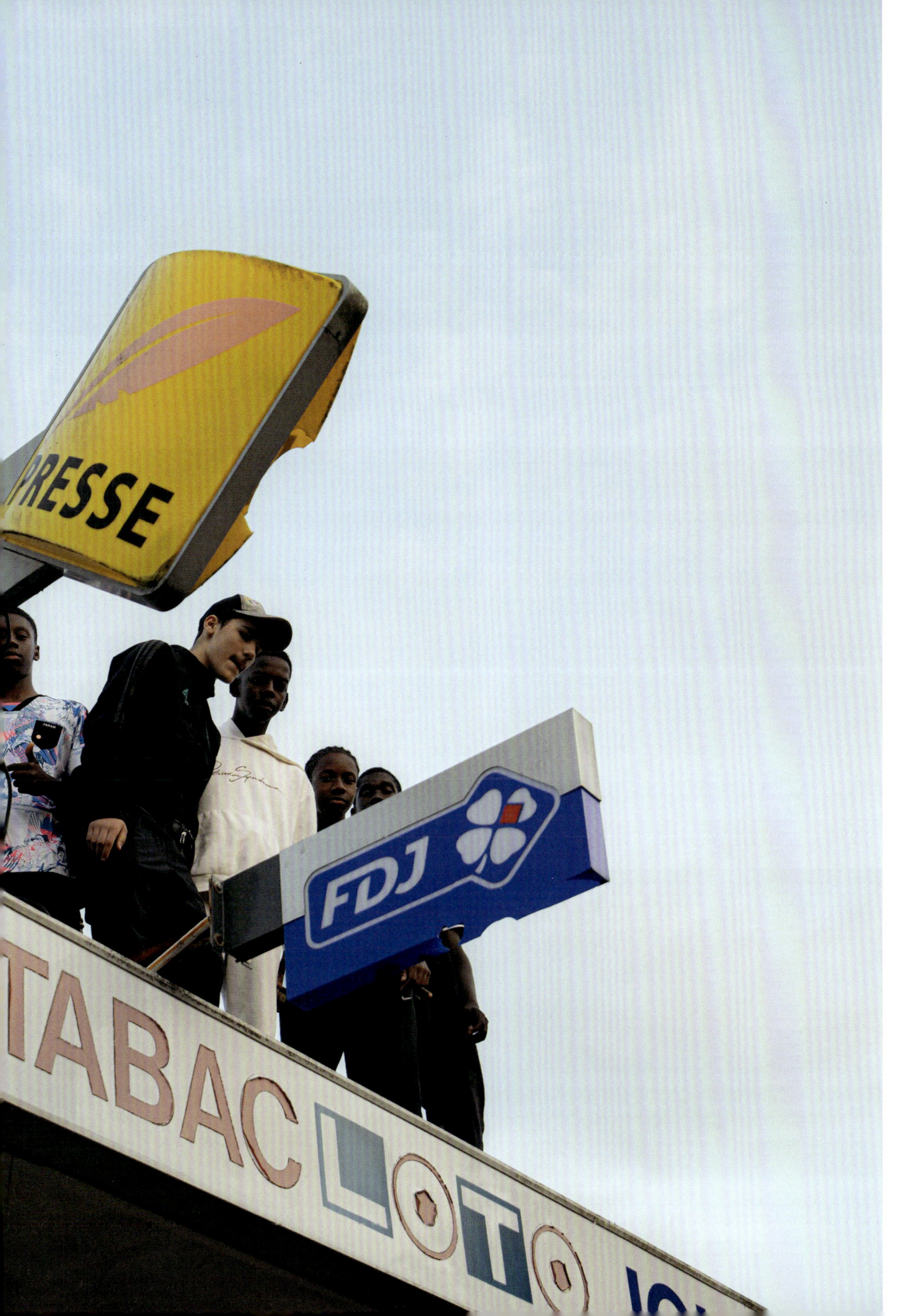
PRESSE
FDJ
TABAC LOTO

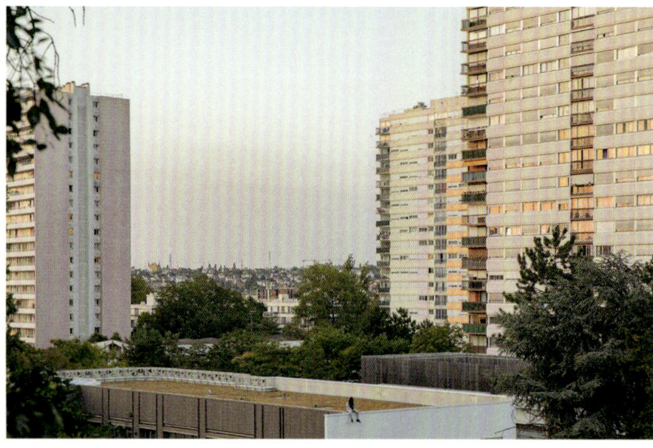

Local resident Ysnear sits on the roof of École élémentaire Paul Langevin in the La Zup housing project. Fontenay-sous-Bois, France, 19 July 2023

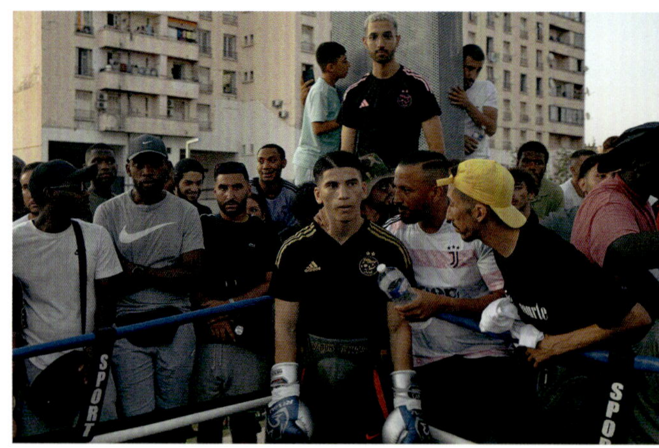

Mehdi, of Algerian origin and originally from the Bosquets housing project in Montfermeil, competes in a street fight organized by CanalPourss, a local initiative that uses boxing to reduce violence. Marseille, France, 27 July 2024

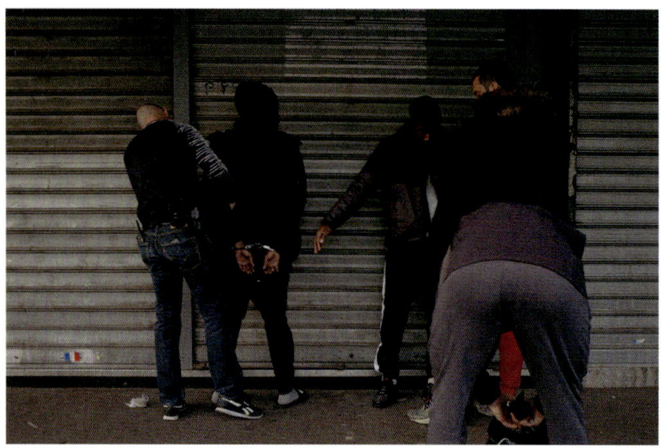

Officers of the anti-crime brigade (BAC), a unit of the national police, arrest men connected to a drug trafficking point under surveillance. Blanc-Mesnil, France, 13 April 2022

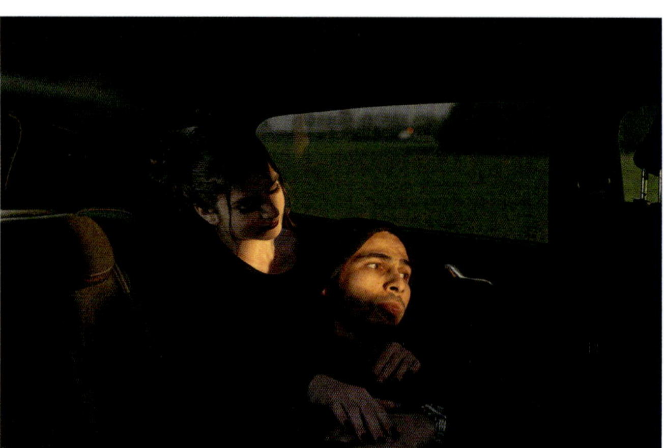

Younes and Sandra embrace in a car close to Villepinte. Seine-Saint-Denis, France, 18 April 2024

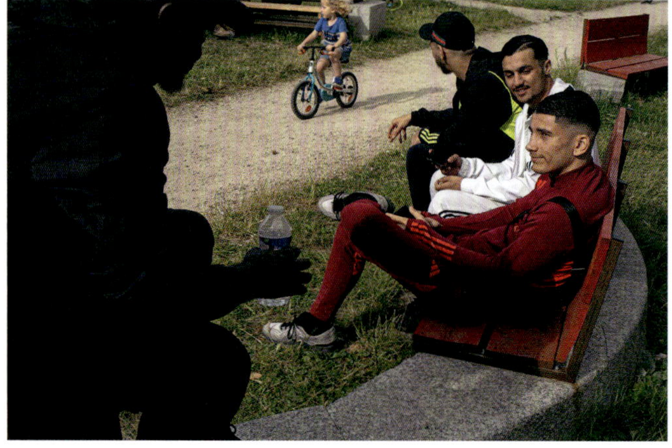

Mehdi, a young boxer of Algerian origin, with friends at the Bosquets housing project. Montfermeil, France, 6 July 2024

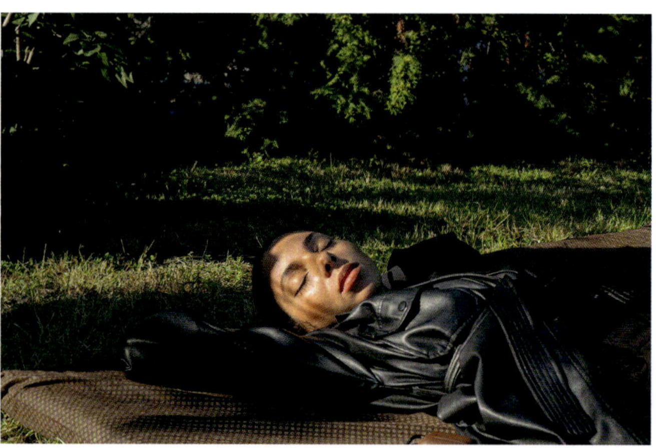

Lobna, of Moroccan and Egyptian descent, rests in a garden during a gathering with friends. She studied advertising and now works for an agency. Aulnay-sous-Bois, France, 28 May 2023

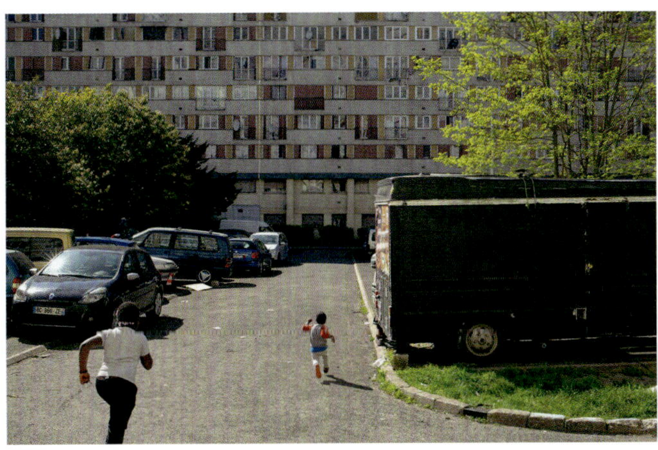

The Chêne Pointu housing project, where riots began in 2005 following the deaths of Zyed Benna and Bouna Traoré, two teenagers of Maghrebian and West African descent who were electrocuted while fleeing police. Clichy-sous-Bois, France, 16 April 2022

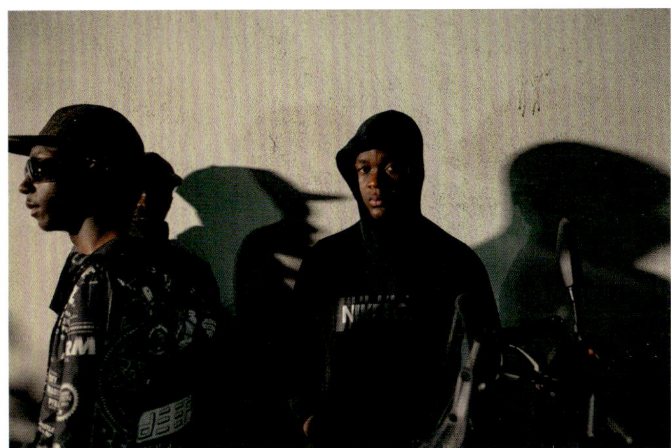

Enzo, a young resident of a working-class neighborhood. Aulnay-sous-Bois, France, 30 June 2025

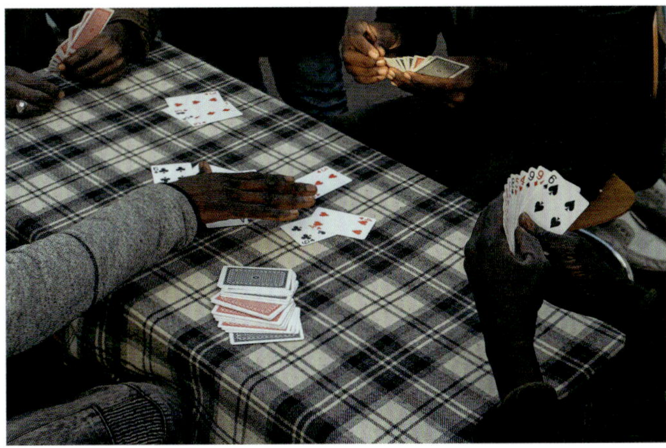

Sudanese migrants spend the afternoon playing cards at the Ecluse camp, an unofficial settlement opposite the Stade de France. Saint-Denis, France, 12 November 2020

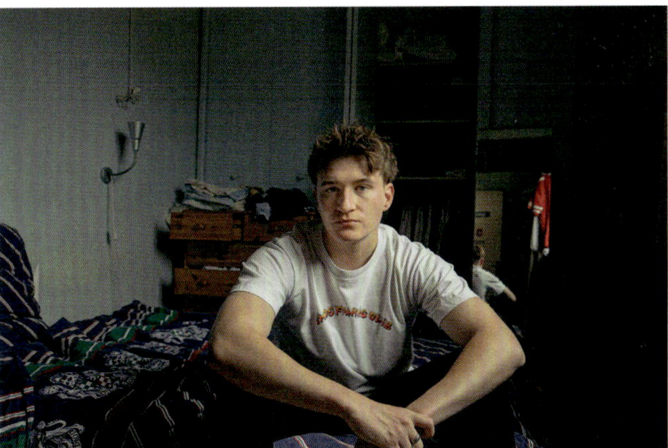

Alexandre Belorgey, of French-Russian descent, lives at home with his parents. He hopes to become a film director. Aulnay-sous-Bois, France, 15 July 2024

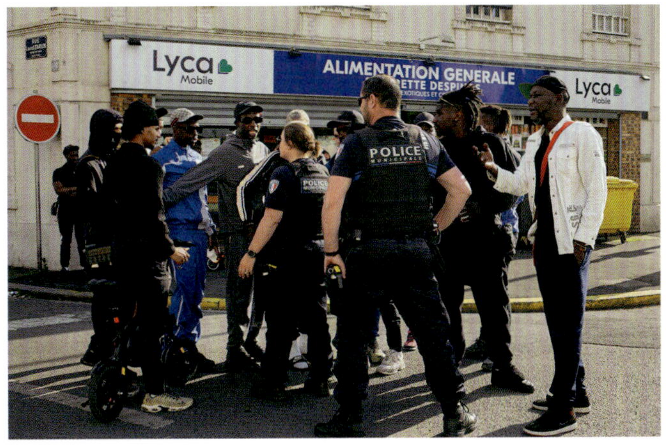

Young people argue with police officers who have ordered them to disperse for "illegal assembly." Creil, France, 10 May 2024

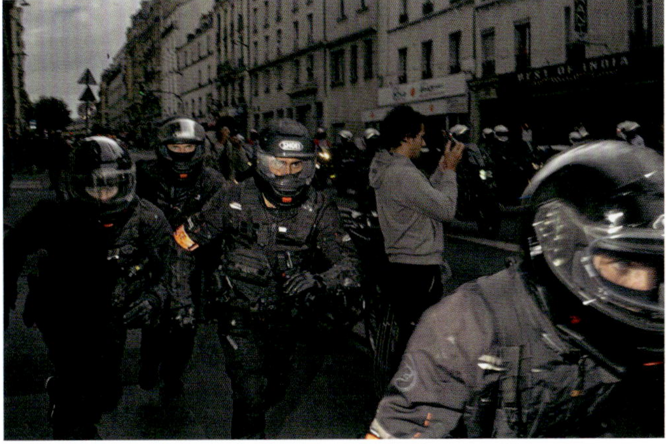

Police charge protesters near Gare du Nord during the "Bloquons tout" demonstrations, a citizen-led movement against the political class and proposed budget cuts. Paris, France, 10 September 2025

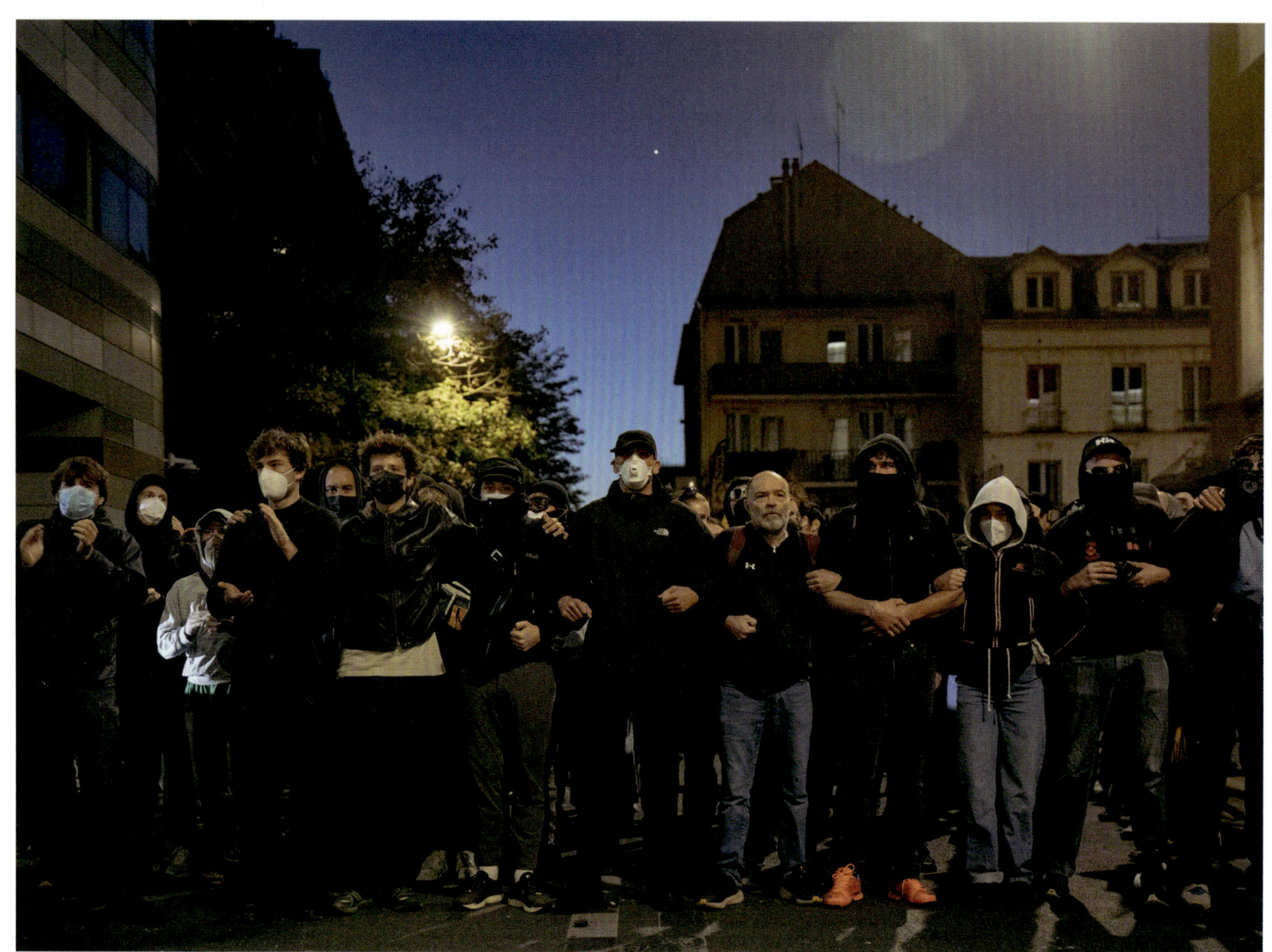

Union members and protesters prepare to face a police charge at dawn during an attempt to block buses from leaving the Lagny bus depot, as part of the "Bloquons tout" movement. Paris, France, 18 September 2025

—

DOES IT MATTER WHO TAKES THE PICTURE?

Authorship can be both
essential and irrelevant.
An outsider's view may
offer distance, while
local connection can
resist a colonial gaze.
Yet often the power
of the image itself can
outweigh the photogra-
pher's identity.

—

Krzysztof Candrowicz,
Europe jury

A professional
photographer should
document reality with
integrity and neutrality,
avoiding judgment or
interference, so the
image can speak for
itself and viewers
remain free to interpret
its meaning.

—

Alfred Yaghobzadeh,
West, Central, and South Asia jury

The photographer's
distinctive voice shapes
a photograph's truth.
Without that human
perspective behind the
camera, we lose the
very thing that gives an
image its integrity.

—

Kira Pollack,
Global jury chair

Photojournalists don't
just record events; they
bring perspective.
The choices they make
shape how we see the
world, and carry real r
esponsibility, often
alongside personal risk.

—

Gael Almeida,
South America jury

Who takes the
photograph matters,
especially in relation
to the subject. A local
perspective can be vital
for accurate reporting,
while an outsider
may notice what feels
ordinary to others and
expand the overall view.

—

Michael Robinson Chávez,
North and Central America jury

Lived experience,
cultural knowledge,
and trust within a
community shape how
stories are framed,
ensuring accurate,
sensitive, and respectful
representation.

—

Tsvangirayi Mukwazhi,
Africa jury

Authorship may
not always matter.
Photographs made
under real risk can
teach us something
essential, and some-
times safety demands
anonymity. But knowing
a photographer's
identity can sometimes
deepen understanding.

—

Yasuyoshi Chiba,
Asia-Pacific and Oceania jury

NORTH AND CENTRAL AMERICA

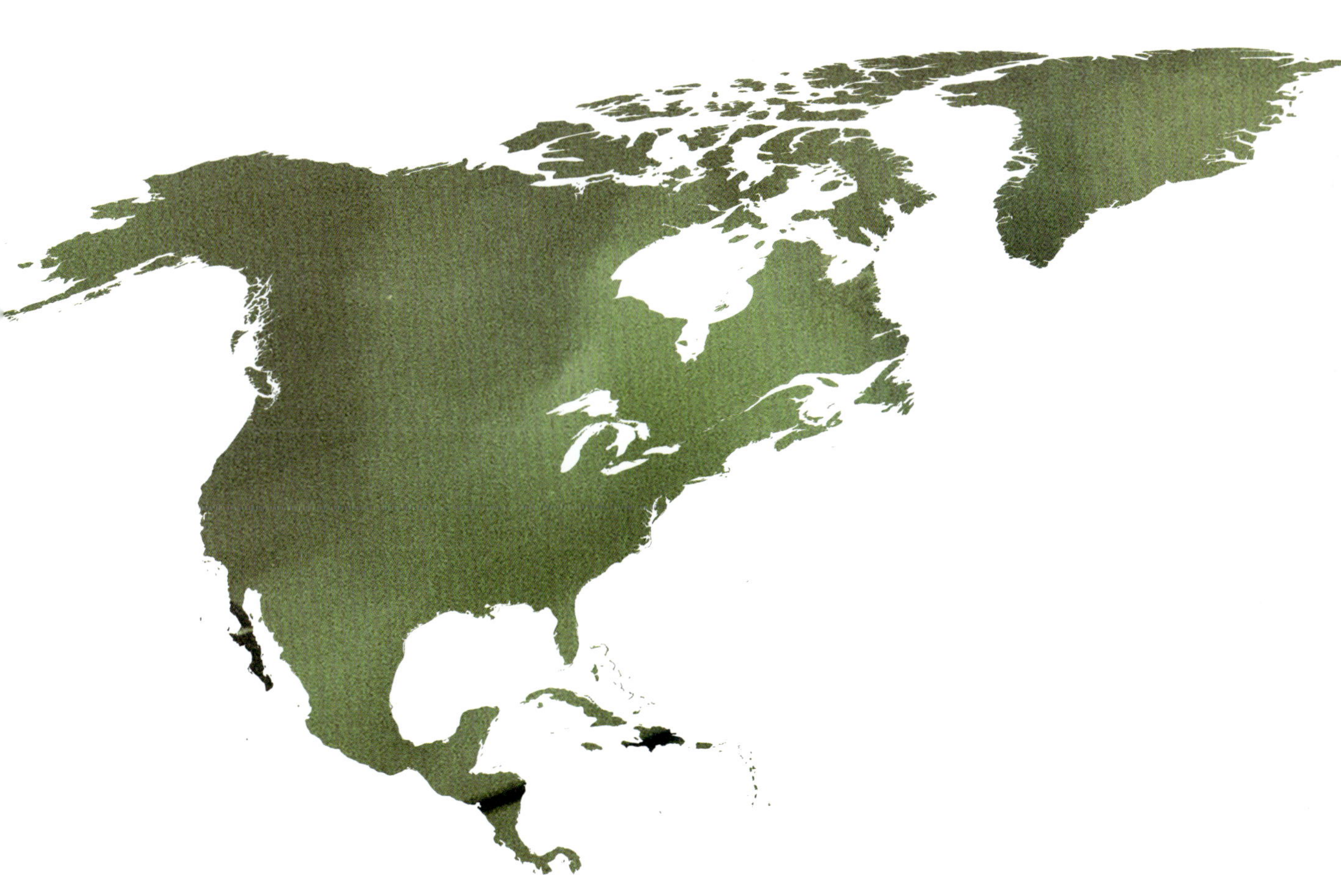

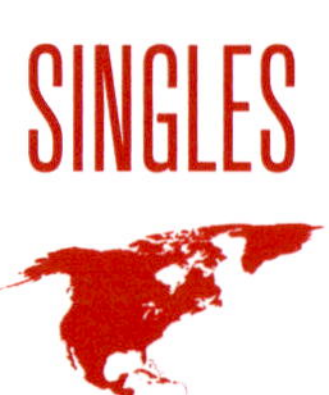

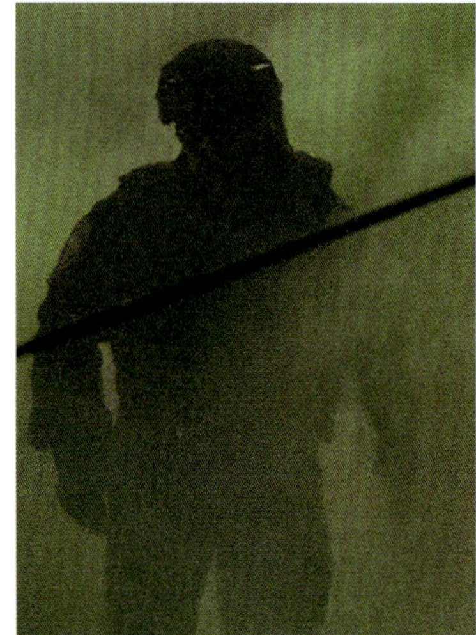

PORTLAND PROTESTS ICE

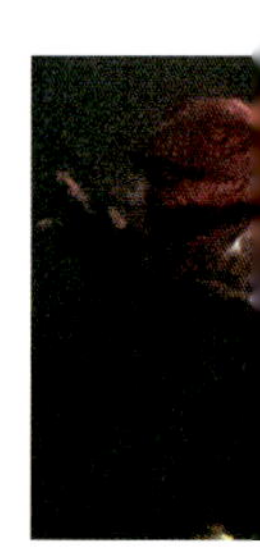

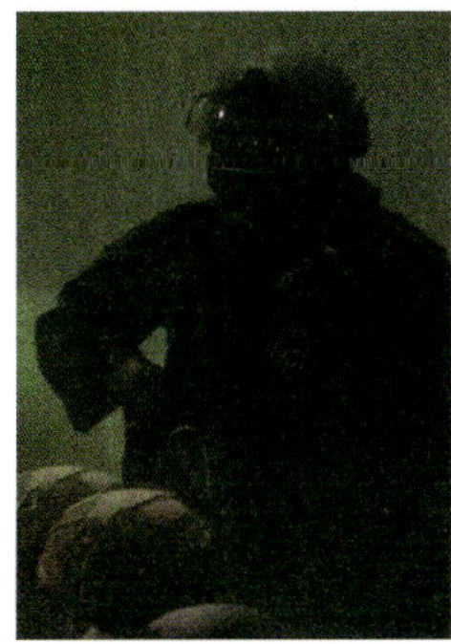

In 2025, the Trump administration shifted its immigration enforcement from the border to the US interior, aiming for 3,000 arrests per day and abandoning protections for schools, hospitals, courthouses, and places of worship. In response, Portland, a "sanctuary city" that prohibits its own state and local law forces to cooperate with federal immigration enforcement, became a flashpoint for resistance. During the nationwide "No Kings" demonstrations in June, localized protests escalated into nightly clashes outside the city's Immigration and Customs Enforcement (ICE) facility.

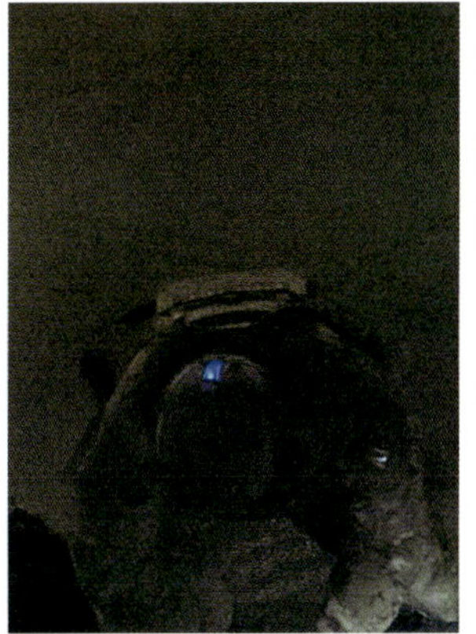

JAN SONNENMAIR

Officers from the Department of Homeland Security and other federal agencies clash with demonstrators outside an ICE processing center. The intense summer protests centered on opposing the administration's escalating mass-deportation agenda. Portland, Oregon, United States, 24 June 2025 / Jan Sonnenmair

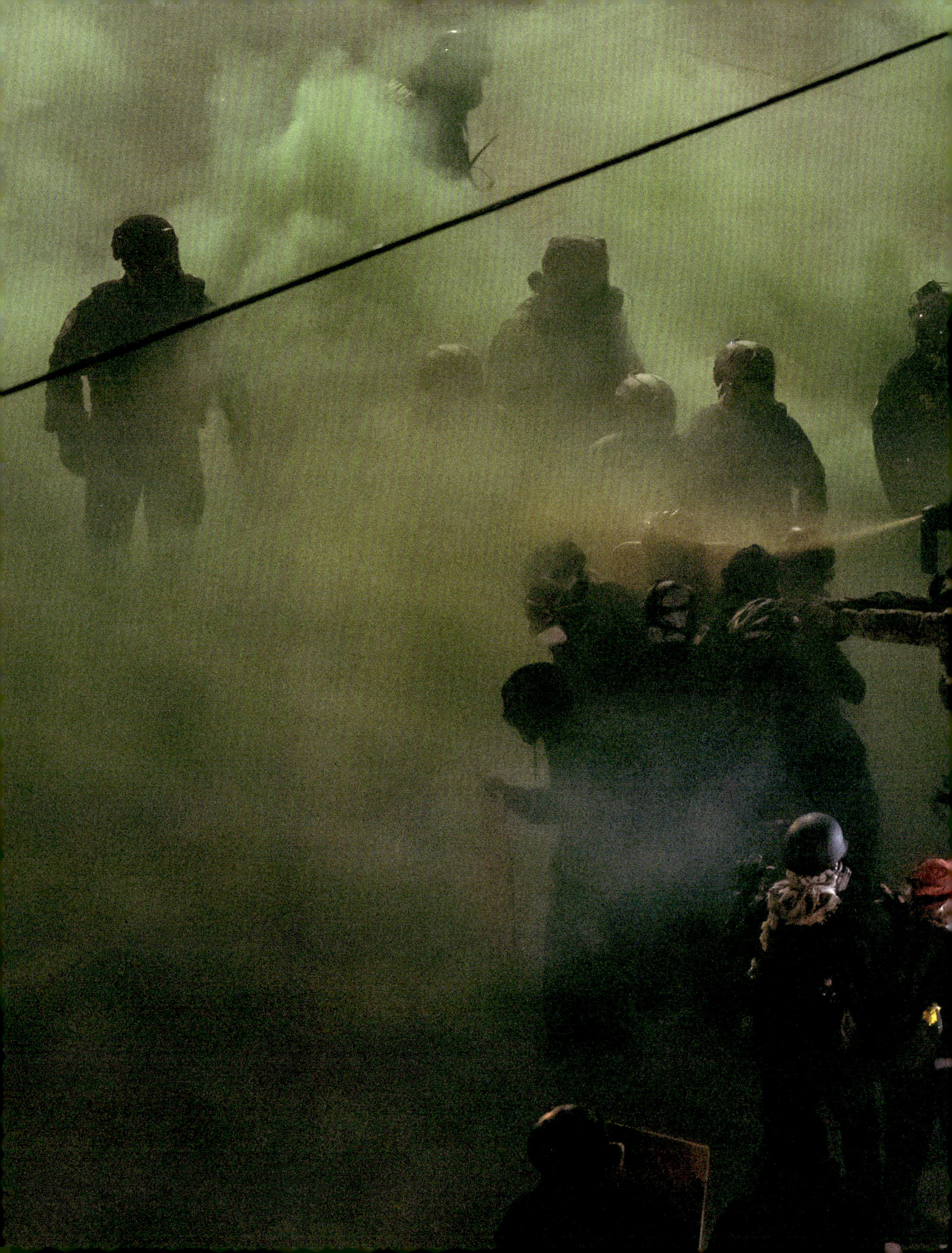

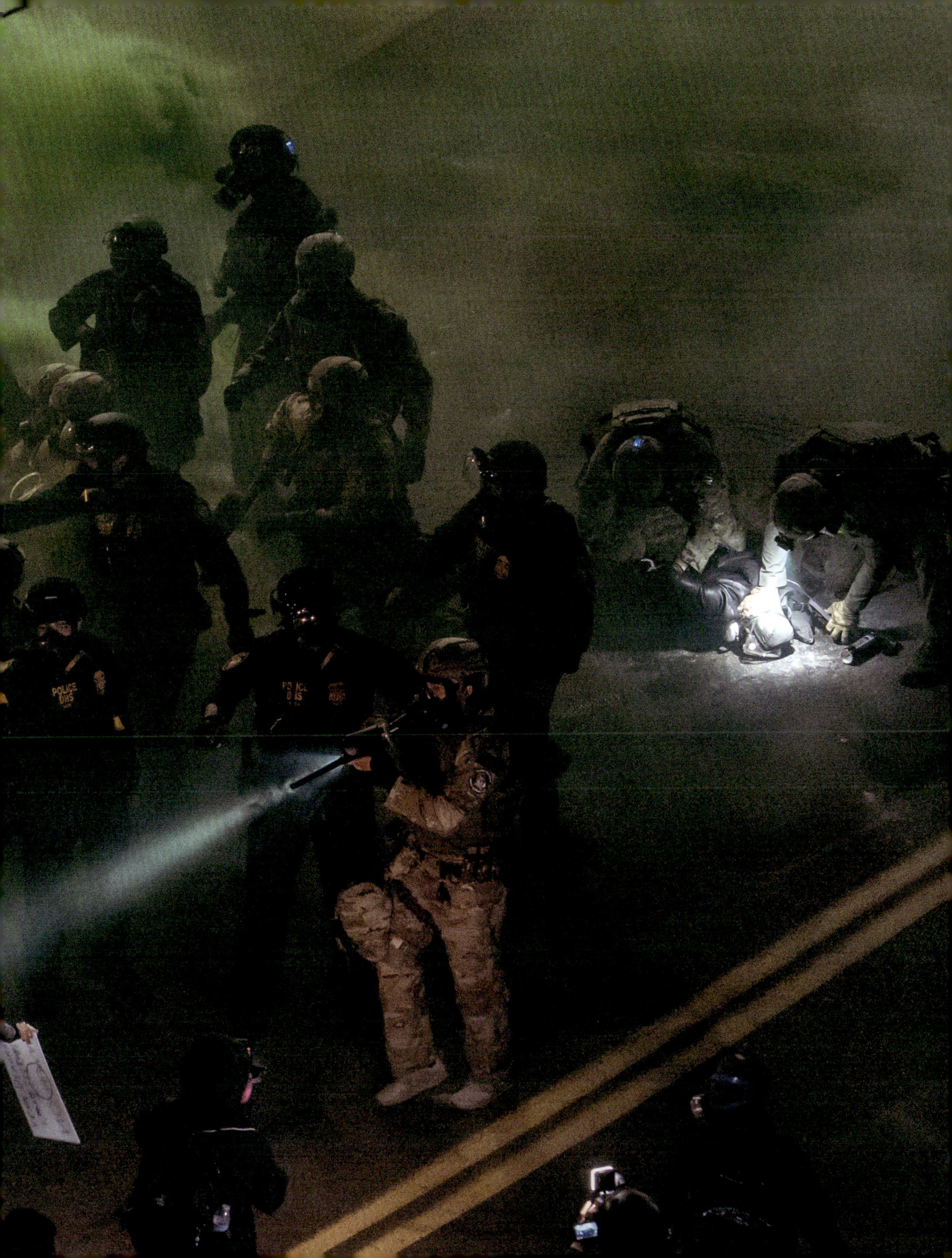

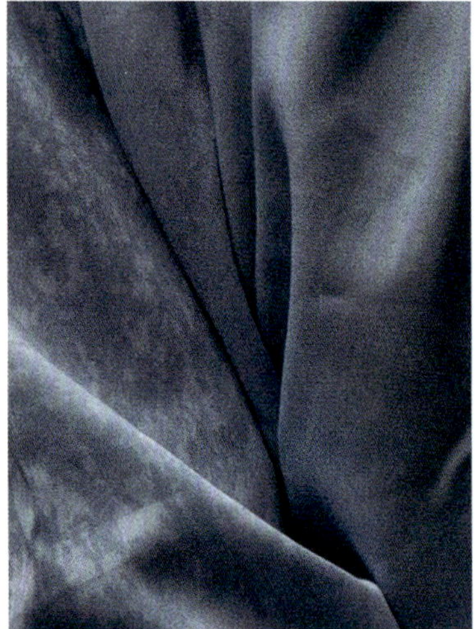

Facing intense political pressure to limit pro-Palestine demonstrations, many US universities became focal points in a national conflict over free speech and institutional independence. At Columbia University, the Trump administration suspended $400 million in federal funding to force a crackdown on campus protests, causing severe administrative upheaval. The students were caught in this institutional crossfire, but many members of the graduating class of 2025 as well as alumni chose to exercise their first amendment rights in protests and demonstrations.

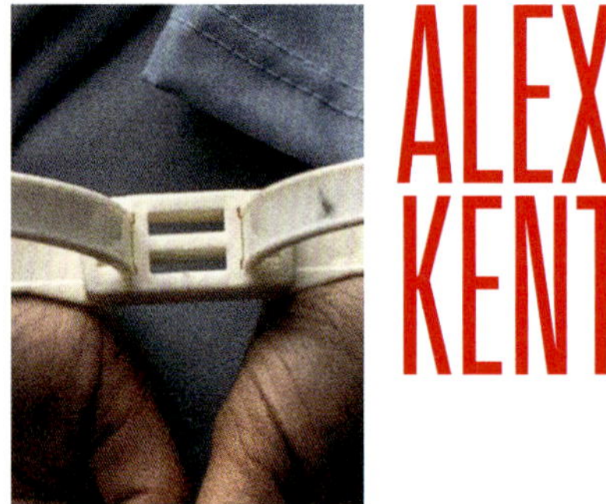

ALEX KENT

COLUMBIA UNIVERSITY PRO PALESTINE PROTESTS

Barnard College alumna Jesse Pearce is arrested outside Columbia University's commencement ceremony. Along with current students, alumni protested the institution's ongoing financial ties to Israel. New York City, New York, United States, 21 May 2025 / Alex Kent, for *The New York Times*

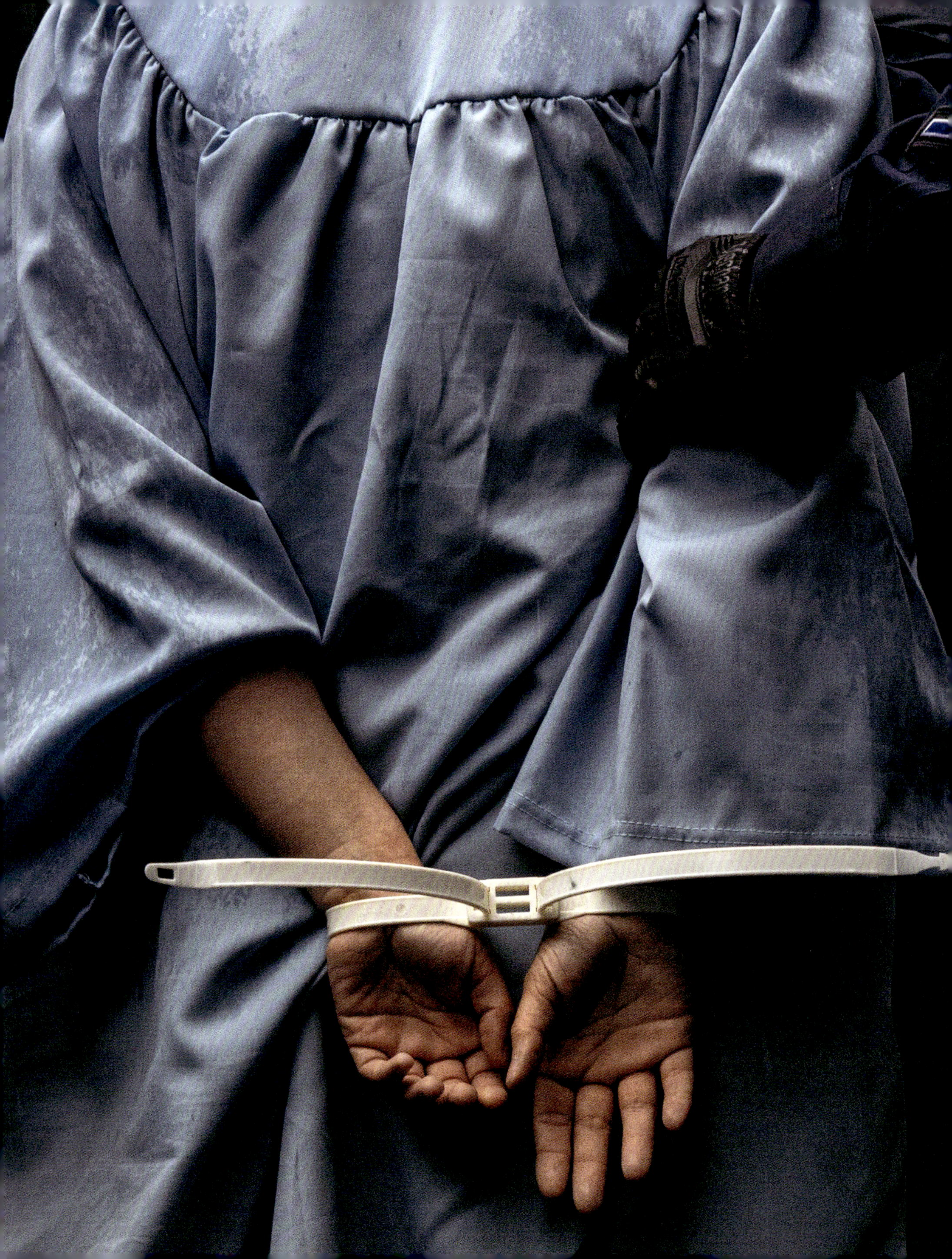

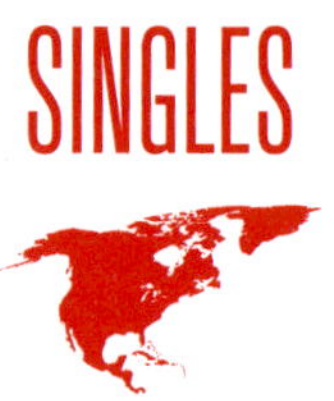

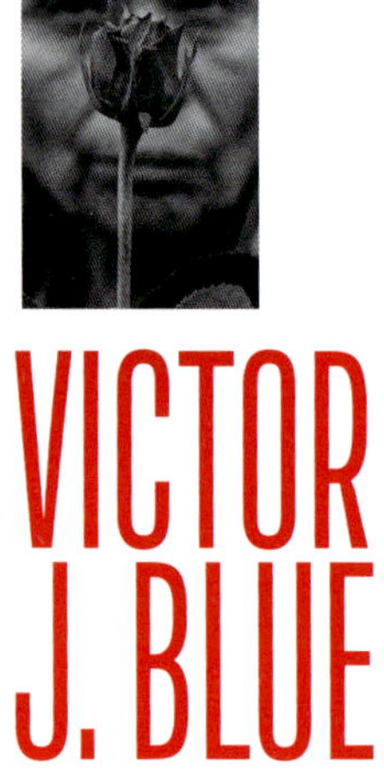

VICTOR
J. BLUE

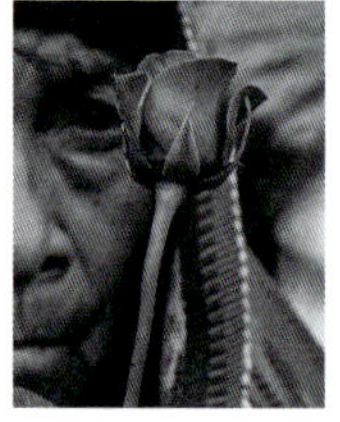

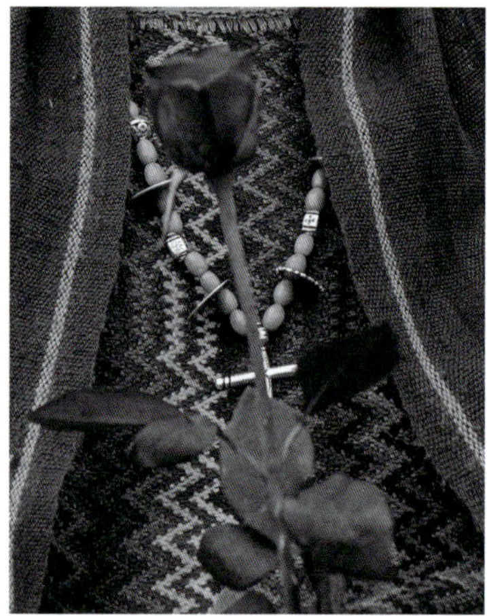

For four decades, a group of Indigenous Maya Achi women in Rabinal lived in the same communities as the men who had raped them, sometimes as neighbors. Guatemala's civil war led to the genocide of thousands of Maya Achi people by the military and local state-backed paramilitary forces, who used sexual violence as a systematic weapon to subjugate Indigenous communities. In 2011, 36 women broke their silence, launching and winning a 14-year legal battle against their abusers. Their collective resilience is transforming a legacy of wartime impunity into a historic victory for justice.

THE TRIALS OF THE ACHI WOMEN

Doña Paulina Ixpatá Alvarado stands with other Achi women outside a Guatemala City court. That afternoon, three ex-civil defense patrollers were found guilty of rape and crimes against humanity and sentenced to 40 years in prison each.
Guatemala City, Guatemala, 30 May 2025 / Victor J. Blue, for *The New York Times Magazine*

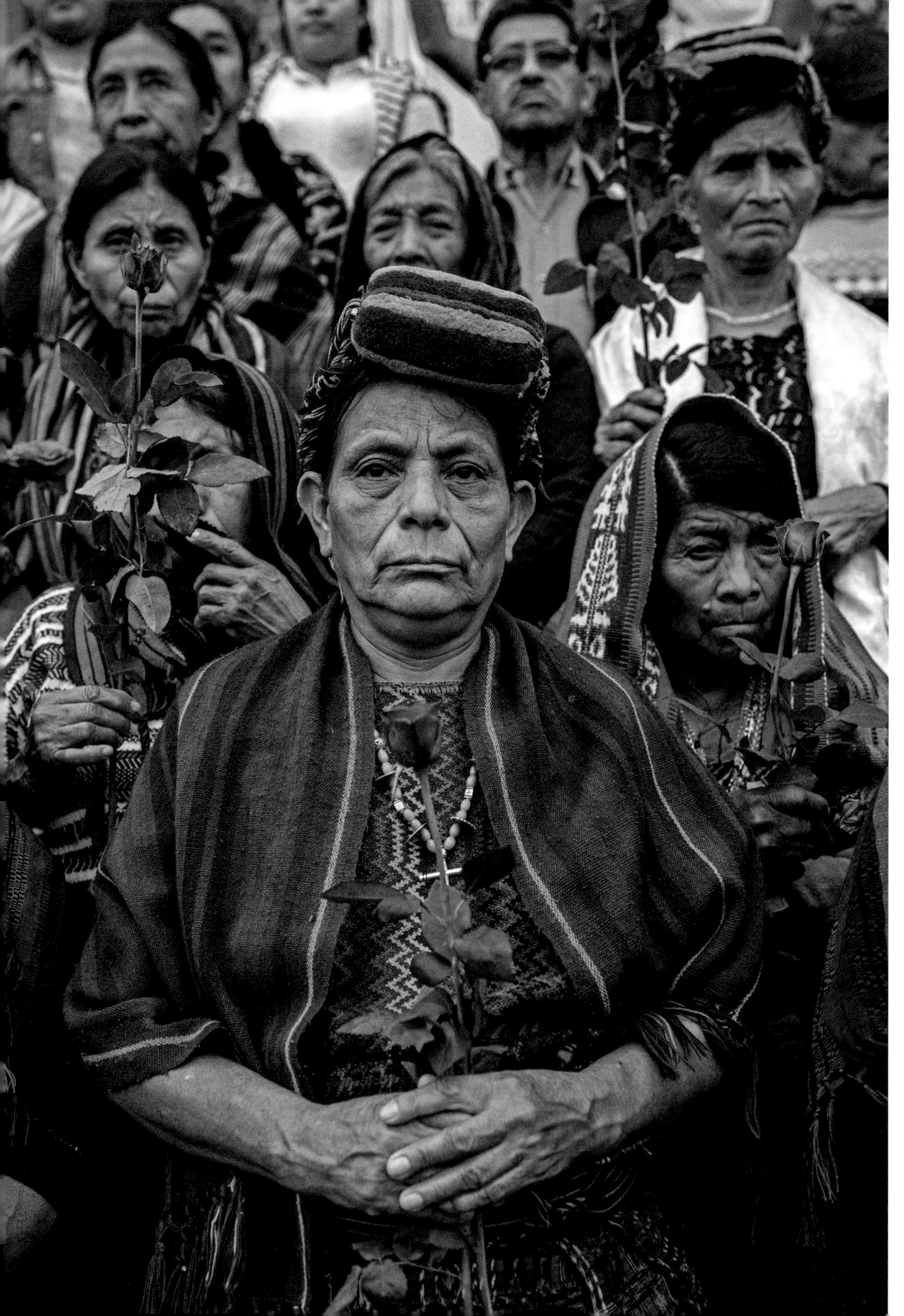

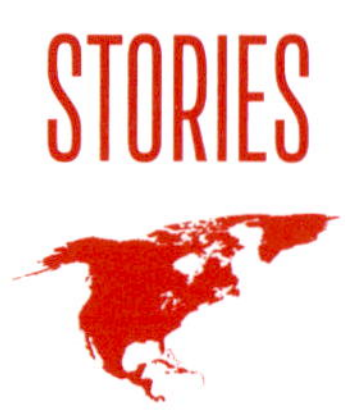

JAHI
CHIKWENDIU

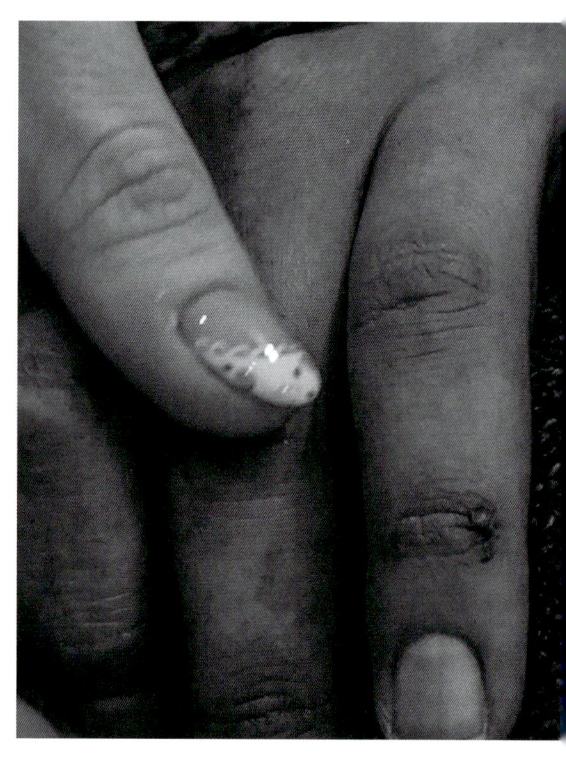

TANNER'S SONG

Diagnosed with Stage 4 colon cancer at age 25, Tanner Martin and his wife, Shay, raced to build a family despite a terminal prognosis. This intimate story documents the final months of Tanner's life, culminating in the birth of his daughter, AmyLou, just 41 days before his death at age 30. His experience puts a human face on a staggering global trend: people born in 1990 now face a 200 to 300% increased risk of some early-onset cancers compared to previous generations.

Tanner and Shay hold hands after a family dinner. While cancer primarily affects those over 65, incidence rates for US-citizens under 50 have risen steadily since the late 1990s. South Jordan, Utah, United States, 9 February 2025 / Jahi Chikwendiu, *The Washington Post*

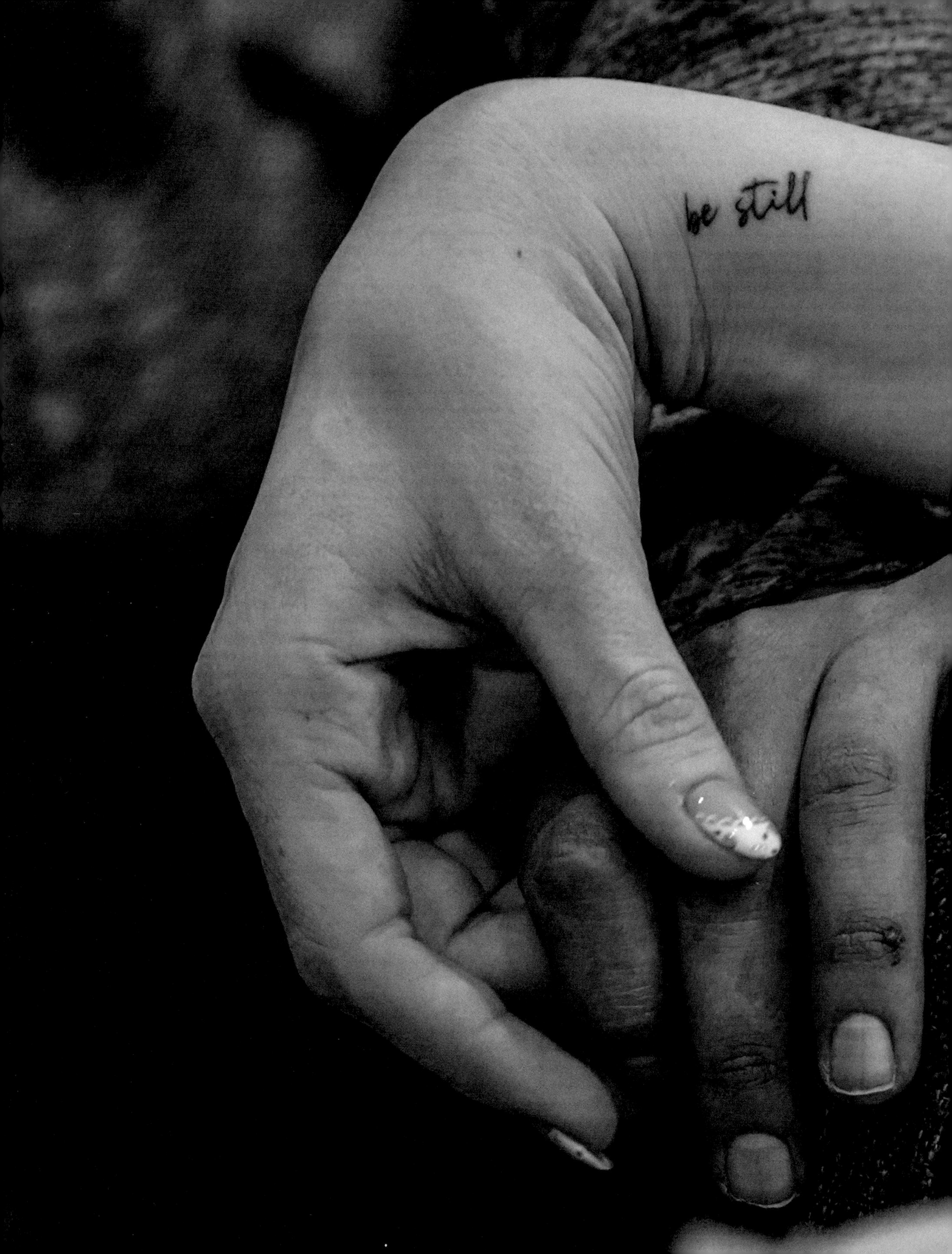
be still

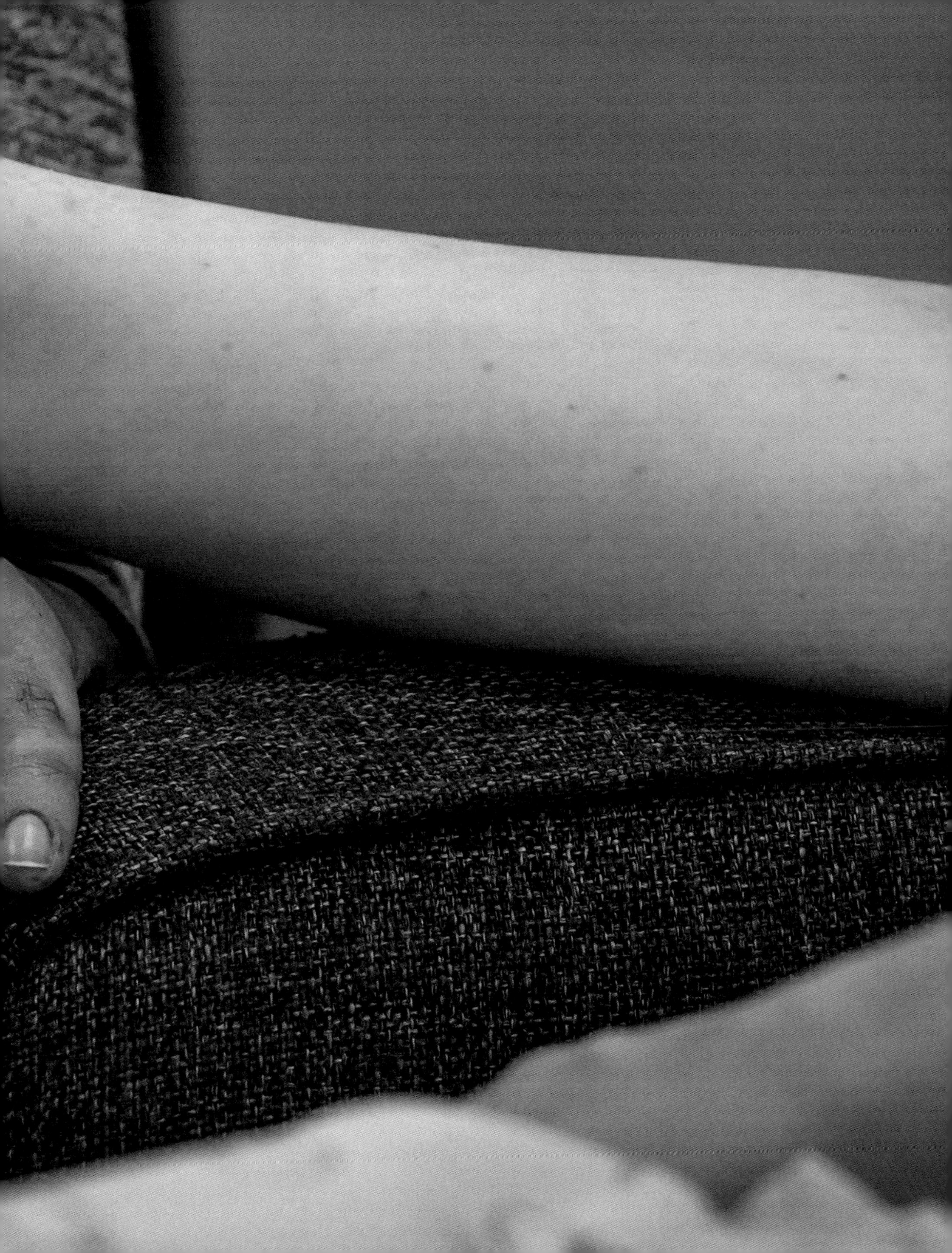

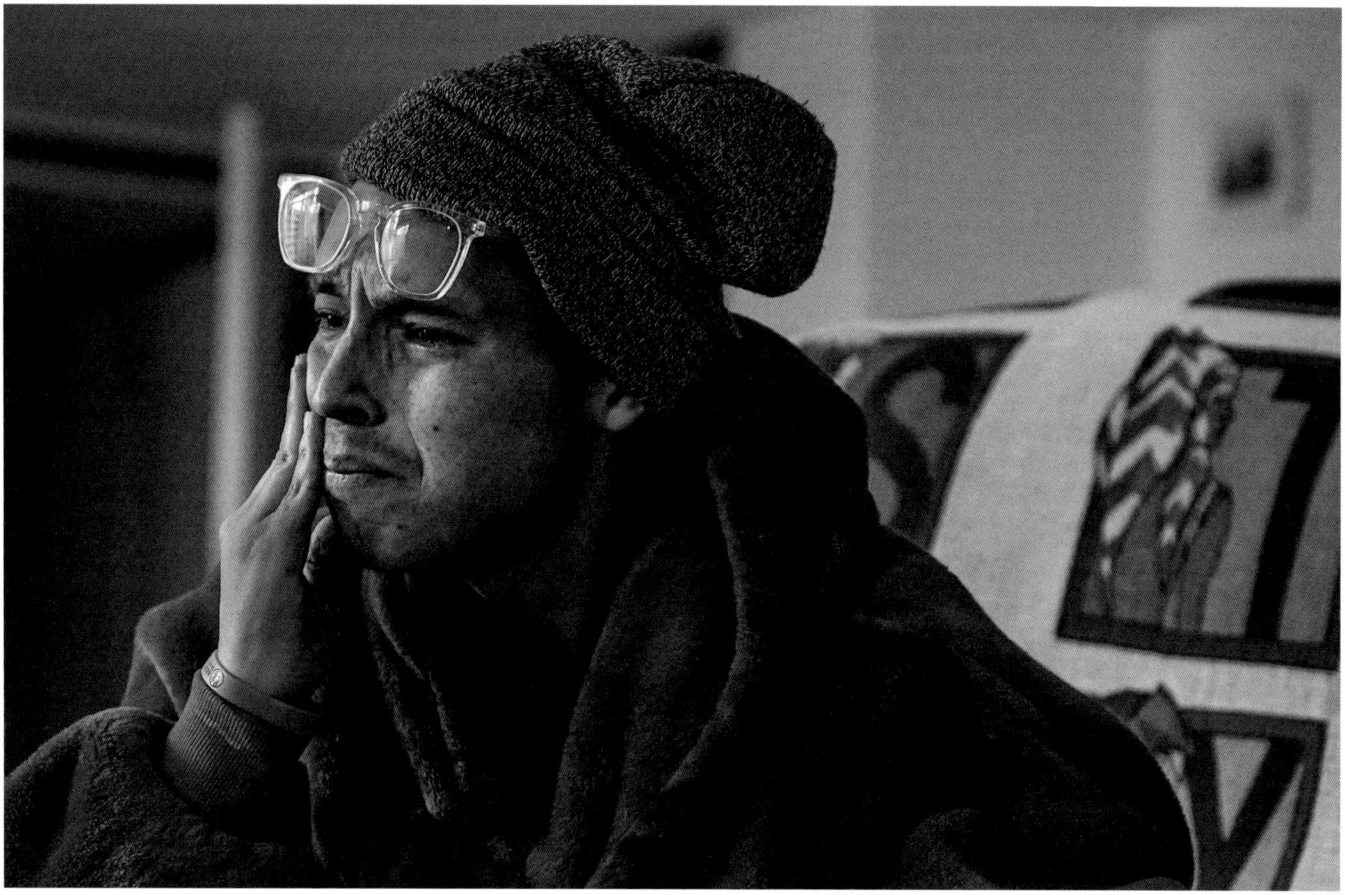

Tanner contemplates his family's future without him. For young adults, early-onset cancer disrupts a period of life traditionally defined by good health and financial productivity. American Fork, Utah, United States, 8 February 2025

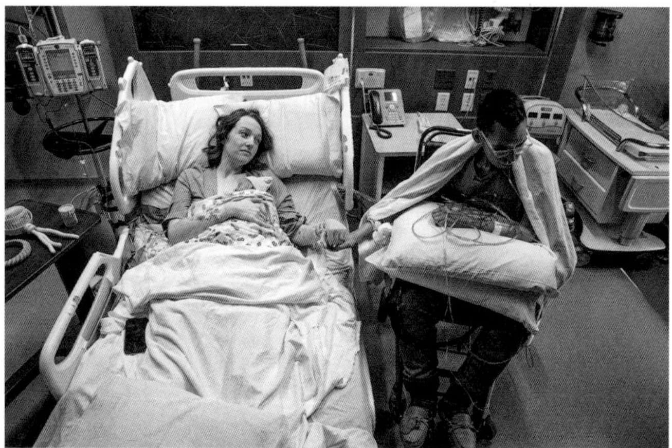

Shay holds her newborn daughter, AmyLou. On the day of her birth, Tanner managed to stay at the hospital for over four hours – remarkable considering he could not stay awake for more than 30 minutes at a time in recent weeks. American Fork, Utah, United States, 15 May 2025

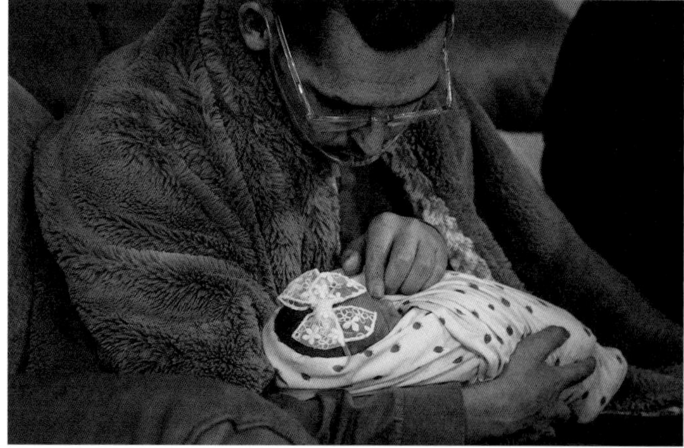

Tanner cradles AmyLou two days after her birth. Too weak to stand, Tanner held his daughter on his lap while Shay filmed a father-daughter dance for their daughter's future wedding. American Fork, Utah, United States, 17 May 2025

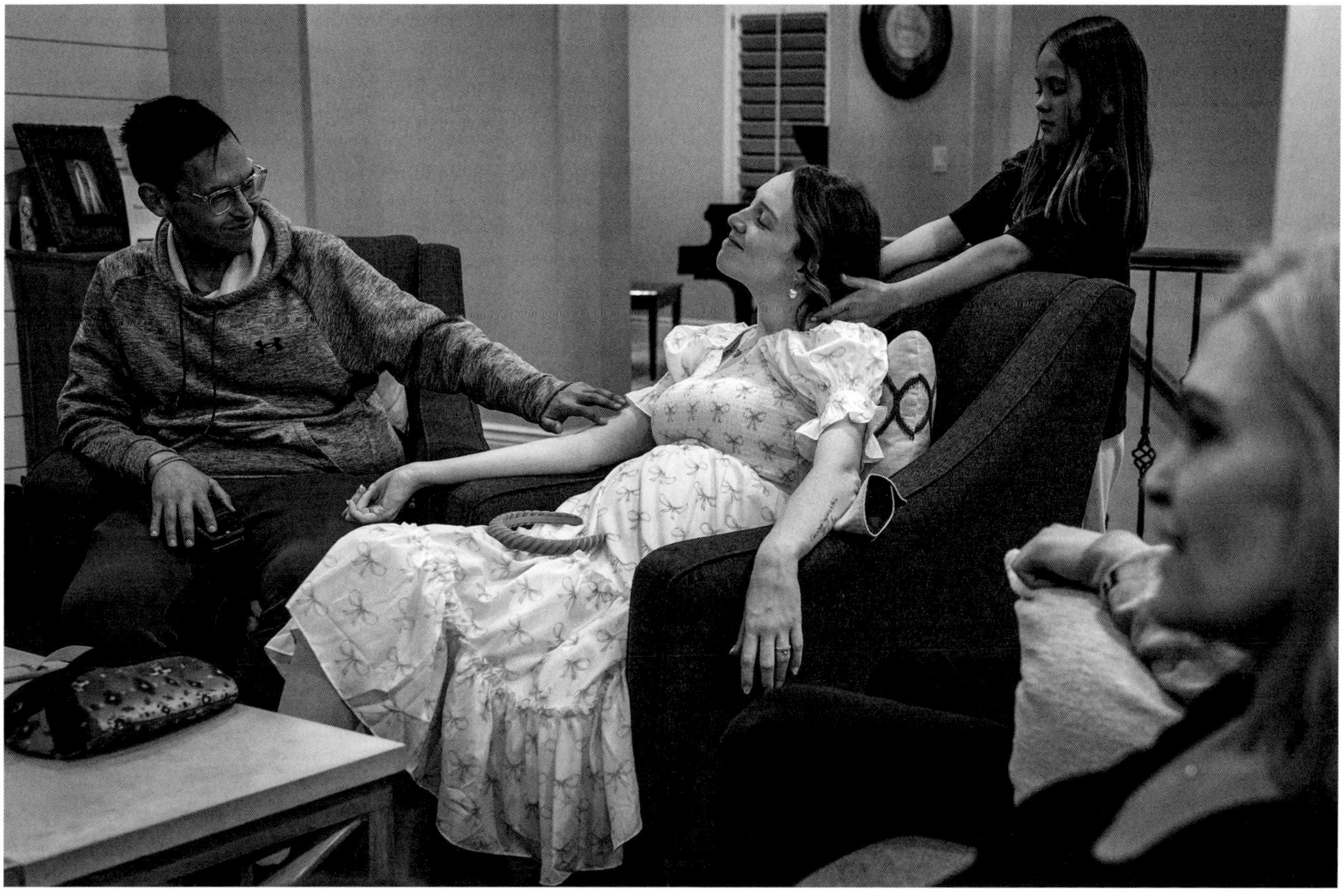

Tanner strokes Shay's arm as her cousin plays with her hair. Between 2010 and 2019, approximately 200,000 people aged 15 to 49 were diagnosed with cancer annually in the US. South Jordan, Utah, United States, 9 February 2025

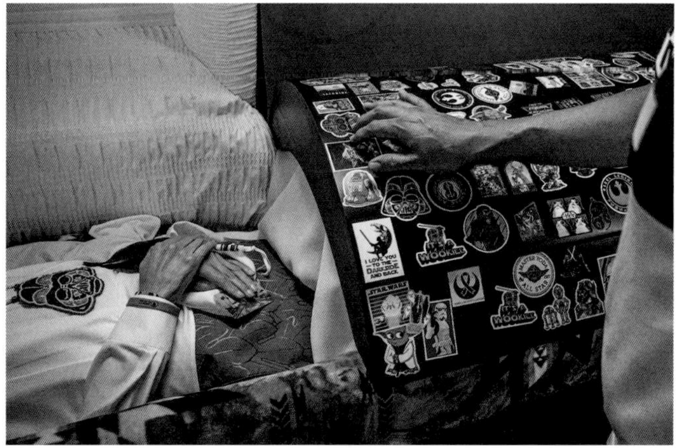

Star Wars stickers, placed by family and friends, cover Tanner's casket during his viewing. Tanner passed away at the age of 30. American Fork, Utah, United States, 3 July 2025

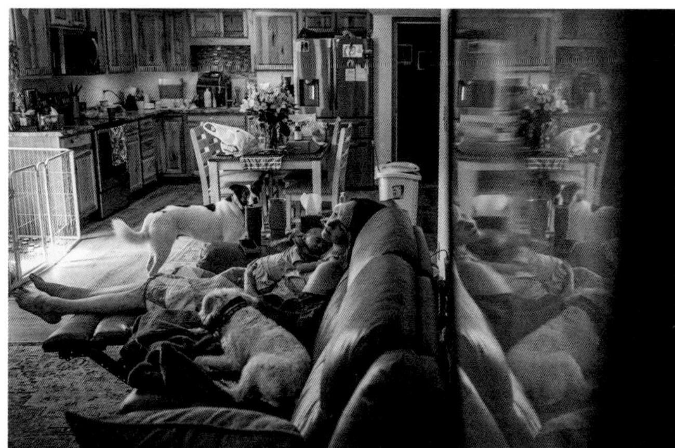

Shay relaxes with AmyLou in the spot where Tanner used to sit. Before his death, the couple documented their experience on social media, reaching millions of viewers worldwide. American Fork, Utah, United States, 3 July 2025

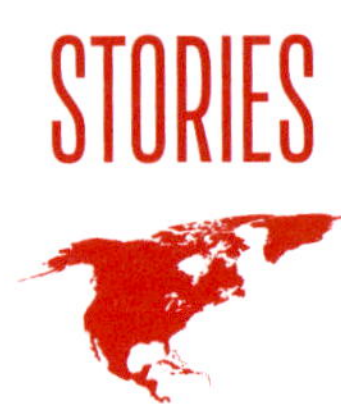

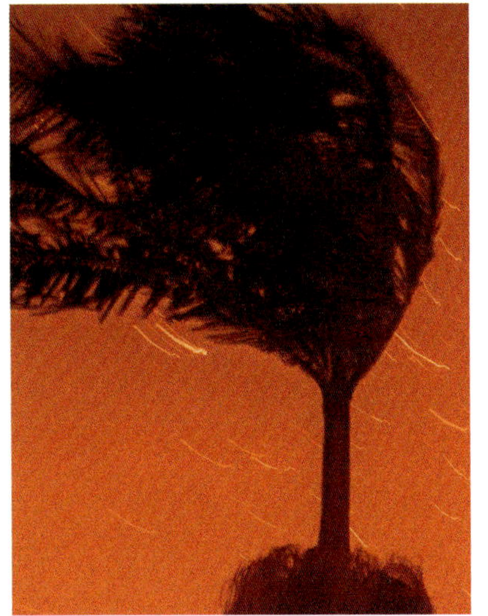

ETHAN
SWOPE

LOS
ANGELES
ON FIRE

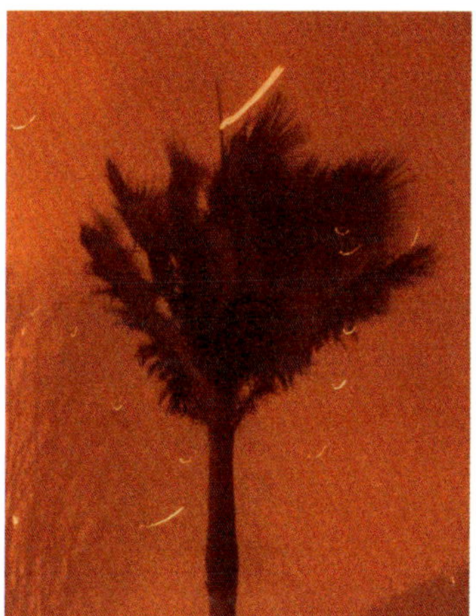

In January 2025, severe drought and 100-mph (roughly 160-kph) Santa Ana winds fueled 14 devastating wildfires across Los Angeles, destroying over 18,000 buildings and displacing 200,000 residents. While officials reported 31 direct fatalities, public health studies estimate 440 excess deaths linked to toxic smoke and disrupted medical care. In the disaster's aftermath, a stark wealth divide has defined recovery efforts, with lower-income residents facing displacement while wealthier communities leverage private resources to rebuild.

The Palisades Fire ravages a neighborhood amid high winds. The Los Angeles blazes inflicted between $28 and $53.8 billion in property damage, disrupting thousands of local businesses. Los Angeles, California, United States, 7 January 2025 / Ethan Swope, for Associated Press

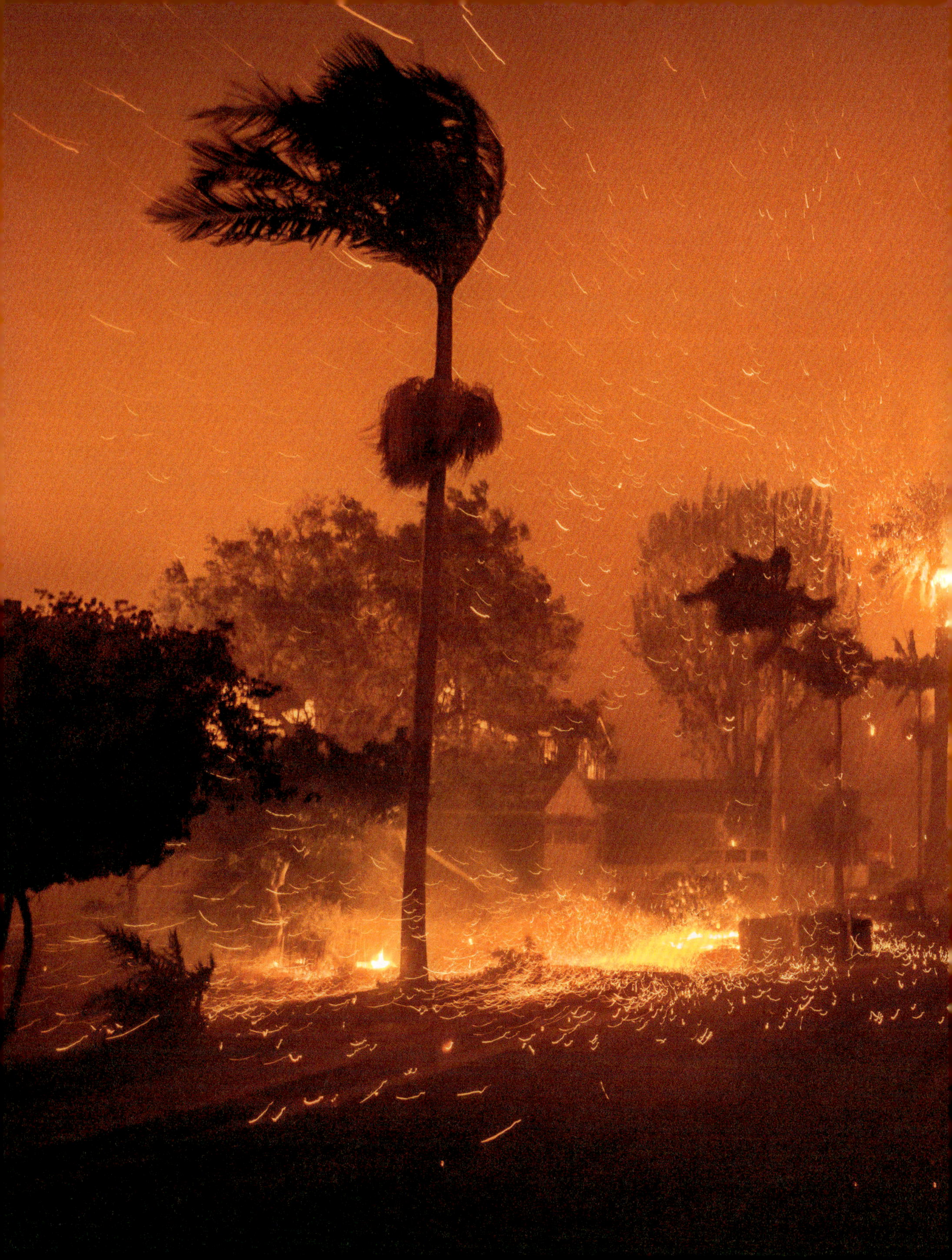

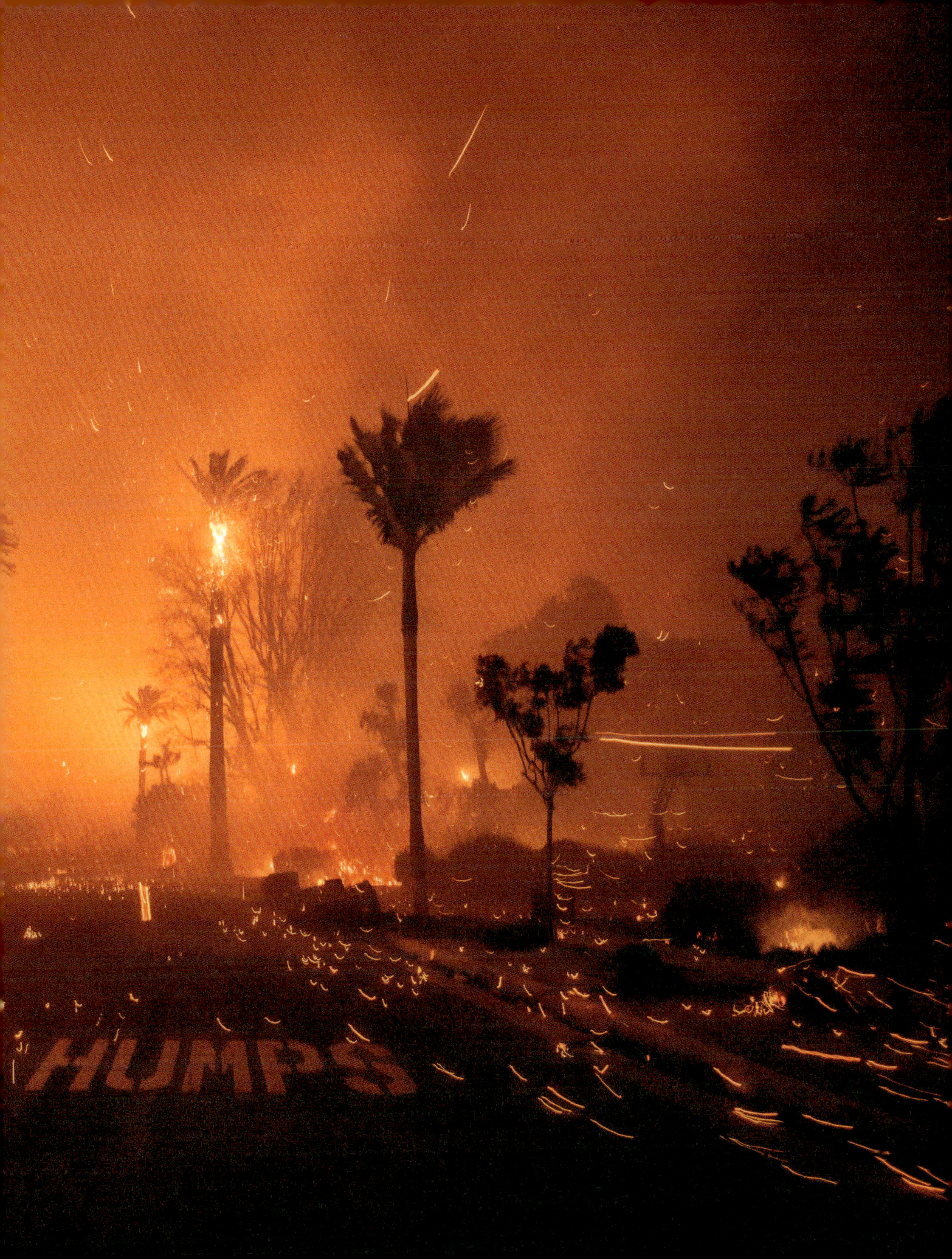
HUMPS

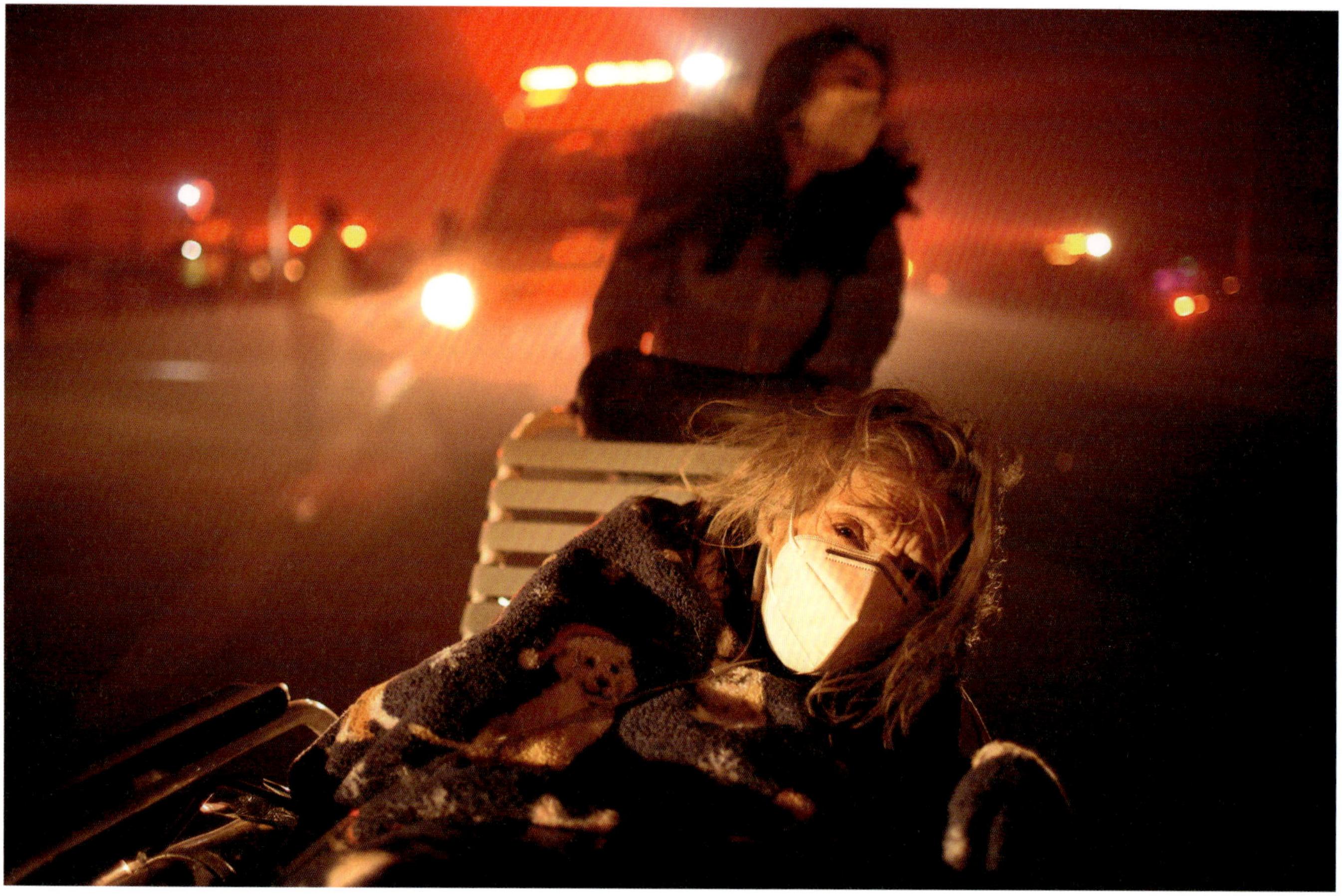

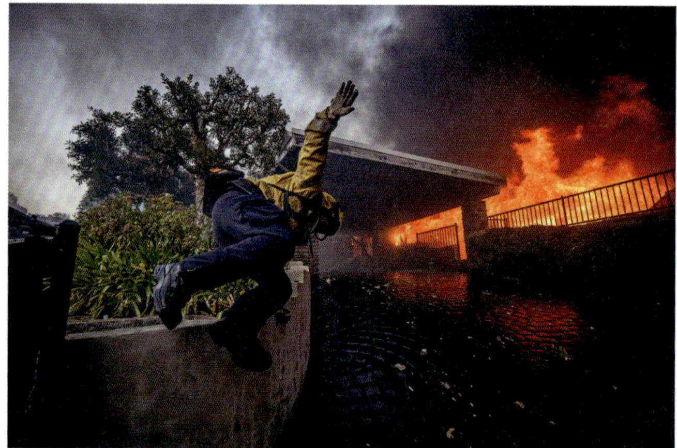

A senior center resident evacuates as the Eaton Fire approaches. Wildfires release massive amounts of toxic particles and carbon monoxide, causing severe respiratory issues that linger for weeks. Altadena, California, United States, 7 January 2025

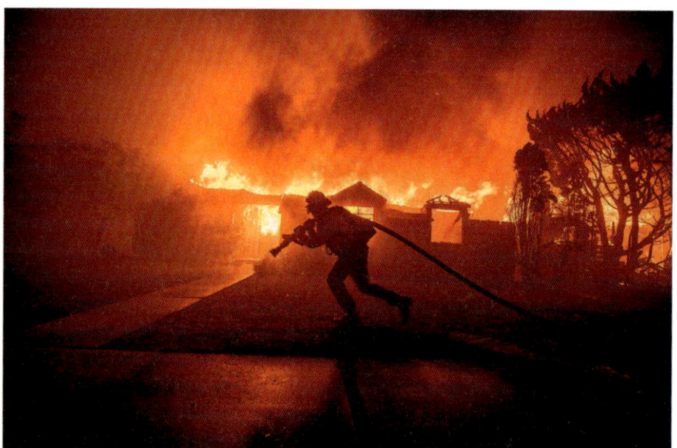

A firefighter jumps over a fence while battling the Palisades Fire. More than 7,500 emergency personnel, including incarcerated firefighters and the National Guard, were deployed to combat the rapidly spreading blazes. Los Angeles, California, United States, 7 January 2025

A firefighter battles the Palisades Fire as a structure burns. Population growth near dry, grassy landscapes in Los Angeles makes the city more vulnerable to man-made sparks that ignite fires. Los Angeles, California, United States, 7 January 2025

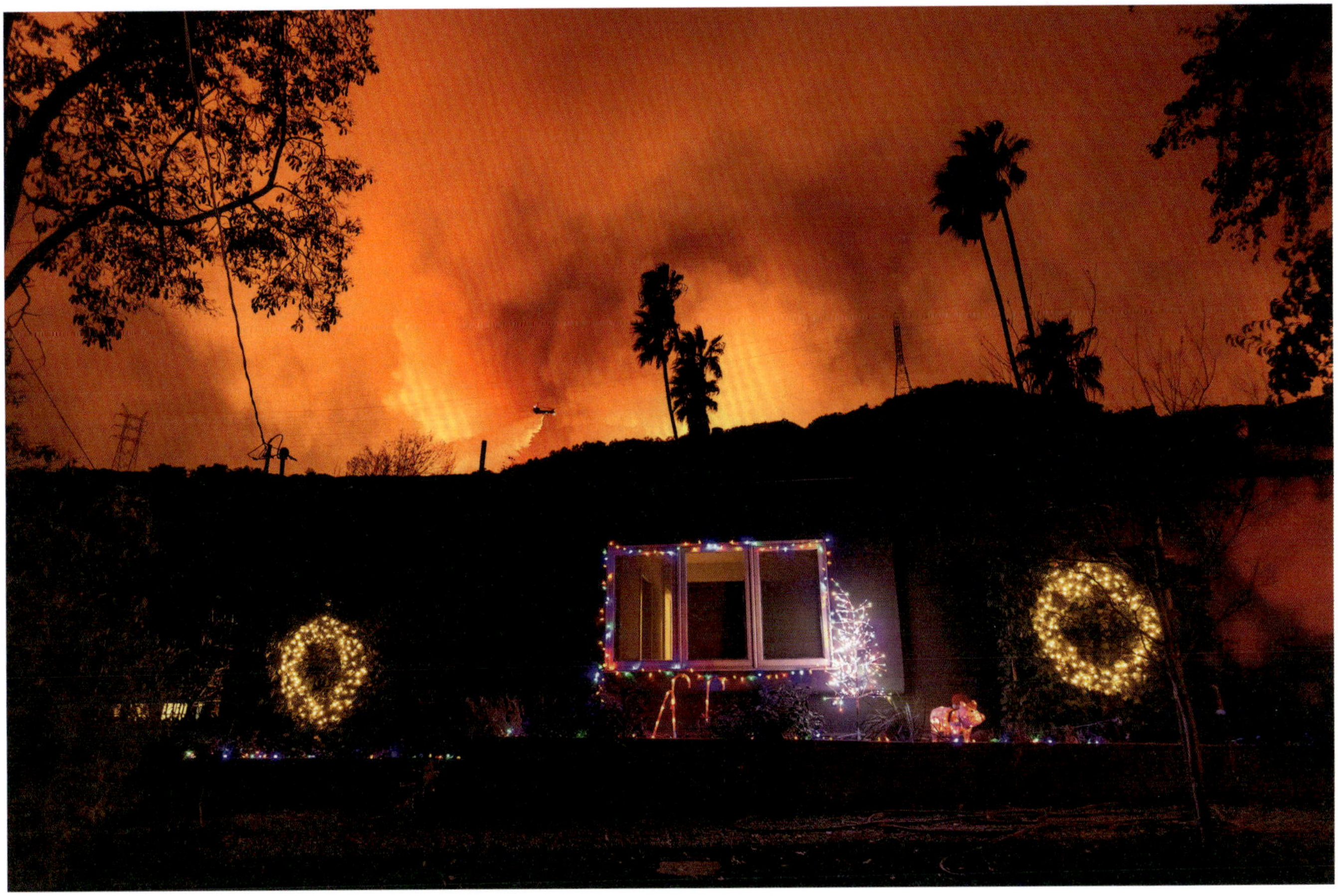

A helicopter drops water behind a Mandeville Canyon home still decorated with Christmas lights. Firefighting efforts were severely hindered by the extreme Santa Ana winds driving the blazes. Los Angeles, California, United States, 10 January 2025

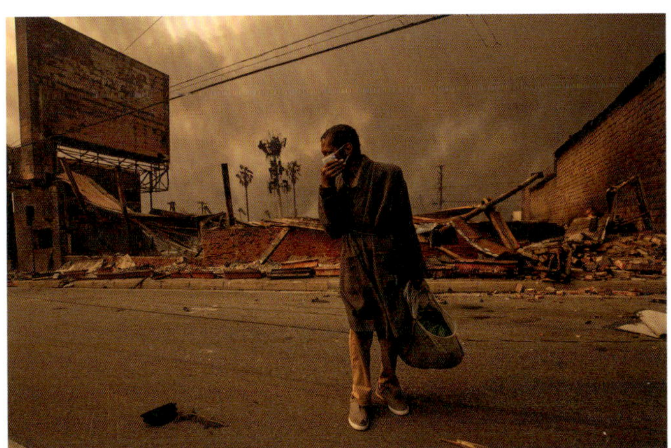

A man walks past a business ruined by fire. The Eaton Fire heavily impacted working-class neighborhoods, where many underinsured homeowners now face gentrification and displacement. Altadena, California, United States, 8 January 2025

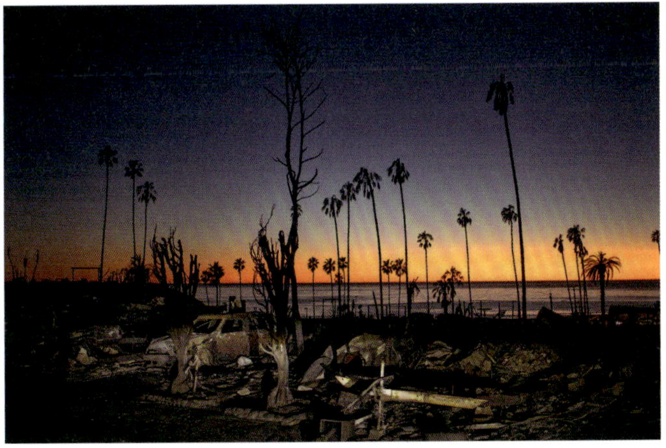

The devastation of the Palisades Fire is visible at sunset. Experts emphasize that the extended, drier fire seasons in Southern California are exacerbated by human-caused global warming trends. Los Angeles, California, United States, 14 January 2025

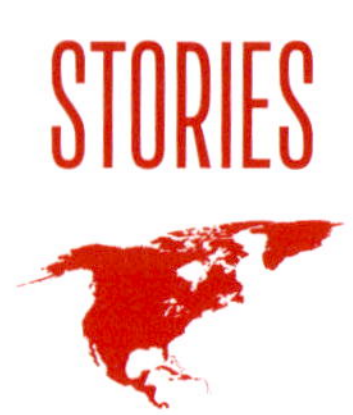

ICE ARRESTS AT NEW YORK COURT

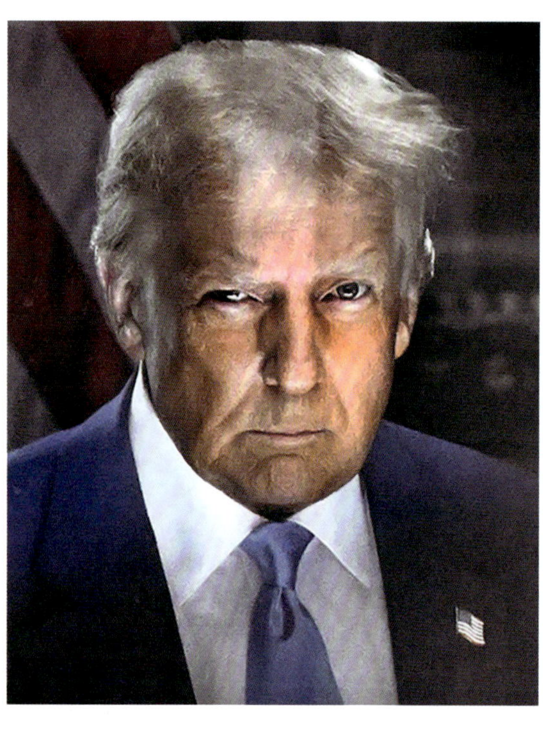

In 2025, shifts in US immigration policy transformed courthouses into focal points for mass deportation efforts by US Immigration and Customs Enforcement (ICE). Masked ICE agents detained undocumented migrants immediately following their hearings, often leading to deeply traumatic family separations. These aggressive tactics, coupled with severely overcrowded and unsanitary conditions at the 10th-floor holding facility in the Jacob Javits Federal Building in New York, prompted fierce public protests, class-action lawsuits, and the arrest of local elected officials demanding accountability.

CAROL GUZY

Migrants line up in the lobby of the Jacob Javits Federal Building. In 2025, ICE pushed for a target of 3,000 daily arrests, heavily targeting interior locations away from the border, like schools, hospitals, and immigration courts. 5 August 2025
All photos taken in New York City, New York, United States / Carol Guzy, ZUMA Press, iWitness, for *Miami Herald*

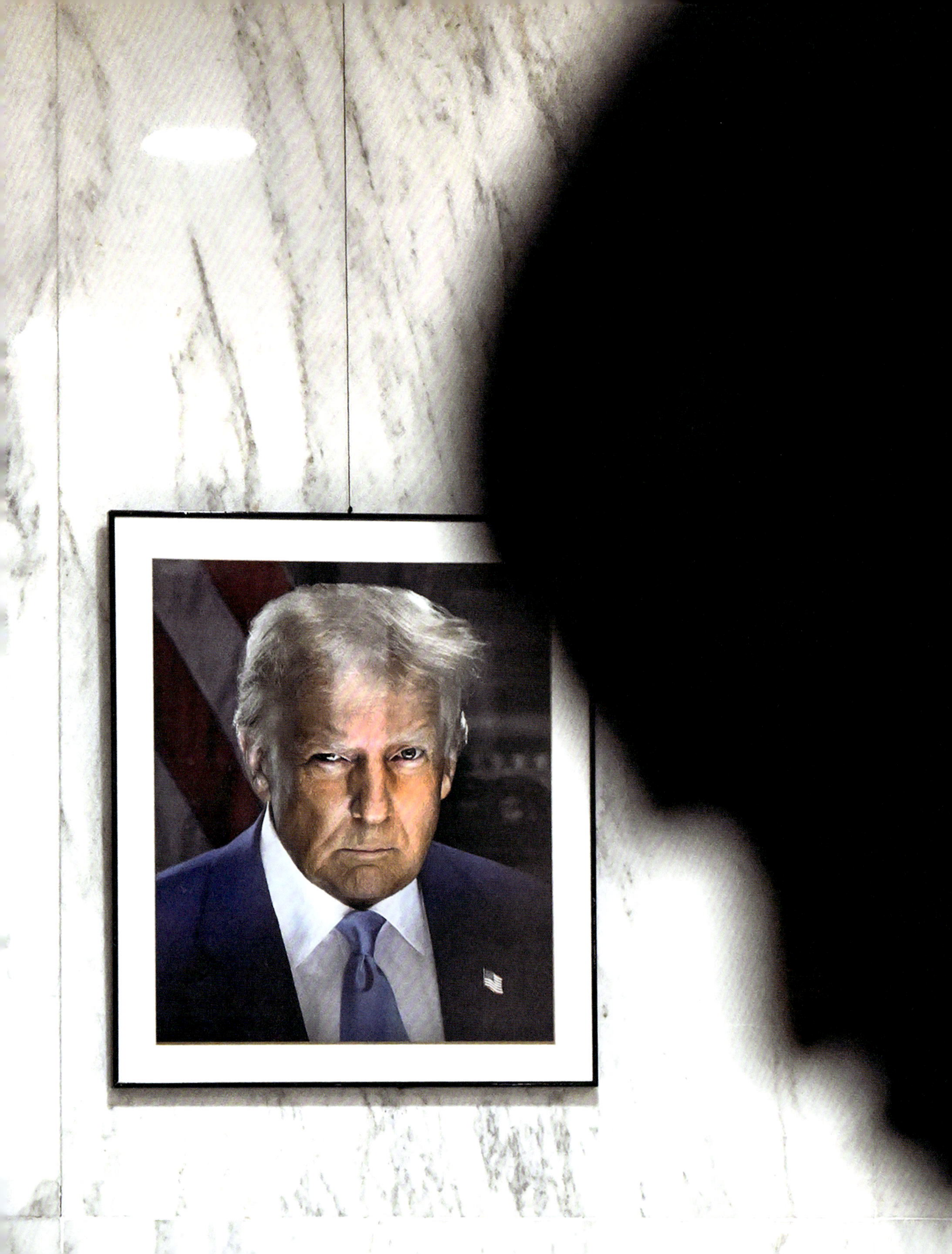

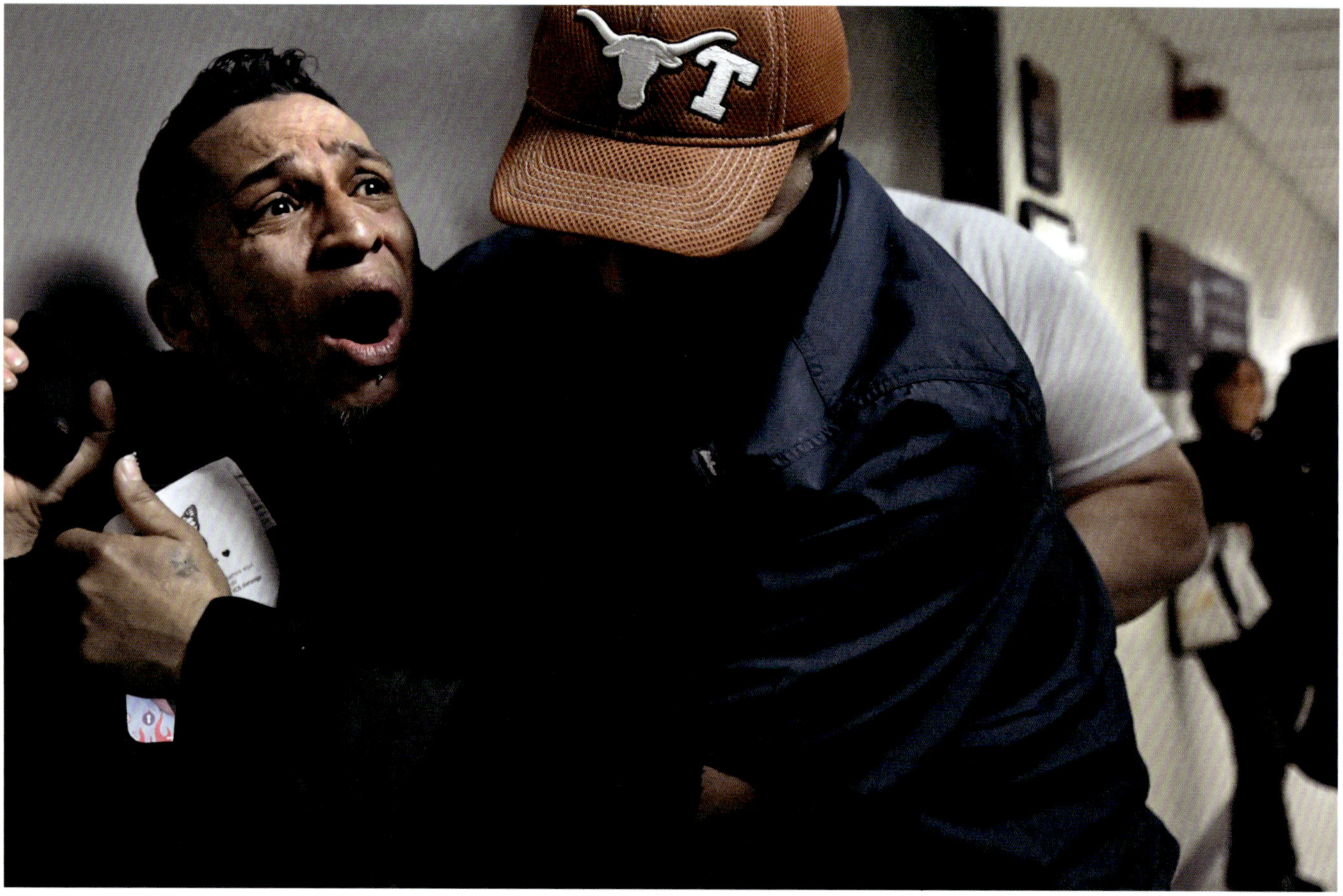

A Colombian migrant struggles as federal agents detain him. Critics argue that conducting arrests at courthouses deters undocumented individuals from participating in the justice system or seeking legal asylum. 27 October 2025

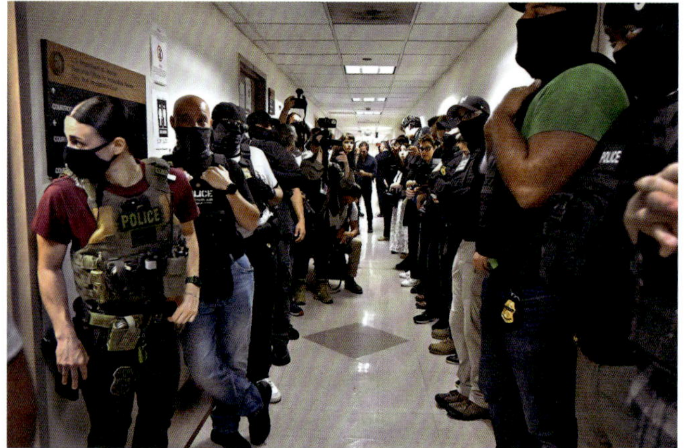

Masked federal officers wait outside courtrooms holding target photographs. While ICE claims masks protect the identity of agents and their families, critics argue the practice erodes accountability and public trust. 8 July 2025

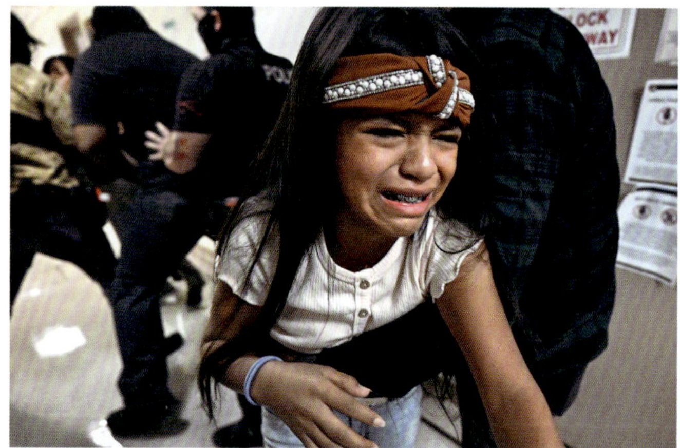

Rosa (12) is pulled away from her father, Ruben. Between 2017 and 2021, over 4,600 children were separated from their parents; at least 1,360 children have yet to be reunited with their families as of early 2025. 25 September 2025

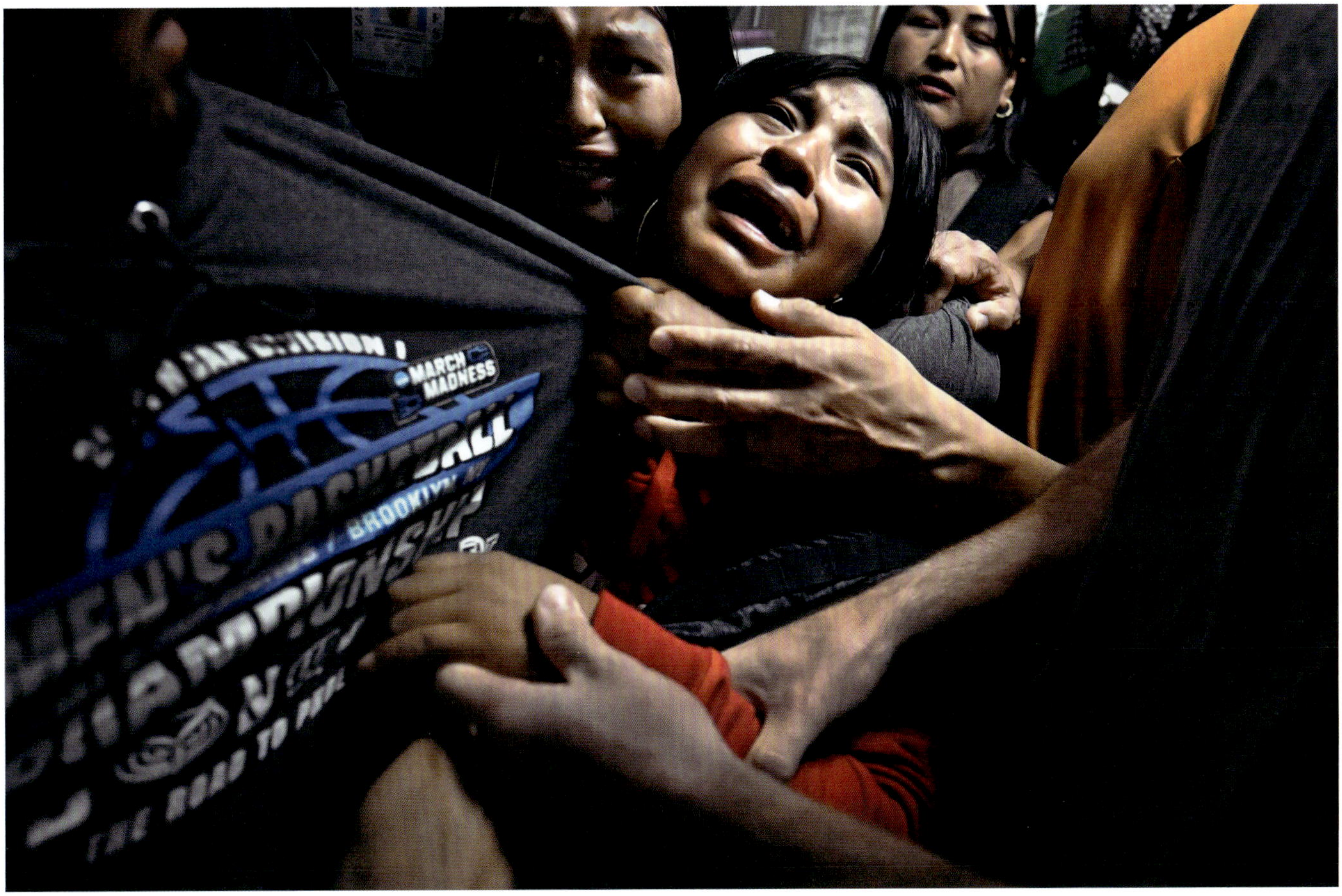

Distraught girls cling to their father, Luis, as ICE detains him following an immigration hearing. Luis served as the sole breadwinner for his family. 26 August 2025

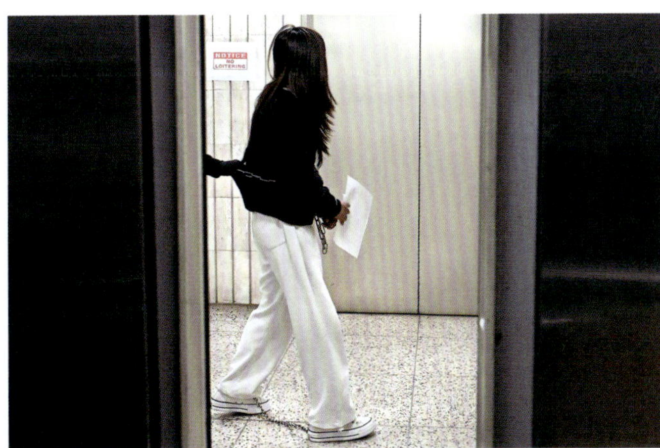

A woman is led in shackles through the Jacob Javits building's 10th floor. A 2025 injunction required ICE to improve "deplorable" conditions at this facility, which was off-limits to inspectors until 19 December 2025. 2 October 2025

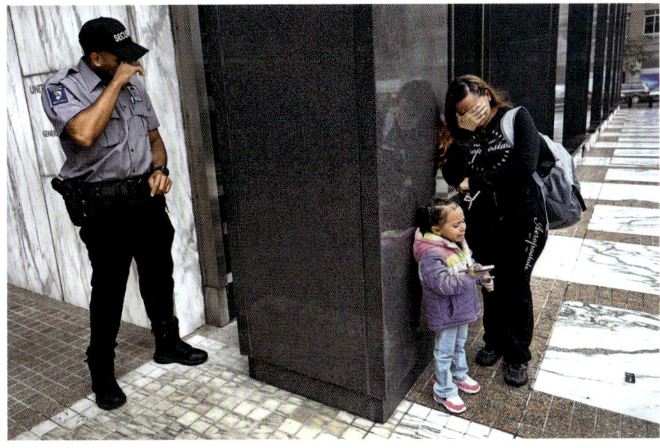

A security guard breaks down while witnessing a family separation. Security personnel frequently find themselves caught between federal agents, desperate families, and protesters in the increasingly volatile courthouse environment. 20 August 2025

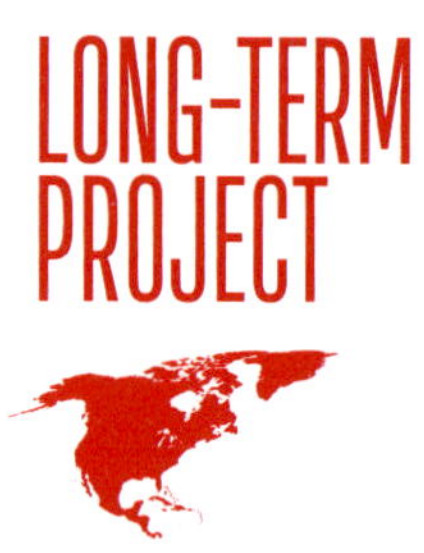

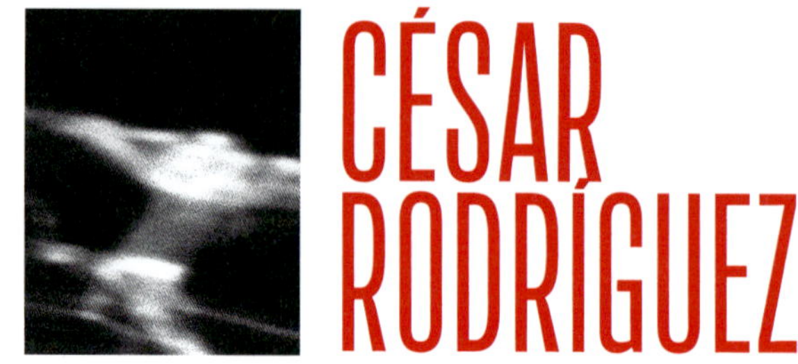

CÉSAR RODRÍGUEZ

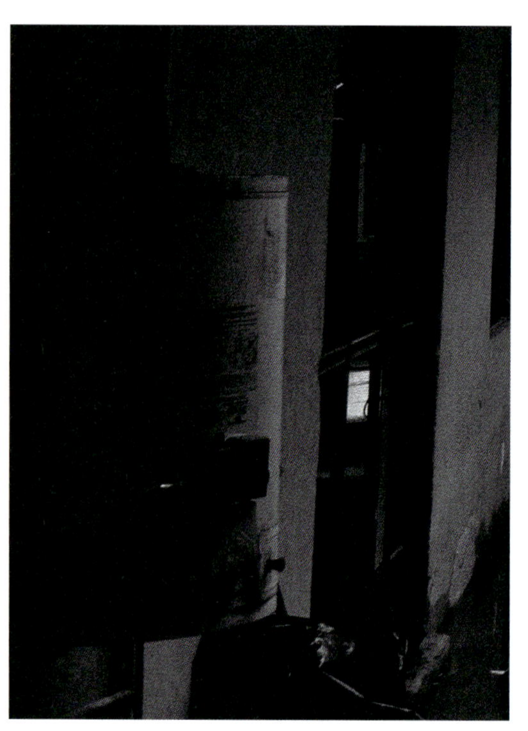

MEXICO, A CHANGING CLIMATE

Mexico is especially vulnerable to climate extremes, with 52% of its territory situated in arid or semi-arid zones. Over the last two decades, environmental disasters have internally displaced approximately 2.7 million people, a figure projected to reach up to 8 million by 2050. This project documents the enormous cost of these changes on a human scale: from the rapid erosion of Tabasco's coastlines, where sea levels are rising three times faster than the global average, to the systemic water scarcities in Monterrey and the State of Mexico, where renewable water availability has plummeted by 81% since 1950.

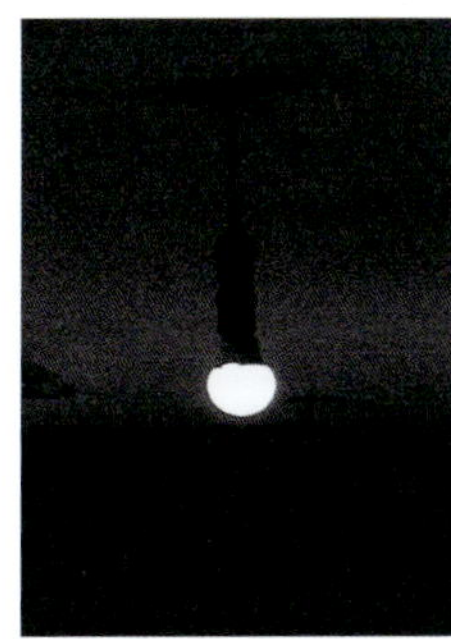

A child runs up to the second floor of a partially submerged home. The 2024 floods affected 7,000 residents. Many families lost personal belongings like photographs and other cherished items.
Chalco, State of Mexico, Mexico, 19 August 2024 / César Rodríguez, Norwegian Red Cross, SNCA, *The New York Times*

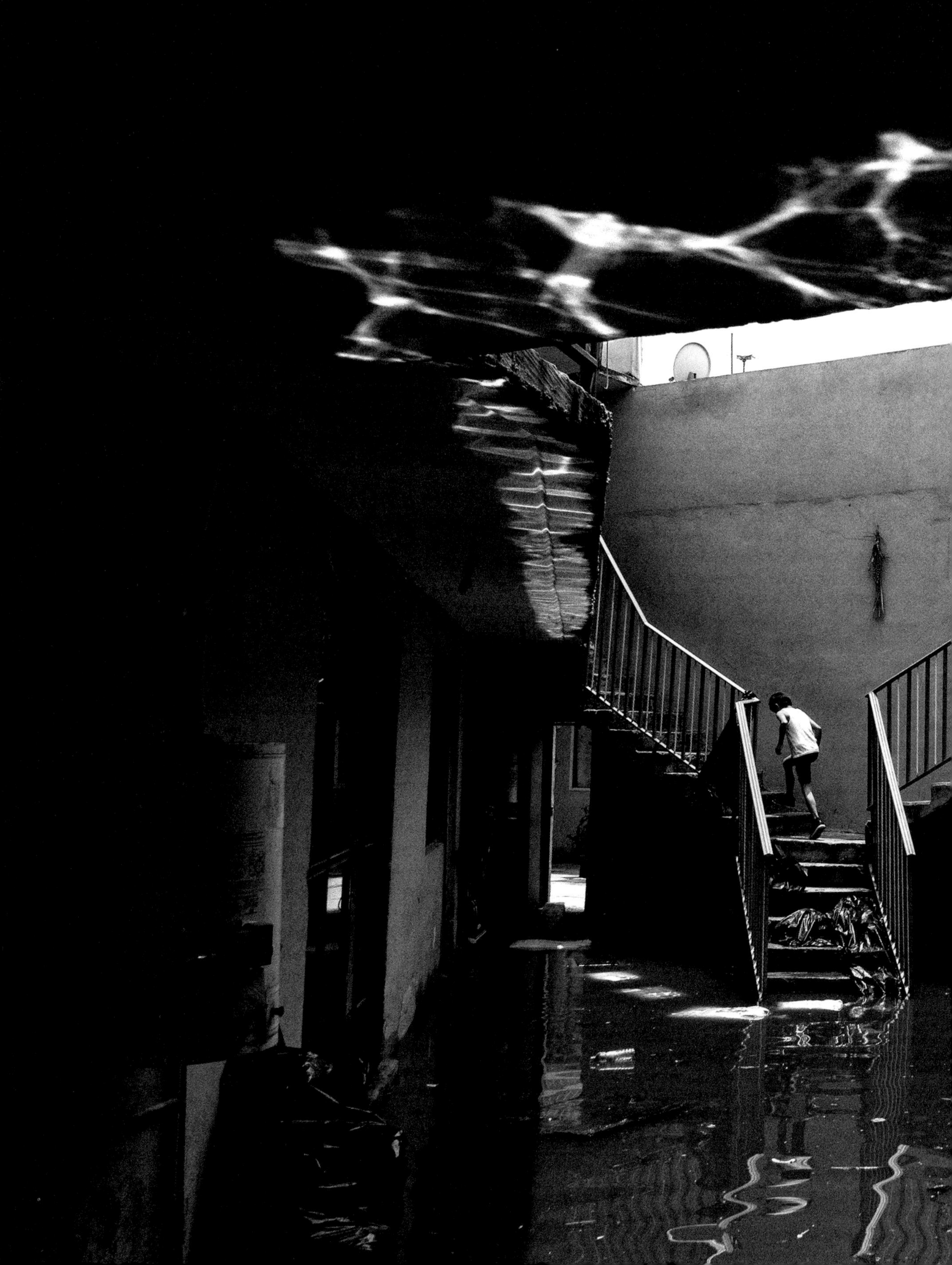

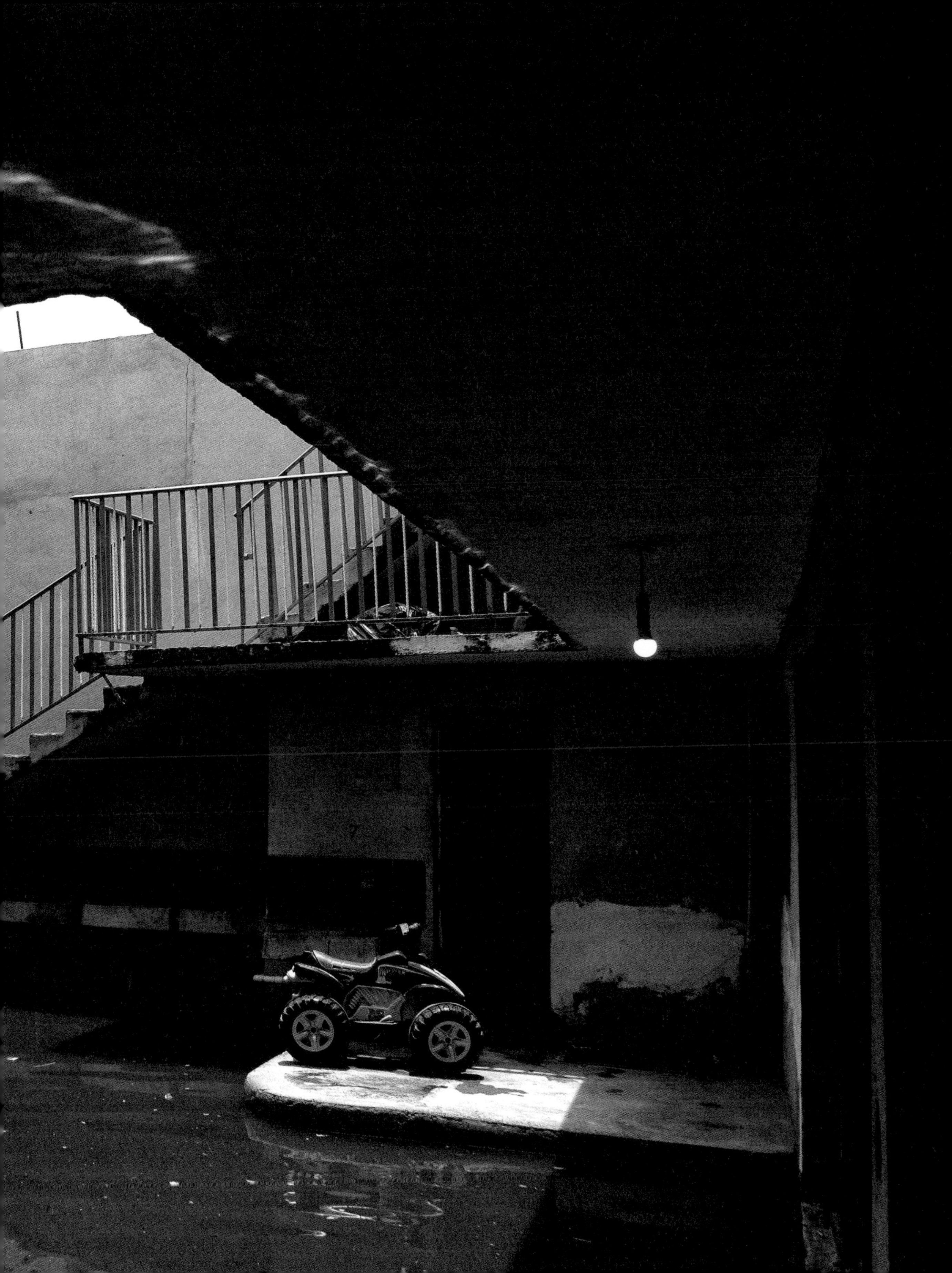

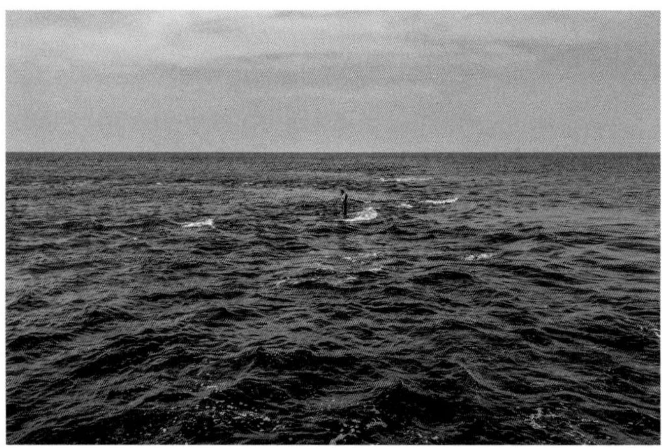

A man stands on the remains of a breakwater in Sánchez Magallanes. Coastal erosion in Tabasco has consumed over 500 meters of land since 2005. Tabasco, Mexico, 5 September 2021

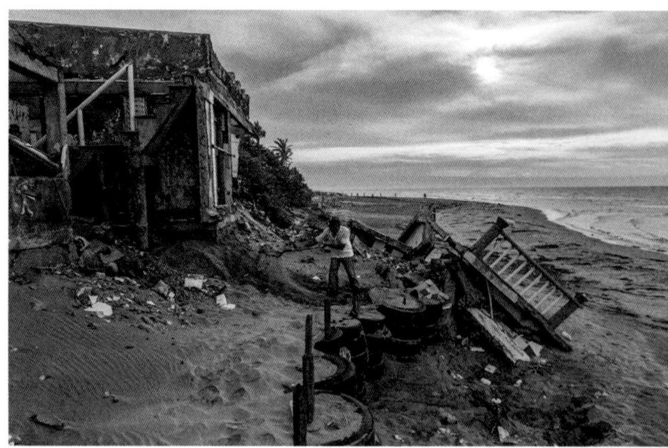

Juan Izquierdo shovels sand to shore up his home's foundation. Seven days after this photograph was taken, another section of the house collapsed. Sánchez Magallanes, Tabasco, Mexico, 2 September 2021

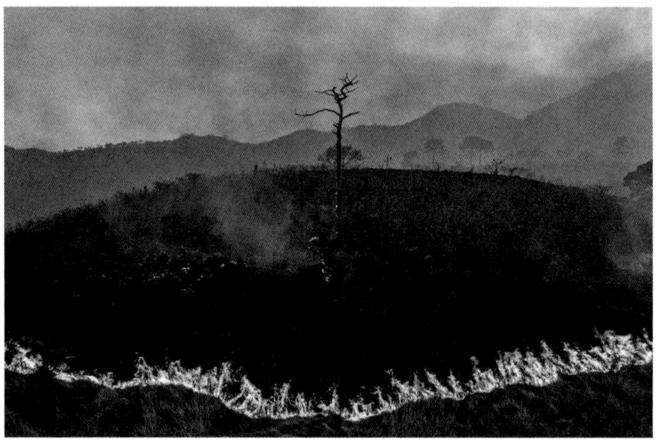

A forest fire burns on Cerro de San Juan. Fueled by drought, the fires consumed over 950 hectares, threatening the biodiversity of the Nayarit highlands. Tepic, Mexico, 17 April 2023

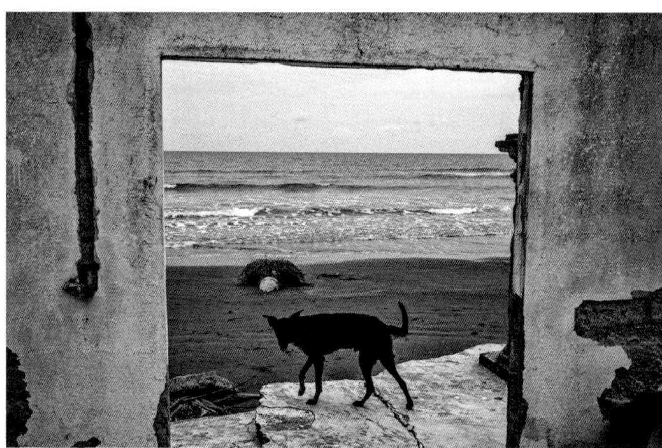

A dog wanders the vanishing coastline of Las Barrancas. Fishermen and families who depend on the ocean struggle to survive; many are forced to relocate. Veracruz, Mexico, 10 March 2025

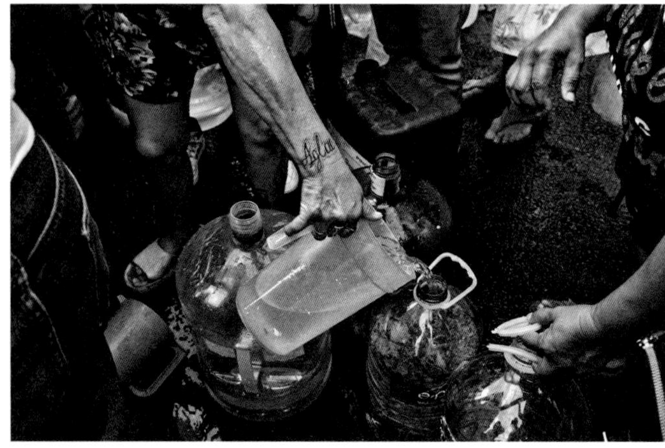

Residents fill containers after eight days without running water. In July 2022, about 48% of Mexico's territory was suffering from drought. Monterrey, Nuevo Leon, Mexico, 21 June 2022

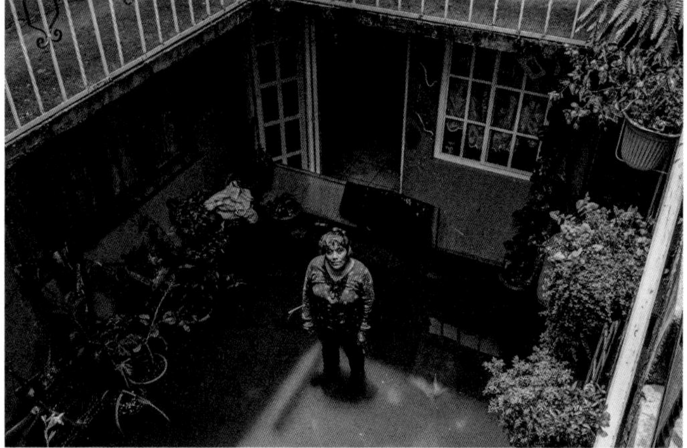

A woman stands in her flooded patio in Chalco. Sewage-infused floodwaters submerged over 2,000 homes for 40 days in 2024. State of Mexico, Mexico, 19 August 2024

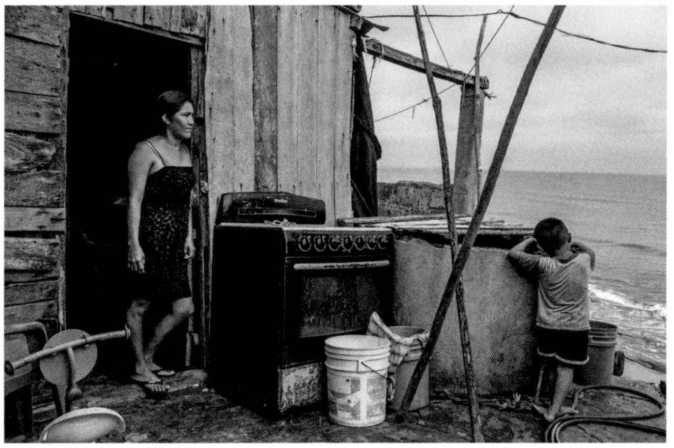

Ms. Marlit watches her son play in the remains of their home, having lost over half the structure to the sea. Sánchez Magallanes, Tabasco, Mexico, 5 September 2021

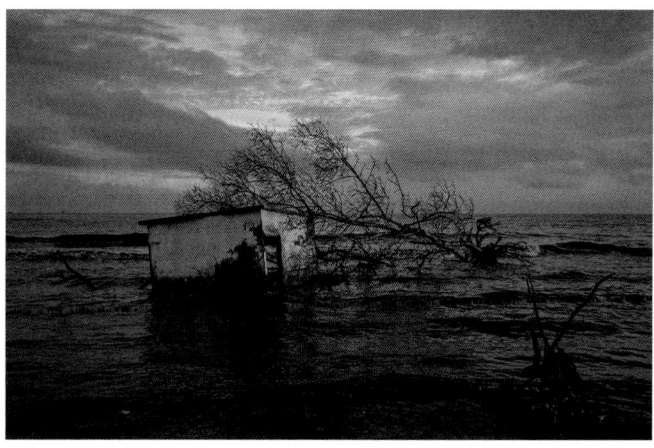

A house sits partially submerged by the sea in El Bosque, the first Mexican community officially recognized as displaced by climate change. Tabasco, Mexico, 5 December 2023

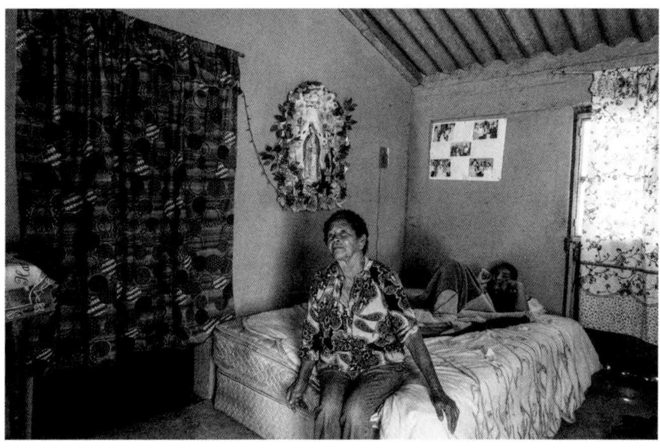

María Elvira and her grandson in their new home. They are part of the community that fled the sinking village of Palmar de Cuautla. Nuevo Palmar de Cuautla, Nayarit, Mexico, 30 March 2025

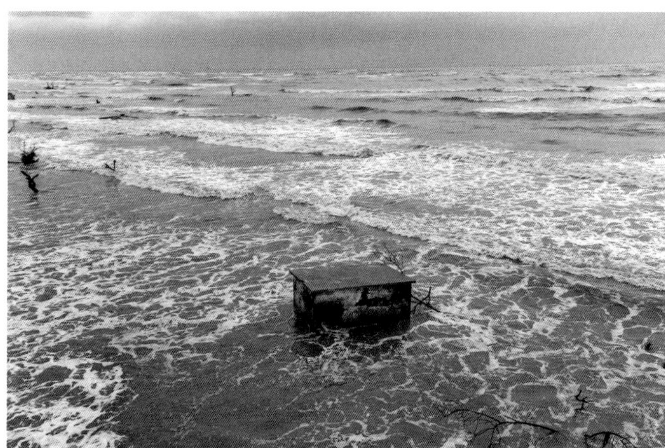

An aerial view shows the remnants of El Bosque. The community once housed 700 residents; today, rising sea levels have left barely a dozen. Centla, Tabasco, Mexico, 12 December 2024

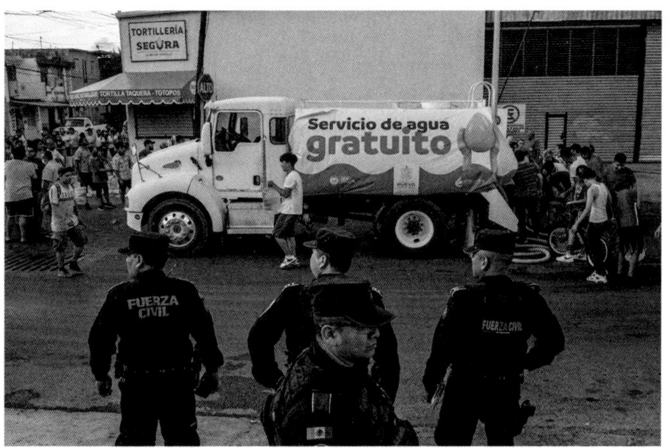

Police monitor a water distribution point to prevent altercations. In 2022, the state government was forced to ration water for 5 million residents. Monterrey, Nuevo Leon, Mexico, 21 June 2022

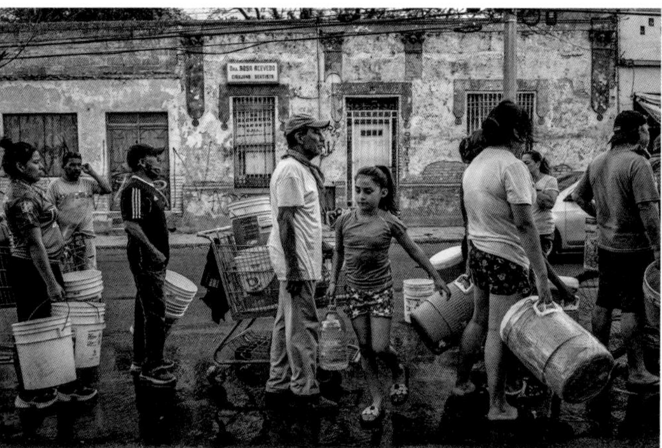

Residents in Monterrey line up for water. Some blocked streets to demand water service. In response, large trucks delivered water daily to the city's most vulnerable neighborhoods. Nuevo Leon, Mexico, 21 June 2022

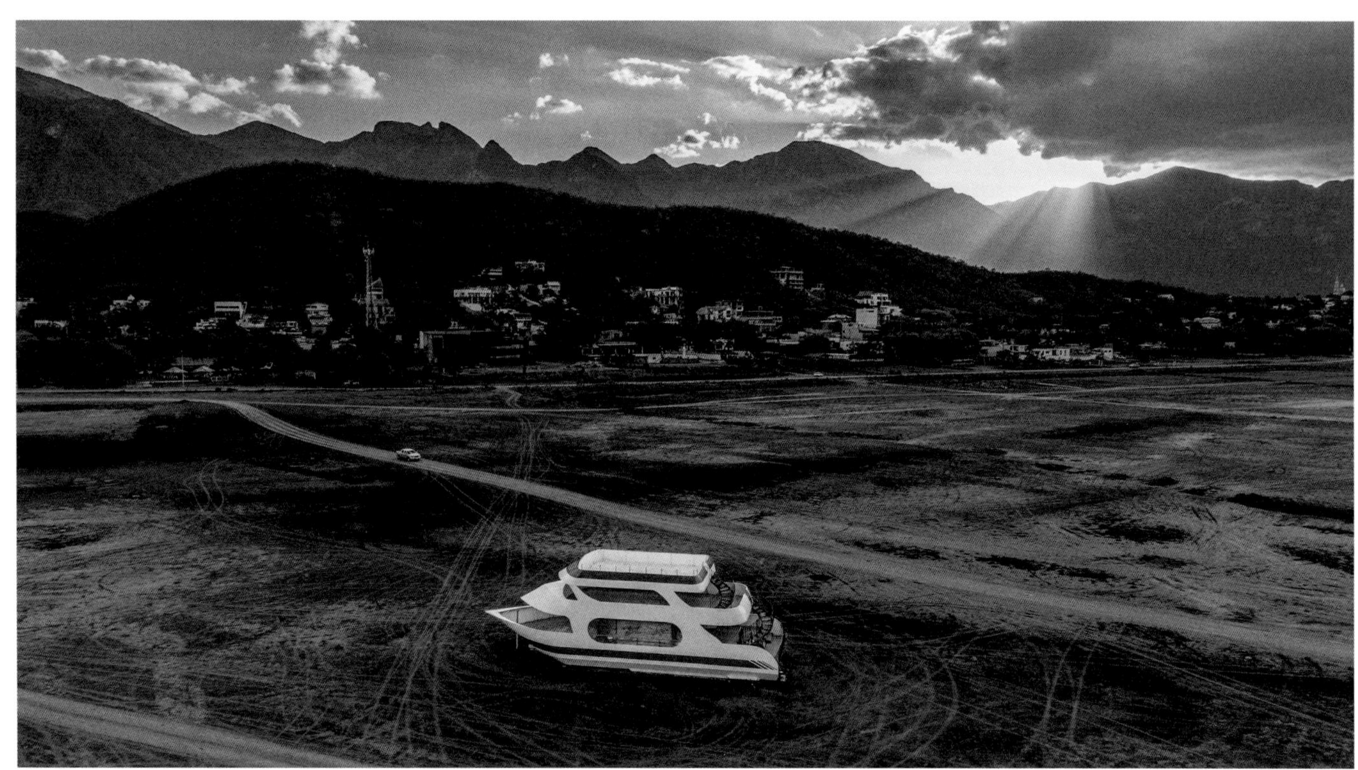

A tourist boat sits grounded after the La Boca dam dropped to 8.5% capacity during the 2022 drought.
Monterrey remains caught between extreme water scarcity and catastrophic, climate-driven flooding.
Santiago, Nuevo Leon, Mexico, 20 June 2022

DO WE NEED TO SEE GRAPHIC CONTENT TO UNDERSTAND WHAT IS HAPPENING IN THE WORLD?

Graphic content can confront difficult truths, but must be made with compassion, respecting dignity. The challeng is to capture powerful emotions and shape images that help us understand reality, rather than merely shock us into looking away.

—

Kira Pollack,
Global jury chair

A story can be told effectively without graphic content; however, at times nothing is as shocking as visceral depictions of world events. What is "too graphic" is highly subjective, depending on the story and intended audience.

—

Vivek Prakash,
Asia-Pacific and Oceania jury

When used responsibly, graphic content can cut through indifference, confront audiences with uncomfortable realities, and deepen understanding of human suffering.

—

Tsvangirayi Mukwazhi,
Africa jury

Graphic content can be necessary, but if violence is all we see, despair becomes the dominant story. We need images that show dignity, complexity, and different perspectives.

—

Gael Almeida,
South America jury

When shown with respect for human dignity and the audience, graphic content can foster awareness, empathy, and accountability.

—

Alfred Yaghobzadeh,
West, Central, and South Asia jury

Unfortunately, graphic content often needs to exist to document atrocities.Photographs provide undeniable evidence and historical records, making suffering visible and countering denial.

—

Marie A. Monteleone,
North and Central America jury

Graphic content may awaken empathy, yet risk creating harm. Without visual literacy, looking is insufficient, especially in a post-truth era. Learning how to see is essential to understanding reality without losing our humanity.

—

Krzysztof Candrowicz,
Europe jury

SOUTH AMERICA

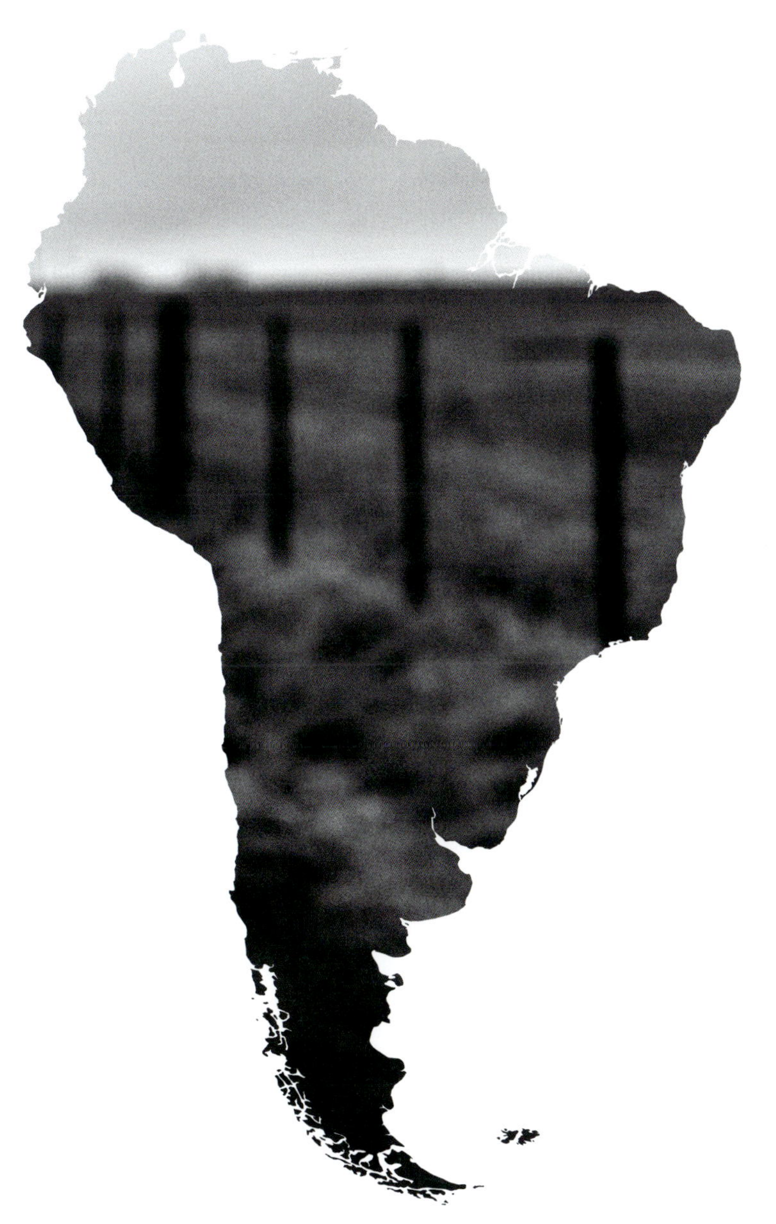

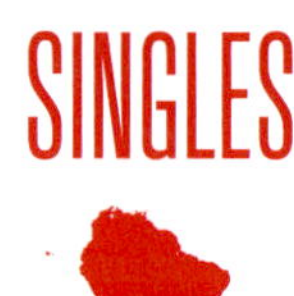

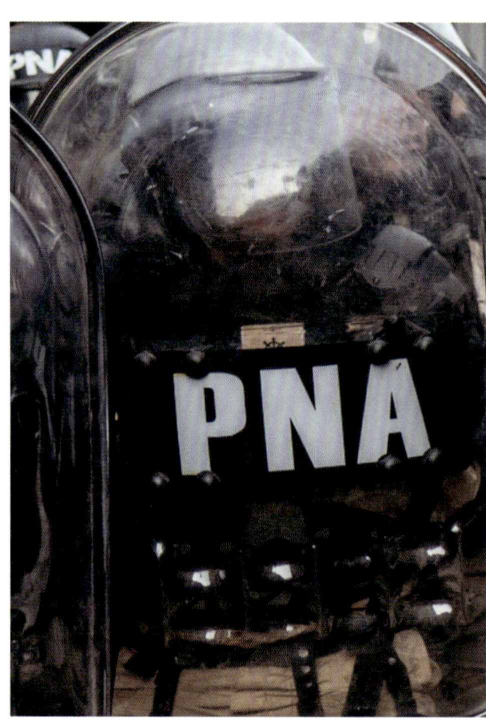

MILEI'S ARGENTINA

TADEO BOURBON

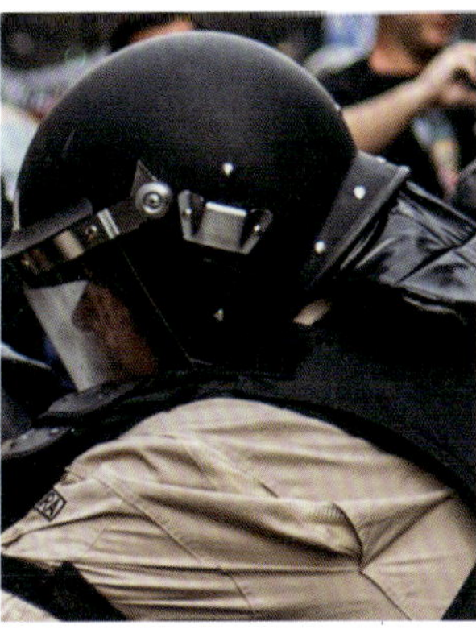

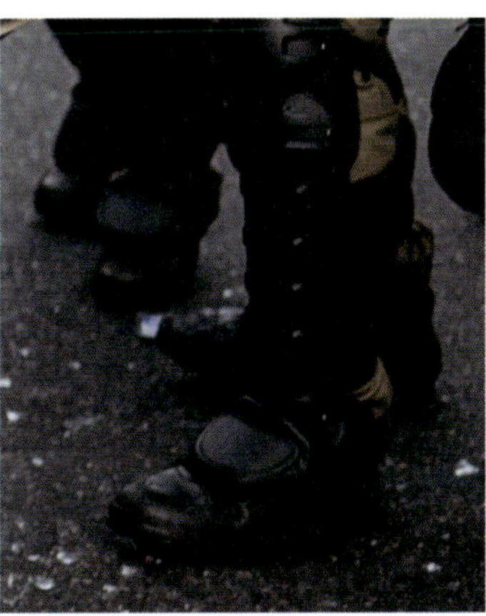

In Argentina, aggressive austerity measures aimed at curbing 200% inflation have plunged the nation's older people into a desperate struggle for survival. With the minimum pension hovering around $300 – less than half the estimated basic cost of living – many retirees are forced to ration food and forgo essential medical treatments. Every Wednesday, pensioners gather outside the National Congress to protest low pensions and cuts to free medication programs. These demonstrations are frequently met with heavily militarized police responses, drawing international condemnation.

Police detain Father Jorge "Chueco" Romero during a pensioners' protest. Members of the "Opción por los Pobres" (Option for the Poor) clergy have joined weekly demonstrations against pension freezes and cuts to essential medical coverage. Buenos Aires, Argentina, 14 May 2025 / Tadeo Bourbon, for *Revista Mu*

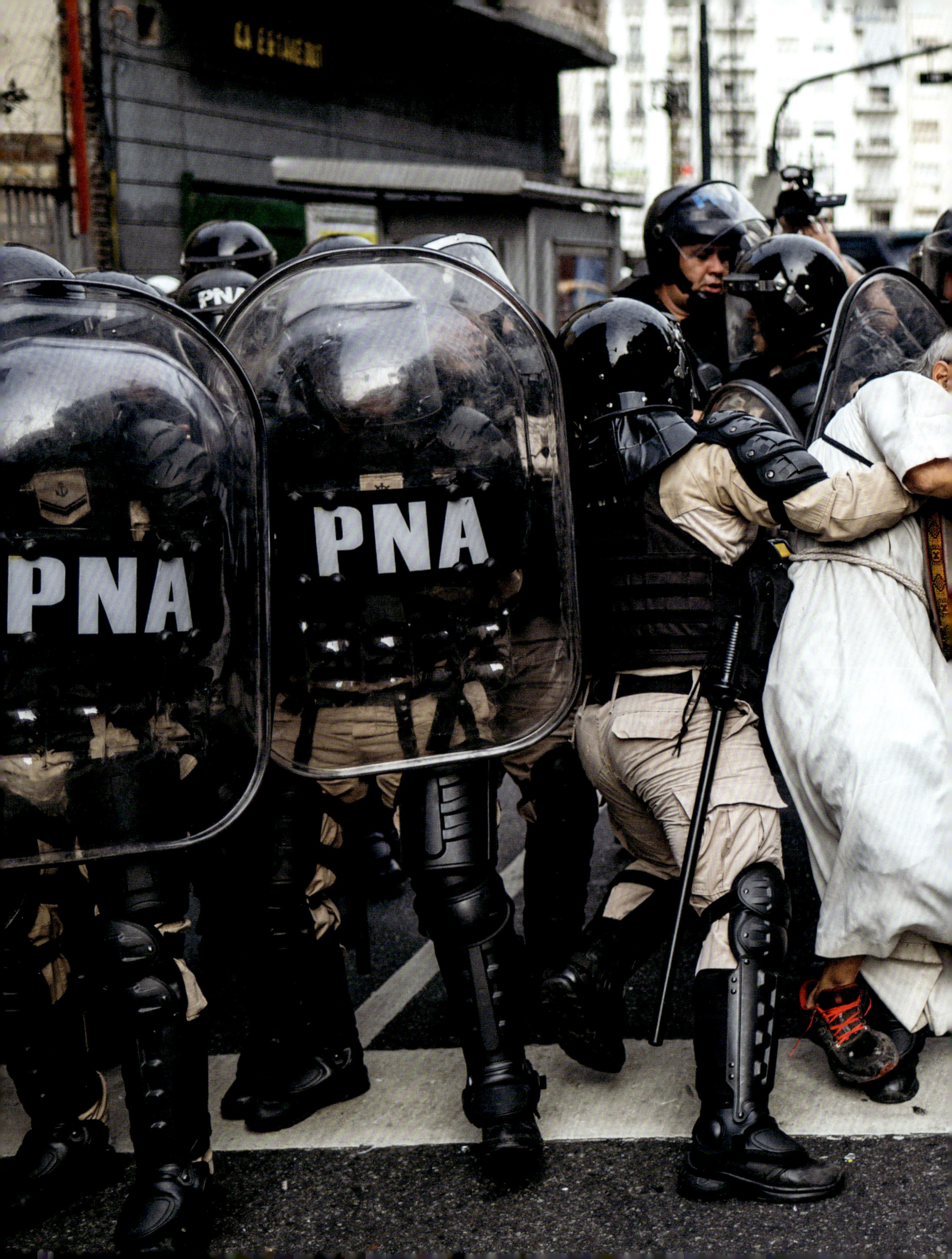

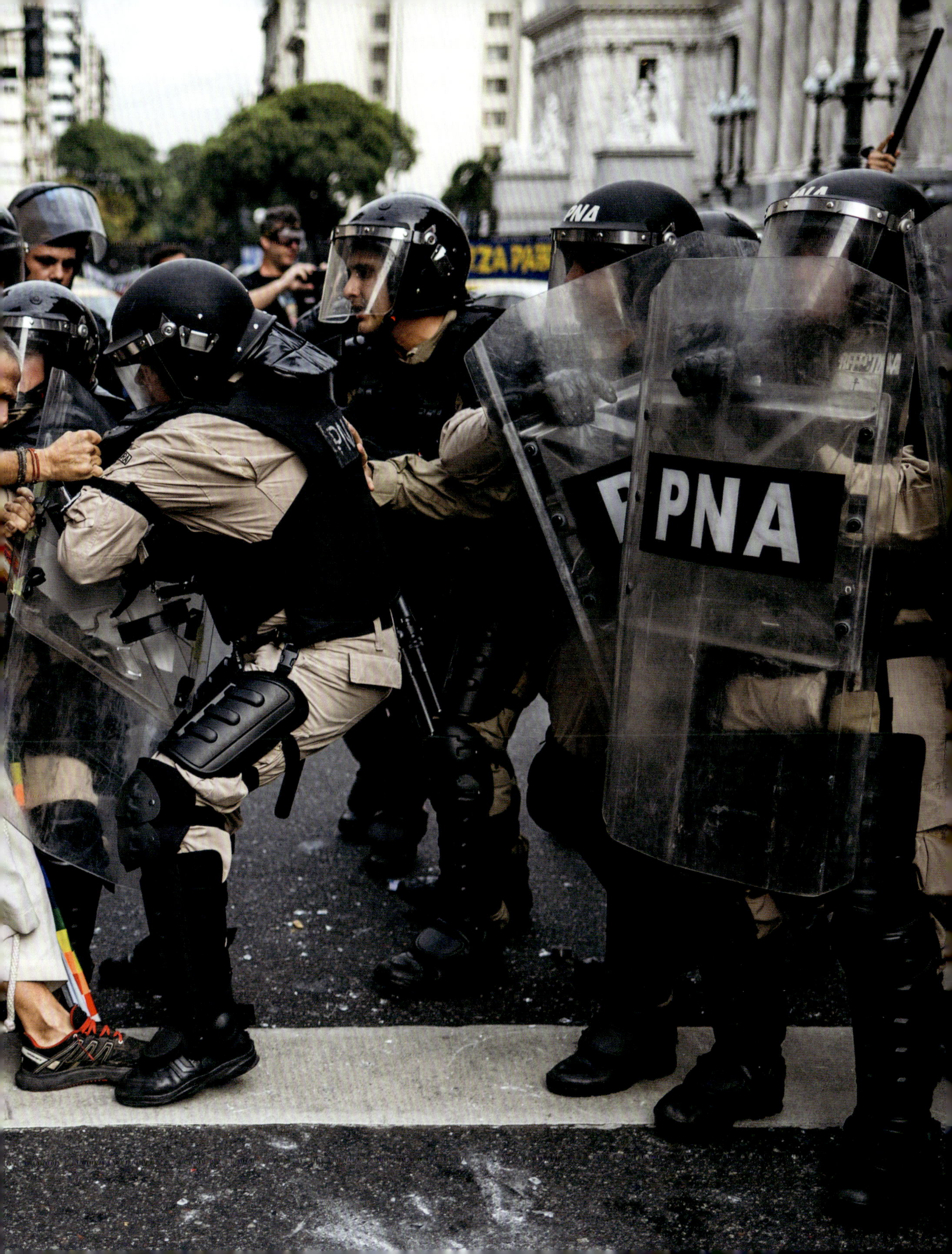

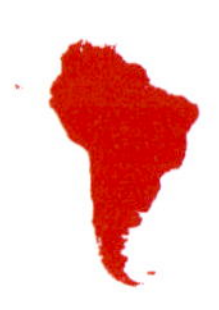

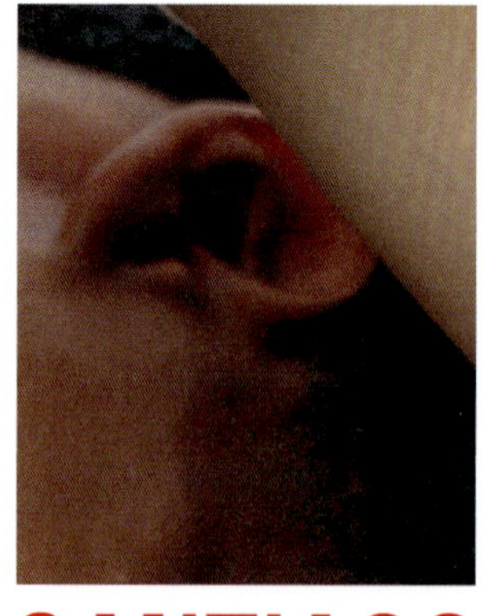

SANTIAGO ARCOS

Ecuador's militarized crackdown on transnational gangs has transformed vulnerable communities into targets for state violence. In December 2024, four Afro-Ecuadorian boys – aged 11 to 15 – disappeared after a neighborhood football practice in Guayaquil. The government initially denied involvement, then attempted to label the children as criminals. The discovery of their burned remains near an air force base shattered the Las Malvinas community and exposed the dangers of security policies that racially profile and criminalize marginalized youth.

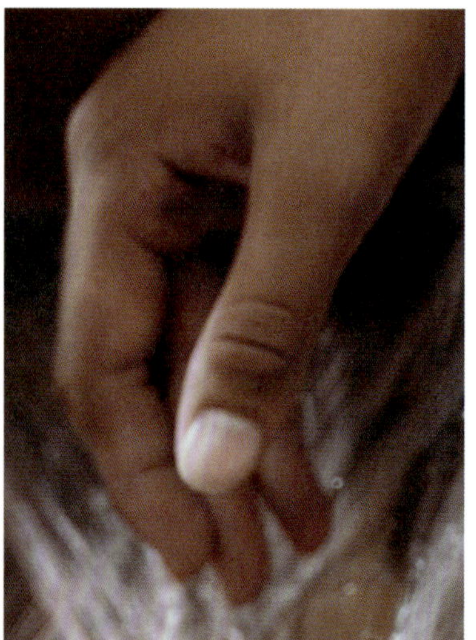

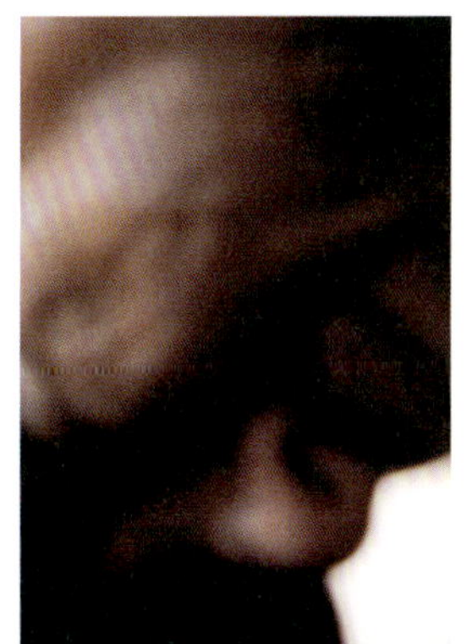

FUNERAL FOR "THE FOUR OF MALVINAS"

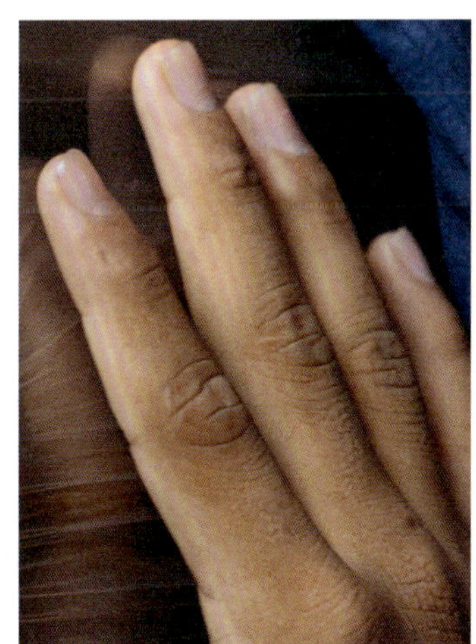

Teammates mourn Ismael Arroyo (15) who was tortured and murdered by Air Force personnel. Families, neighbors, and residents of Las Malvinas accompanied the coffins from their homes to the cemetery, turning the funeral into a massive public act of grief and protest. Guayaquil, Ecuador, 1 January 2025 / Santiago Arcos, for Reuters

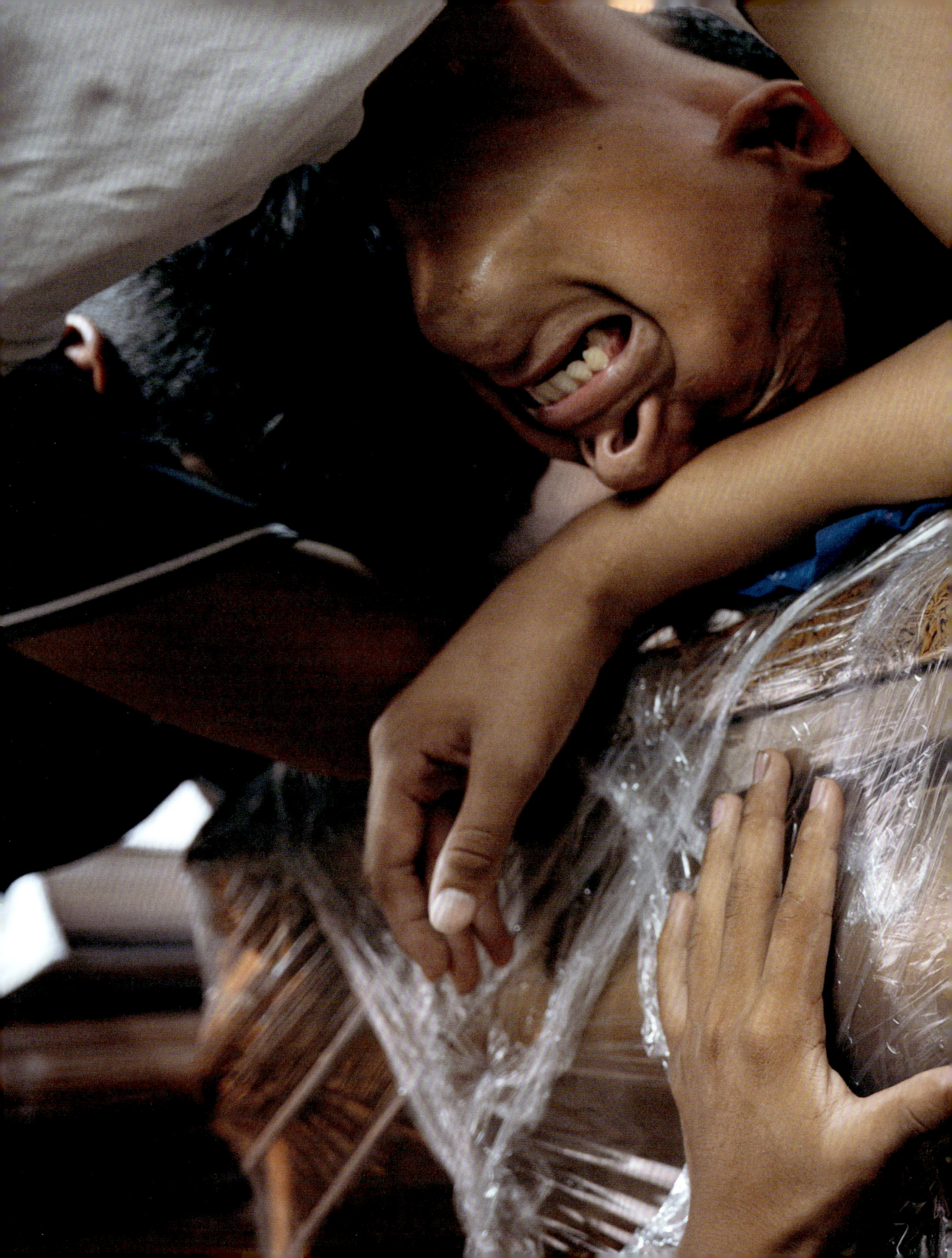

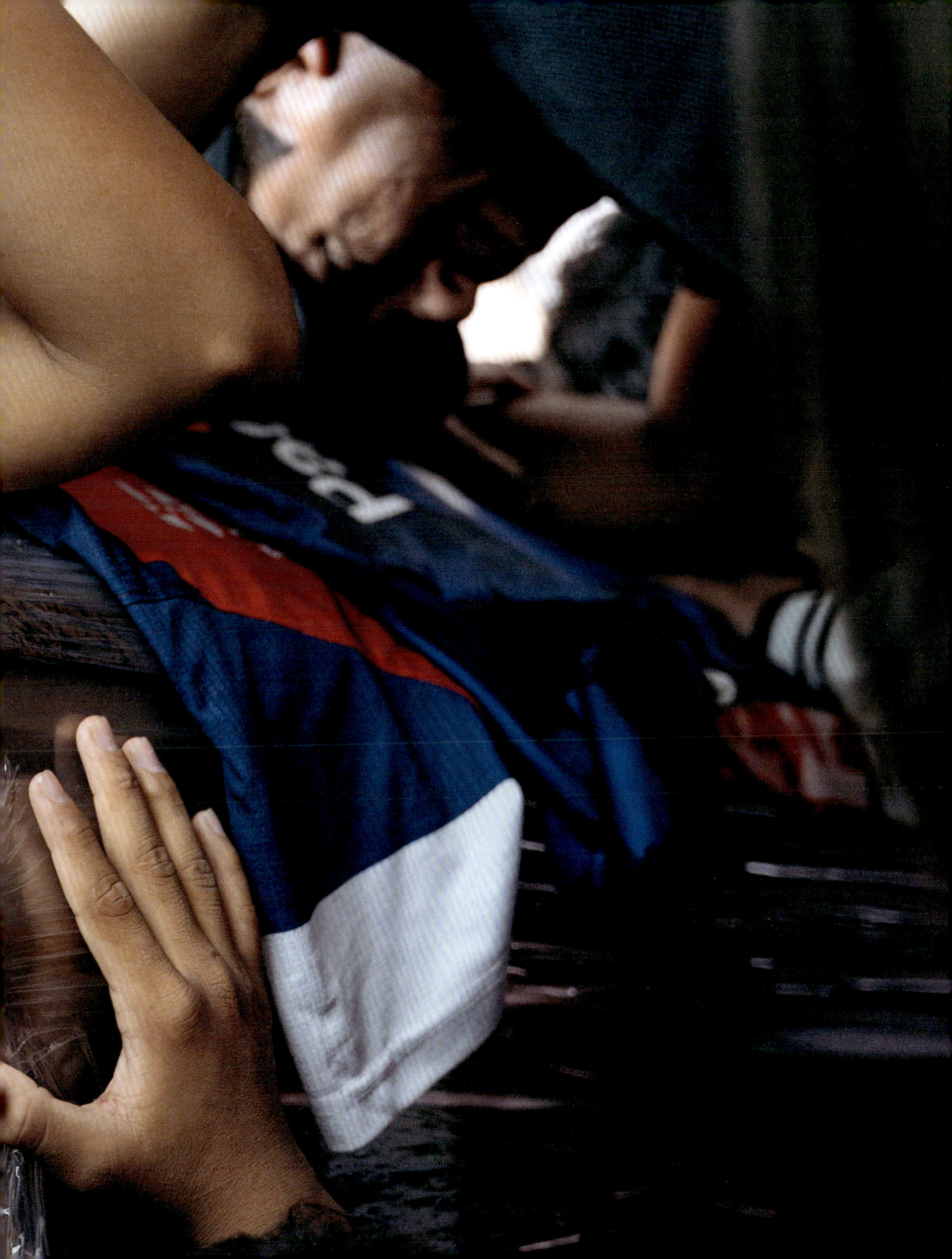

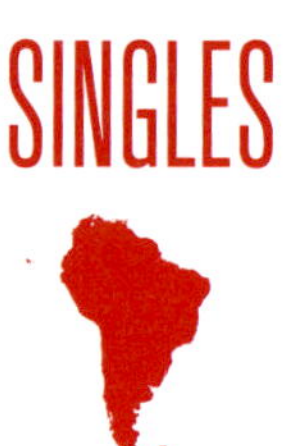

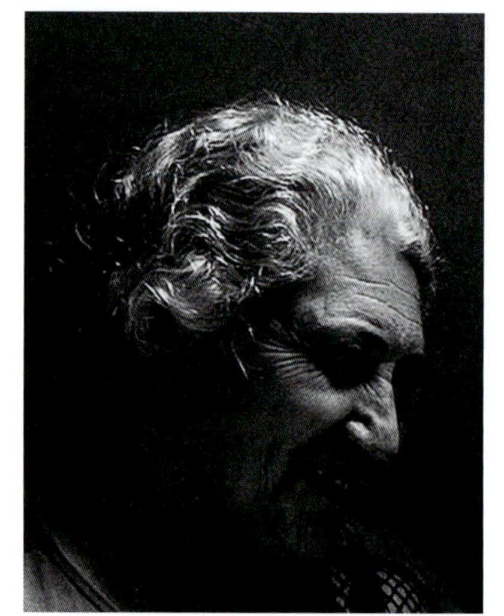

A TERRIT OF HOPE

PRISCILA RIBEIRO

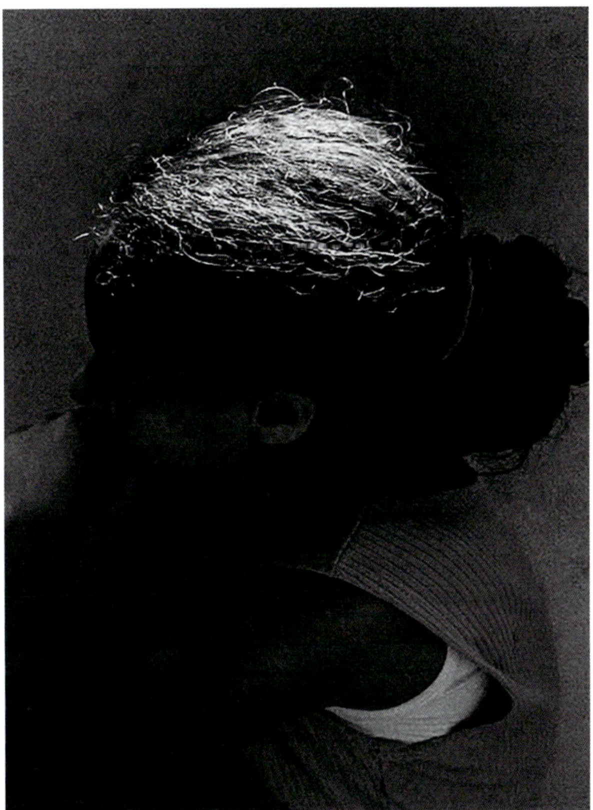

Millions of Brazilians lack safe and affordable housing, with a national shortage of 5.9 million homes forcing approximately 16.4 million people into informal settlements. In the city of Colombo, the Parque dos Lagos occupation is home to 200 families living without official access to water, sewage disposal, or electricity. This project examines the struggle for land regularization, the legal process of converting informal possession into property rights. For Sandra Mara Siqueira and these communities, legal tenure is the essential gateway to credit, permanence, and dignity.

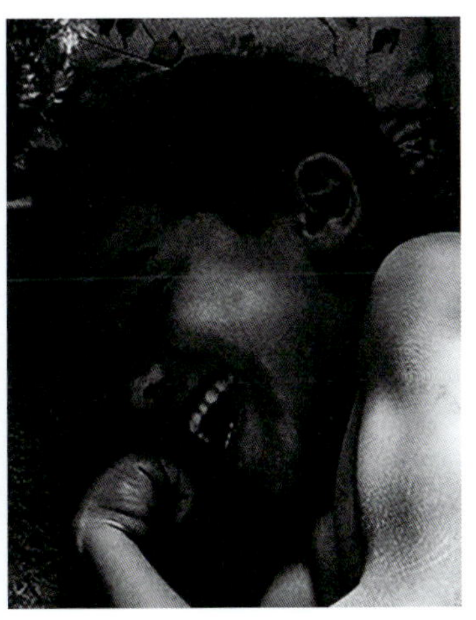

Sandra Mara Siqueira rests with her grandchildren, Micael, Davi, Ana Flávia, and Vitória. Living in the Parque dos Lagos occupation since 2013, the family seeks land regularization to guarantee access to basic infrastructure. Colombo, Paraná, Brazil, 15 November 2025 / Priscila Ribeiro

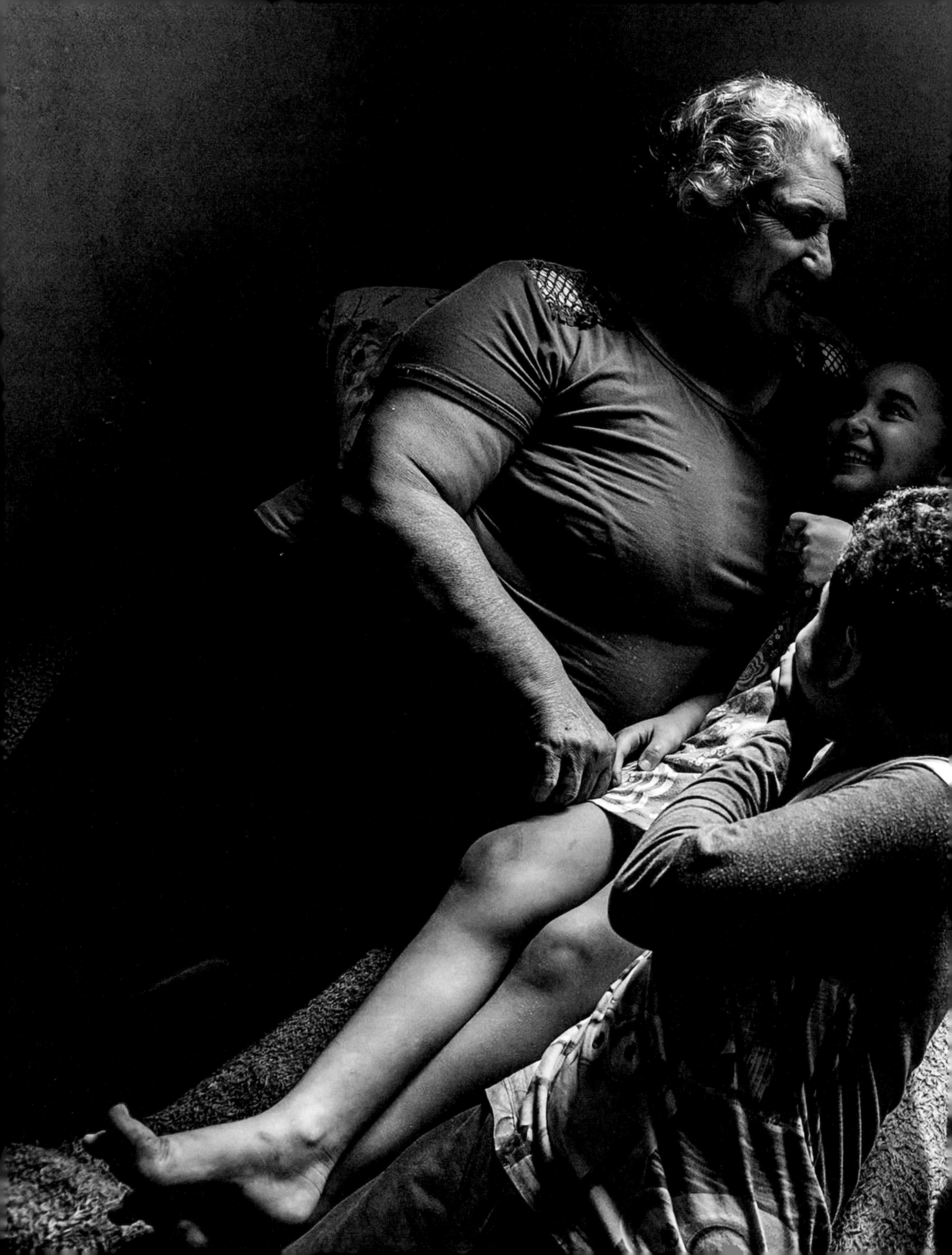

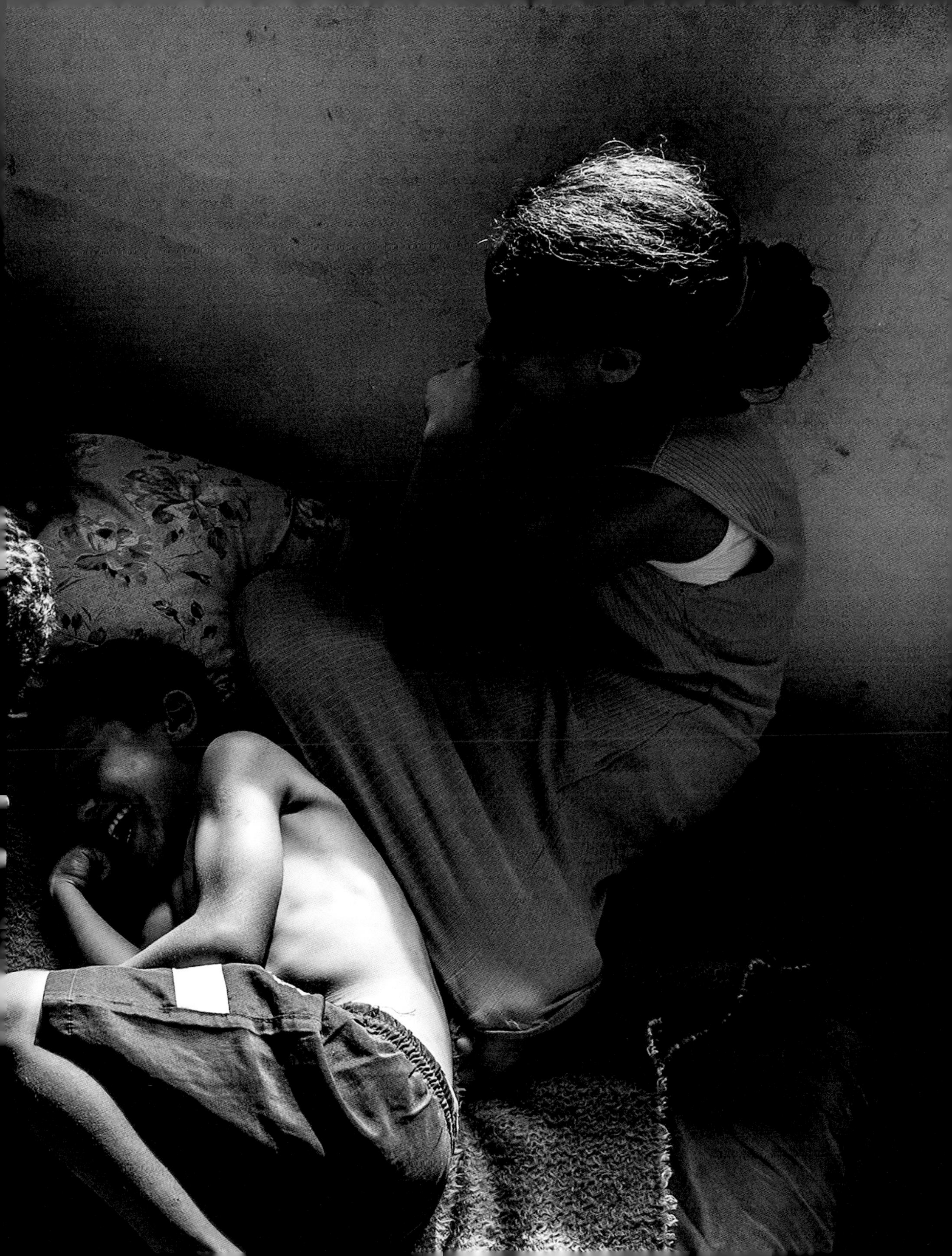

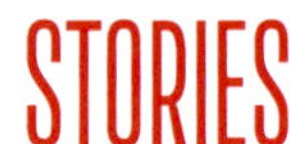

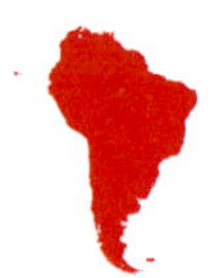

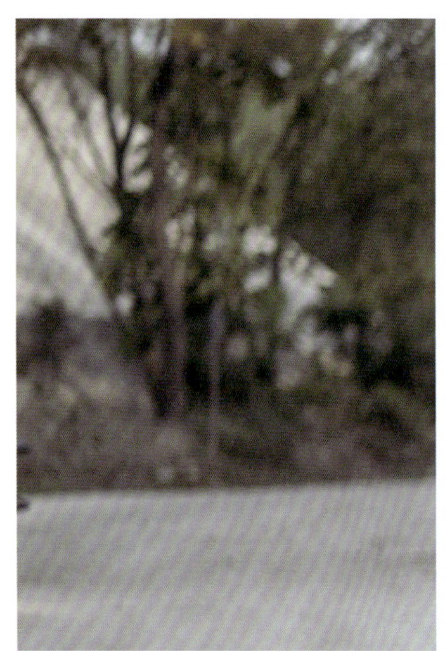

THOSE WHO CARRY THE DEAD

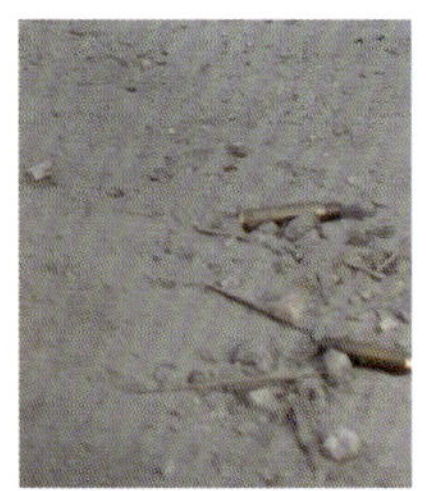

EDUARDO ANIZELLI

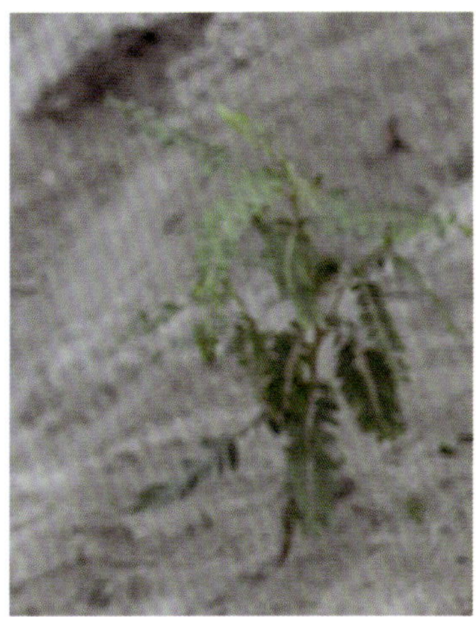

In October 2025, a massive police operation targeting
the Comando Vermelho criminal syndicate unfolded in
Rio de Janeiro's Complexo do Alemão and Penha favelas.
Deploying a record 2,500 local and military officers, the
raid was the deadliest police operation in Brazilian
history. Of the 122 who were killed, the vast majority
were Afro-Brazilians. In the aftermath, authorities
failed to deploy forensic teams, forcing the community
to bear the physical and emotional weight of carrying
their own dead.

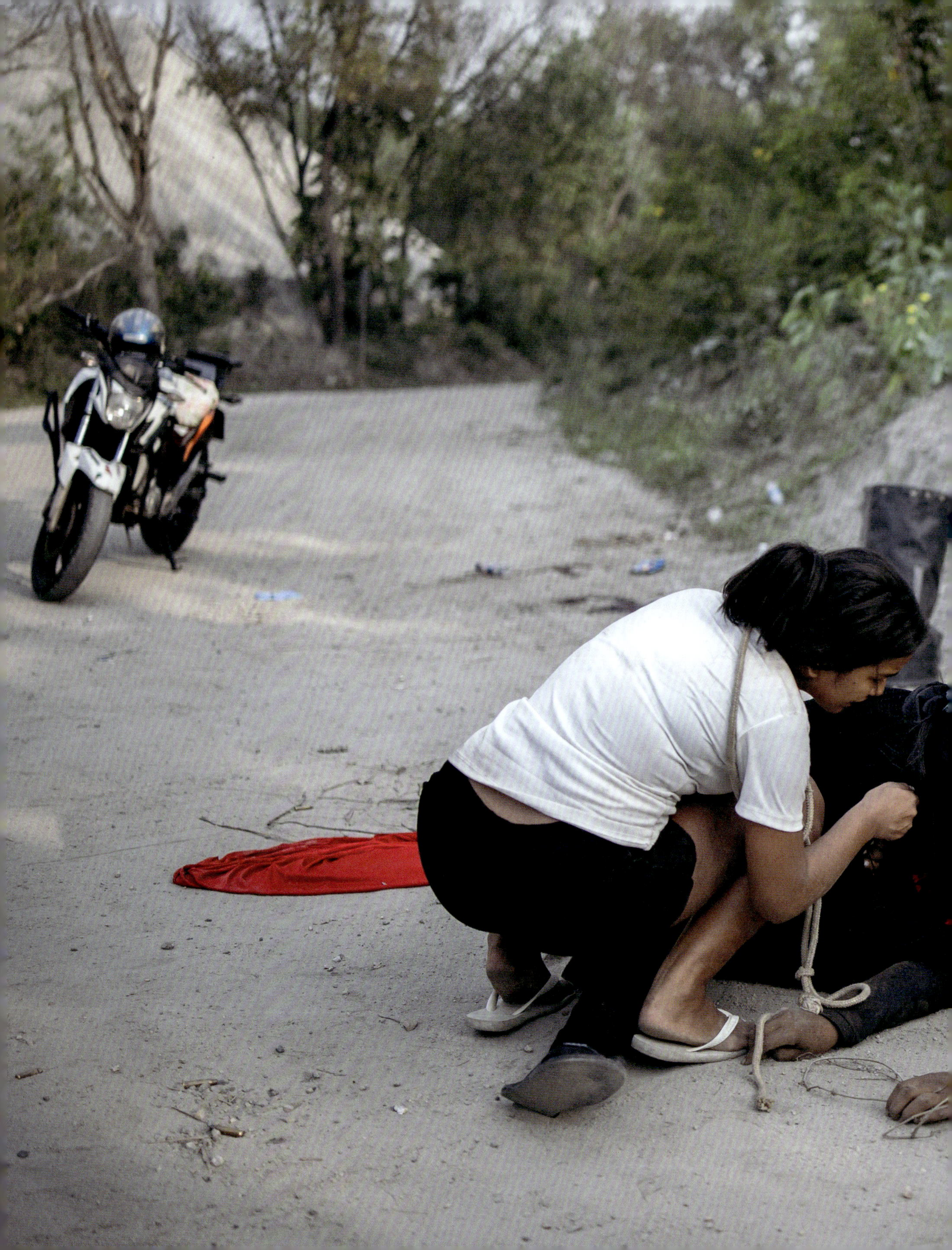

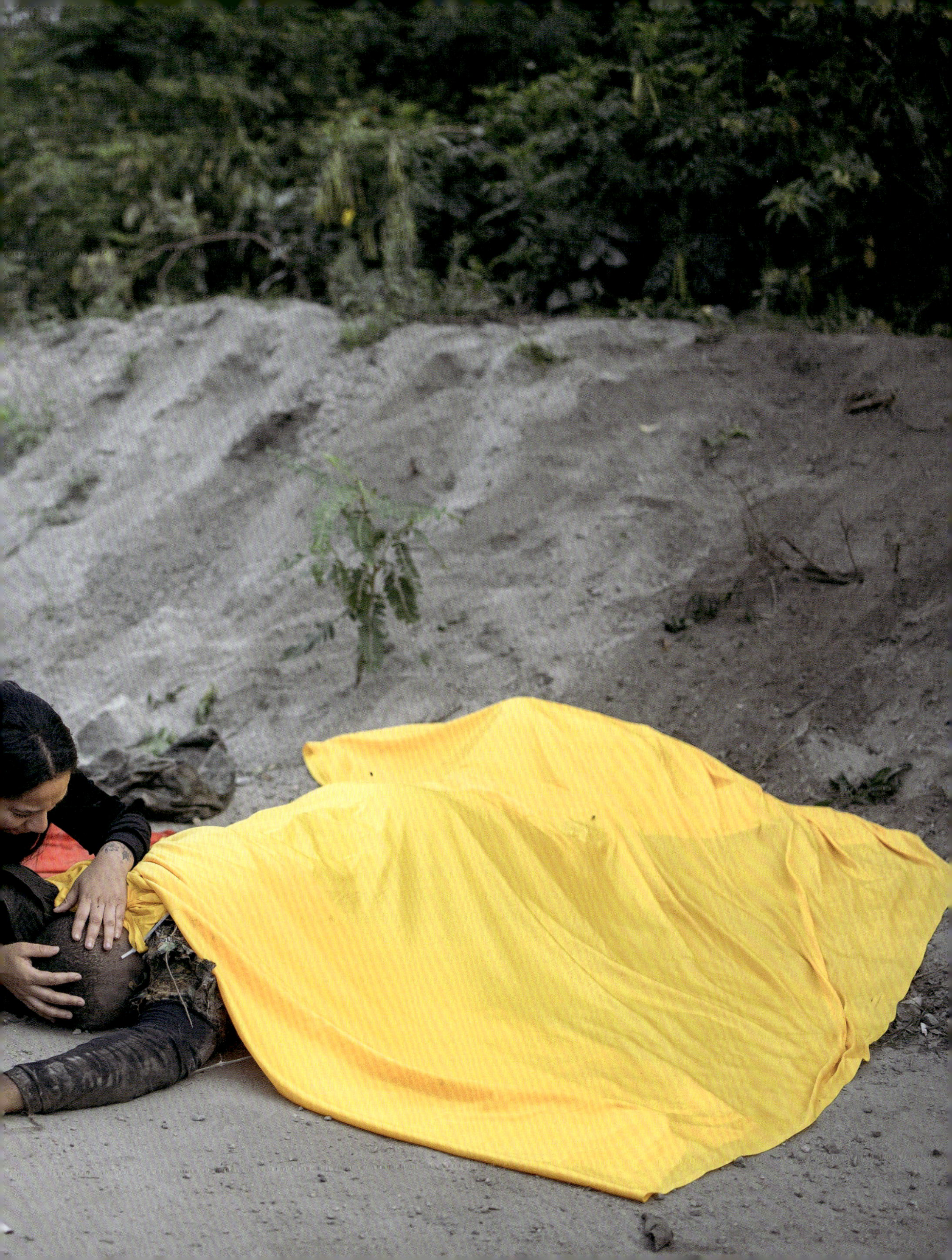

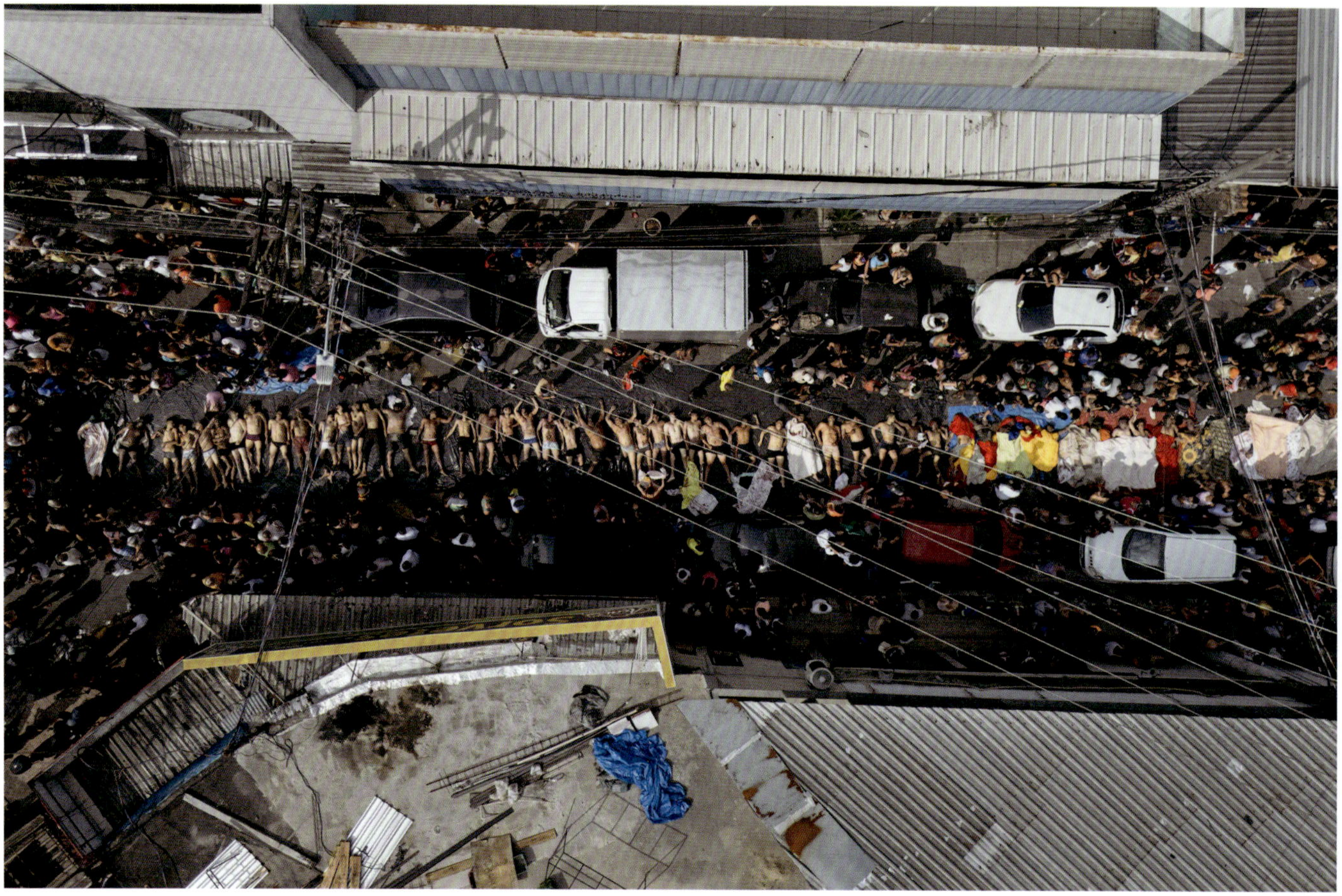

Recovered bodies lie in São Lucas Square. It took four days for authorities to officially identify and release all the victims, disrupting Brazilian funeral and mourning practices. 29 October 2025

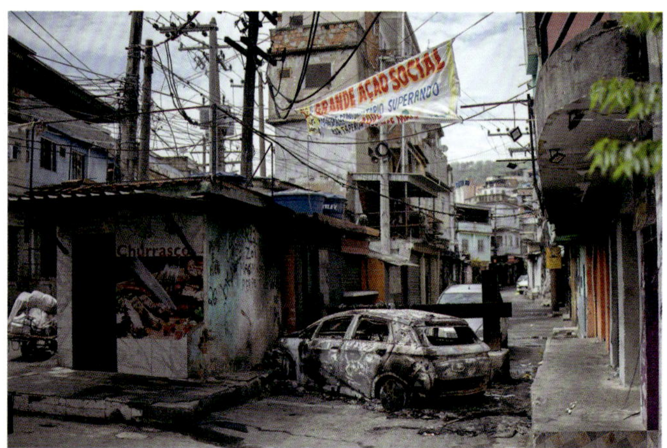

A vehicle burned by drug traffickers smolders at a barricade, hindering police access to the Penha complex. Setting vehicles ablaze is a common tactic to delay advancing law enforcement. 28 October 2025

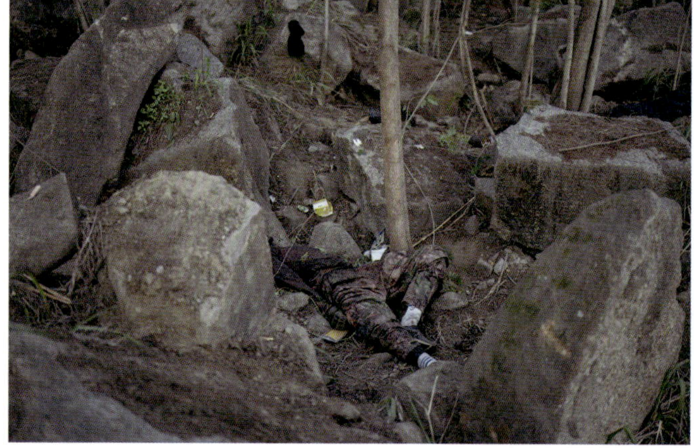

A body lies in the Vacaria forest between the Penha and Alemão favelas. Police ambushed fleeing individuals here, leaving victims overnight. 29 October 2025

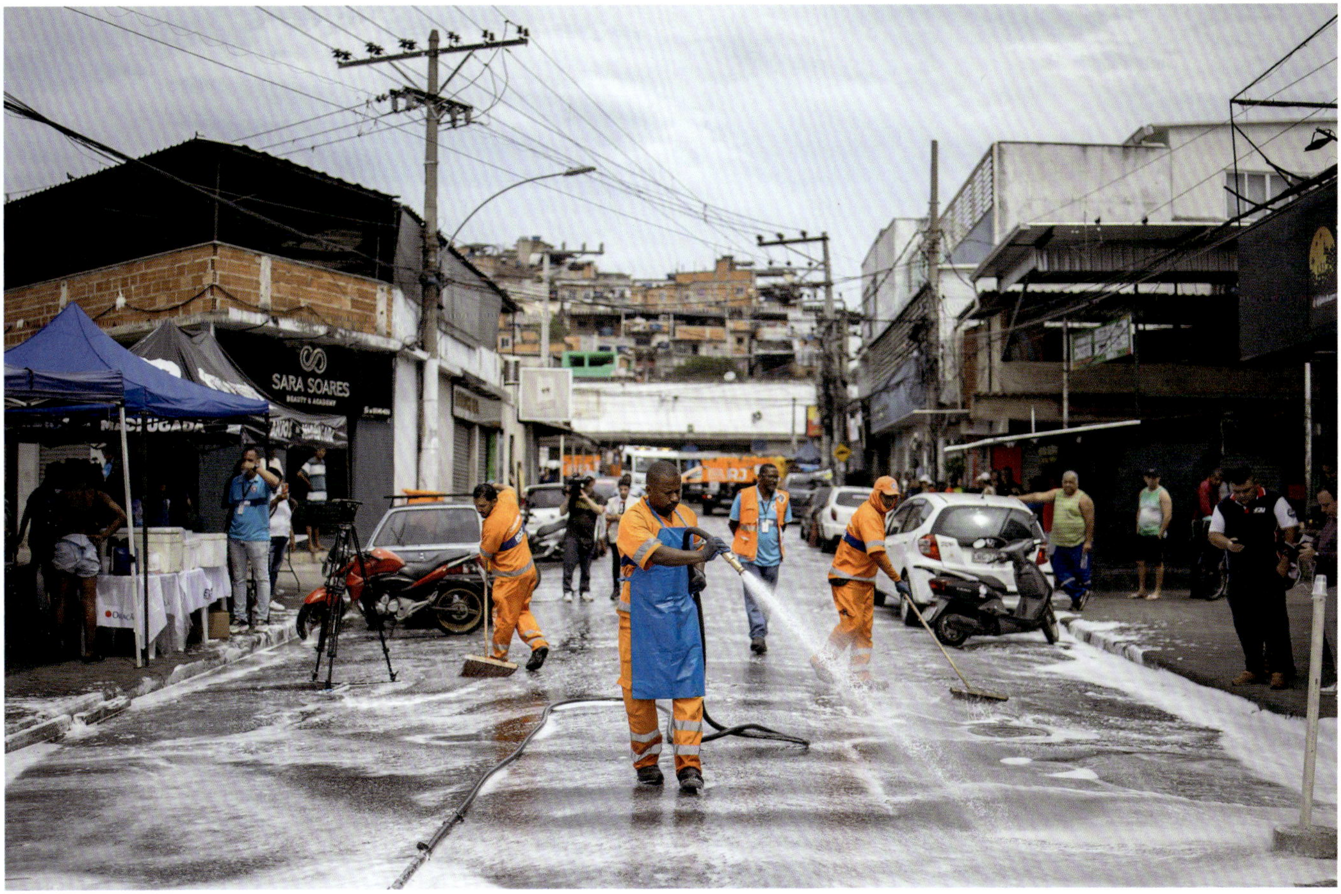

Municipal workers wash away blood in São Lucas Square. Despite the unprecedented death toll and failure to apprehend key gang leaders, the state government declared the operation a success. 29 October 2025

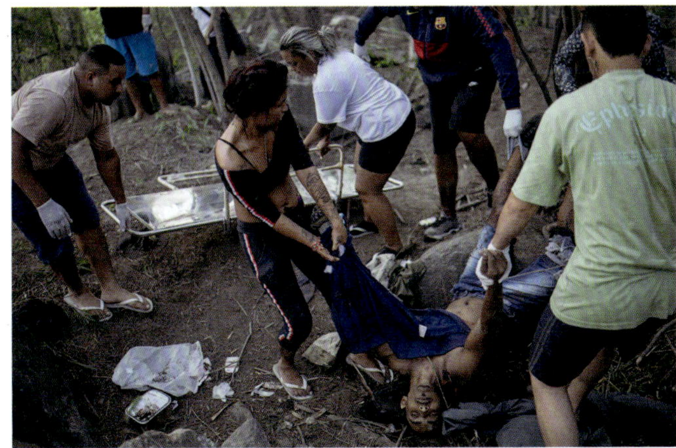

Residents carry a body out of the Vacaria forest. In the complete absence of state rescue or forensic teams, the community was forced to recover their own dead. 29 October 2025

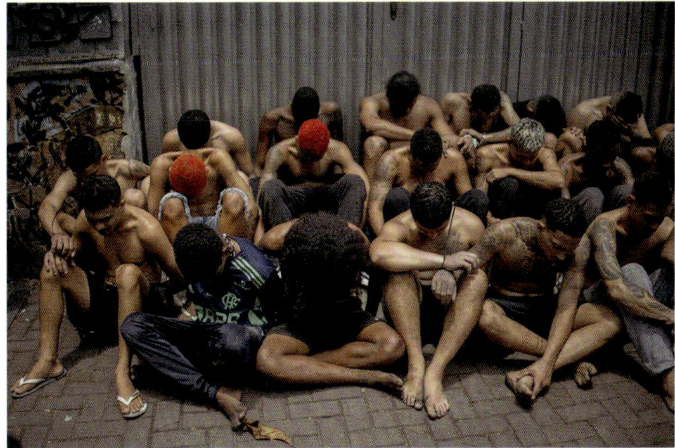

Suspects sit with their heads bowed to protect their identities. Authorities targeted over 50 individuals in the operation, but only a few of these were arrested and none were killed. 28 October 2025

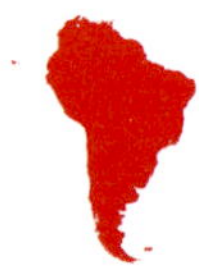

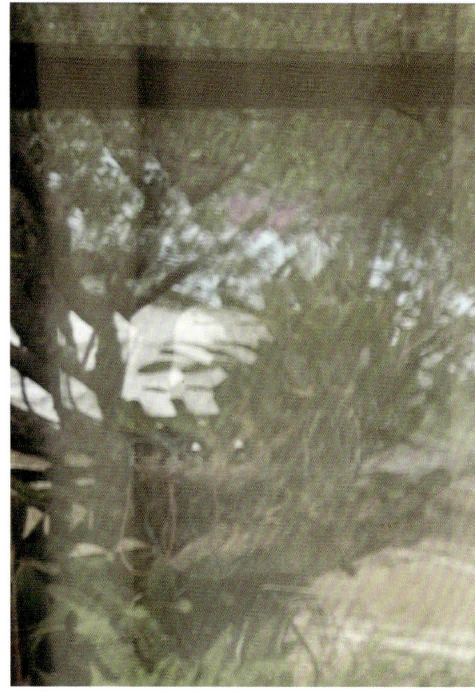

NAME THE ABSENCE

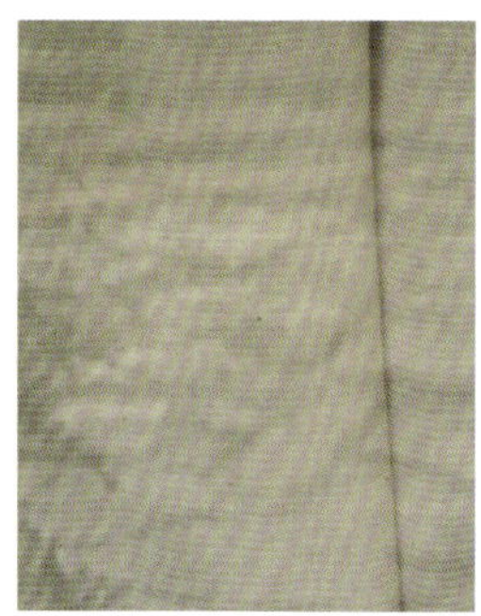

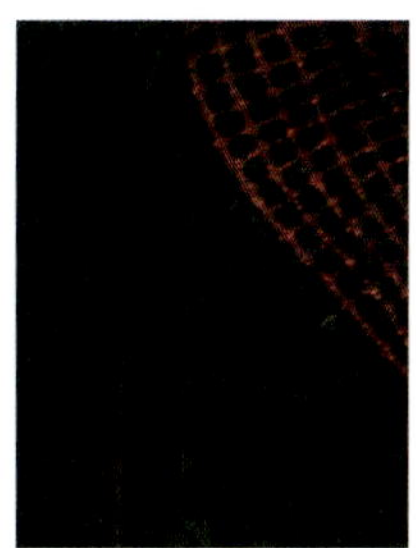

Colombia has the world's highest rate of single mothers. The photographer and his family experience this reality not as a statistic but as a "recurring wound." In 1999, Ferley Ospina's father was murdered in the border region of Norte de Santander, forcing him to flee with his mother. Photographing the women in his extended family, Ospina seeks to understand the "weight of absence" and the systemic and personal impact of "growing up incomplete."

FERLEY
A. OSPINA

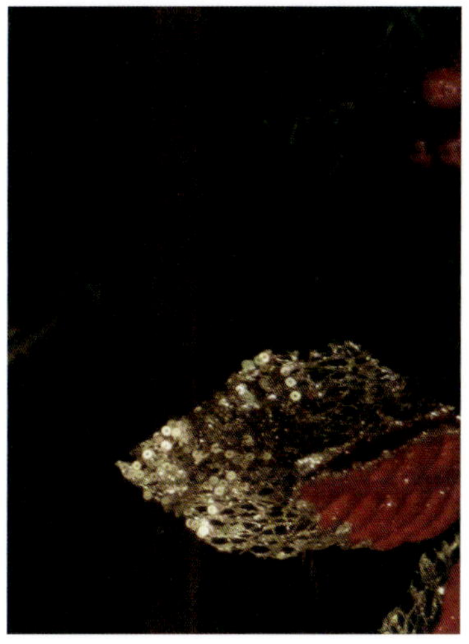

María (20), the photographer's cousin, watches television with her grandmother, Orfelina. In Ospina's family, there are 12 women, including mothers, sisters, and daughters, but only three adult men. 9 December 2025
All photos taken in Los Patios, Norte de Santander, Colombia / Ferley A. Ospina

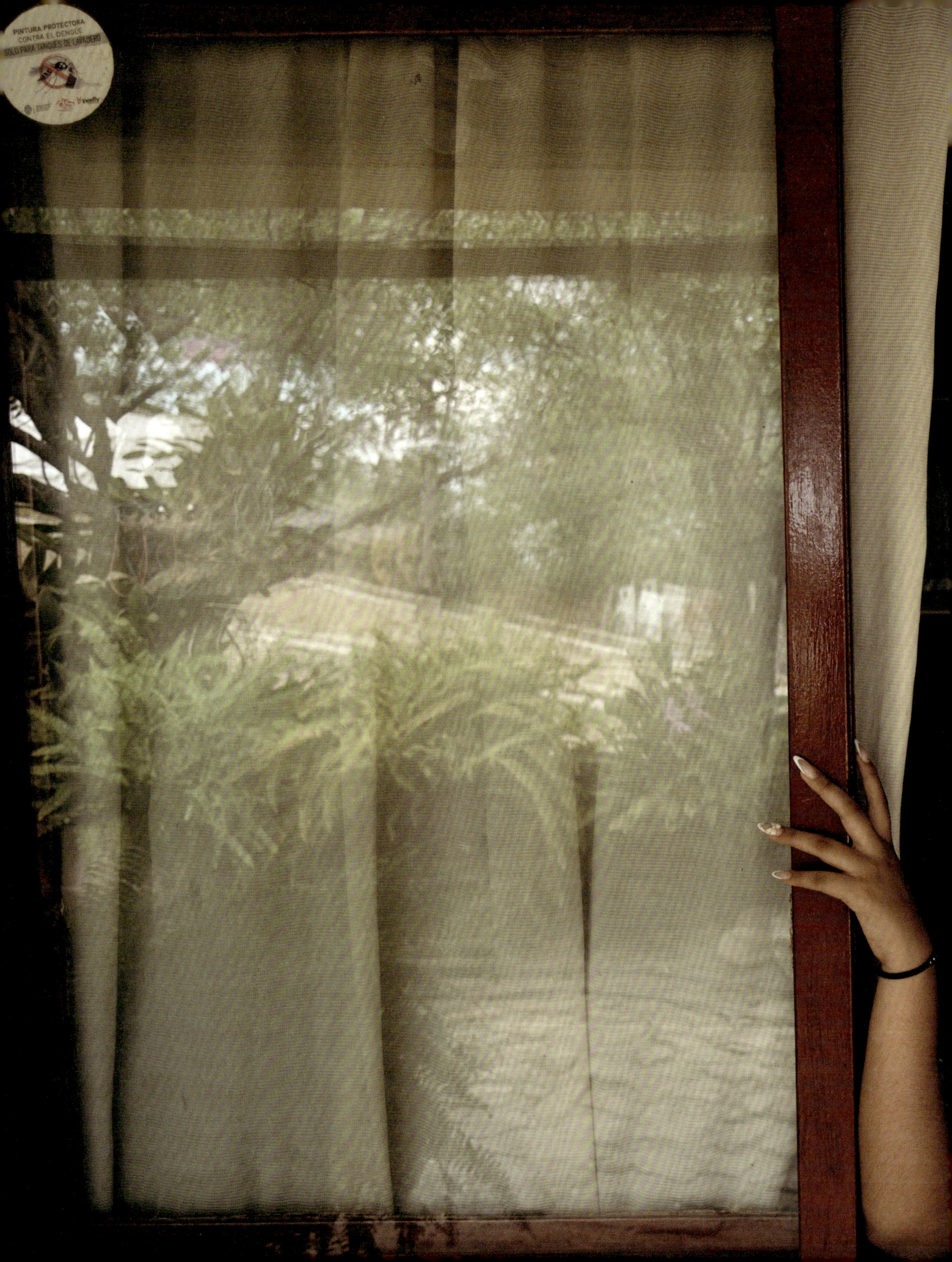

PINTURA PROTECTORA
CONTRA EL DENGUE
SÓLO PARA TANQUES DE LAVADERO
Firefly

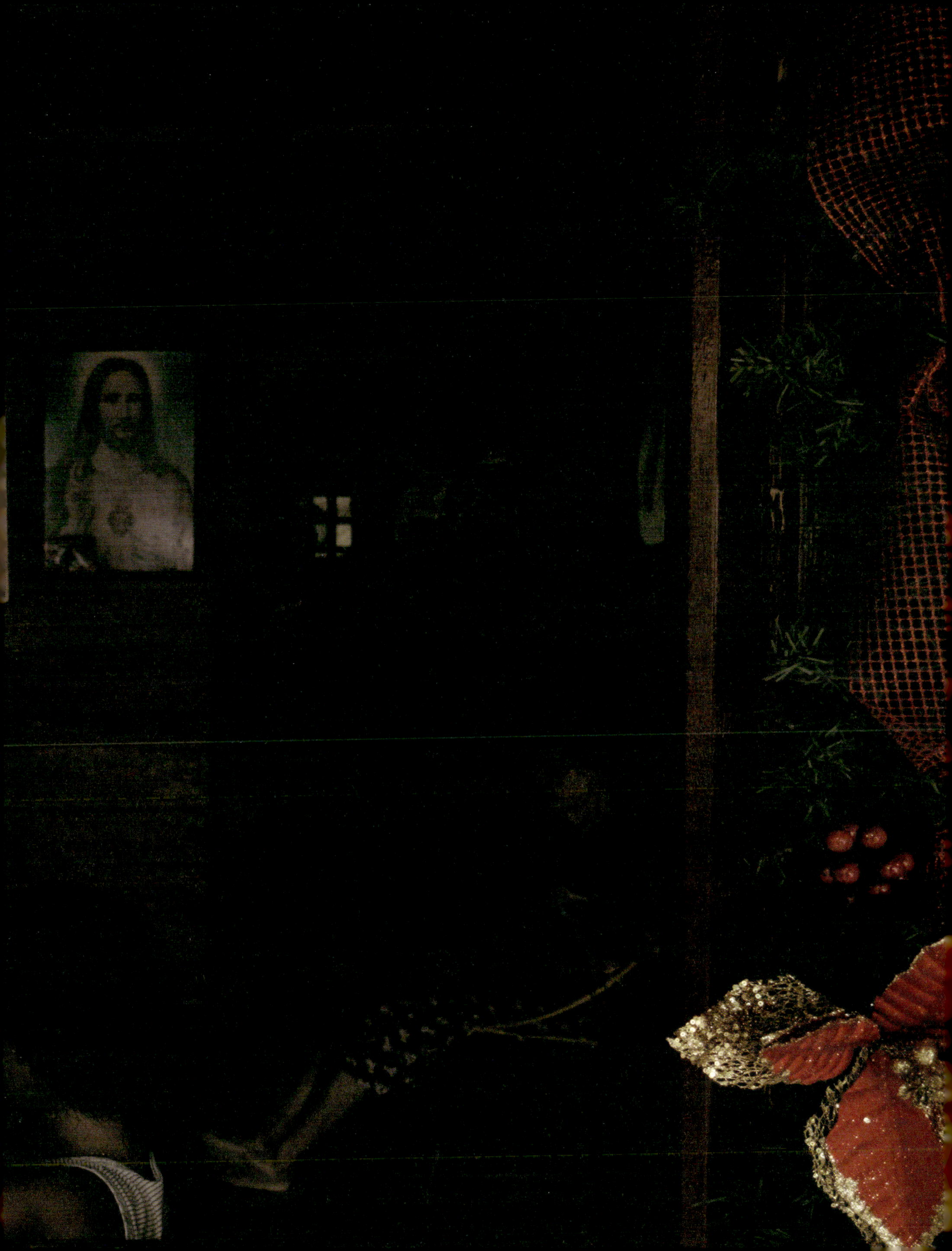

Emma (3) is the family's youngest member. Weeks after this photograph was taken,
her mother left the home to sue Emma's father for child support. 24 September 2025

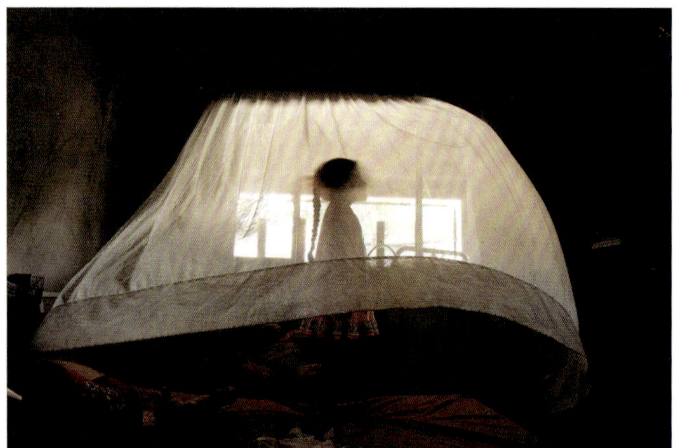

Valeria (5) plays behind a curtain at her aunt's house. She is raised solely
by her mother. In her region, 30% of households are headed exclusively
by women. 10 September 2025

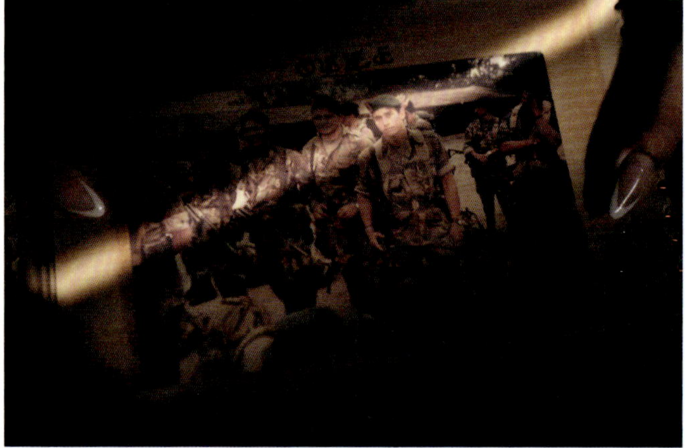

A photograph of the photographer's father, Ferley. He deserted the
Colombian army to raise his son but was murdered during the 1999
paramilitary massacres in Norte de Santander. 18 December 2025

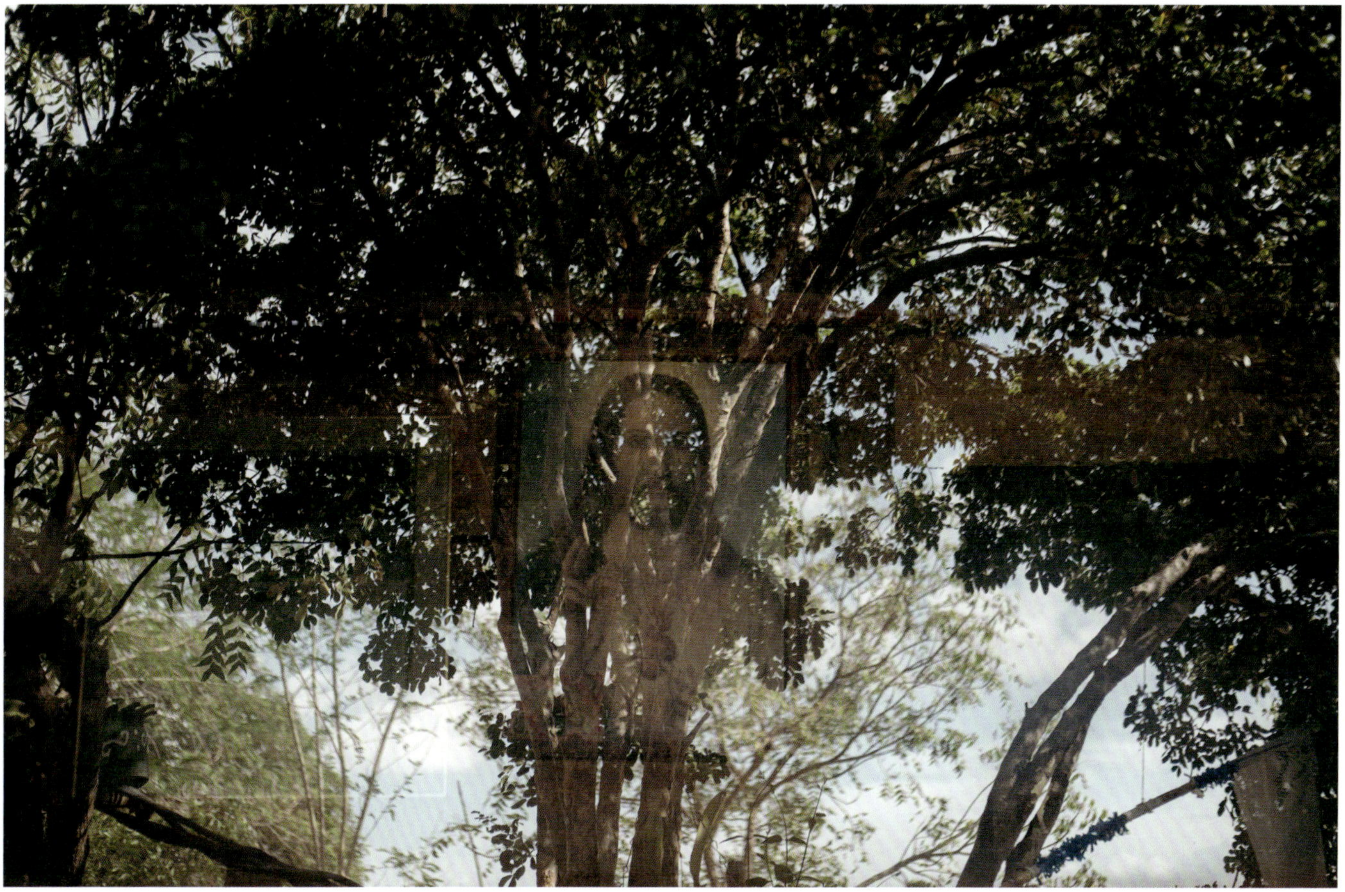

A painting of Jesus Christ is reflected by the window. Placed by the photographer's late grandfather,
it is the sole male presence remaining inside grandmother Orfelina's home. 5 November 2025

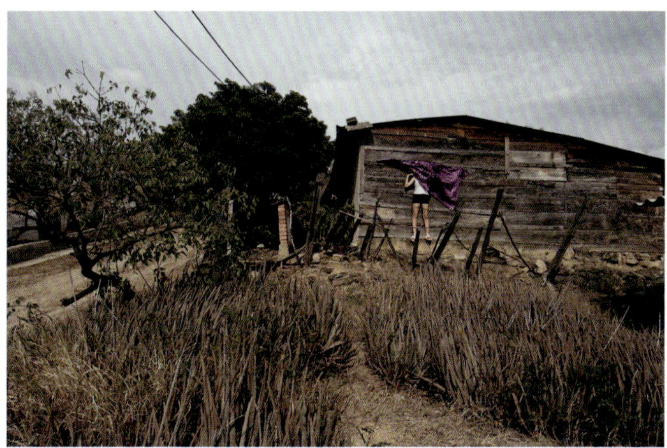

Gabriela (12) hides behind a cloth at her grandmother's house.
The house was built by her grandfather and uncle, who died in 2016
and 2023 respectively. 22 September 2025

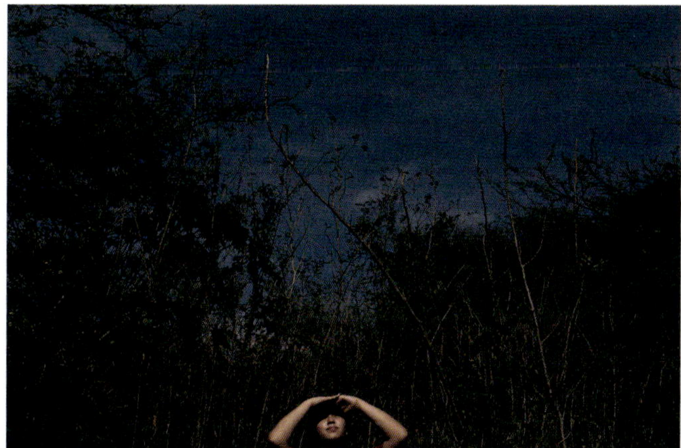

Nicole (17) was raised by her grandfather when her father abandoned her
family. In Colombia, extended families are pivotal in providing shelter and
support to unpartnered mothers. 15 October 2025

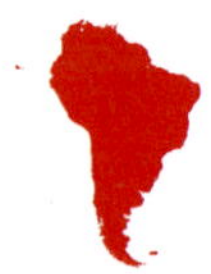

MANACILLOS: A RETURN TO LIFE

EVER ANDRÉS MERCADO PUENTES

Juntas is an Afro-descendant community deep in the Colombian Pacific rainforest, accessible only by a ten-hour boat journey up the Yurumanguí River. Settled by descendants of enslaved Africans brought to the region in the 1700s, the community faces threats from illegal mining, logging, and armed conflict. Fiesta de los Manacillos is a traditional ritual enacted by the community during Holy Week activities that blends Catholicism with African spiritual traditions. More than just a celebration, the festival is a homecoming for a diaspora, representing a profound affirmation of cultural resilience.

Guerilla, paramilitary, and drug cartel groups contest this region of the Yurumanguí River for control of illicit activities like coca cultivation and mining. Their clashes lead to the displacement of hundreds from the area. 28 March 2024
All photos taken in Juntas, Buenaventura, Colombia / Ever Andrés Mercado Puentes

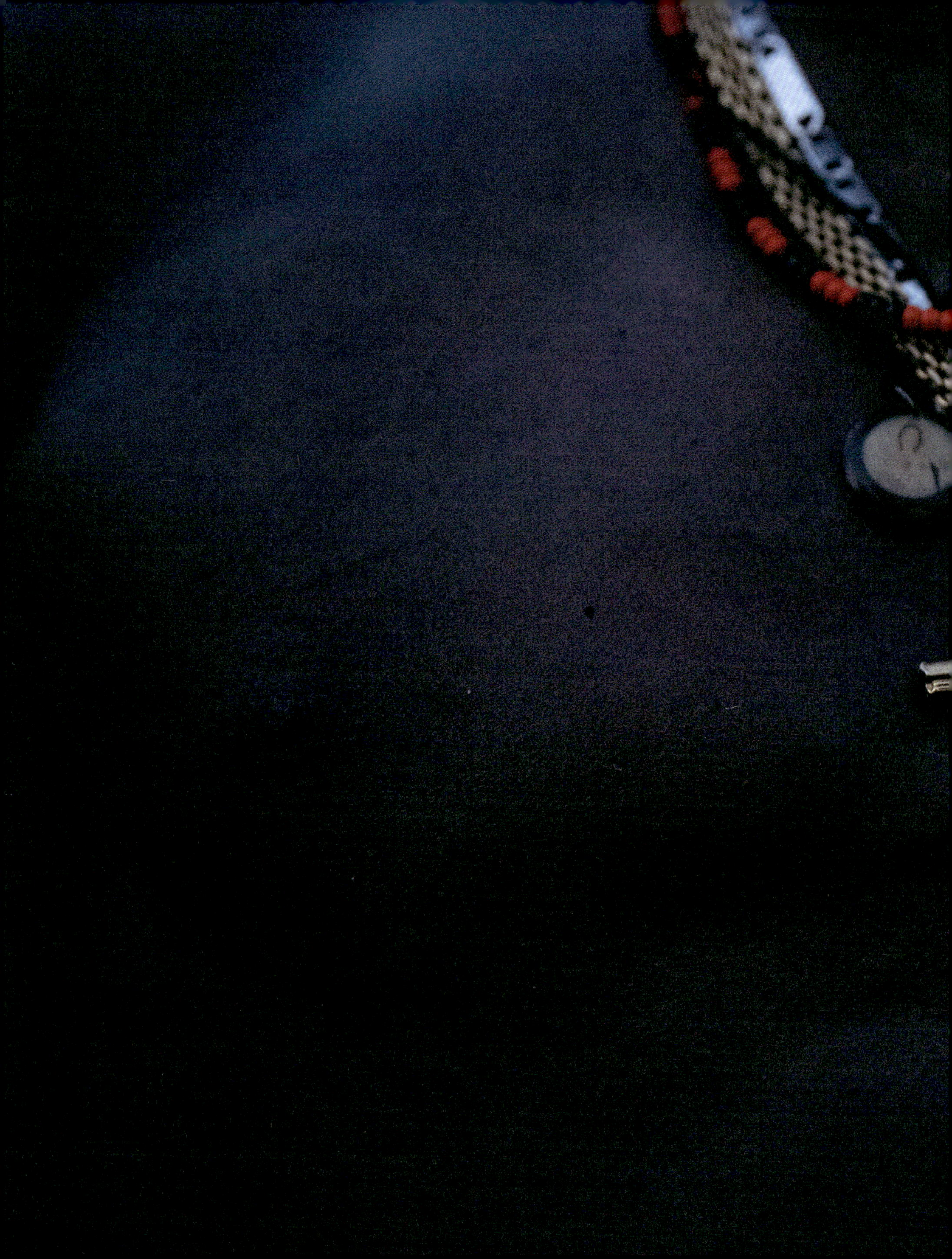

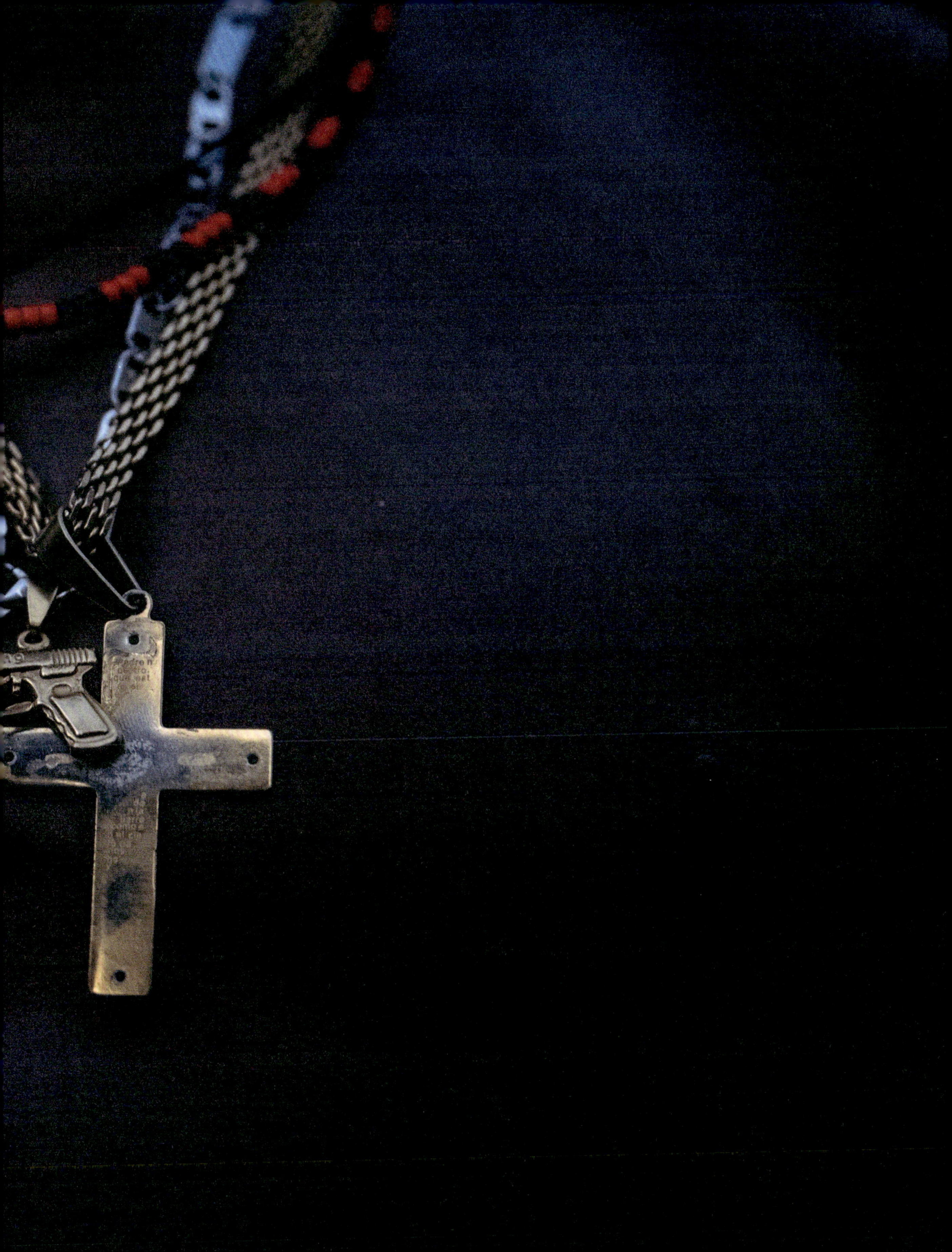

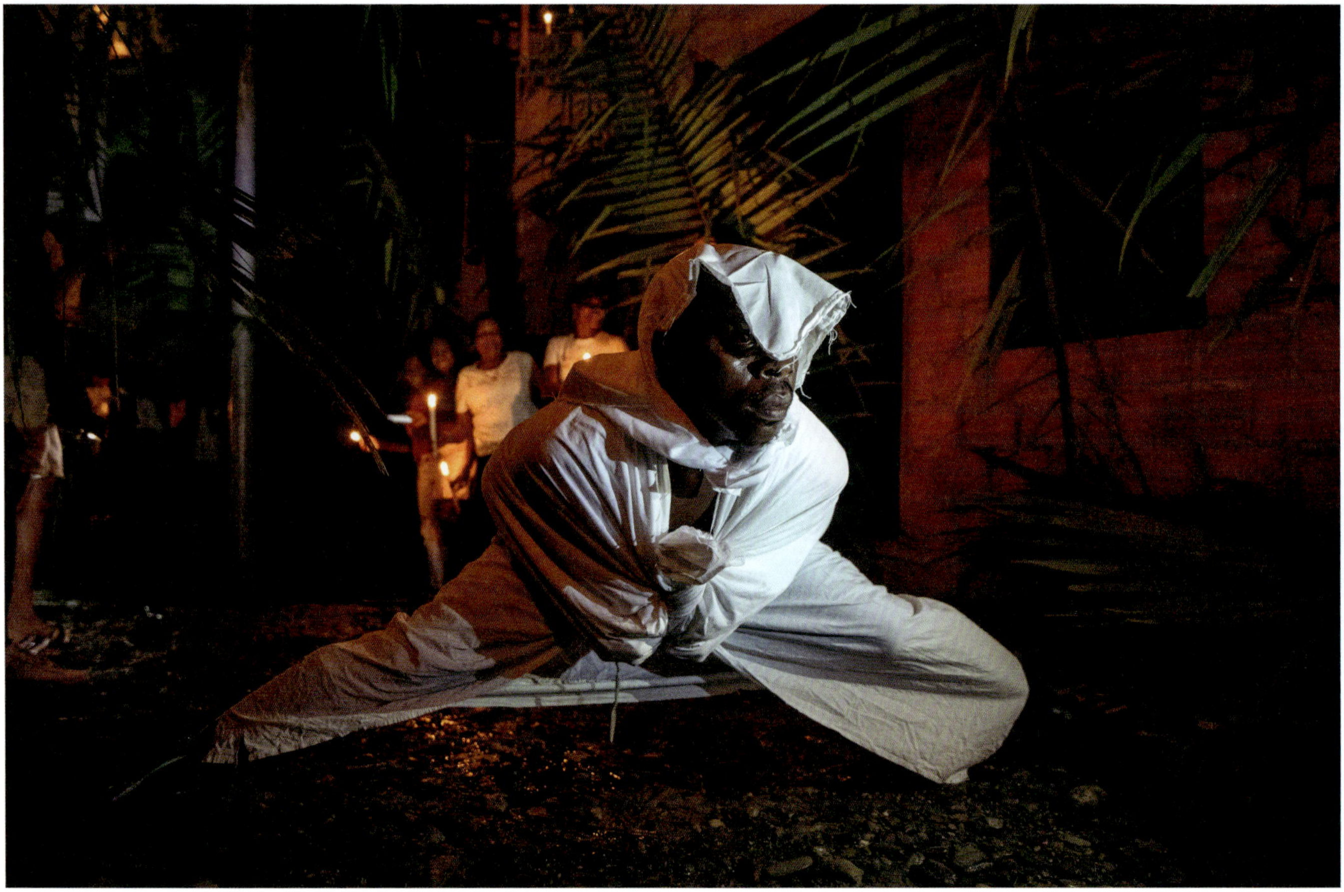

Luis Aramburo dresses in a white sheet to represent the *Ánimas Solas* (solitary souls). Trembling and whispering,
he descends to prepare the community for the arrival of the Manacillos. 18 April 2025

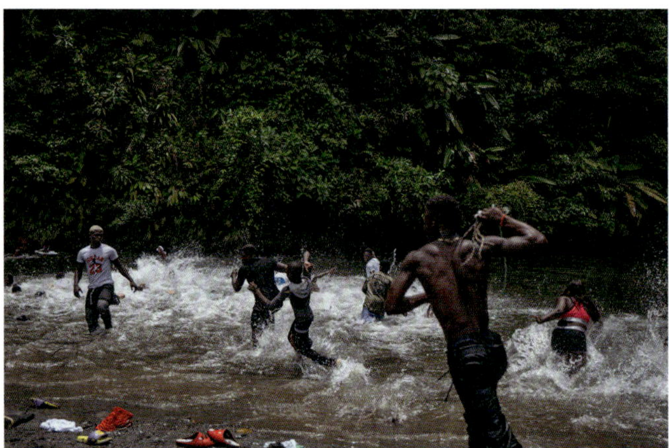

Participants in the Fiesta de los Manacillos engage in a ritual whipping
game. The act represents both the soldiers who crucified Jesus and the
enslavers who whipped the community's African ancestors. 31 March 2024

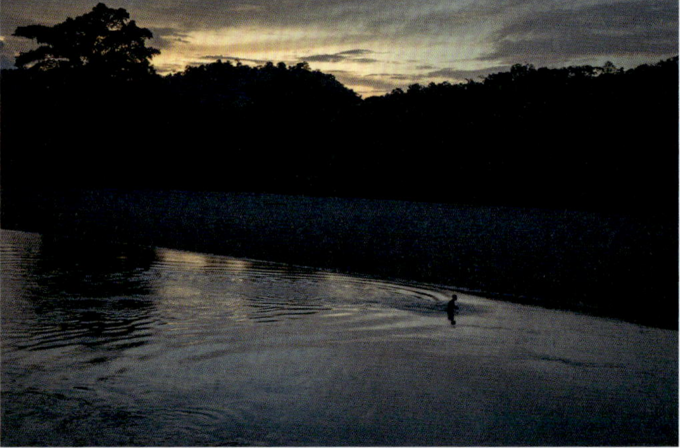

Participants return to their daily lives. For the Yurumanguí diaspora,
returning for Manacillos is a cultural and political act that reaffirms
their connection to their ancestral territory. 26 March 2024

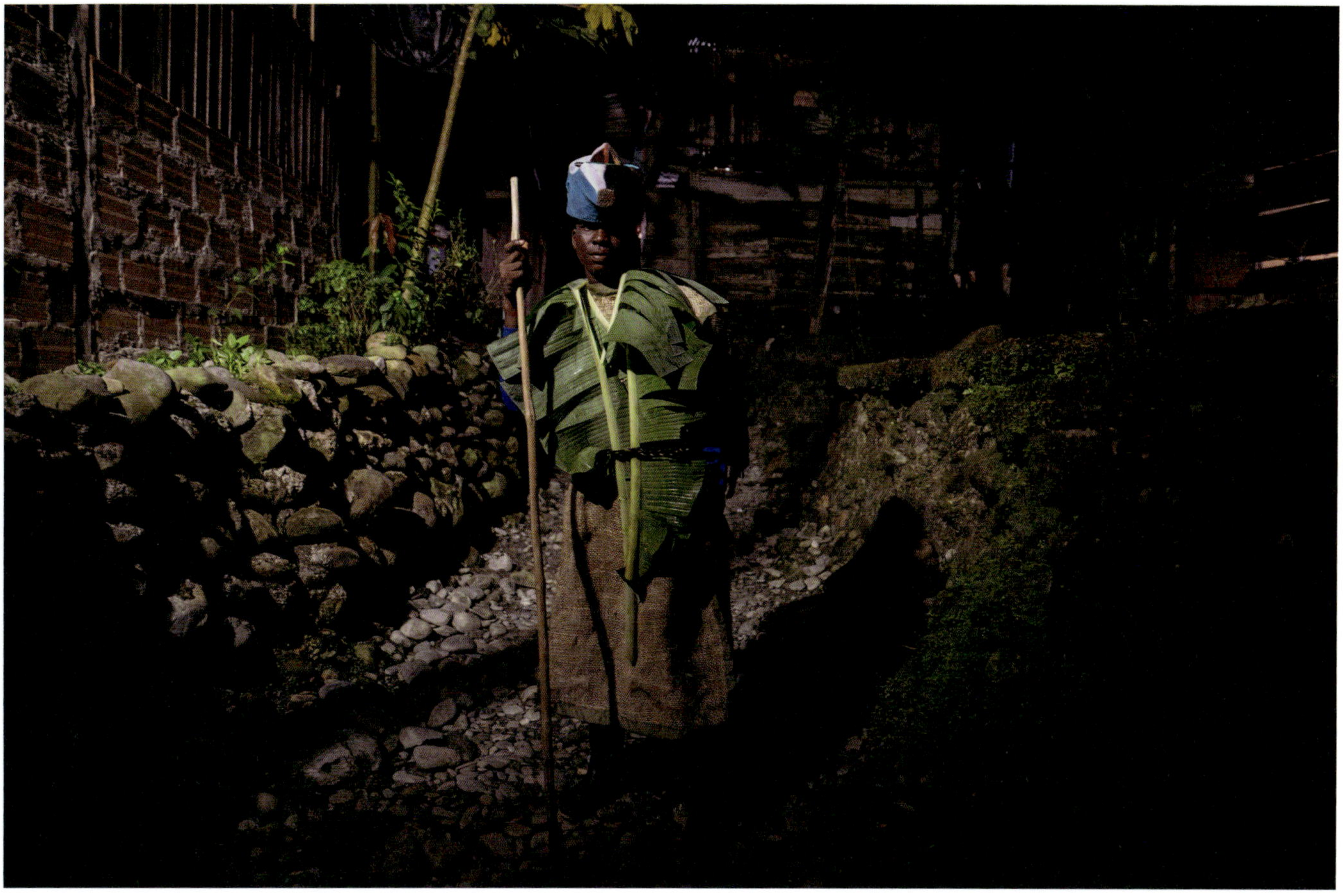

Eider Calimeño is one of 33 men who act as *Matachín*: those who commit to participating in the Manacillos.
This responsibility is inherited from close male relatives and honors deceased or displaced ancestors. 29 March 2024

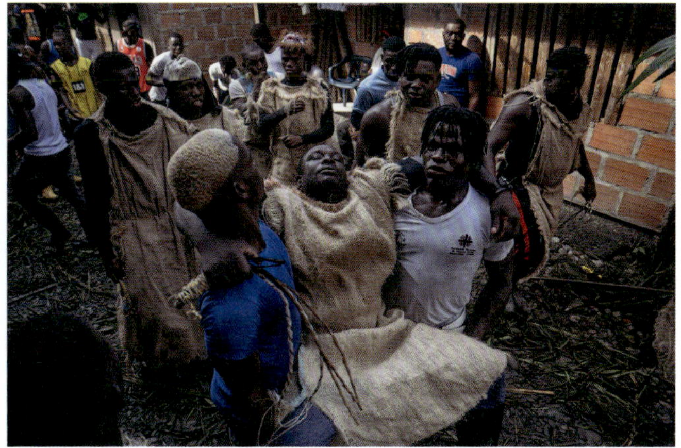

Two people carry an exhausted Manacillo. Tradition dictates that
Manacillos cannot sleep for the first 48 hours of the festival; those
who fall asleep are ritualistically whipped. 19 April 2025

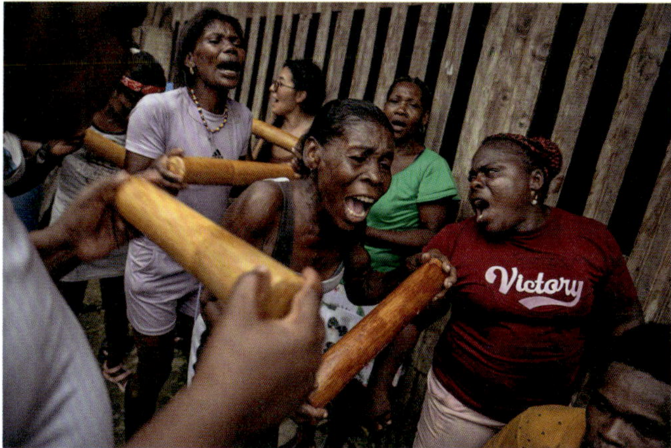

Mercedita and others sing traditional songs during a house-to-house tour.
Her singing plays an important ritual role, creating a mystical trance that
invokes ancestral presences. 30 March 2024

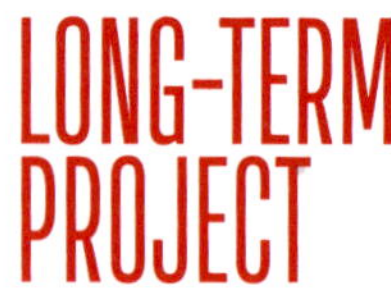

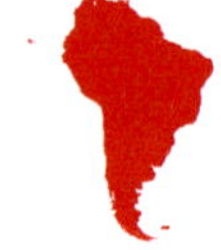

PABLO E.
PIOVANO

THE HUMAN COST OF AGROTOXINS

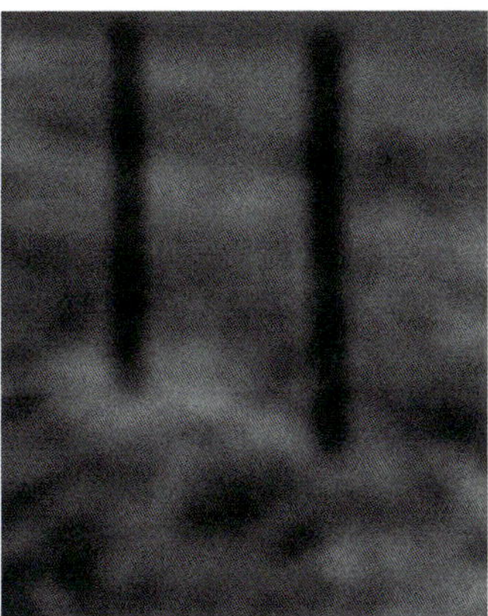

In 1996, Argentina approved genetically
modified, herbicide-resistant soybeans
paired with glyphosate-based herbicides,
a policy adopted without independent
research. In three decades, pesticide use
skyrocketed from 40 million to 580 million
liters annually. Today, 60% of Argentina's
cultivated land is sprayed, affecting 14 million
people. Despite independent studies linking
exposure to increased risks of cancer and
congenital malformations, regulations
continue to loosen even as agrochemical
usage moves closer to human settlements.
This project documents the human cost
of an economic model that prioritizes
agro-industrial profit over the lives of
its rural citizens.

Former land applicator Alfredo Cerán shows his burned fingernails. After years of mixing chemical products without adequate
protection, he developed non-alcoholic cirrhosis and underwent a liver transplant. Cordoba, Argentina, 23 September 2015
Pablo E. Piovano, Manuel Rivera-Ortiz Foundation, Philip Jones Griffiths Foundation, Lawen.doc

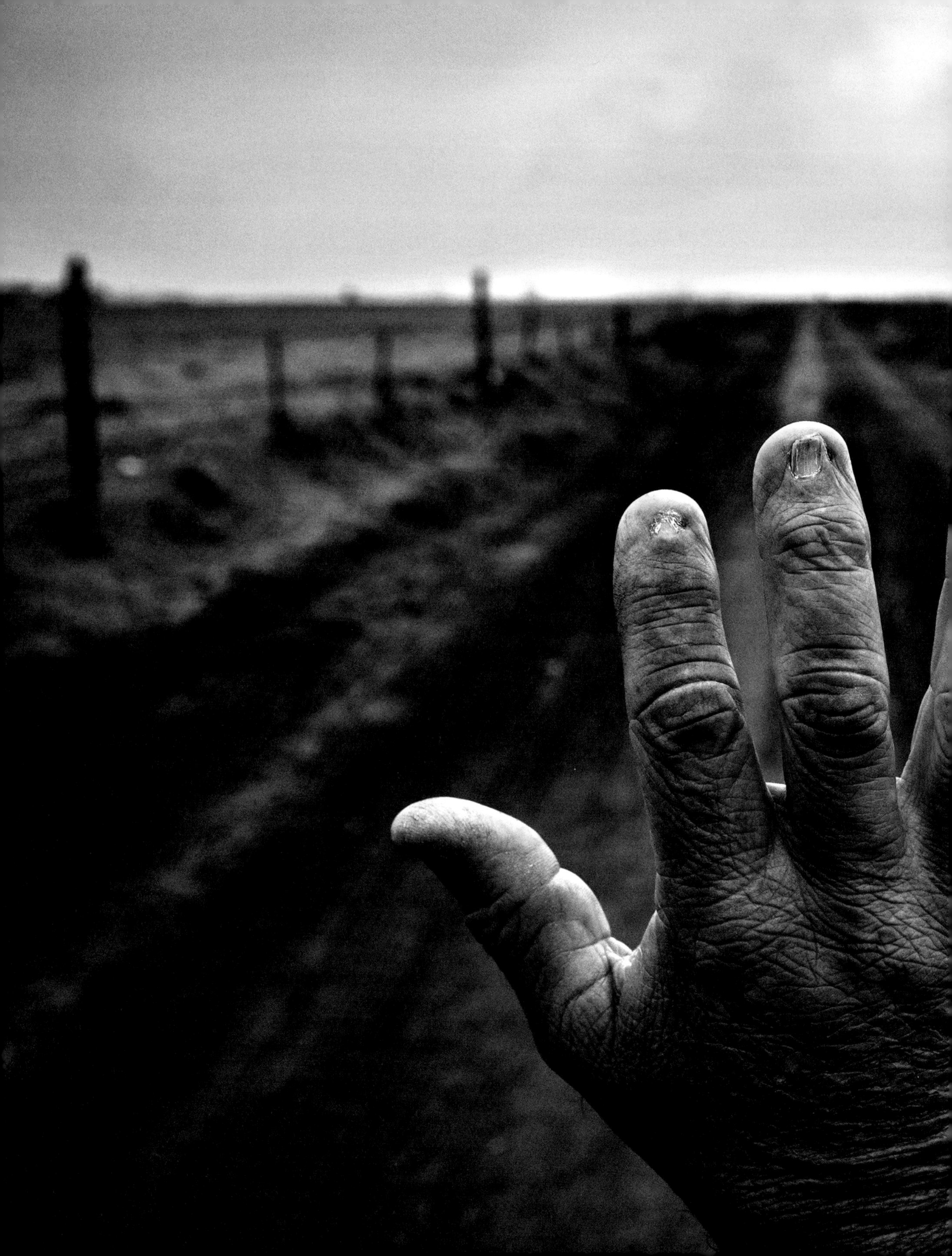

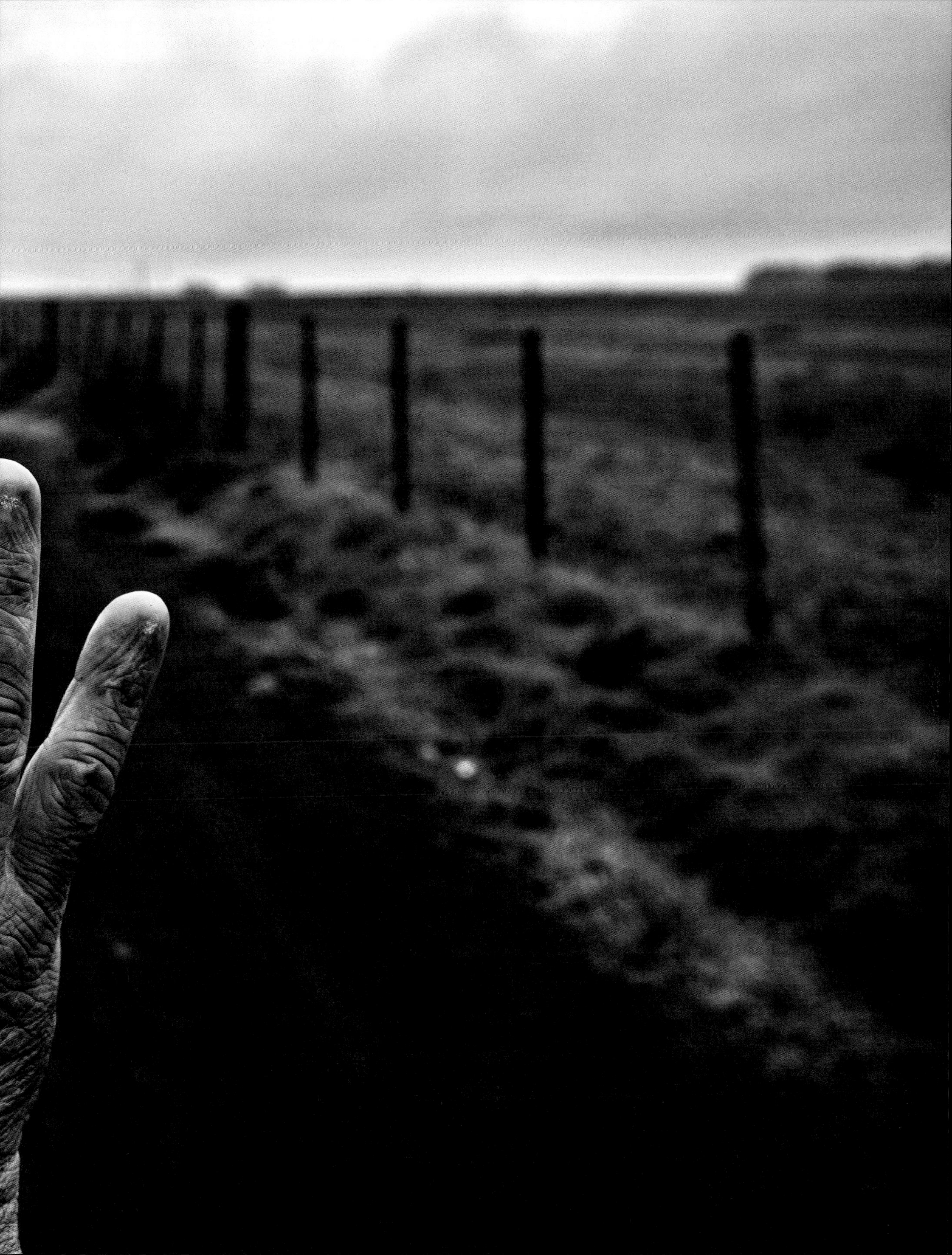

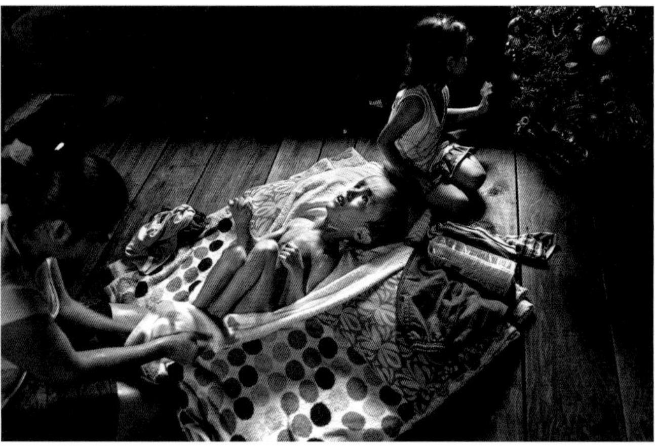

Cándida Rodríguez dries the feet of her son, Fabián Piris, who has hydrocephalus. Cándida handled agrochemicals on tobacco plantations during her pregnancy. Misiones, Argentina, 11 December 2014

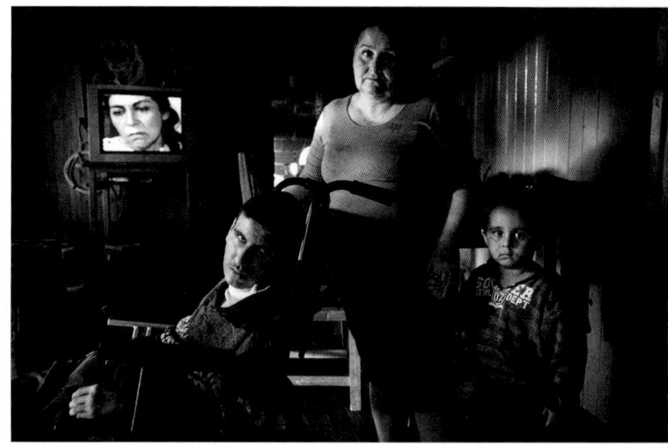

Leonardo Lorenzo, who has cerebral palsy, lives in San Vicente. In his neighborhood, disability rates are high among families living in proximity to intensive agricultural spraying zones. Misiones, Argentina, 6 April 2015

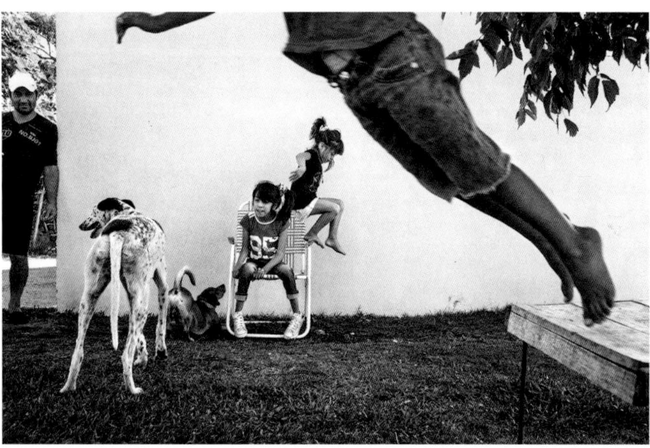

Maribella Alexandra Duarte (centre) was born with congenital malformations. Her family lives 30 meters from soybean fields. Entre Ríos, Argentina, 22 November 2014

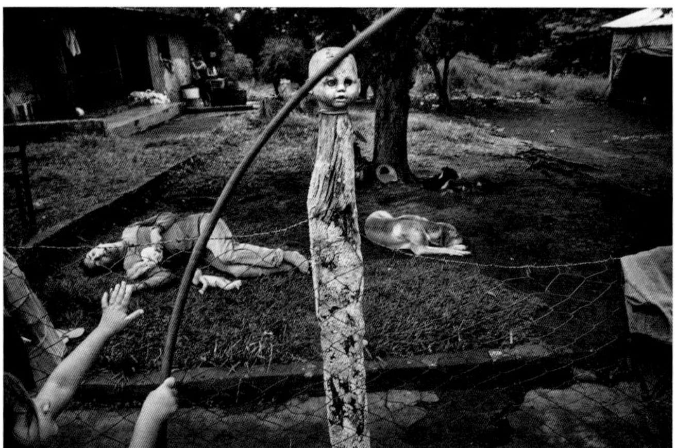

The youngest of the Gotin family (bottom left). Her sister suffers from motor dysfunction and kidney failure from inhaling methyl bromide, and her brother (left) lives with mental disability. Misiones, Argentina, 15 April 2015

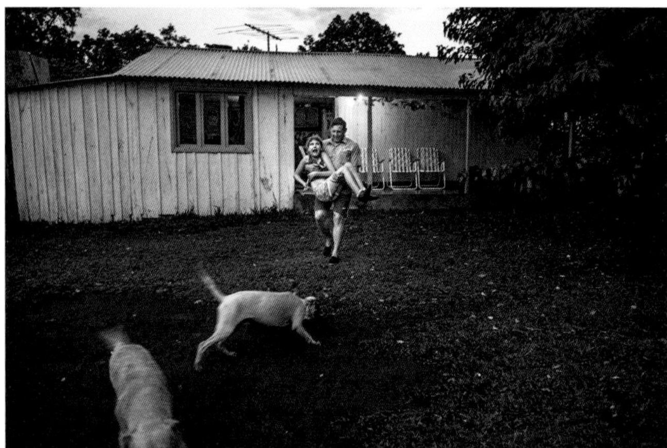

Talia Belén Soroco was born with congenital malformations and required heart surgery. Her parents, formerly tobacco workers who handled banned insecticides like Furadan, have since transitioned to sustainable, chemical-free horticulture. Misiones, Argentina, 8 December 2014

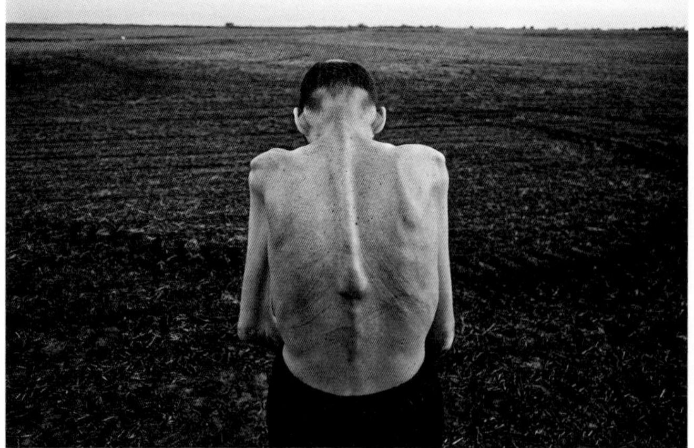

Fabián Tomasi, a former agrochemical worker, suffered from severe toxic polyneuropathy and became a global face of the fight against agrotoxins. He passed away in 2018. Entre Ríos, Argentina, 25 October 2016

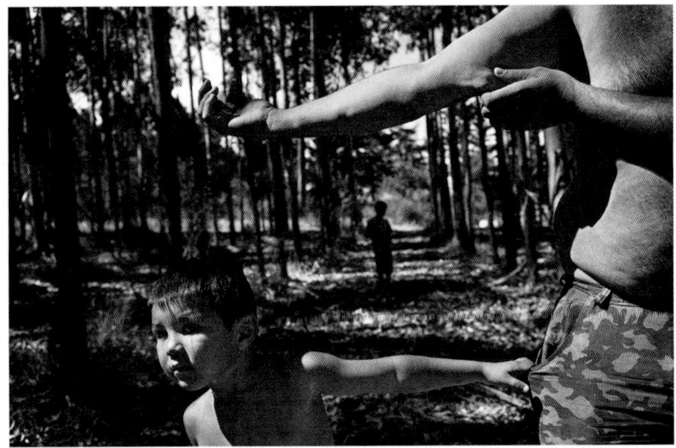

Mario Lovatto, a former citrus worker, suffers from multiple lipomatosis with roughly 100 tumors. His children also face severe health issues. Entre Ríos, Argentina, 22 December 2016

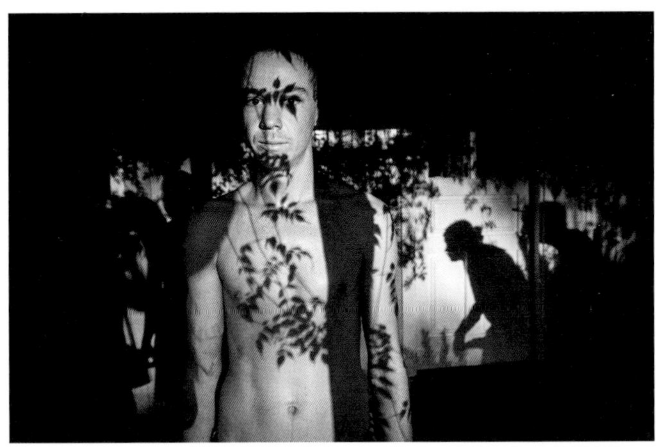

Marcos spent years awaiting a kidney transplant after developing leukemia at the age of 10. His mother was hospitalized for chemical poisoning during her pregnancy. Misiones, Argentina, 6 December 2014

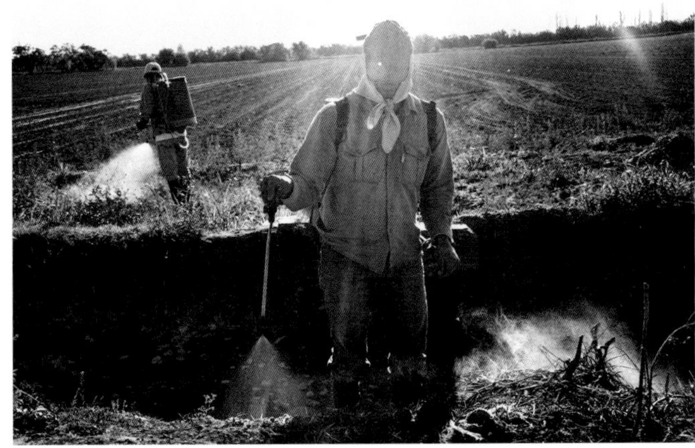

Agrochemical applicators work in Cordoba. A national agency identified 83 active pesticide ingredients on Argentine produce; 49% of these substances are classified as probable or possible carcinogenic agents. Cordoba, Argentina, 17 September 2015

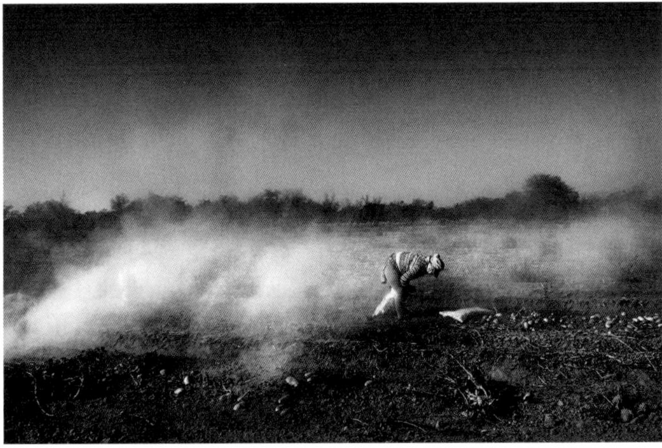

Workers harvest potatoes in Cordoba. Potato cultivation in Argentina is intensive, with official reports indicating that up to 40 different agrochemicals are applied. Cordoba, Argentina, 17 September 2015

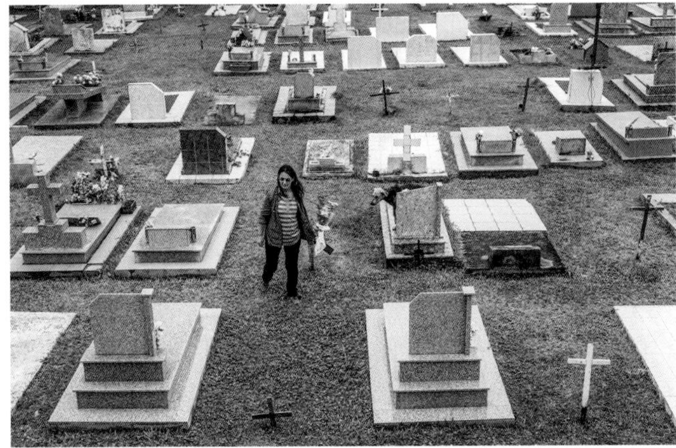

Mirta María Velzi visits the grave of her daughter, who died from a brain tumor at age 17. Her father worked for years on farms exposed to multiple chemical substances. Entre Ríos, Argentina, 21 November 2014

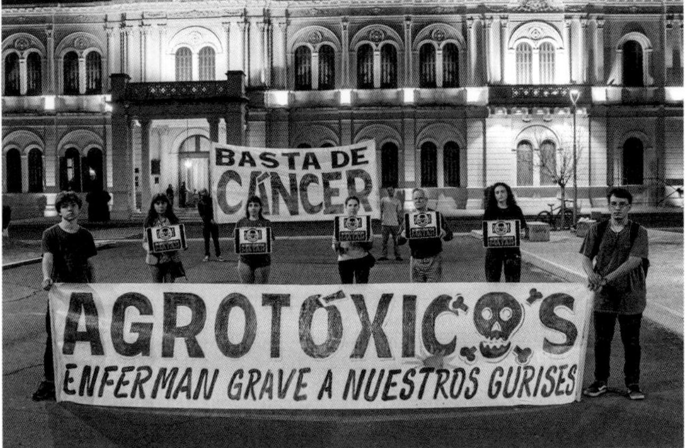

The coalition "Basta es Basta" (Enough is Enough) protests in Entre Ríos. In 2024, the province enacted laws allowing pesticide spraying as close as 10 meters from homes. Entre Ríos, Argentina, 30 September 2025

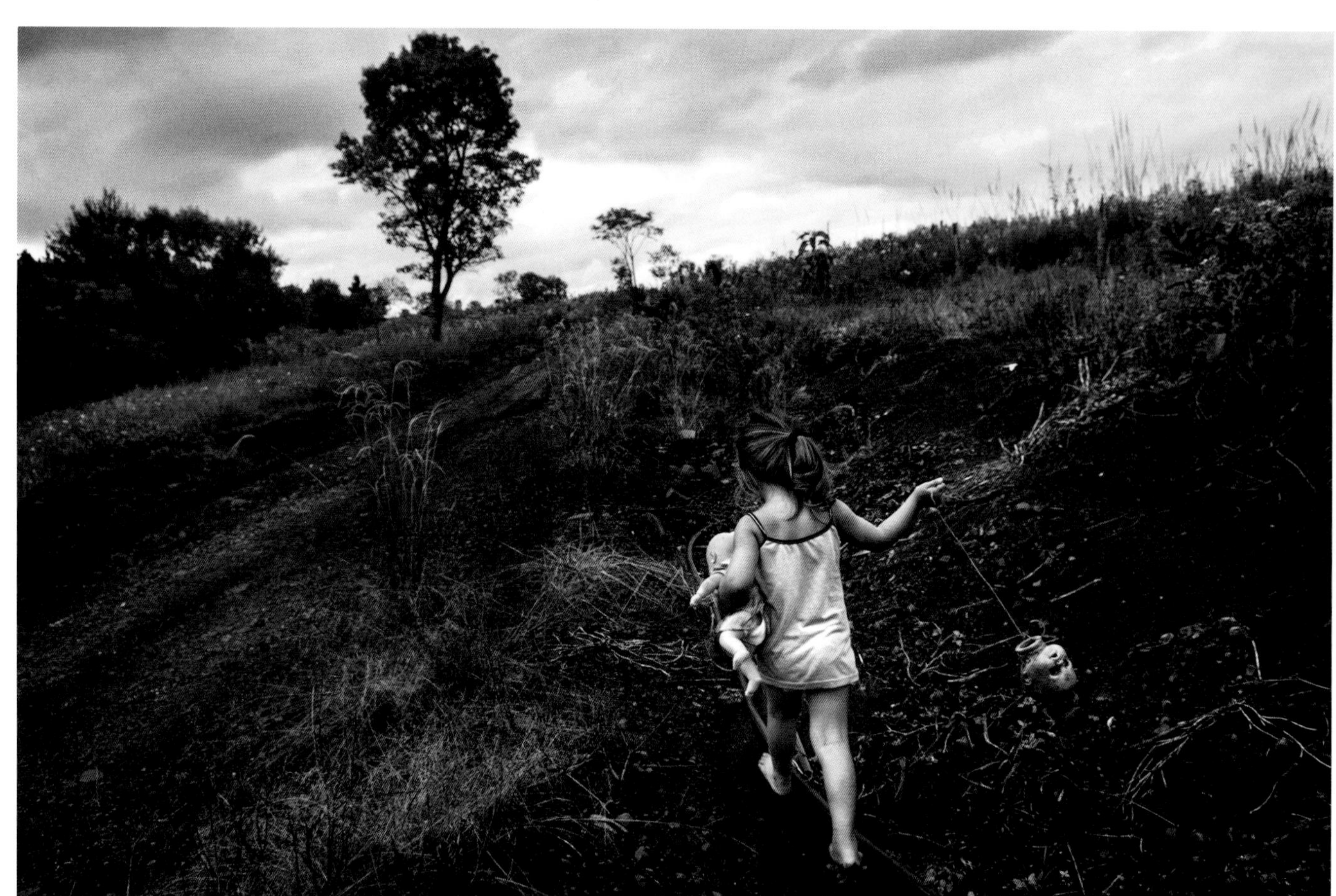

A girl runs through fields near the Brazilian border. Her siblings have disabilities and organ failure attributed to their father's 30-year career handling methyl bromide on tobacco plantations. Misiones, Argentina, 15 April 2015

—

IN THE AGE OF AI, WHY IS IT IMPORTANT TO HAVE A PERSON BEHIND THE CAMERA?

Unlike AI, photographers carry ethical responsibility for accuracy, context, and intent, grounding images in lived reality and preserving truth, credibility, and public trust beyond simulation, manipulation, or distortion.

—

Marie A. Monteleone,
North and Central America jury

At a time when truth feels fragile, having a professional behind the camera matters more than ever. Photojournalists bear witness at personal risk; AI cannot replace the human act of presence, judgment, and responsibility.

—

Kira Pollack,
Global jury chair

When a real person stands behind the camera, a photograph becomes testimony, not merely an image.

—

Yasuyoshi Chiba,
Asia-Pacific and Oceania jury

Honest storytelling requires a person witnessing events firsthand. In the age of AI, we must protect ethical photojournalistic values or risk losing photojournalism itself.

—

Sima Diab,
West, Central, and South Asia jury

A human behind the camera means responsibility for what is shown, how it is obtained, why it enters the public space, and the perspective that is shown. That accountability cannot be automated.

—

Gael Almeida,
South America jury

In an unregulated AI era, users need guarantees that images and stories come from ethical professionals. Crediting authorship reassures audiences, safeguards trust, and is vital for the credibility and survival of the media.

—

Silvia Omedes,
Europe jury

AI lacks human connection and risks turning people's lived experiences into mere simulations. Photojournalism is inherently informative and grounded in truth. The fabrication of images stands in direct opposition to those core principles.

—

Maheder Haileselassie,
Africa jury

WEST, CENTRAL, AND SOUTH ASIA

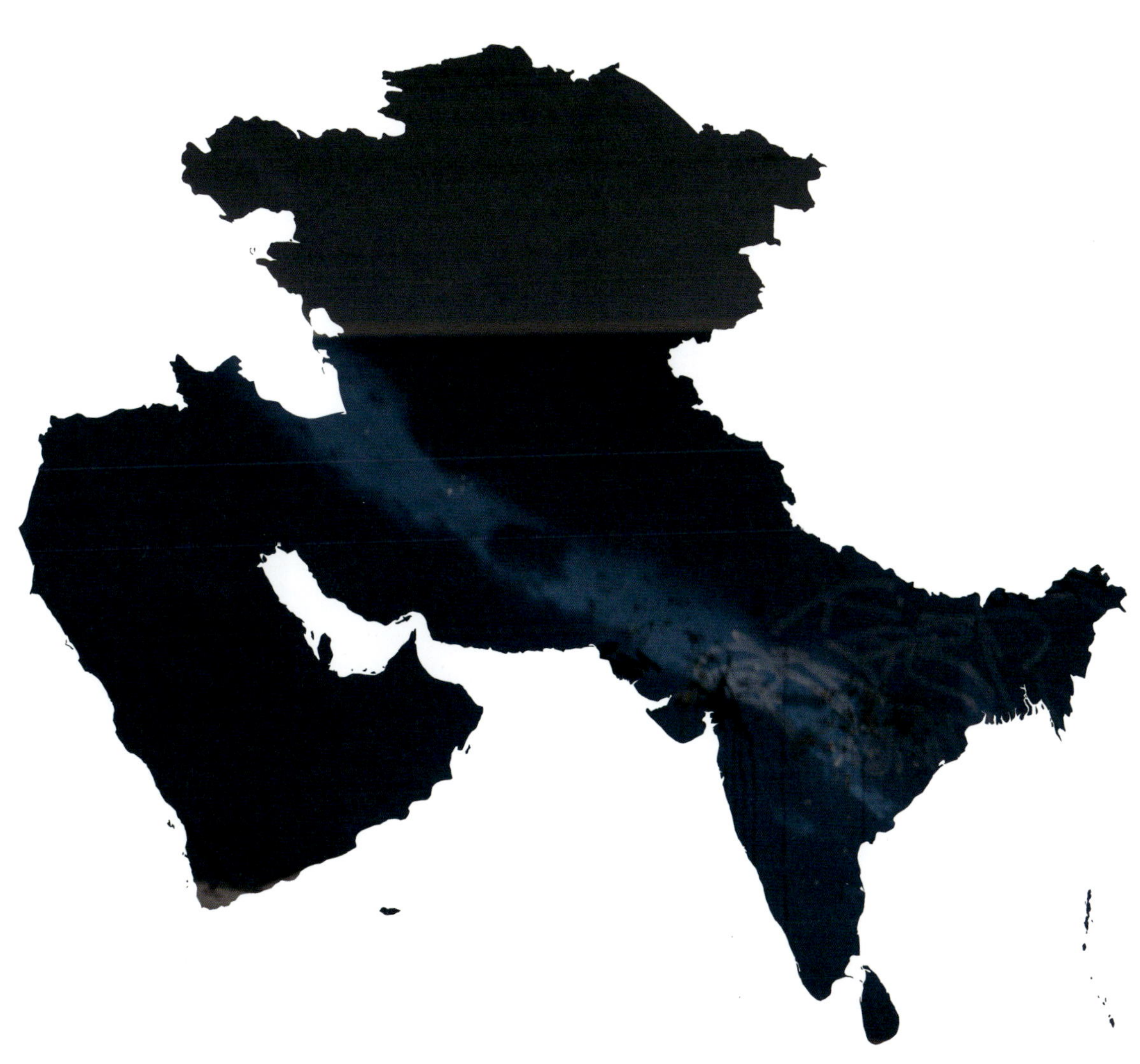

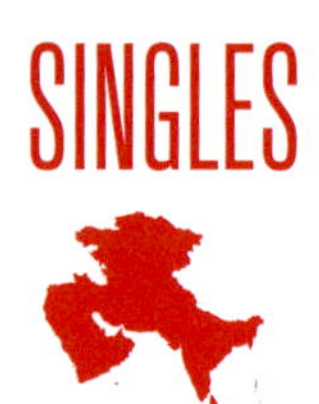

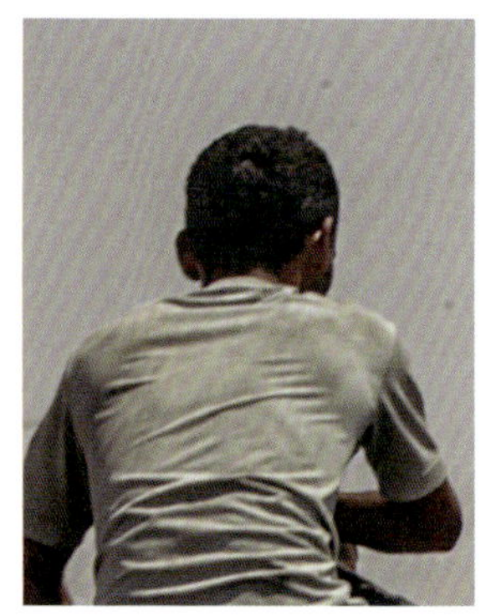

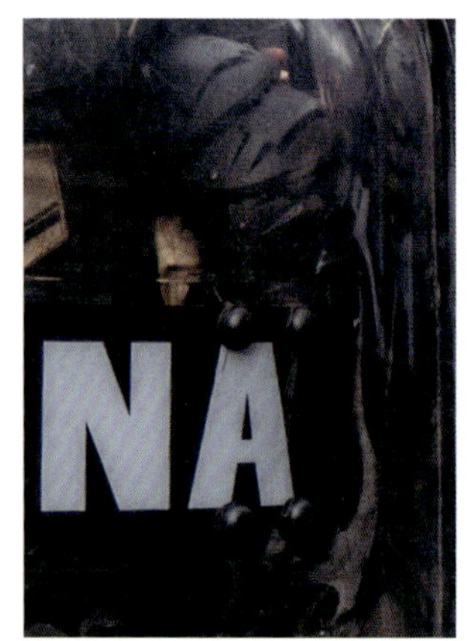

AID EMERGENCY
IN GAZA

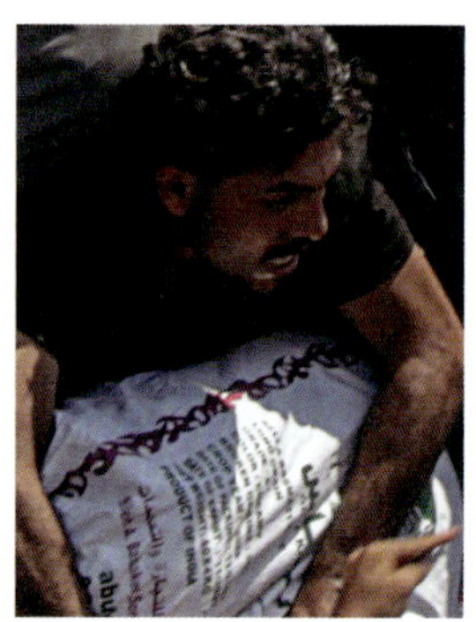

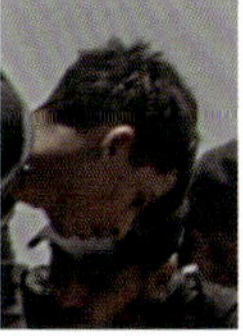

In 2025, famine took hold amid what
a UN Commission has concluded is a
genocide in Gaza, which Israel disputes.
Israeli authorities imposed a complete
aid blockade in March, a tactic described
by humanitarian organizations as the
weaponization of starvation. The UN
reports that between 27 May and 31 July
at least 1,373 Palestinians seeking food
were killed at or near aid distribution
sites. Despite a ceasefire agreement in
October, more than 75% of the population
still face hunger and malnutrition. The
photographer was born in Gaza and
has documented life there since 1997.

SABER NURALDIN

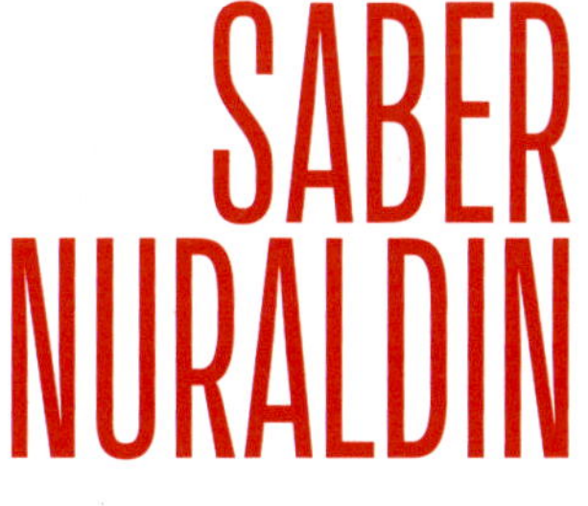

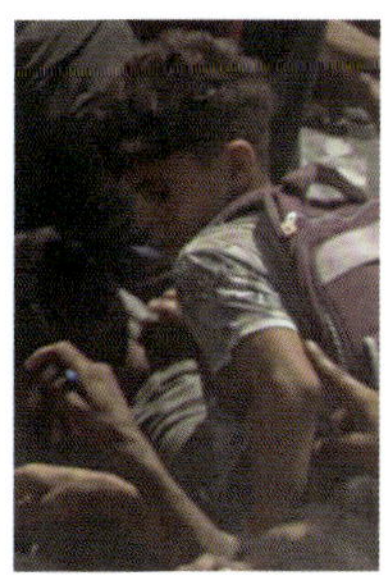

Palestinians climb onto an aid truck as it enters the Gaza Strip via the Zikim Crossing in an attempt to get flour, during what the Israeli
military called a "tactical suspension" in operations to allow humanitarian aid through. 27 July 2025 / Saber Nuraldin, EPA Images

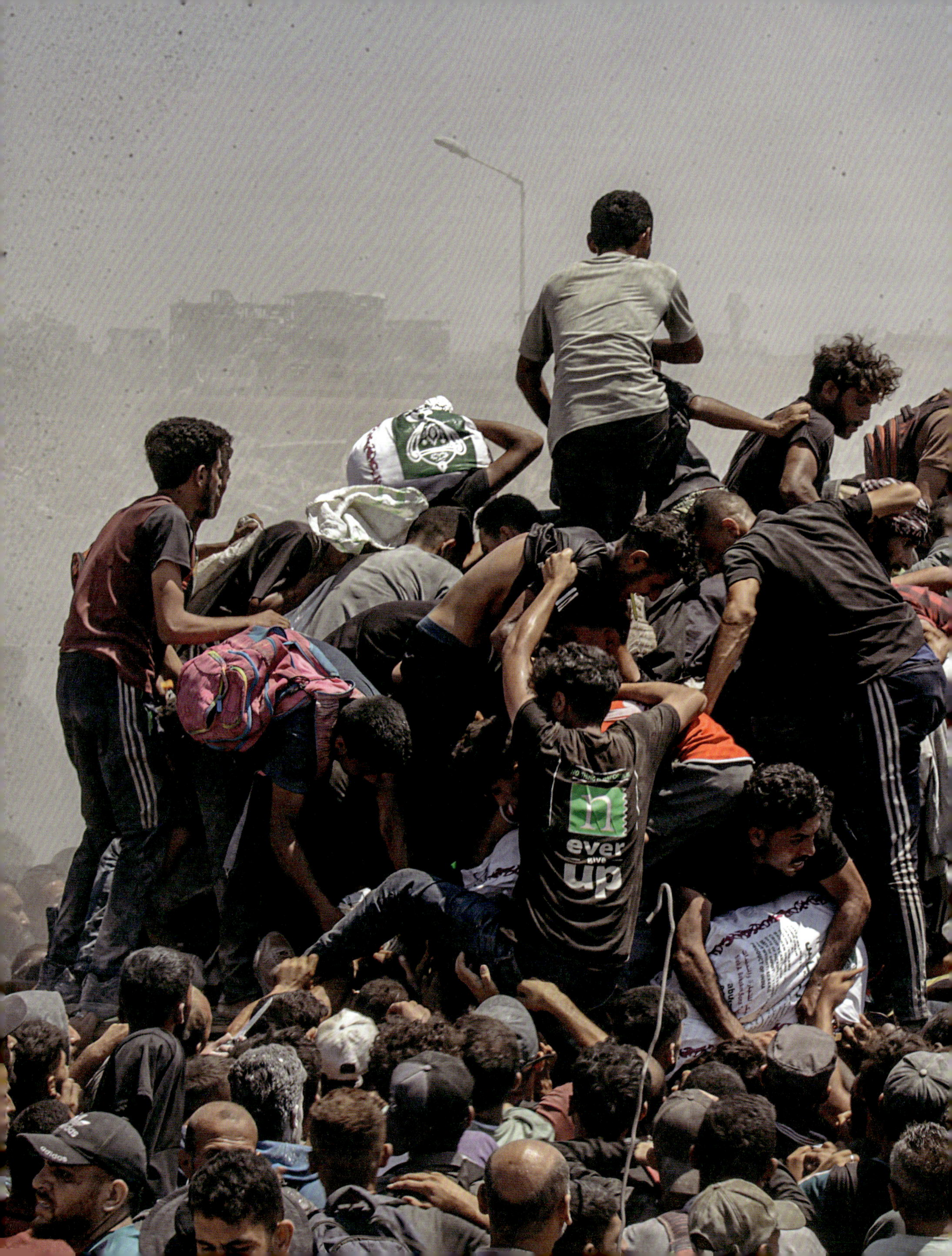

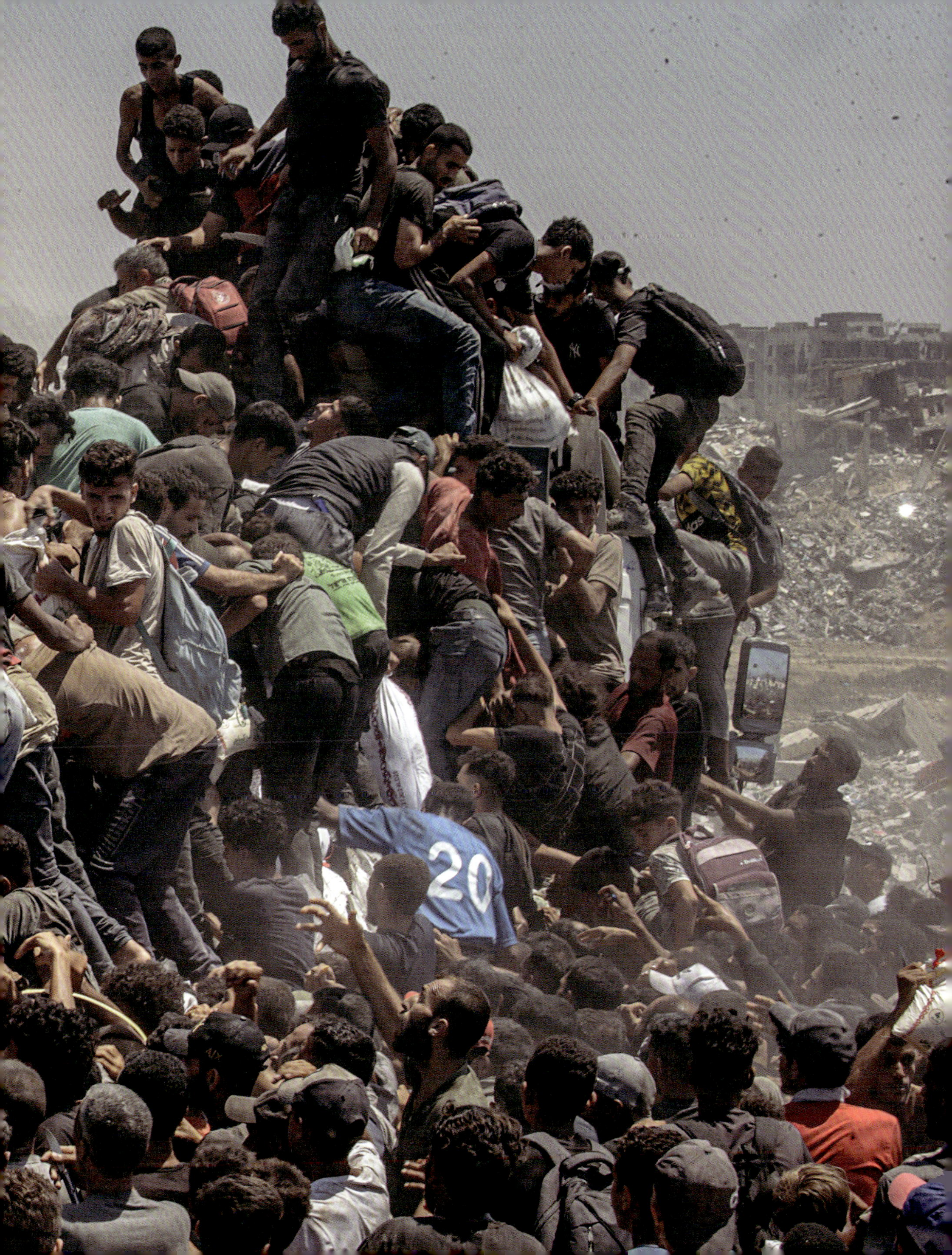

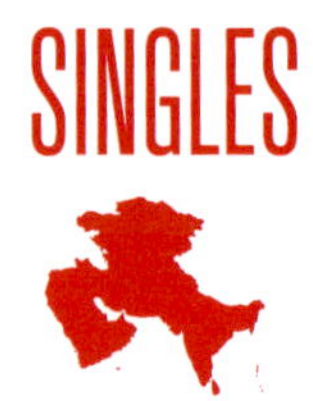

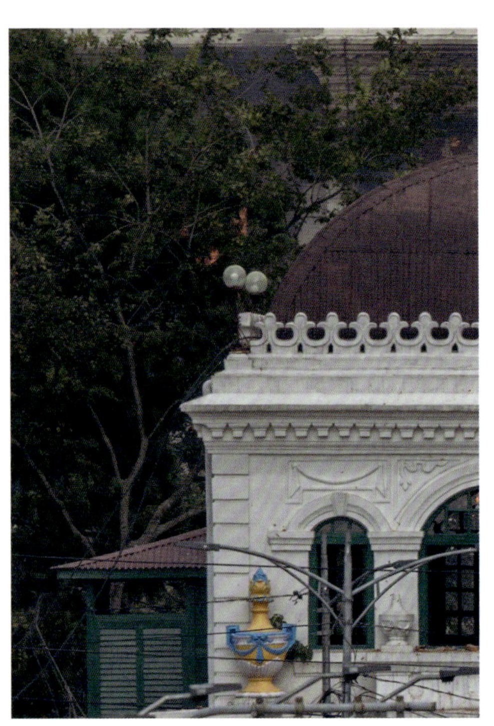

NEPAL'S GEN Z UPRISING

A government ban of 26 social media platforms on 4 September 2025 was the breaking point for Nepal's youth. On 8 September, thousands took to the streets, part of a generation of young people around the world refusing to accept systems that perpetuate corruption, unemployment, and economic hardship. Within two days, 76 people were dead, most of them young demonstrators killed by police. Thousands more were injured. On 9 September, following Prime Minister KP Sharma Oli's resignation, protesters stormed and set fire to Singha Durbar, the historic complex at the heart of Nepal's government.

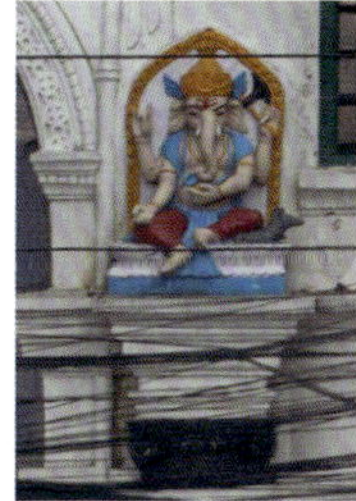

NARENDRA SHRESTHA

Fire and smoke engulf Singha Durbar after protesters stormed and set the government complex alight during violent demonstrations. Kathmandu, Nepal, 9 September 2025 / Narendra Shrestha, EPA Images

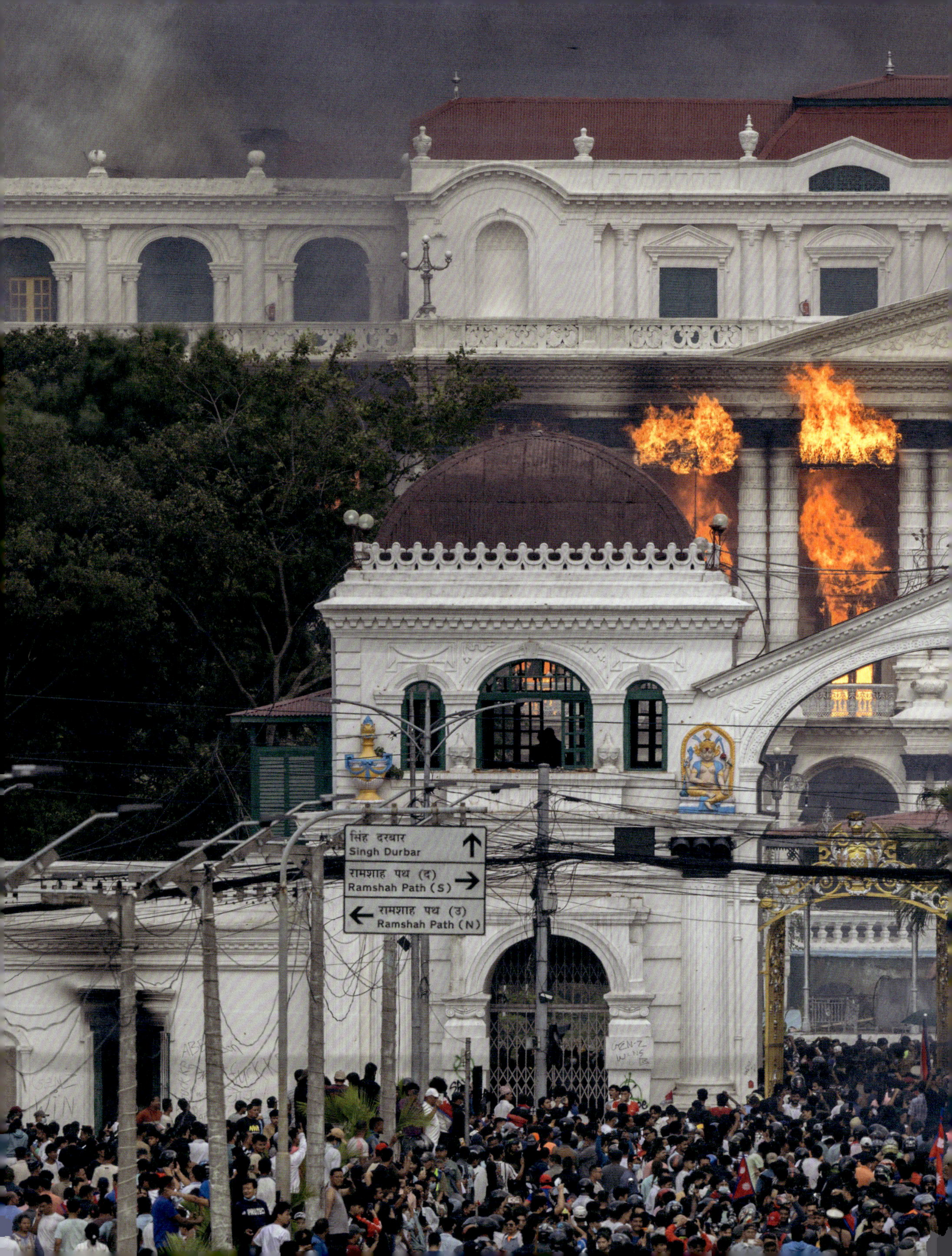
सिंह दरबार
Singh Durbar
रामशाह पथ (द)
Ramshah Path (S)
रामशाह पथ (उ)
Ramshah Path (N)
GEN-Z
WINS
GEN
WIN

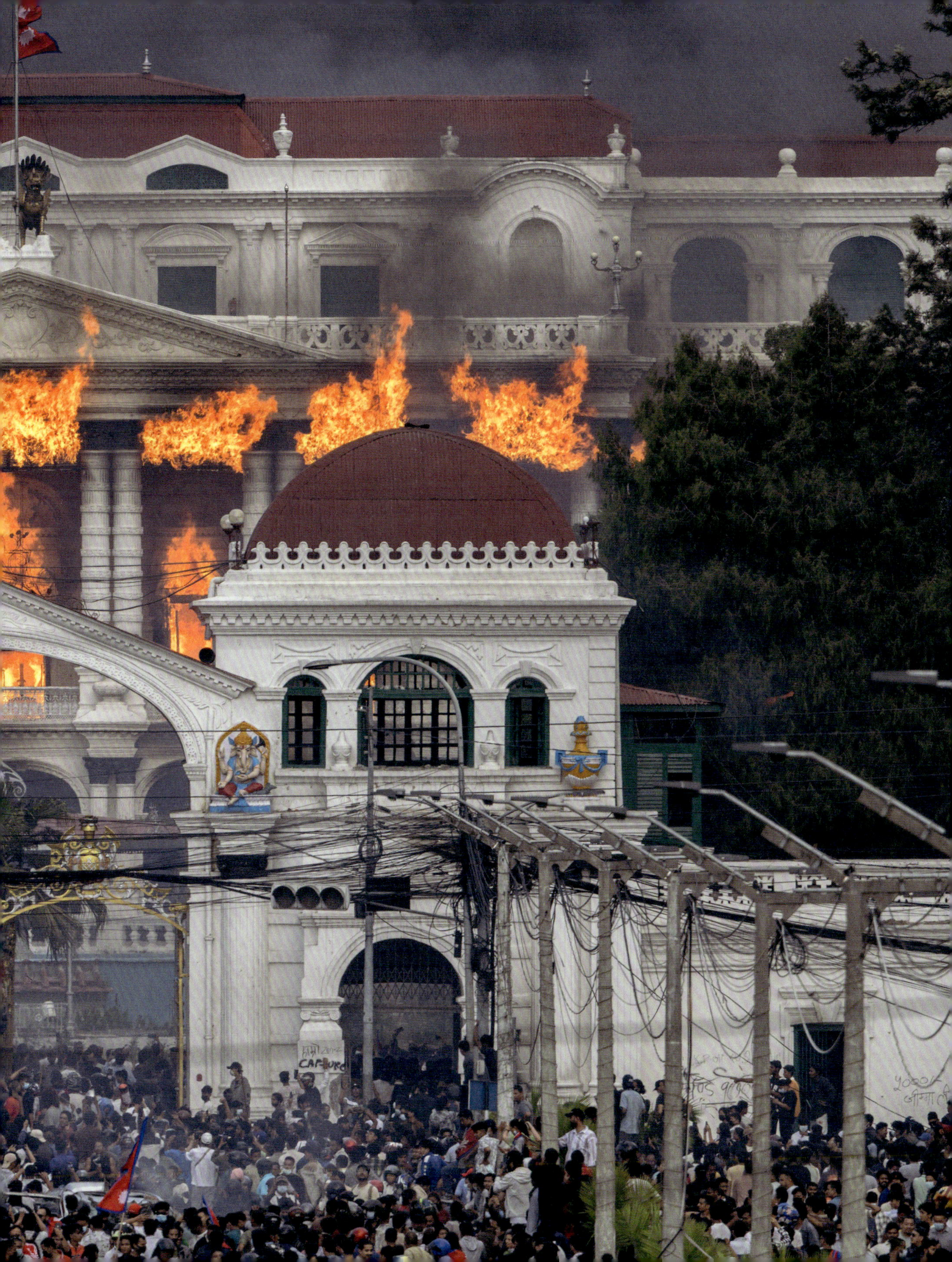

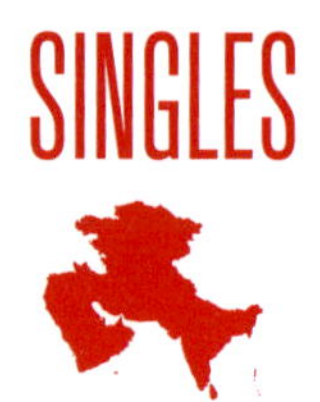

A DAUGHTER'S GRIEF IN KASHMIR

YASIR IQBAL

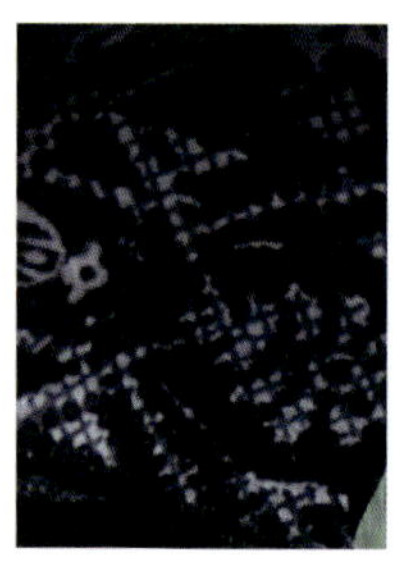

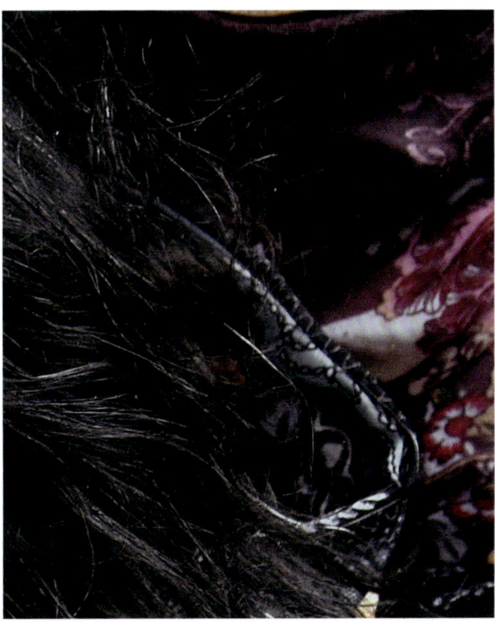

The Kashmir region has been contested between India and Pakistan since the 1947 partition of British India, a territorial dispute that has fueled decades of conflict. On 22 April 2025, an attack on tourists in Pahalgam killed 26 people. India blamed Pakistan-backed militant groups and responded with strikes on 7 May. Four days of intense cross-border shelling, drone attacks, and airstrikes followed. Thousands of civilians were displaced, dozens killed, and homes and infrastructure along the Line of Control (the de facto border) were destroyed. Widespread international pressure secured a ceasefire on 10 May, averting further escalation between the two nuclear-armed rivals.

Sanam Bashir (21) collapses with grief at her mother's funeral. Nargis Begum (45) died from shrapnel wounds after a mortar shell struck while the two were fleeing their home. Uri, Jammu and Kashmir, India, 9 May 2025 / Yasir Iqbal, *Outlook India Magazine*

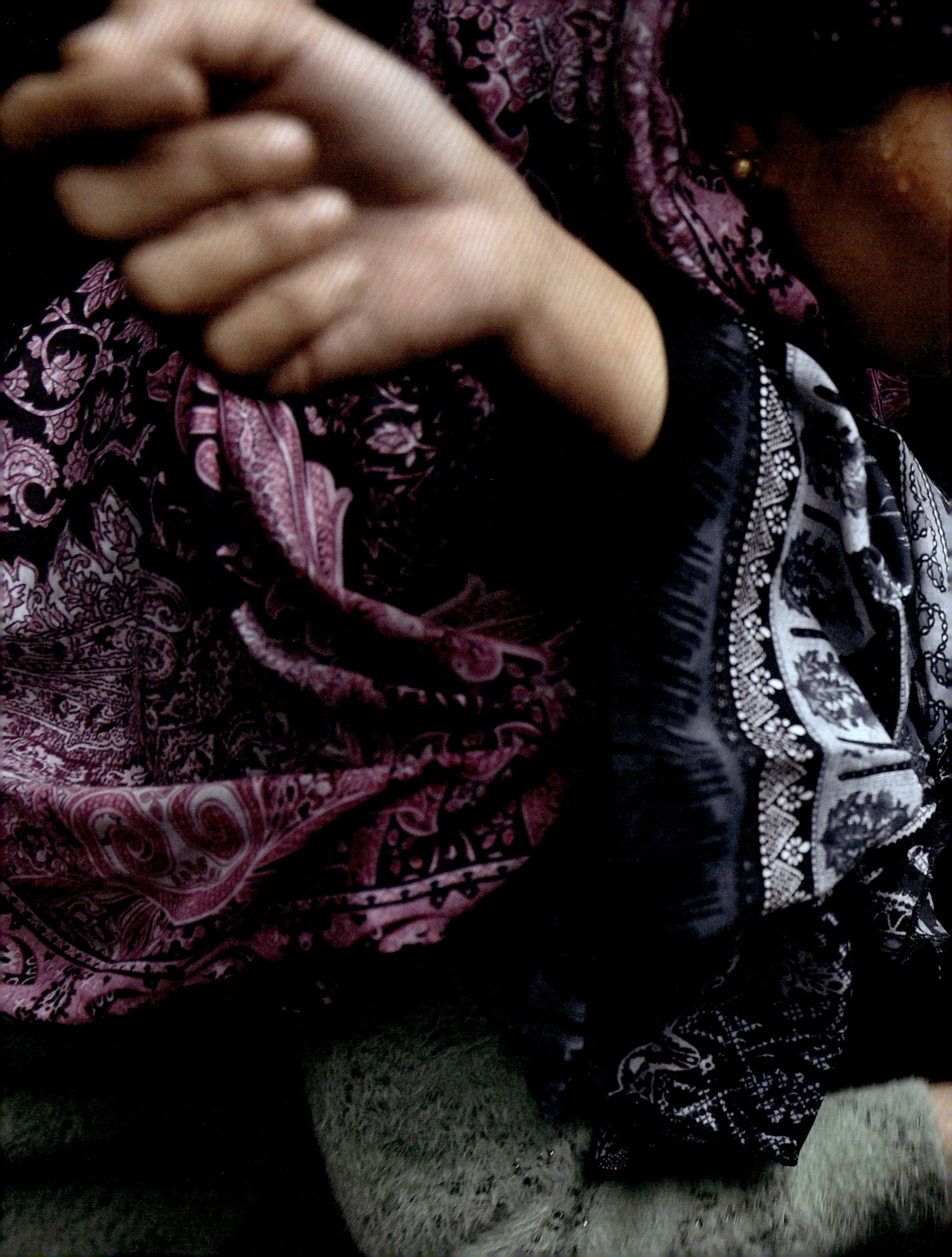

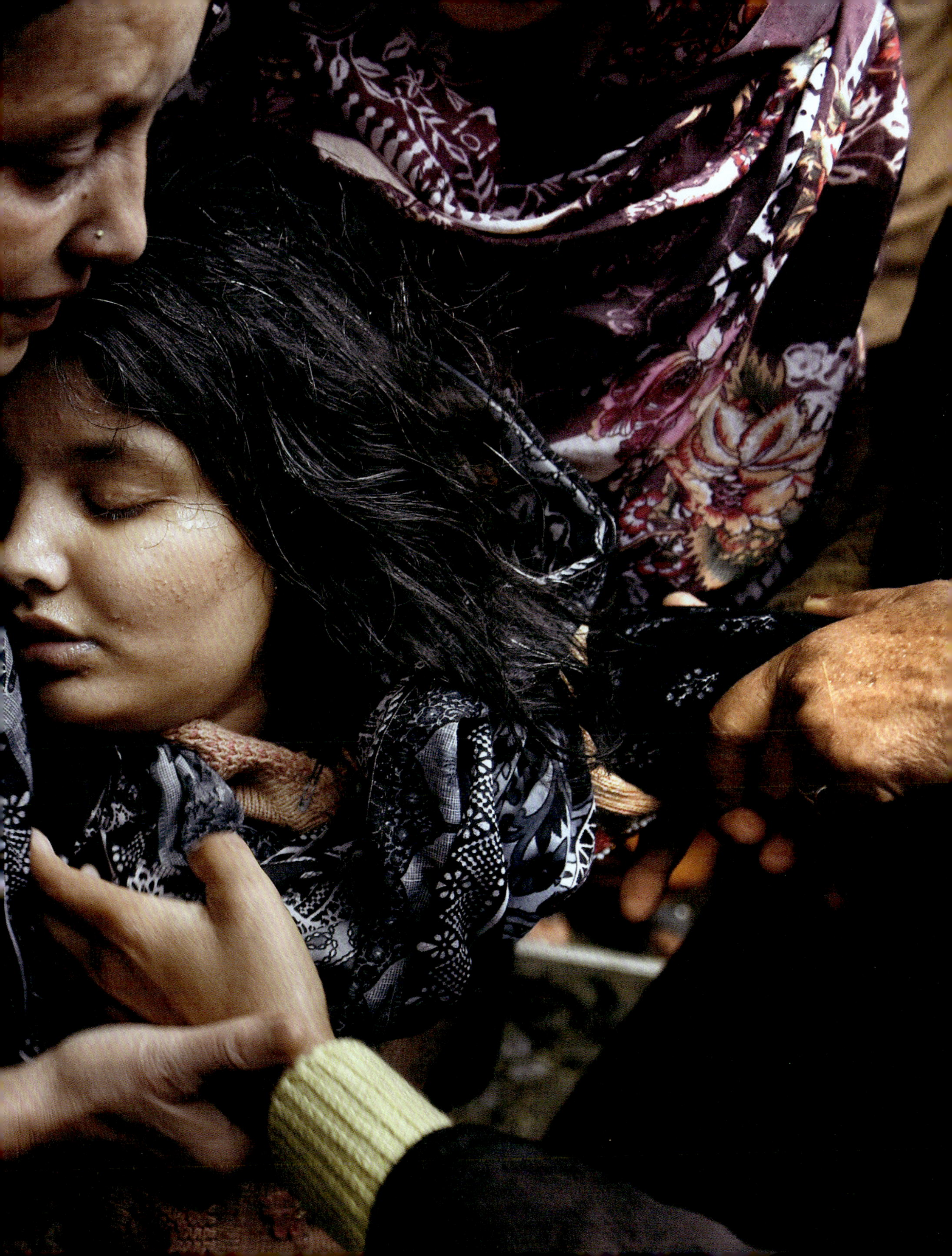

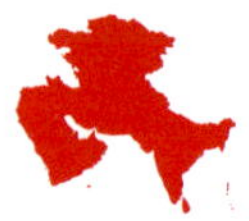

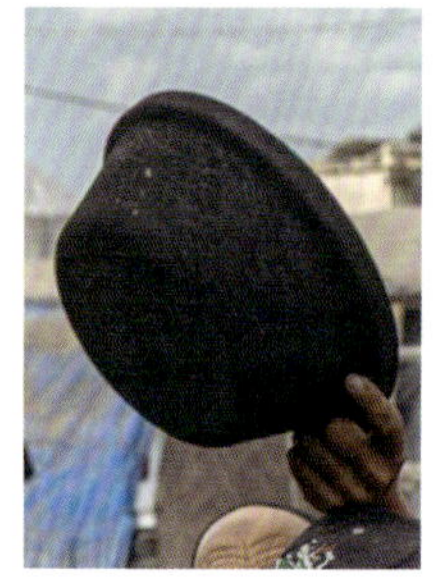

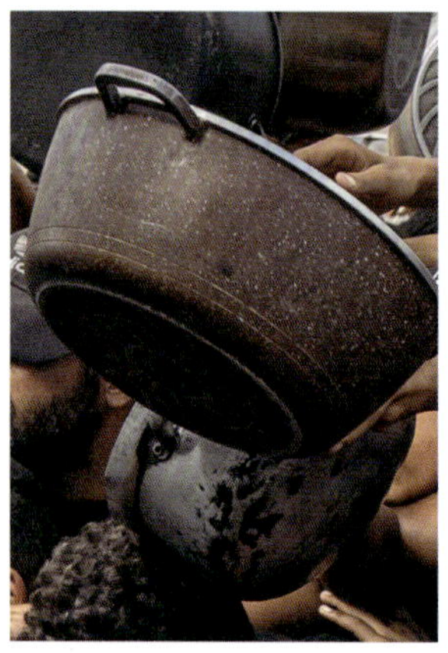

SAHER ALGHORRA

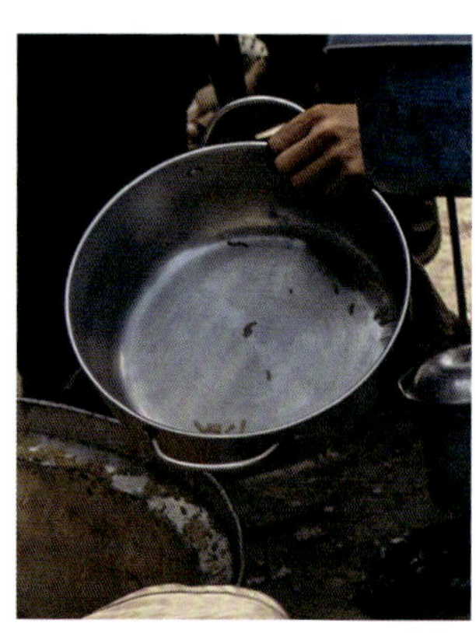

In 2025, civilians in Gaza endured starvation, famine, and relentless bombardment as the death toll surpassed 75,000 and Israeli authorities severely restricted the flow of humanitarian aid. A ceasefire agreement in October has yet to bring meaningful relief. Palestinian journalists – living through the reality they document – are the world's few witnesses to what a UN Commission has concluded is a genocide. Israel disputes this. The photographer worked under immense danger, driven by a refusal to let the world turn away. "Even when everything around me told me to stop, I couldn't – silence would mean surrender."

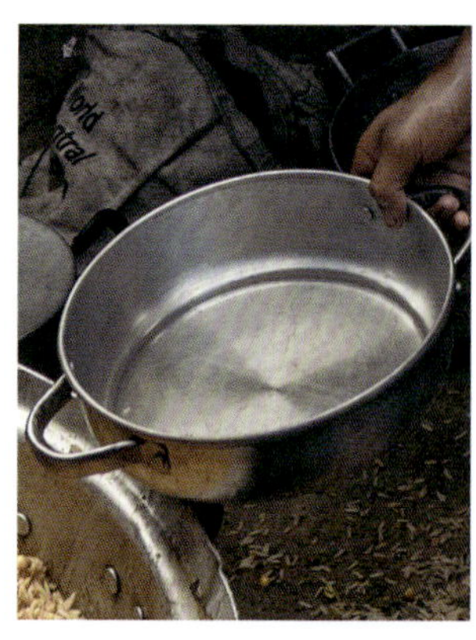

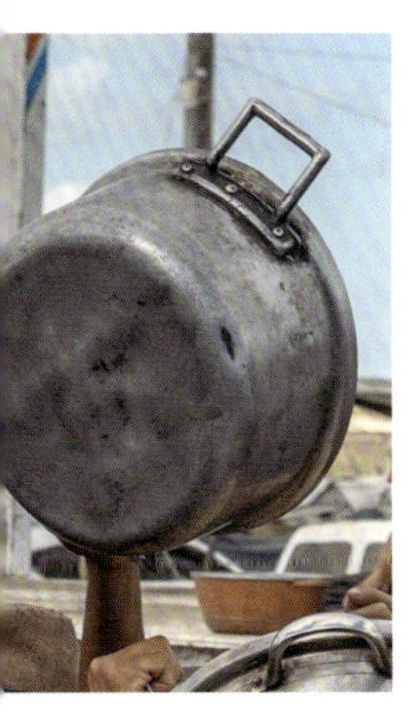

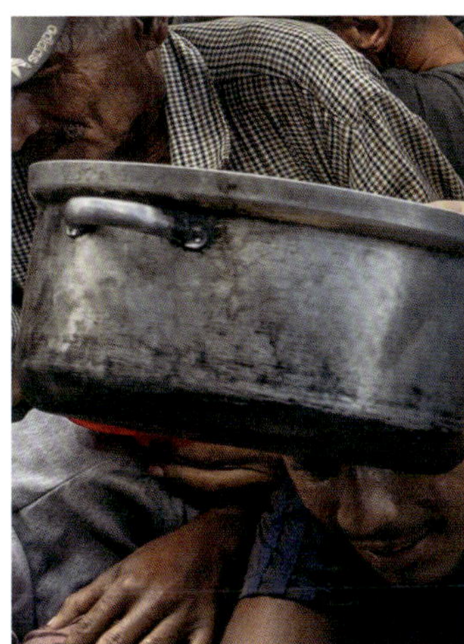

WITNESSING GAZA

Palestinians at Al-Mawasi displacement camp wait for a meal. Local charity kitchens were one of the only food sources for many of Gaza's displaced. Khan Younis, Gaza Strip, 21 September 2025 / Saher Alghorra, for *The New York Times*

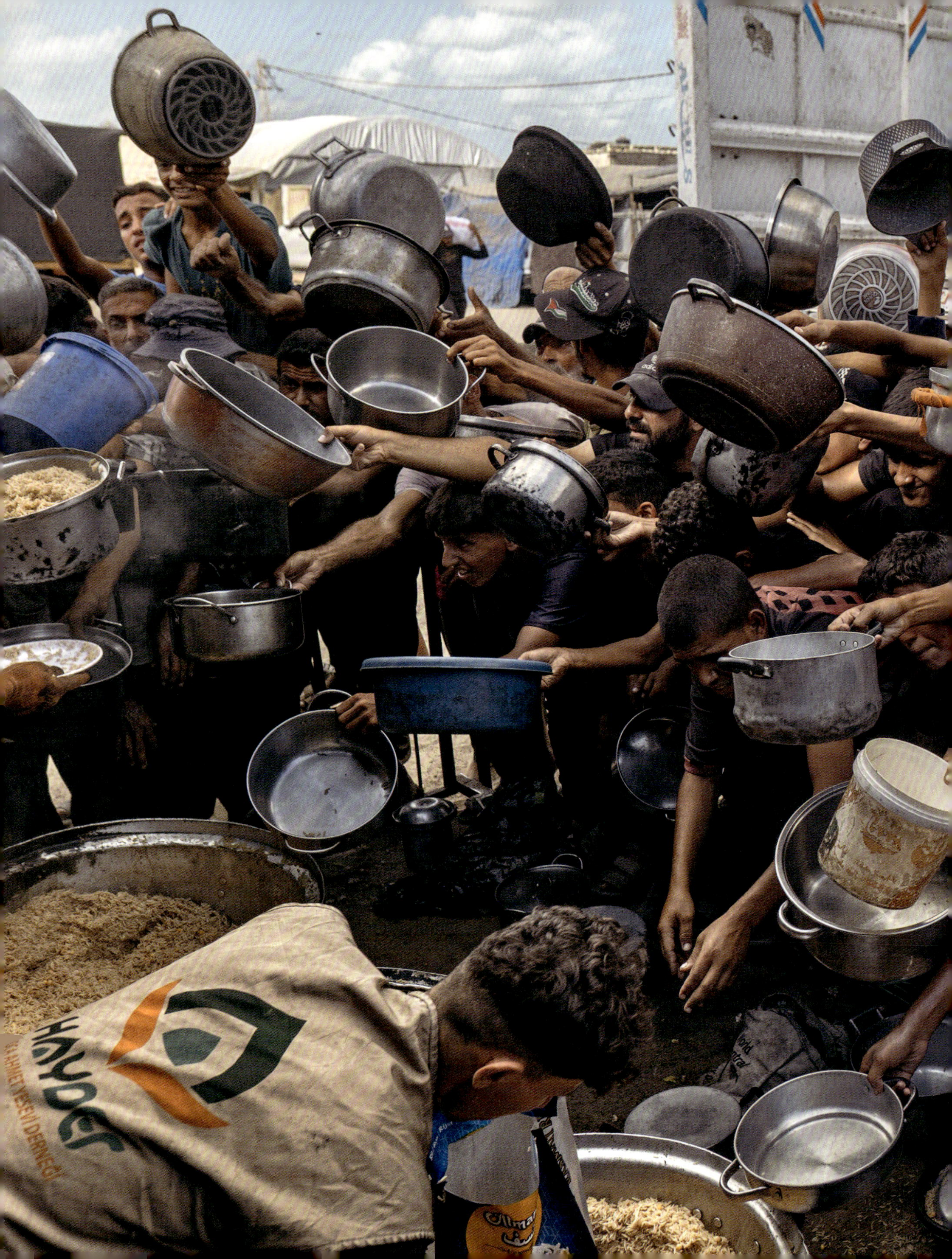

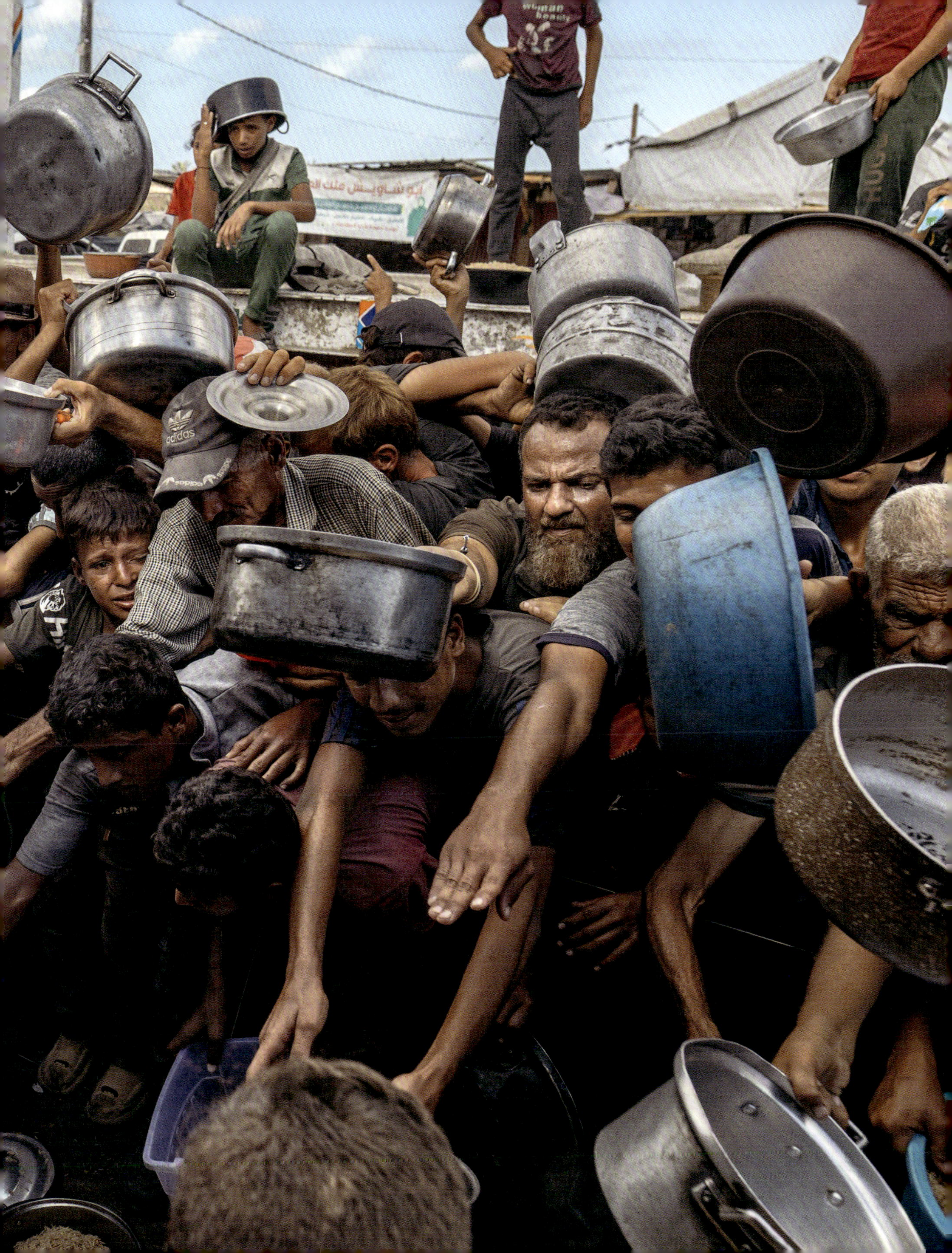

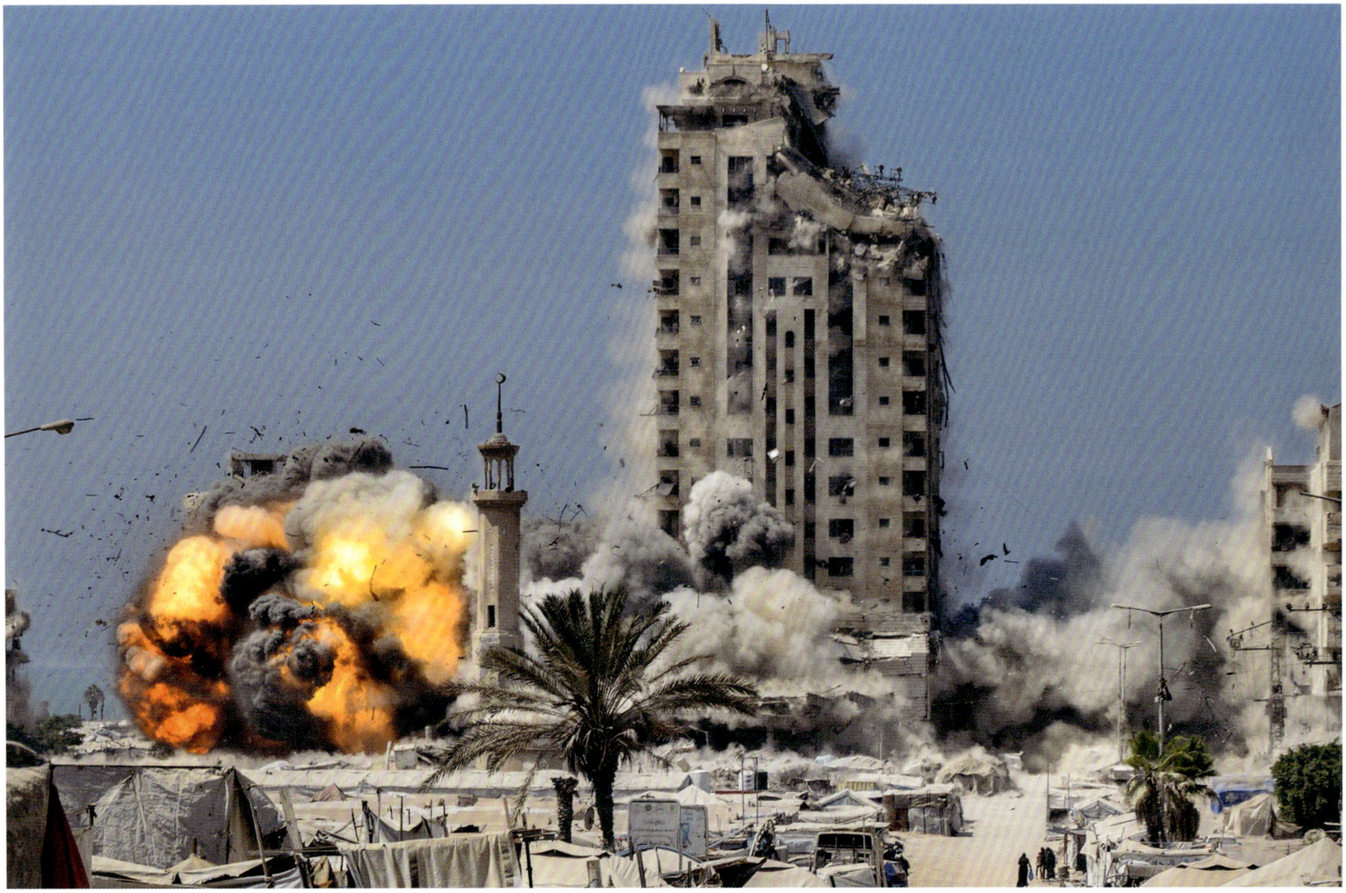

The Mushtaha Tower collapses in a military strike, amid hundreds of makeshift tents sheltering
displaced Palestinians, as Israel's offensive on Gaza City intensified. Gaza Strip, 5 September 2025

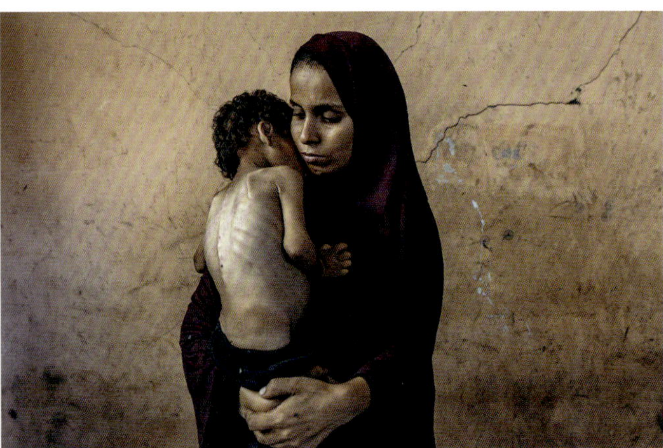

Yazan Abu al-Foul (2) with his mother, Naeema, who cannot find
enough food to feed him. Nearby hospitals were short on resources,
and could not provide him with inpatient care. Al-Shati Refugee Camp,
Gaza City, Gaza Strip, 19 July 2025

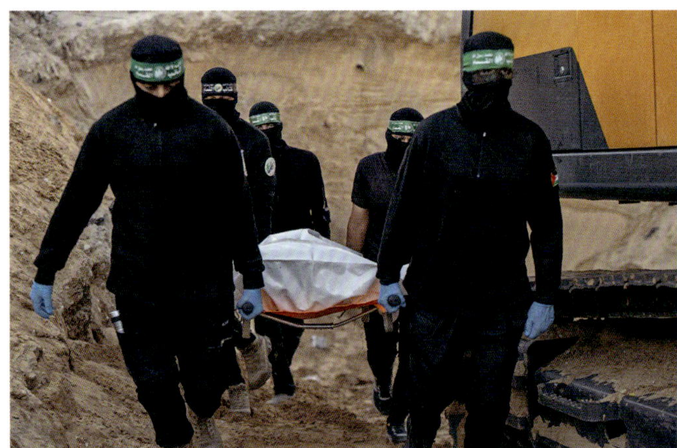

Members of Hamas carry what are believed to be the remains of an Israeli
hostage. Following the ceasefire agreement, Hamas returned all 20 living
hostages and 28 bodies. Khan Younis, Gaza Strip, 28 October 2025

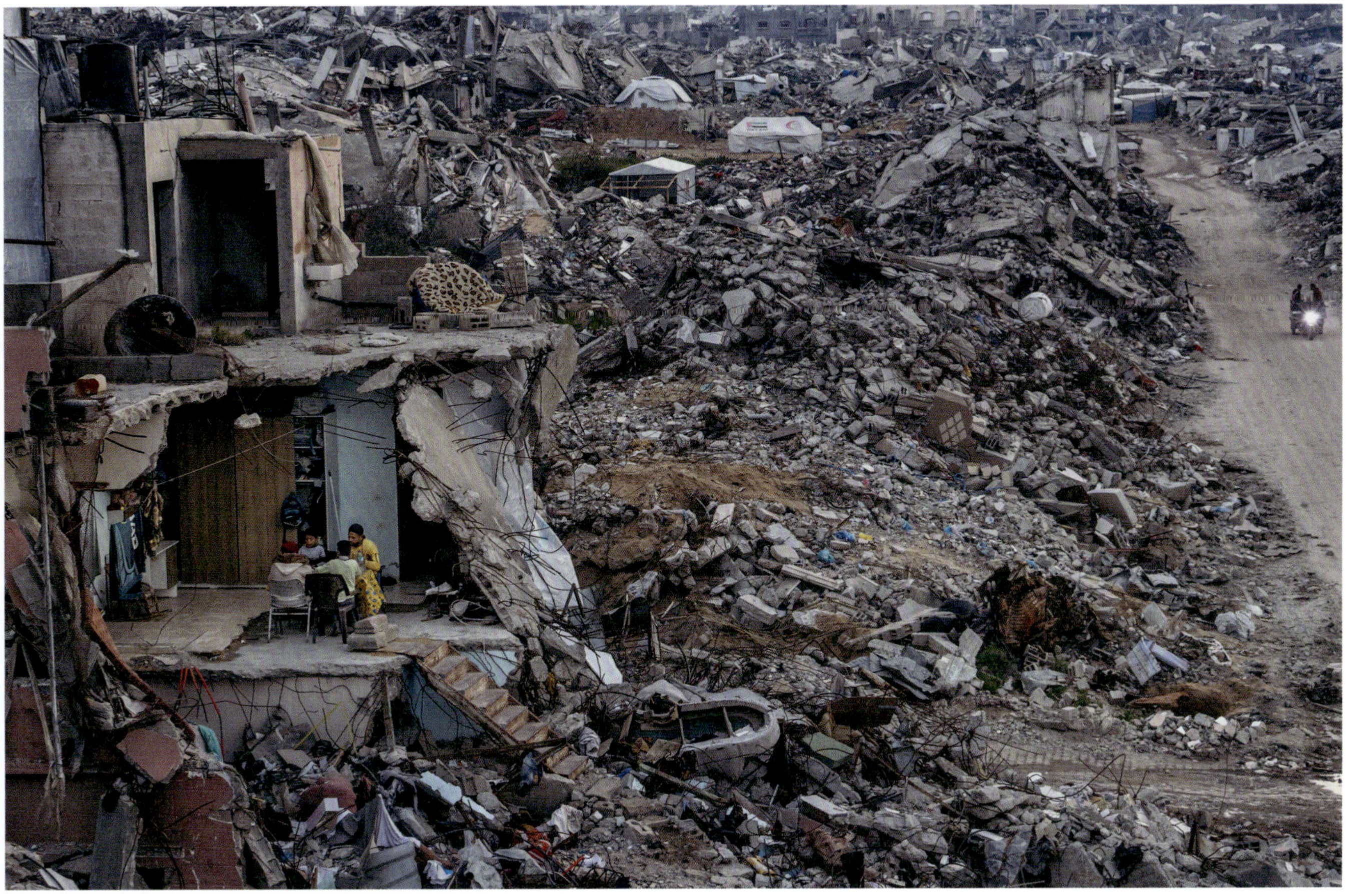

Tamer Hassan al-Shafei and his family break their Ramadan fast in the remains of their home.
Food shortages meant only basics were served instead of the usual spread. Beit Lahia, Gaza Strip, 4 March 2025

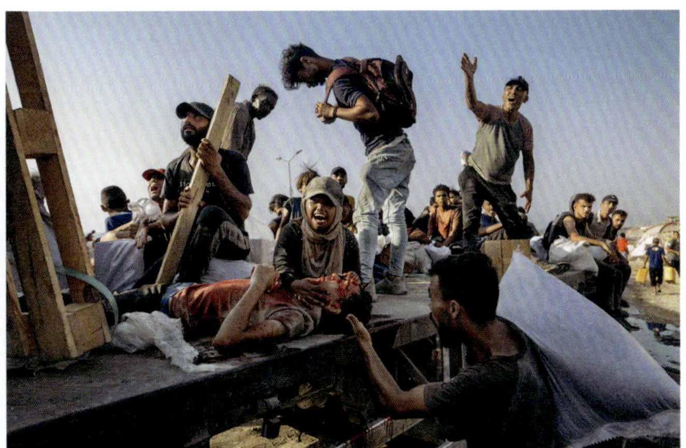

A woman screams for her son who was shot while trying to collect aid
from a truck near the Zikim crossing, in the north of Gaza along the coast,
and is being rushed to hospital on the same truck. Gaza City,
Gaza Strip, 14 August 2025

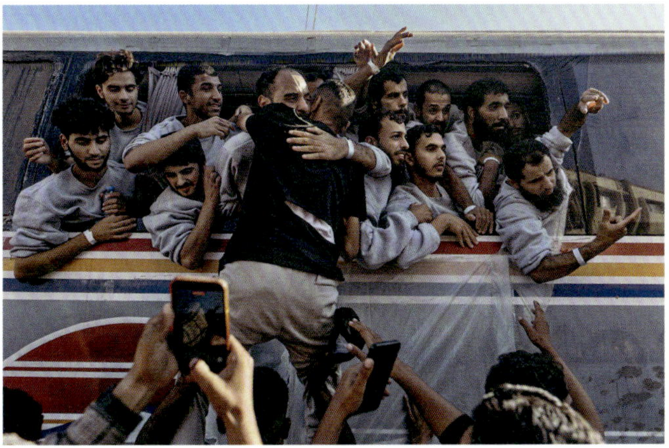

Palestinian detainees and prisoners arrive at Nasser Hospital after being
released from Israeli custody as part of the ceasefire agreement. Israel
freed nearly 2,000 Palestinians. Khan Younis, Gaza Strip, 13 October 2025

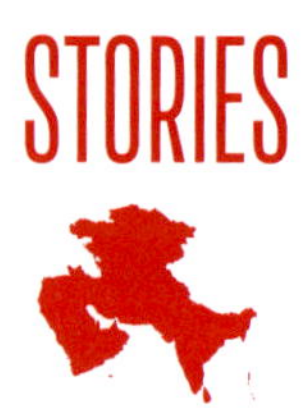

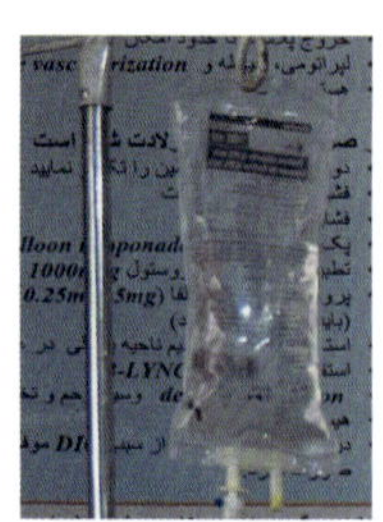

"I'M AFRAID": AFGHAN WOMEN FACE US AID CUTS

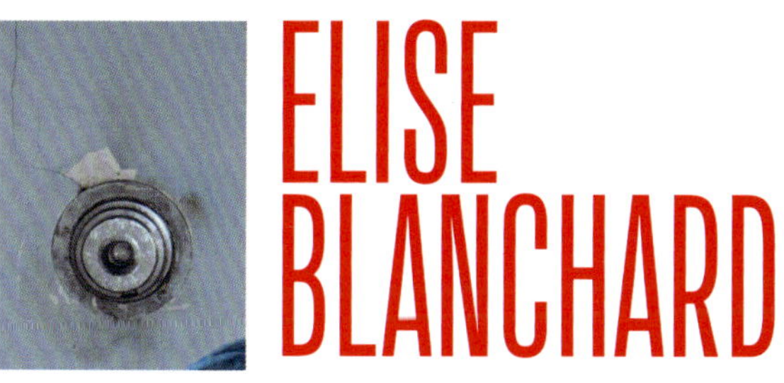

ELISE
BLANCHARD

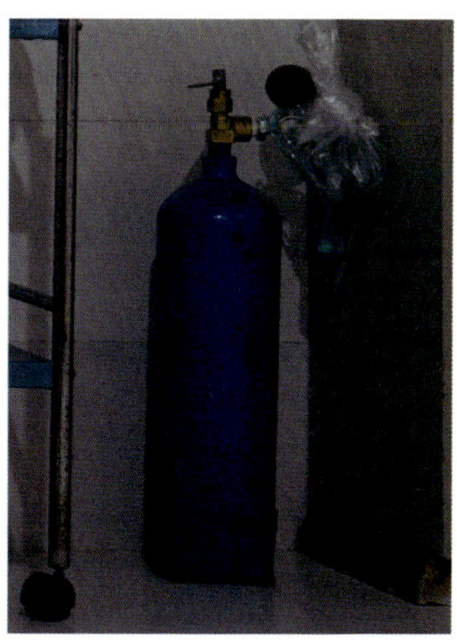

In Afghanistan's remote Daikundi province, US aid cuts have left pregnant women without access to care, forcing many to give birth at home in a country with one of the world's highest maternal mortality rates. The cuts have led to the suspension or closure of 422 health facilities nationwide, including small community clinics staffed by a single midwife, many of whom are now working without salary or supplies. This crisis compounds an already critical situation under Taliban rule; girls are banned from education beyond primary school, preventing a new generation from training as health workers.

Atifa assists in what she says will be her last delivery, having run out of medication and the means to continue, at the Malmastok Family Health House. Shahristan district, 22 July 2025
All photos taken in Daikundi province, Afghanistan / Elise Blanchard, for *Time*

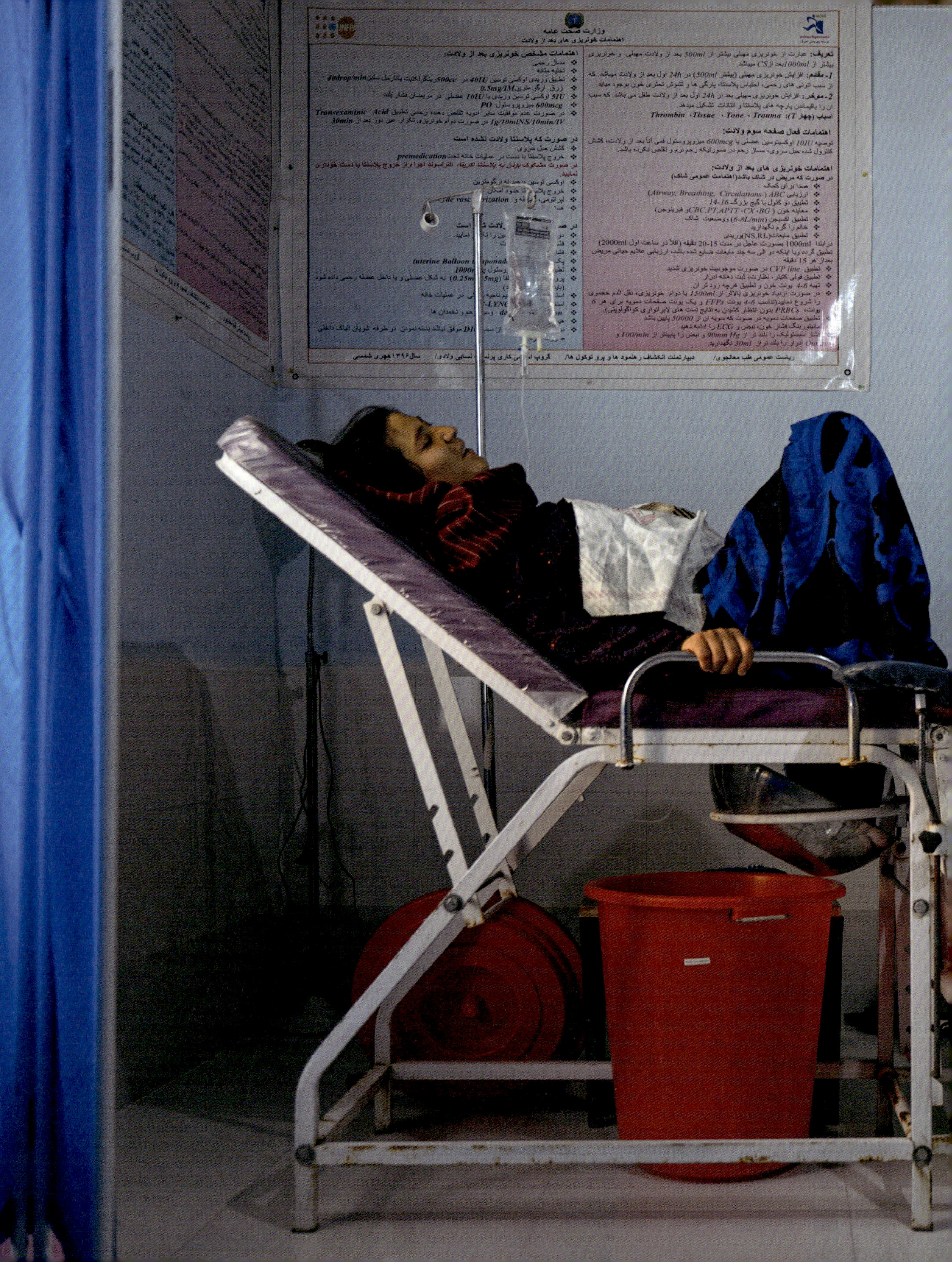

وزارت صحت عامه
اهتمامات خونریزی های بعد از ولادت
اهتمامات مشخص خونریزی بعد از ولادت:

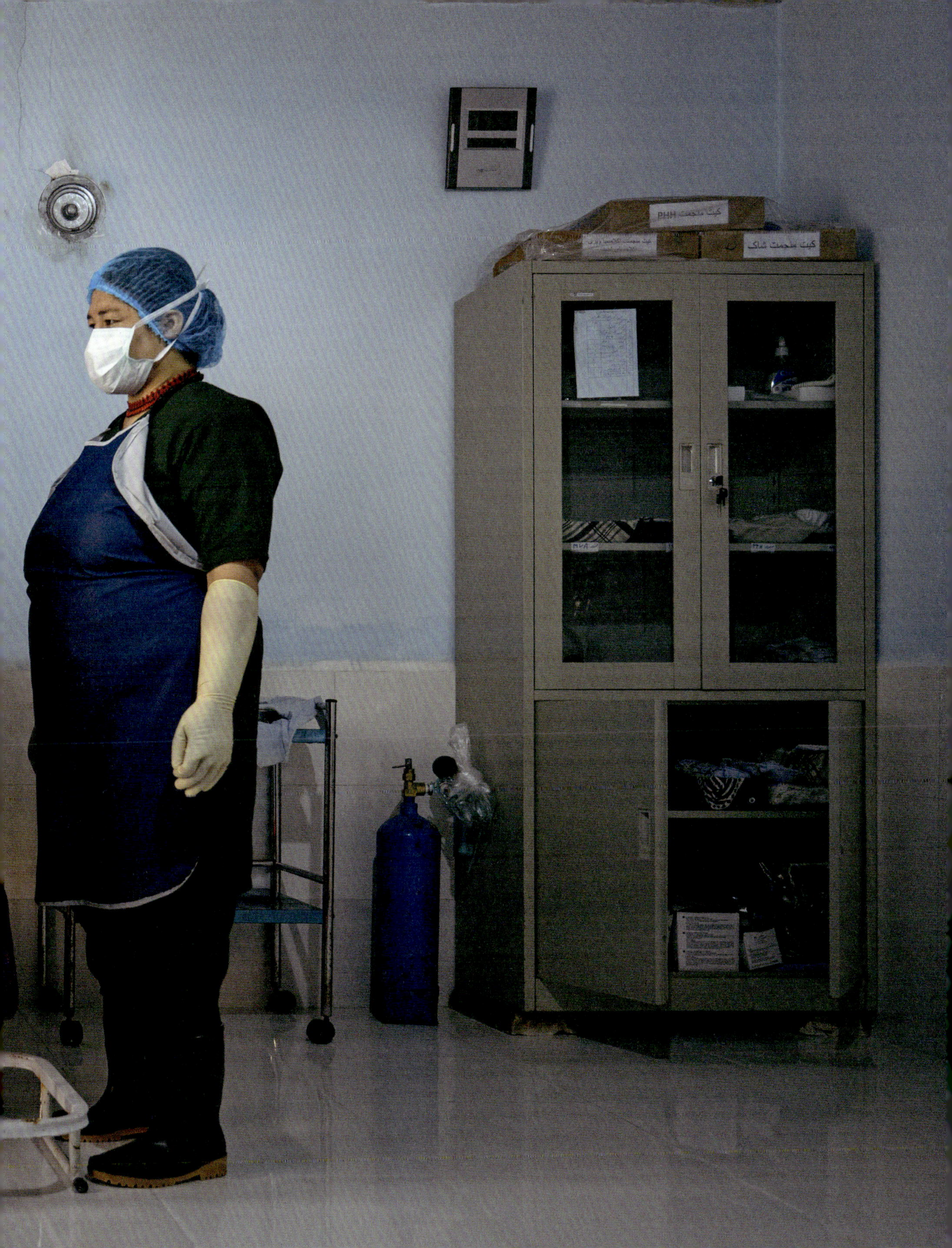
کیت صلحت PHH
کیت صلحت شاک

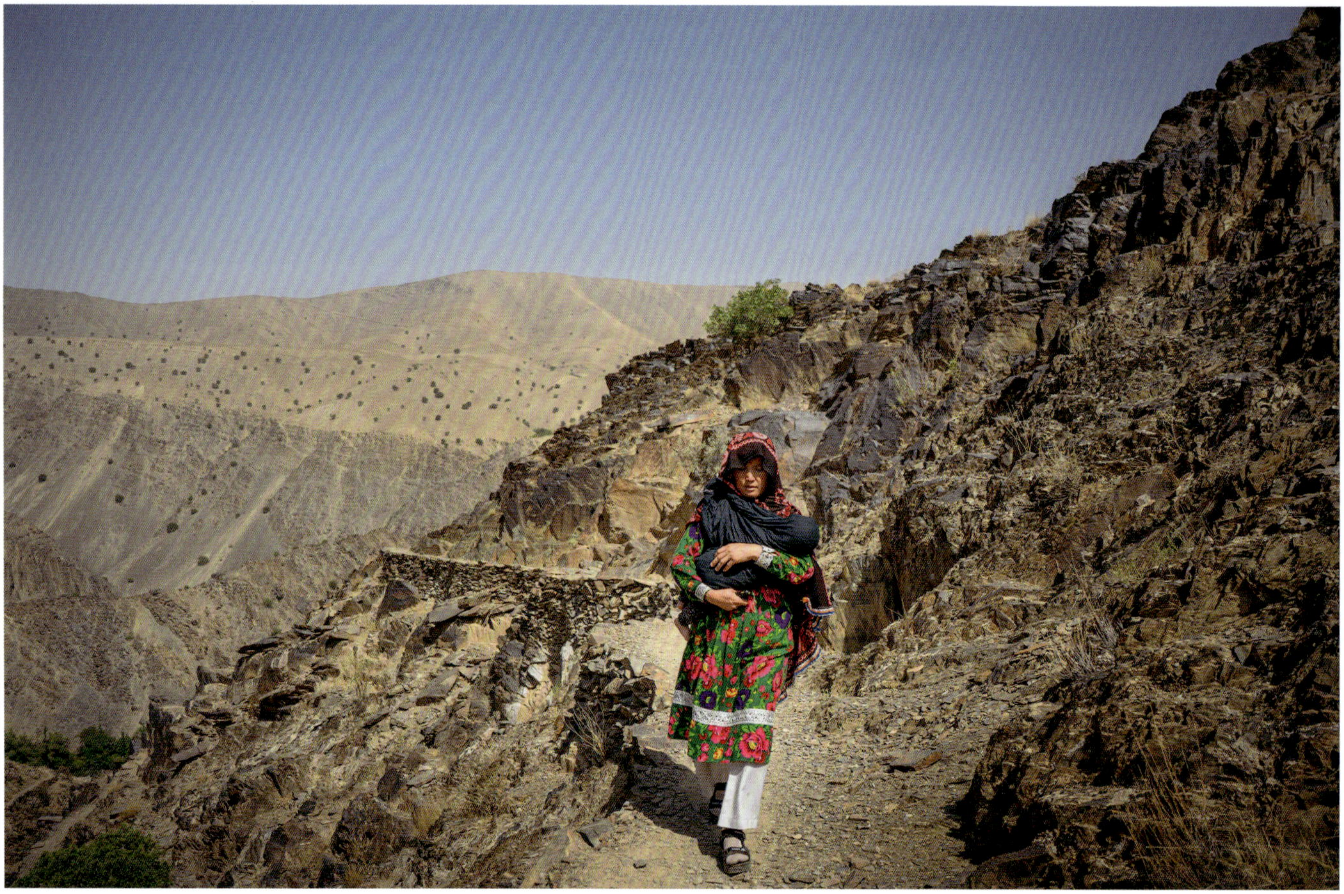

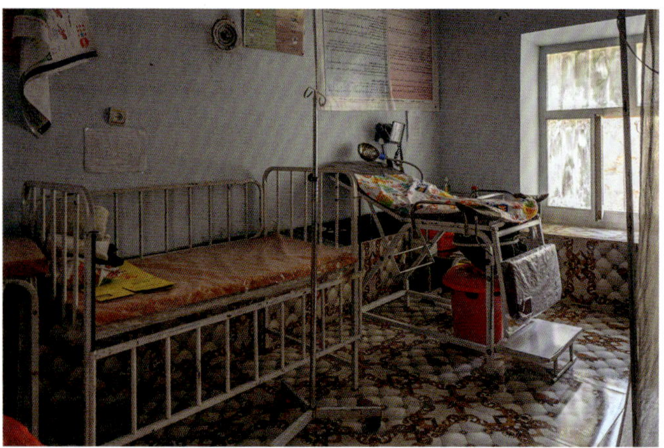

Zahira walks back from visiting a pregnant woman, who is worried she might have to give birth without a midwife. Dahan-e-Tokhomak, Miramor district, 24 July 2025

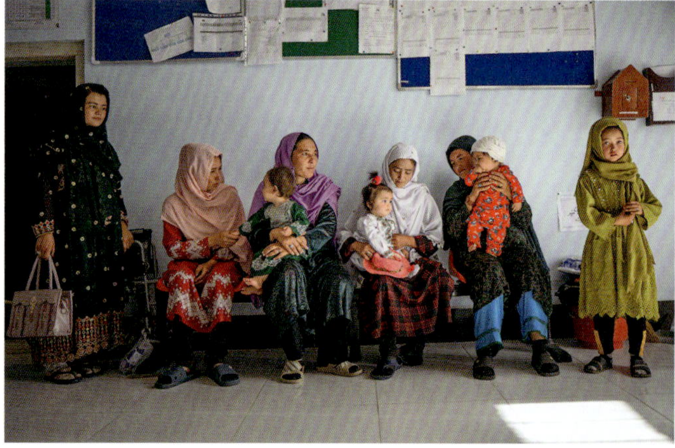

The only clinic serving several remote villages, a Family Health House that closed in April 2025, stands empty, its community now five hours from the nearest hospital. Miramor district, 25 July 2025

Women wait to see Gulshaman, the only midwife at the Waras Family Health House, working without a salary since US aid cuts ended the clinic's funding. Shahristan district, 20 July 2025

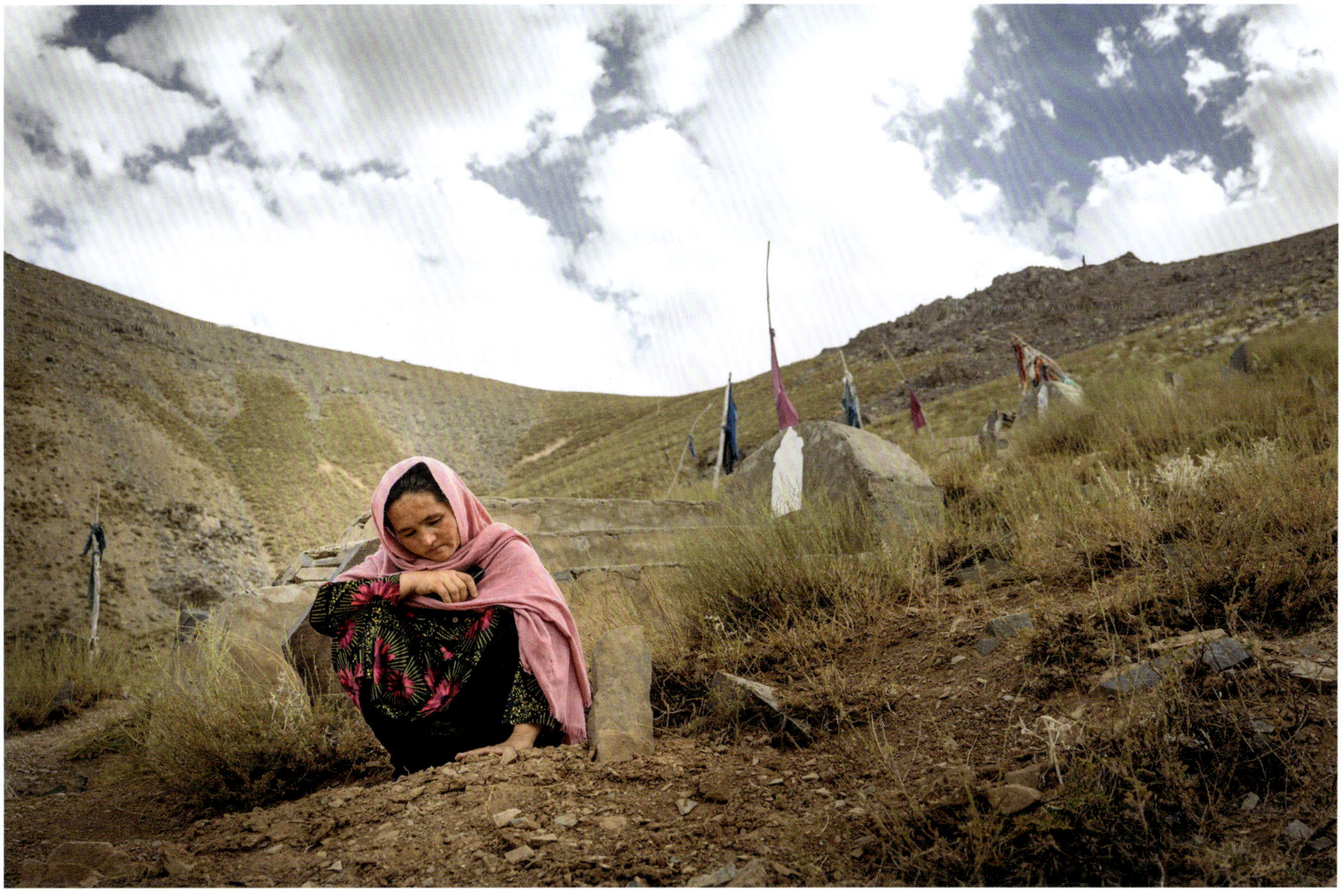

Mahwash visits the grave of her stillborn child for the first time, weeks after waiting two hours outside
the closed Malmastok clinic before reaching another facility. Shahristan district, 22 July 2025

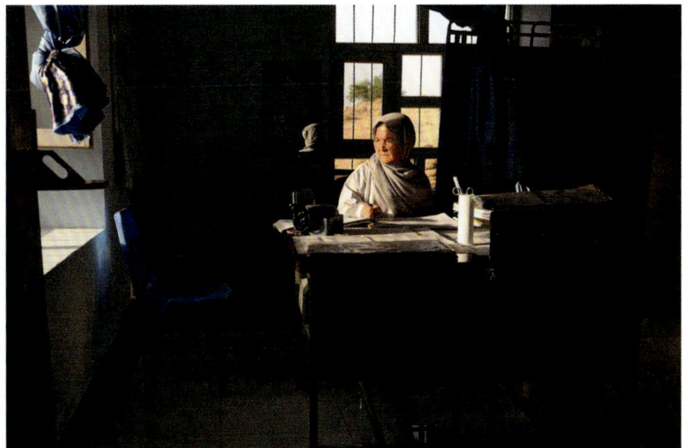

"I cannot abandon the women of my community," says Gulshaman, at her
desk in the clinic she runs alone. Waras, Shahristan district, 21 July 2025

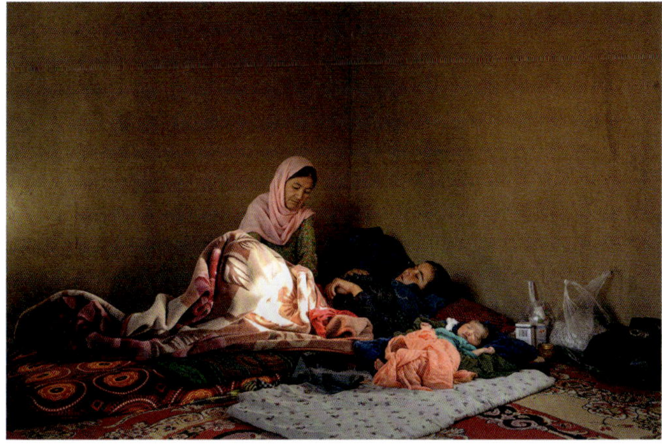

Gulshaman visits Fatemah, whose daughter Yasmin was born the previous
day. Waras, Shahristan district, 27 July 2025

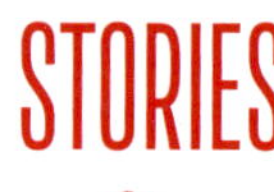

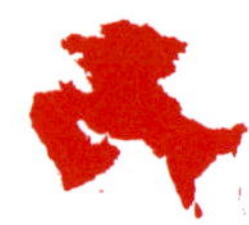

Long neglected by the Syrian state and one of the first cities to rise up in the 2011 revolution, Deir al-Zour endured years of siege, bombardment, and successive occupation by government forces, ISIS, and Kurdish-led fighters. The conflict left around 75% of the city's infrastructure damaged or destroyed. In 2025, the Euphrates River marked a divide; the government controlled one bank, the Kurdish-led Syrian Democratic Forces (SDF) the other, complicating daily movement, trade, and access to services. For those who remained, and those who returned, rebuilding continued regardless.

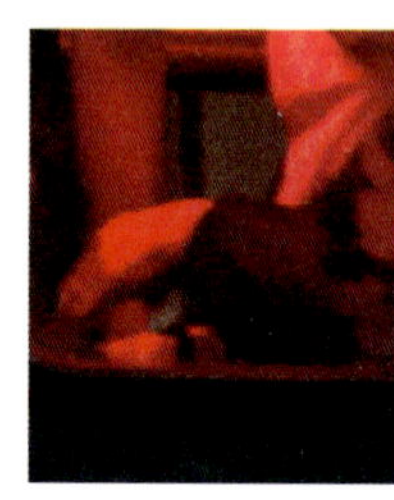

A SYRIAN CITY REBUILDS, STILL DIVIDED

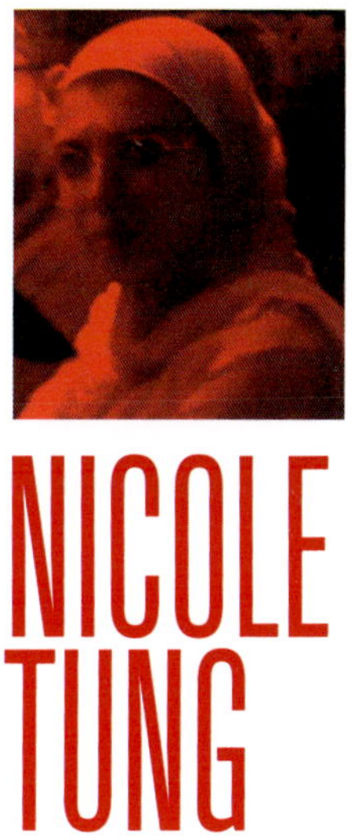

NICOLE TUNG

A member of the Internal Security Command, Syria's national police force, under the Ministry of Interior, patrols a busy square in the eastern city of Deir al-Zour. 20 August 2025
All photos taken in Deir al-Zour, Syria / Nicole Tung, VII Photo, for *The New York Times*

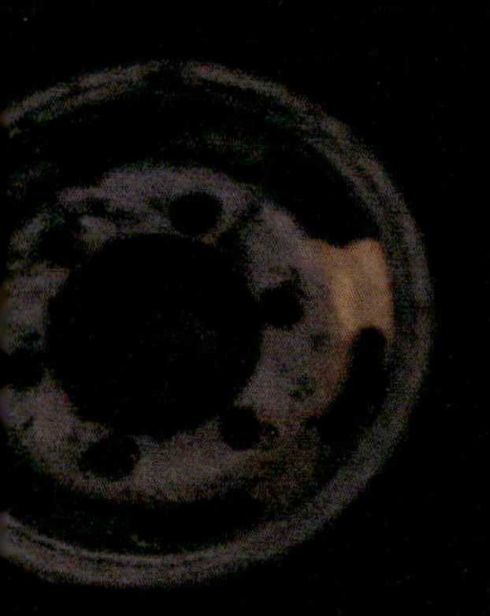

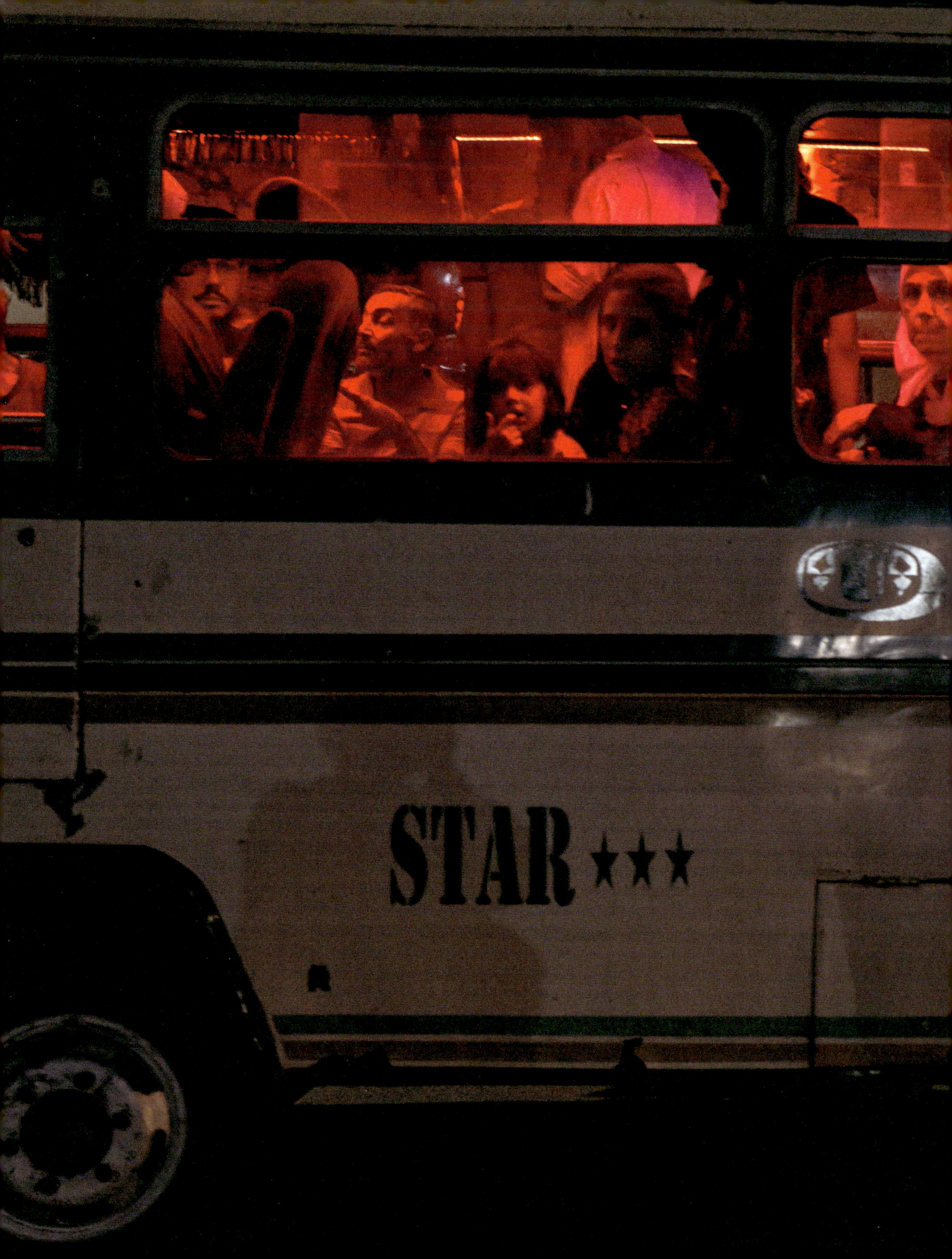

STAR ★★★

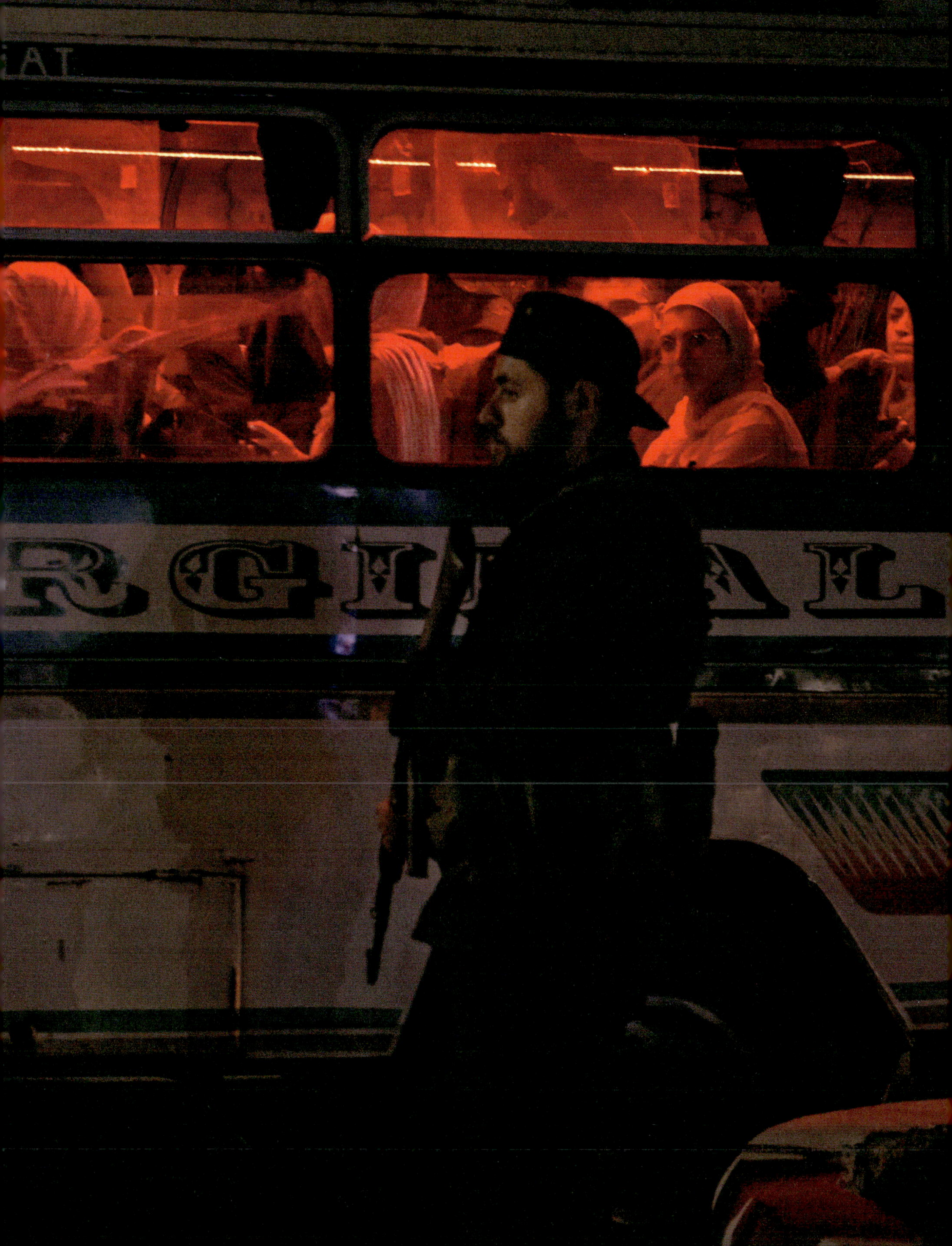

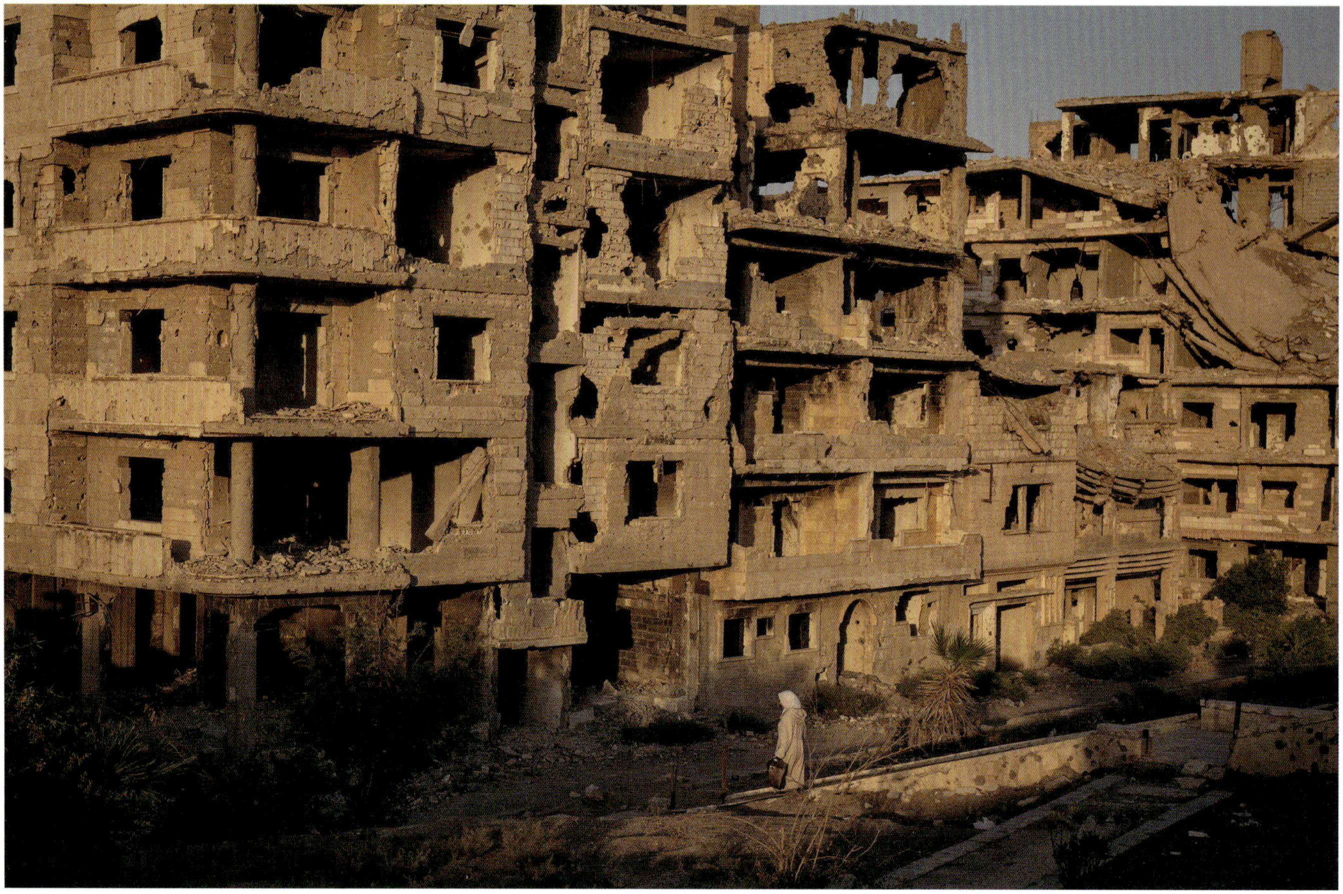

A woman walks through a damaged neighborhood. Seventeen of the city's 25 neighborhoods were almost completely destroyed. 21 August 2025

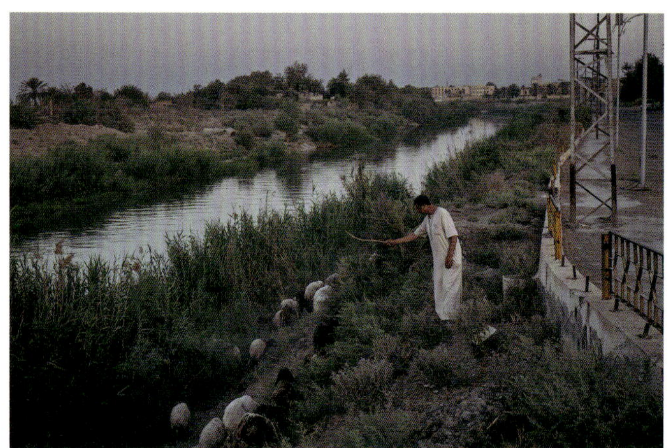

A shepherd herds his flock of sheep on the banks of the Euphrates River. The river divides forces loyal to the new Syrian government and the SDF. 21 August 2025

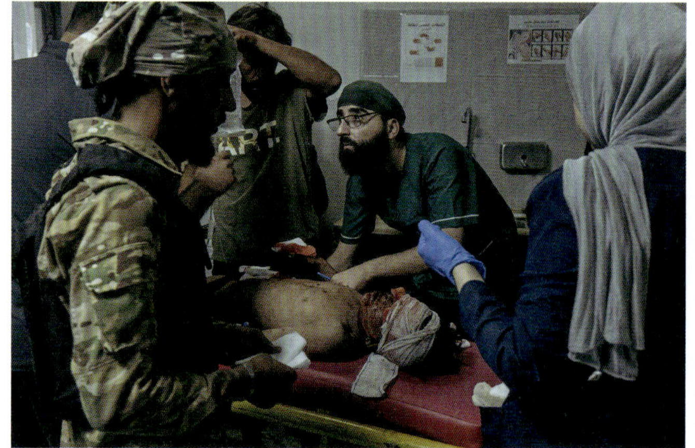

Fadi (13) receives treatment for his injuries at the National Hospital. The boy was injured and his mother was killed as they scavenged for scrap plastic at a dump site, accidentally detonating an unexploded device. 21 August 2025

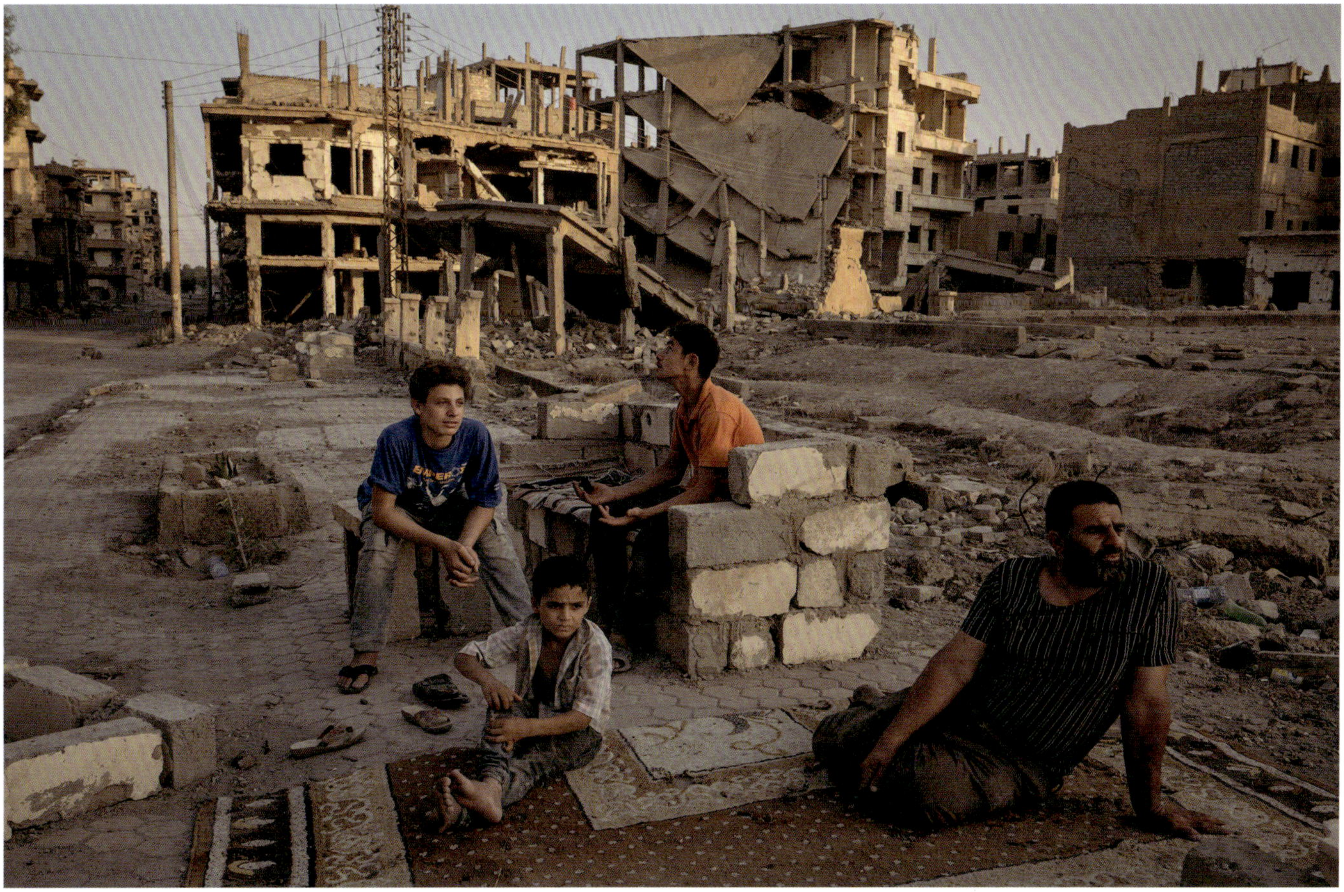

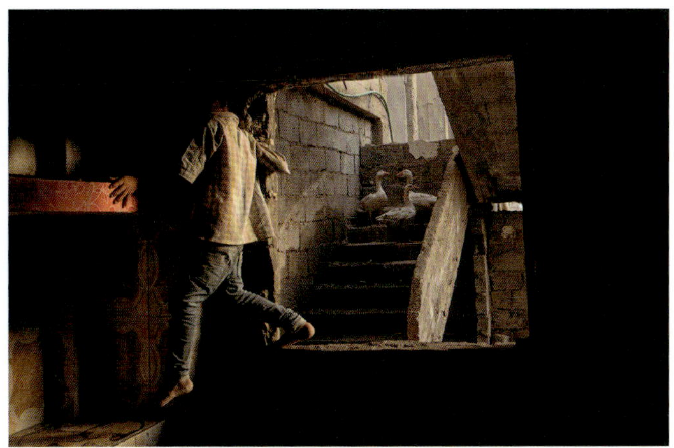

A son of Abdelatif Daham Al Hummada climbs through the kitchen window of the family's heavily damaged home, stripped of copper wiring, tiles, and fittings by looters. 20 August 2025

Abdelatif Daham Al Hummada (right) sits with his sons and nephew on the street outside their heavily damaged home, where the family often sleeps. 20 August 2025

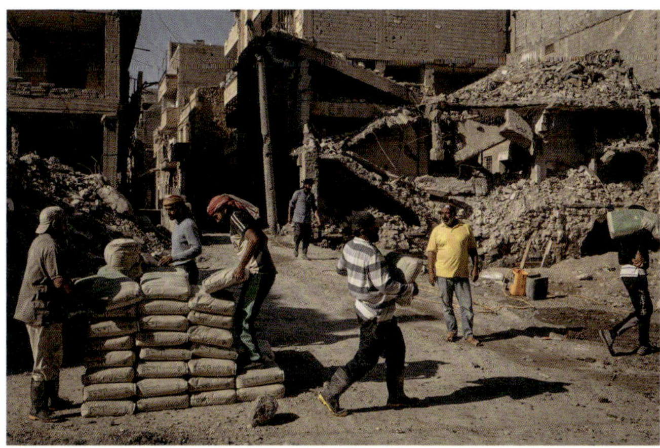

Day laborers prepare cement for mixing at a construction site next to destroyed buildings. 21 August 2025

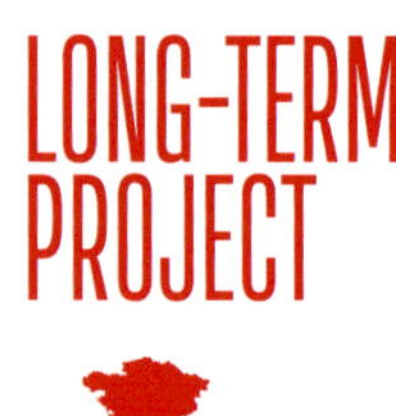

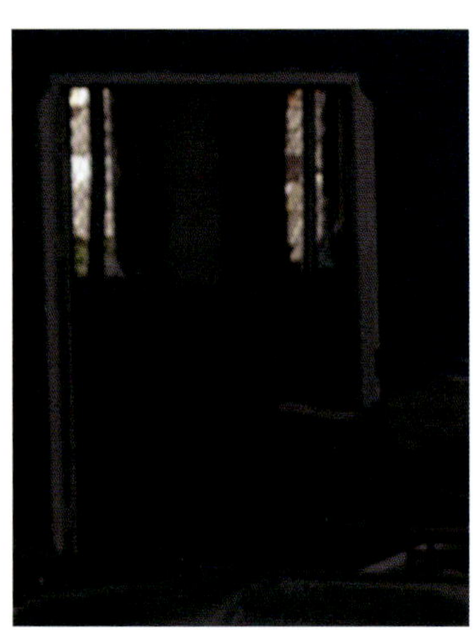

HIJACKED
EDUCATION

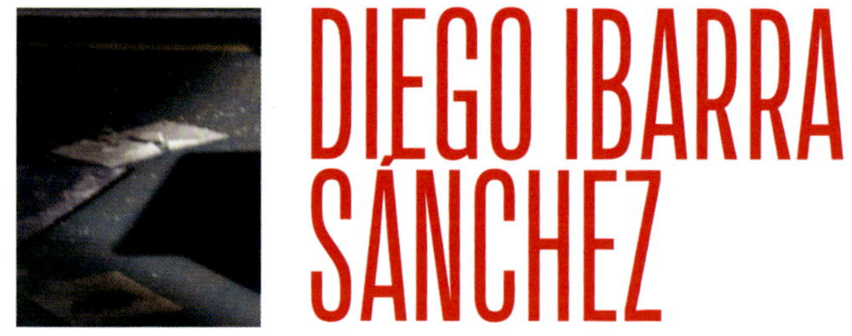

DIEGO IBARRA
SÁNCHEZ

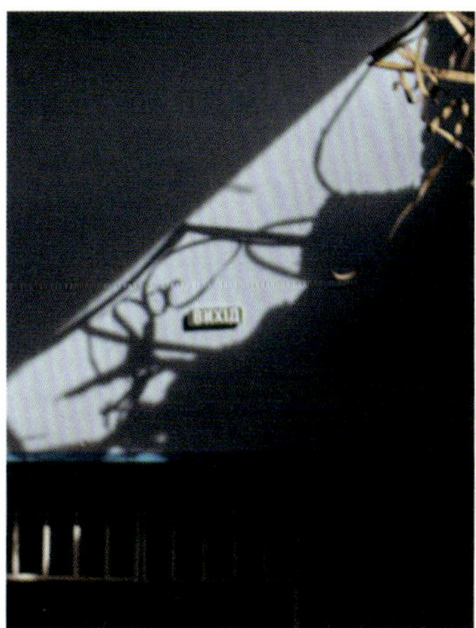

Across the world, war, extremism, and displacement deny children the right to education. Schools are destroyed, teachers killed or forced to relocate, textbooks burned, and classrooms turned into barracks. The UN estimates that 85 million of the 234 million school-age children affected by conflict worldwide have no access to education at all. The consequences extend far beyond the classroom, impacting physical, emotional, social, and cognitive development. Since 2011, the photographer – son of a teacher and father of an 11-year-old – has documented this crisis across nine countries, from Western and South Asia, to Europe and South America.

Daria Kechenovska (16) inside her school, Lyceum #25, destroyed by a missile strike. "I want to become a soldier to defend my country," she says. Zhytomyr, Ukraine, 29 September 2022 / Diego Ibarra Sánchez

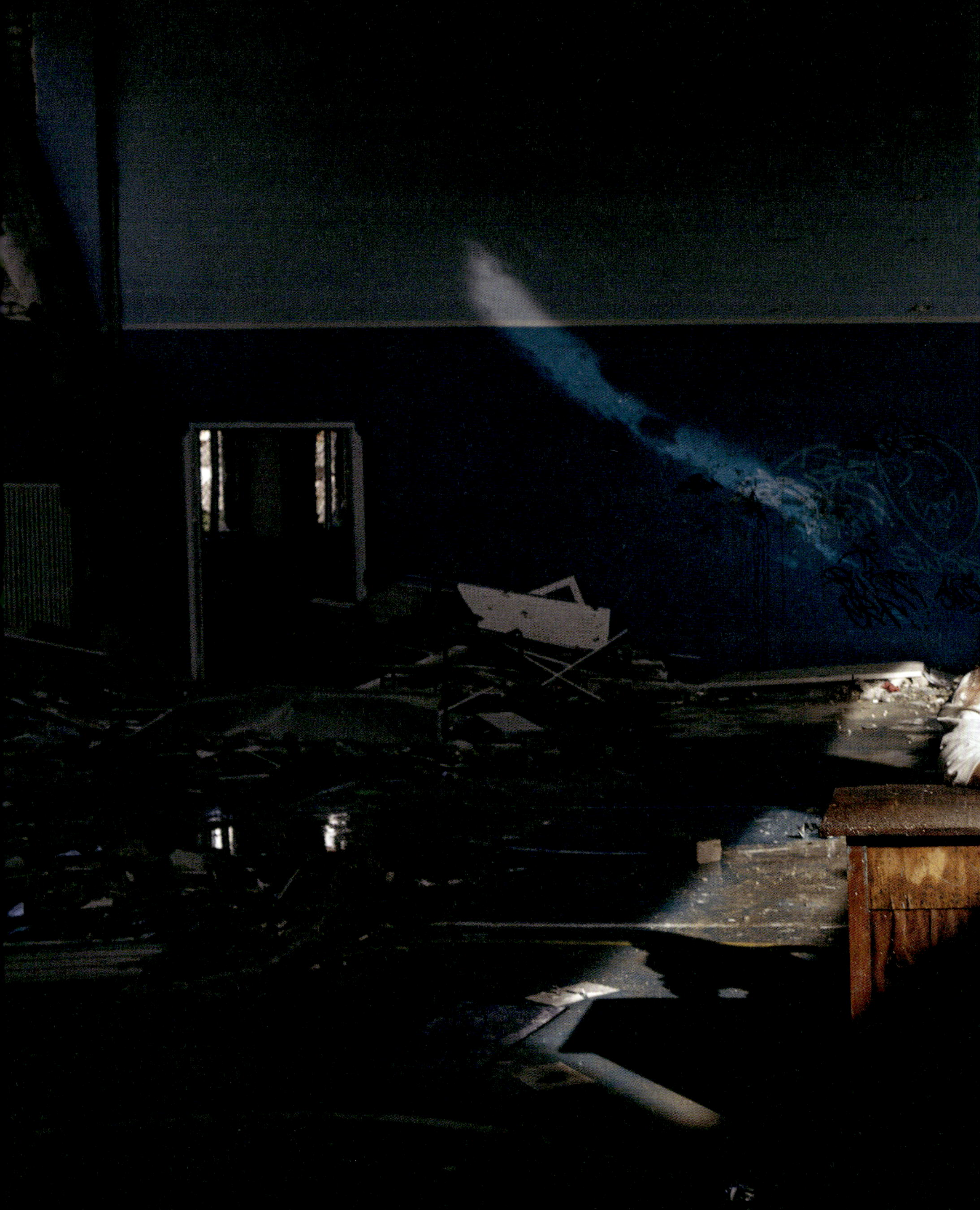

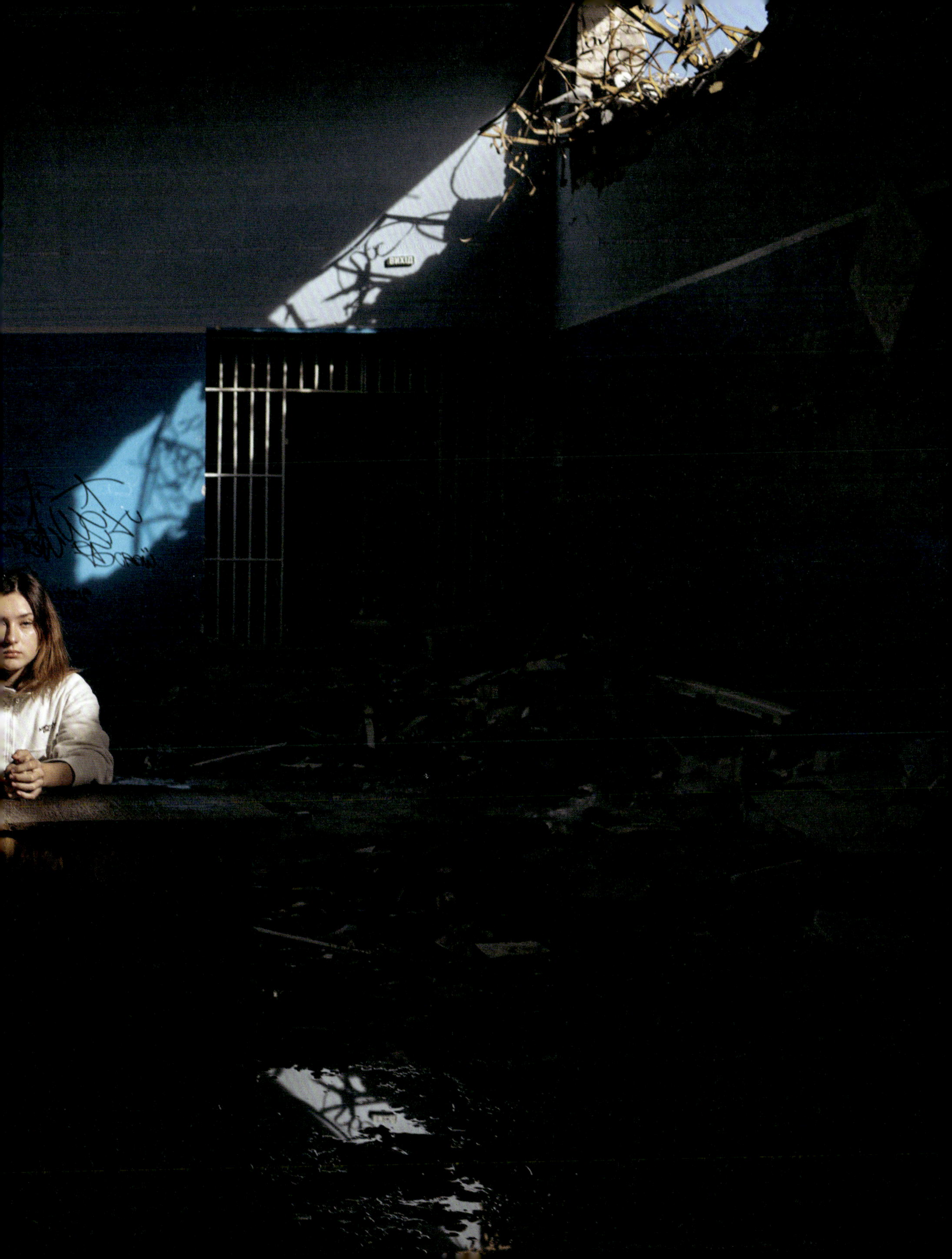
ВИХІД

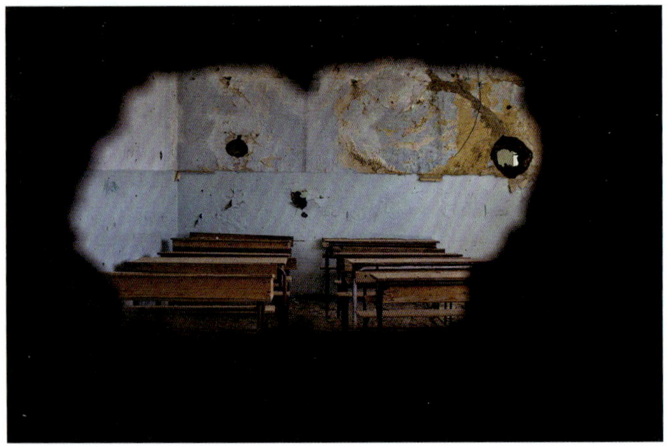

A destroyed classroom seen through a hole in a wall at Tell Ruman school, closed since ISIS attacked it in July 2015. Al-Hasakah, Syria, 13 April 2016

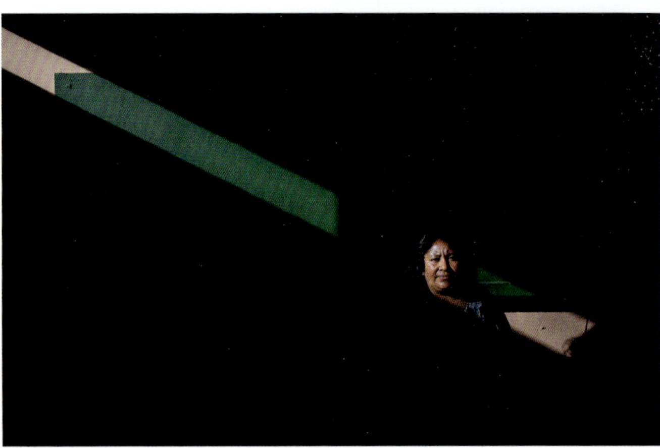

Nora Nancy, a teacher, photographed at her school in Samaniego. In 2008, four teachers were murdered by FARC rebel forces in nearby Guachavés, forcing her to flee her home. Colombia, 25 July 2016

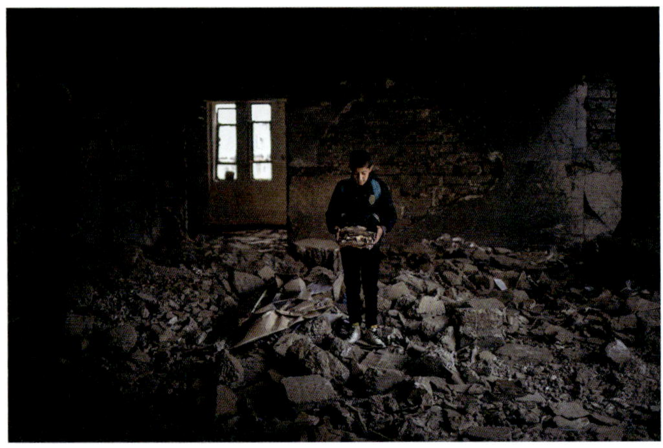

Yousef (12) dreams of becoming a police officer. His school was heavily damaged during the battle for Mosul from 2016 to 2017. Mosul, Iraq, 6 March 2022

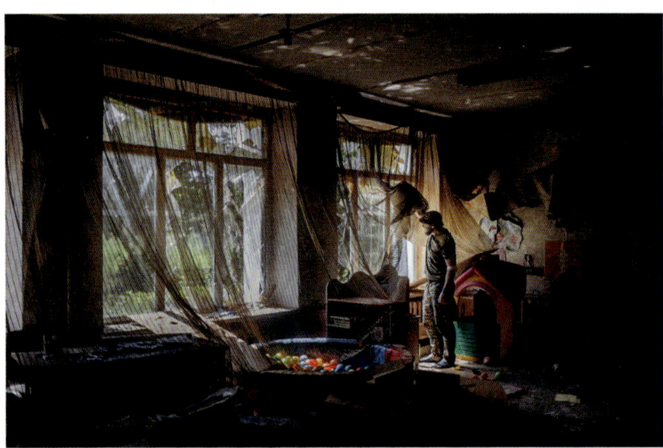

A Ukrainian soldier from the Ares battalion, 129th Territorial Defense Brigade, gazes out of a kindergarten window at the southern front. Donetsk region, Ukraine, 2 August 2023

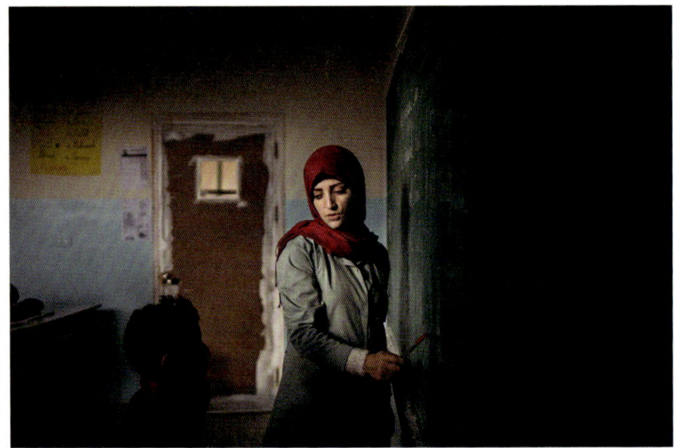

A young Syrian refugee attends a class on the outskirts of Arsal. Limited resources, residency issues, and work restrictions on parents deny many refugee children access to education. Lebanon, 31 October 2017

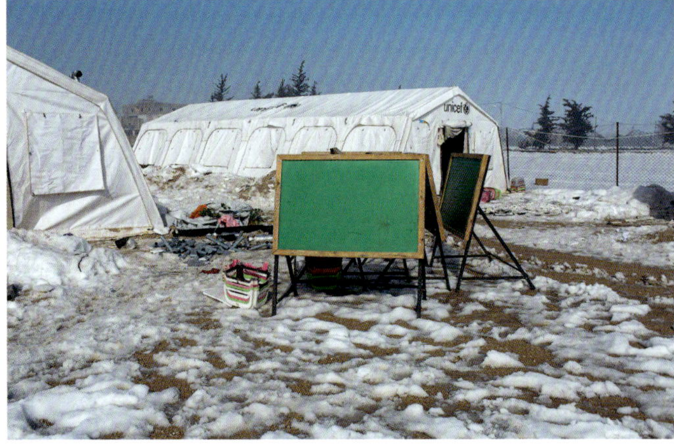

A chalkboard surrounded by snow outside a school for Syrian refugees. Freezing temperatures and lack of secure shelter pose serious health risks for refugees across the region. Zahle, Lebanon, 18 January 2015

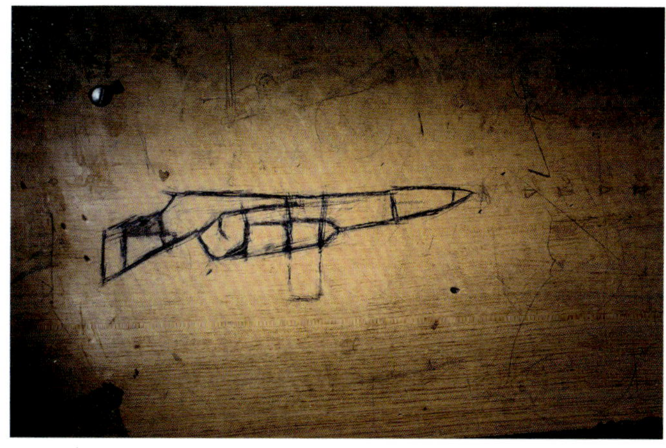

A drawing of a machine gun on a desk at Hajj Ali High School for boys, taken over as a shelter during conflict. Hajj Ali, Iraq, 27 August 2016

Hundreds of textbooks burned by ISIS extremists inside Hani Hakuf's School. At least a quarter of Syrian schools have been damaged or destroyed. Al-Shaddadi, Syria, 11 April 2016

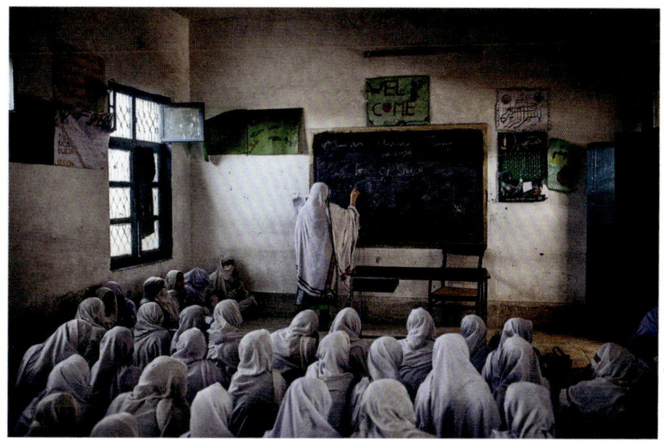

Female students attend class at their school, which was attacked by the Taliban on 21 December 2012 as part of a campaign to prevent girls from accessing education. Swabi, Khyber Pakhtunkhwa, Pakistan, 4 June 2013

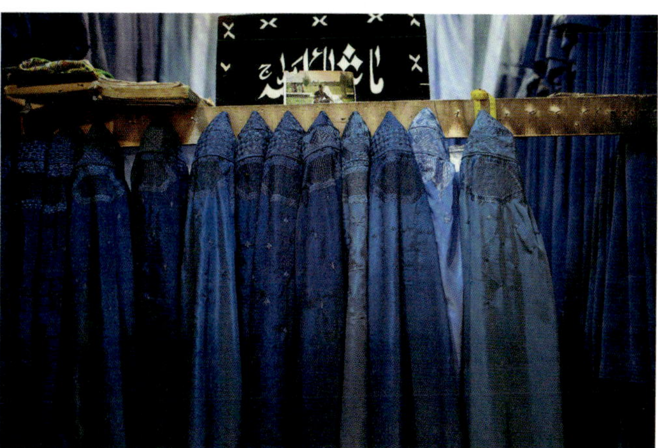

A row of burqas hangs in a vendor's shop in a country where the Taliban has banned girls from secondary and higher education. Kabul, Afghanistan, 16 July 2014

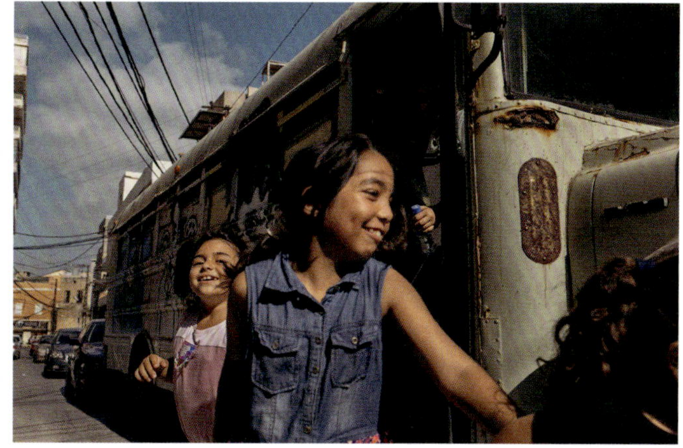

A displaced Lebanese child exits the Peace Art Bus outside the Lebanese National Theater to participate in artistic activities designed to alleviate stress. Tyre, Lebanon, 11 June 2024

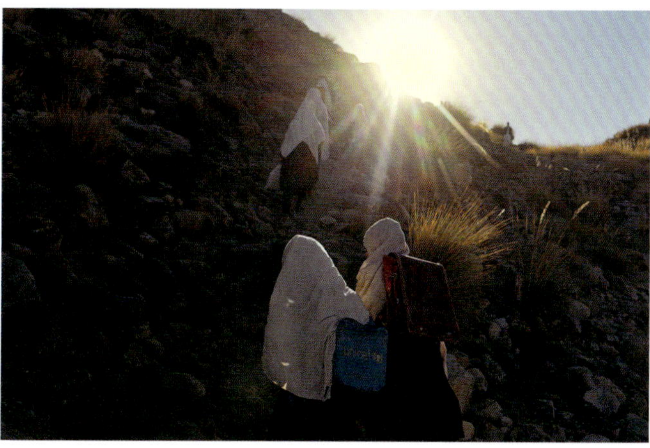

Students walk to Miadad Primary School in Khartanai Village. Hundreds of children across Afghanistan travel long distances on foot to attend classes. Haska Meyna District, Afghanistan, 13 November 2025

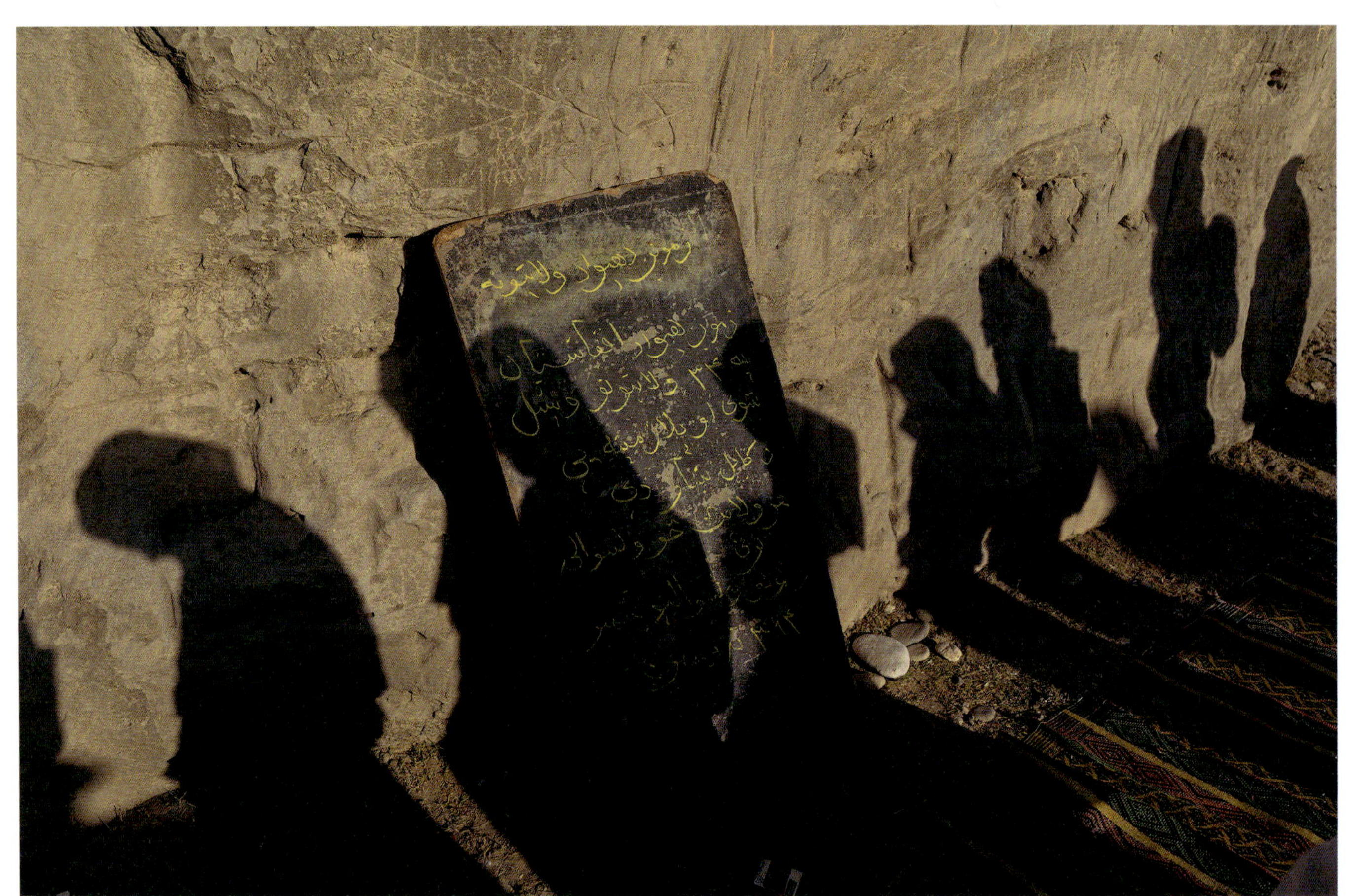

Girls attend an informal open-air school in Chaparhar District. The ban on girls attending school continues to undermine the right to education, affecting nearly 2.2 million students. Afghanistan, 12 November 2025

THE WEIGHT OF WITNESSING

TARA PIXLEY

VISUAL JOURNALIST / DIRECTOR OF THE MASTER OF JOURNALISM PROGRAM, TEMPLE UNIVERSITY, PHILADELPHIA

—

Photojournalism awards carry a dual and enduring responsibility: to enshrine an image as a historical record of its time, and to set the visual standards that will shape journalism in the years that follow. For decades, World Press Photo has occupied this role as one of the most influential institutions for evaluating, awarding, and circulating images of global consequence. Its authority has helped define not only what counts as the "most important" photograph of a given year, but also how the world is seen: who is rendered visible, how suffering is framed, and which visual narratives are legitimized through repetition.

The exhibition *What Have We Done?*, reflecting on 70 years of World Press Photo history, made clear, however, that this legacy is inseparable from its complications. A retrospective examination of more than 70 years of award-winning images surfaced recurring visual tropes that have contributed to enduring stereotypes around race, gender, conflict, and the Majority World.[1] This work of revisiting, interpreting, and recontextualizing the photographic archive is not merely corrective or symbolic; it is necessary labor for making contemporary visual journalism more legible, accountable, and accessible, while opening space for alternative visual futures to emerge.

Today, World Press Photo continues to function as a global visual standard-bearer, but under radically altered conditions. In an era defined by generative AI, widespread public distrust of institutions, and a growing sense of uncertainty about facts online, the authority of photography itself is increasingly contested. Questions of authorship, manipulation, and authenticity now accompany nearly every widely circulated image. As facts are distorted, decontextualized, or algorithmically amplified, the idea of "the real" feels increasingly fragile or negotiable. In this context, photo contests and news organizations alike are being called upon not only to select powerful images, but to actively participate in the work of visual verification and to explain that work to the publics they serve. One recent example of how this transparency can function as a form of trust-building appeared in a *New York Times* Insider essay[2] detailing how the newsroom verified a photograph shared by US president Donald Trump purporting to show Venezuelan president Nicolás Maduro in custody. The *Times* made its editorial reasoning, technical analysis, and points of uncertainty explicit. In the comments section, amid hundreds of responses, readers repeatedly expressed gratitude for this openness, noting that the explanation itself strengthened their confidence in the institution's reporting.

Political power has always relied on visual rhetoric: images deployed to legitimize authority, suppress dissent, or inflame public sentiment. As authoritarian tactics increasingly operate through spectacle and disinformation, the stakes of visual verification have never been higher. Images of detained political leaders, state violence, and human rights abuses now circulate globally within minutes, often stripped of provenance or context. In this environment, photojournalism's credibility hinges not only on what images show, but on how institutions articulate their processes of selection, verification, and publication.

I believe that such transparency, which has long been treated as peripheral or unnecessary, must now be understood as a core ethical and best-business practice of contemporary photojournalism. As organizations like World Press Photo and *The New York Times* continue to shape the visual record of our time, they are uniquely positioned to model how images are assessed, authenticated, and contextualized, helping rebuild trust while redefining visual authority for an unstable media landscape.

Fighting the flood of AI-enabled misinformation and disinformation online is an Orwellian task, one that would require visual journalists to police "truth" itself. That is not our charge. The work of photojournalism is not to discredit the value of

synthetic media wholesale, but to clarify and continually assert the significance of human-made images. Efforts such as Adobe's Content Authenticity Initiative (CAI) gesture toward this future by developing content credential tools that allow photographers to assert authorship from in-camera capture (images recorded with minimal editing or processing) through publication and circulation. While such systems remain unevenly adopted, their promise underscores a larger truth: restoring public trust in images will require collective, industry-wide commitment to verification and disclosure.

Yet the labor of visual verification cannot reside solely within institutions or technical infrastructures. It also falls to individual photojournalists – often those with the least institutional protection – to make their processes visible and legible to audiences. This expectation unfolds against a backdrop of a profoundly precarious labor market that now defines much of the photography profession.

Staff photojournalist positions have steadily declined throughout the 2010s and 2020s, while freelance, contract, and hybrid arrangements have become the norm across the news media industry. To be a photojournalist today is to navigate expanding editorial demands amid shrinking compensation, fewer labor protections, and diminishing long-term security. The same photographers increasingly asked to safeguard the credibility of visual journalism are often doing so without the stability once afforded by staff employment.

This labor uncertainty is not abstract. As this essay was being written, freelance photographers at *The Wall Street Journal* were engaged in a dispute over a proposed 2026 contract revision that would classify their work as "work made for hire," effectively stripping freelancers of their intellectual property rights. For independent photojournalists, an archive is not only a record of a life's work but often the sole form of retirement security. Ownership over one's images is not a symbolic concern, it is a condition of survival.

In the shadow of this compounding economic instability, social media platforms have become a crucial, if imperfect, space for collective visibility. Photojournalists increasingly use these platforms to share experiences, advocate for photographer labor rights[3], and to show how documentary images are actually made. What emerges is not just protest, but pedagogy: an informal, distributed education for audiences about presence, risk, ethical decision-making, and the human labor behind each photograph.

This shift challenges a long-standing norm within photojournalism. For decades, the discipline has equated quality with the erasure of the photographer's subjectivity, aligning itself with Western ideals of objectivity and neutrality. Yet this posture has always obscured a fundamental truth: every photograph is shaped by the body, biases, and perspectives of the person who makes it. To bear visual witness is to be physically present: to see, to feel, and to decide in real time. Embracing that fact means acknowledging the technical and ethical decision-making behind images.

Freelance photographers, by necessity, often become the most public-facing practitioners of this move toward greater transparency. Lacking the institutional distance afforded to staff positions, they more frequently narrate their processes, contextualize their images, and humanize their labor through public platforms and newsletters. Whether demystifying a viral Olympics photo[4] or detailing the processes behind remote portraiture,[5] such moments operate both as marketing opportunities for precariously employed freelancers and visual media literacy education for the broader public. Contemporary photojournalists are increasingly embracing that level of transparency and accessibility as core ethical commitments and a necessary part of their work. In an era of

contested images and unstable truths, this visibility is not a liability. It may be one of photojournalism's most credible paths forward.

Photojournalism is far from dead, despite recurring proclamations of its decline. On the contrary, it performs a critical function in a world that is increasingly visual and perpetually hungry for information. What must change are not the core values of the profession, but the ways in which those values are articulated, defended, and made legible to contemporary audiences. As technologies evolve and images proliferate at unprecedented speed, the inviolable importance of press photography remains: While artificial intelligence can generate images, only humans can bear witness. Documentary photographs are made not simply through technical skill, but through physical presence, ethical judgment, and relational responsibility.

In an era of contested realities, photojournalism's future depends on its willingness to clearly communicate these distinctions. The profession can no longer assume that audiences understand how images are made, verified, or selected for publication. Instead, journalists and institutions alike must actively articulate the human labor behind visual reporting: why being present matters, how decisions are made, and what ethical constraints shape the final image. Transparency, in this sense, is not an auxiliary practice or a defensive response to mistrust; it is a core visual ethic.

Treating image verification as an invisible, internal process only reinforces distance between news organizations and the publics they serve. Making verification accessible through explanation, disclosure, and dialogue invites audiences into a shared process of meaning-making. These verification narratives function as a new form of visual literacy, helping viewers understand not only whether an image is real, but why it matters, how it came to be, and what responsibilities accompany its circulation.

Photo contests and awards institutions, long central to defining the visual language of journalism, have a critical role to play in this shift. Beyond enforcing rules or disqualifying images, they can normalize disclosure as a standard practice by modeling transparency in captions, judging criteria, provenance documentation, and exhibition contexts. In doing so, they help reshape professional norms while signaling to global audiences that visual authority is not rooted in spectacle or certainty, but in accountability. Importantly, news organizations must also value the human labor behind photojournalistic work through fair compensation and preserving photographers' authorship of that work.

Ultimately, humans are driven to connect, to understand the complexities, contradictions, and nuances of our shared world. Photojournalism endures because it answers that impulse through embodied witnessing and ethical care. By embracing transparency, reimagining verification as pedagogy, and reaffirming the human foundations of visual storytelling, the field can move forward not by retreating from technological change, but by clarifying what makes human-made images indispensable in an unstable visual landscape.

—

1 The Majority World is a term referring to the global majority of Black, brown and Indigenous people who reside in nations historically referred to as "Third World" or "developing". Shahidul Alam's 2008 *Amerasia Journal* article "Majority World: Challenging the West's Rhetoric of Democracy" outlined an argument for using this more accurate term.
2 Meaghan Looram, "How The Times Assessed That Photo From Trump of Maduro in Handcuffs", *The New York Times*, 4 January 2026.
3 Aphotoeditor, "Photographers Share the Unsustainability of Working for National Publications", Instagram, 24 June 2024.
4 Katherine Pomerantz, "Behind the Photo: How Olympic Photographer Jerome Brouillet Got the Shot", *Time*, 30 July 2024.
5 Dina Litovsky, "How I Photographed 50 Remote Portraits Of Workers Fired By the Trump Administration For *The Atlantic*", In The Flash, Substack.com, 15 January 2026.

WORLD PRESS PHOTO OF THE YEAR

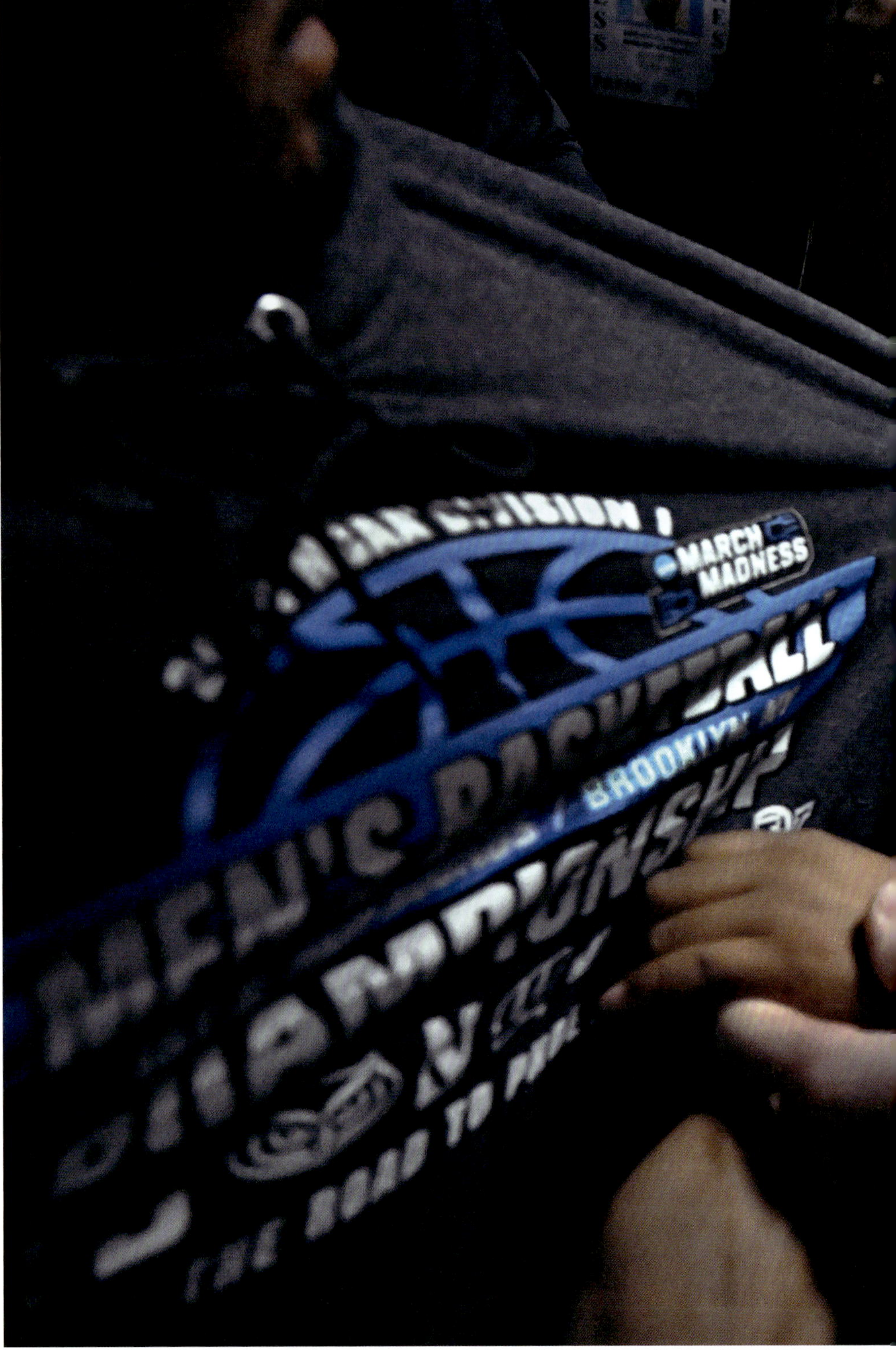

"Please understand we are coming here for a better opportunity, not just for ourselves, but for our children," said Cocha, after her husband, Luis, was detained by ICE agents following an immigration court hearing at the Jacob Javits Federal Building. Luis, an Ecuadorian migrant whom his family says has no criminal record, served as the household's sole provider. This photograph, taken inside one of the few US federal buildings where photographers were granted access,

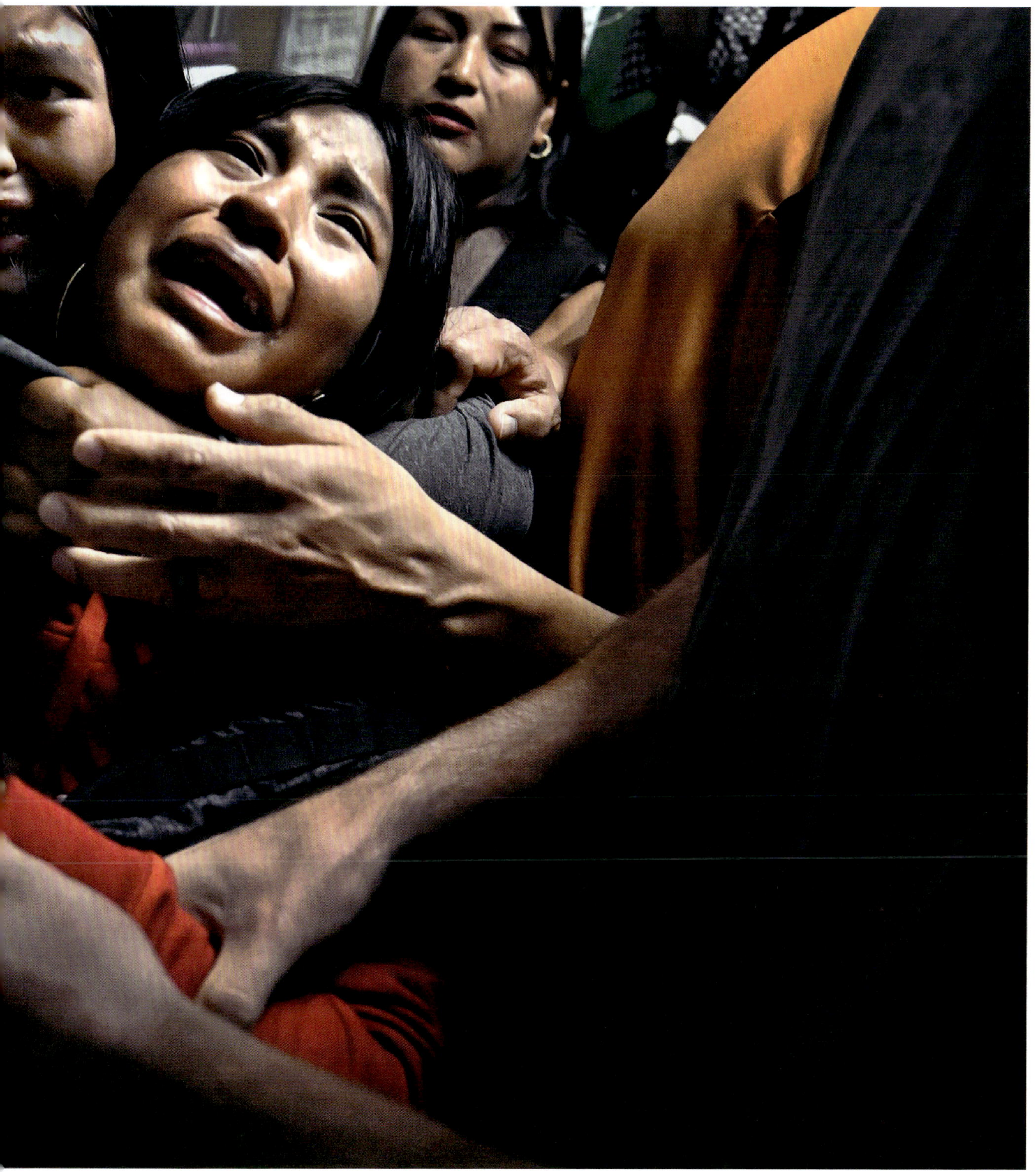

captures a harrowing moment: a family separated by the state. What Carol Guzy has documented is not an isolated instance, but a policy indiscriminately applied to people who arrive for hearings in good faith. Cocha and their three children – ages seven, 13, and 15 – were left inconsolable, facing immediate financial hardship and profound emotional trauma. In a democracy, the camera's presence in that hallway is an essential witness to a policy that has turned courthouses into sites of shattered lives.

FINALISTS

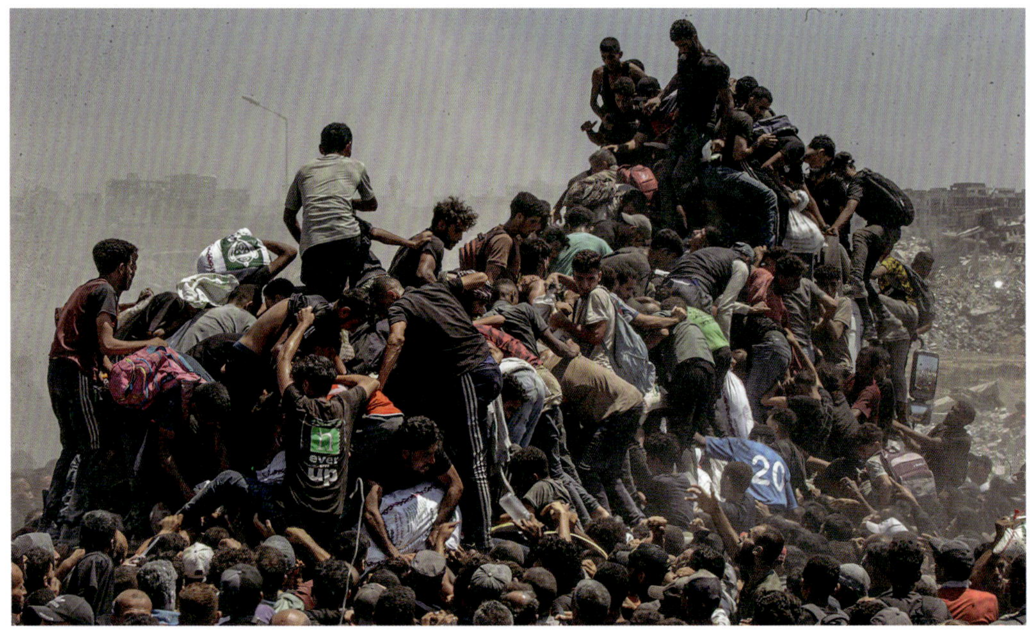

AID EMERGENCY IN GAZA
—
SABER NURALDIN
—
Palestine,
EPA Images

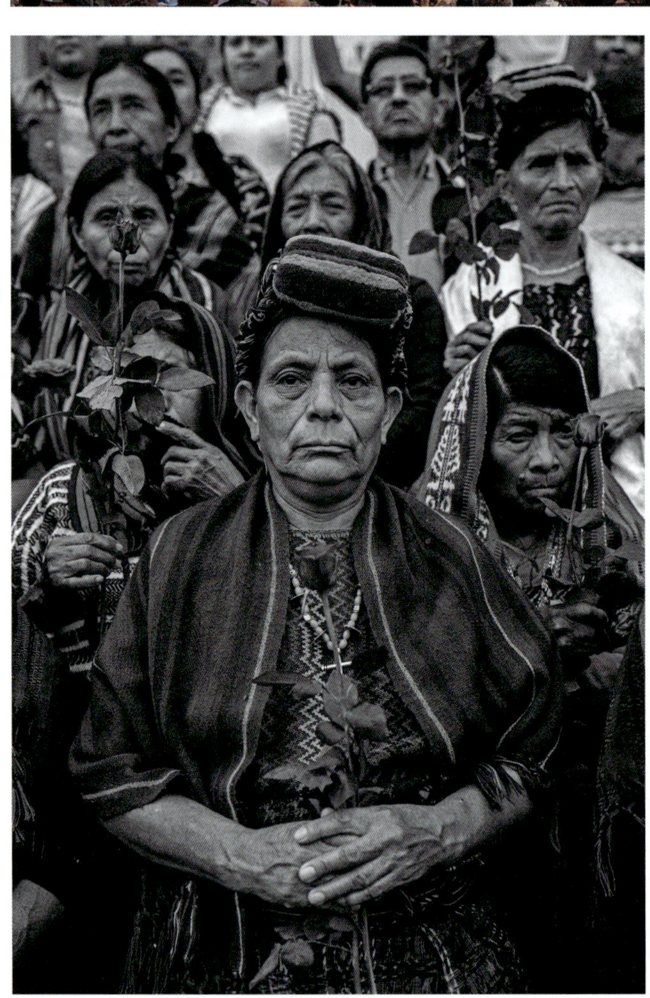

THE TRIALS OF THE ACHI WOMEN
—
VICTOR J. BLUE
—
United States,
for *The New York Times Magazine*

JURIES & WINNERS

AFRICA JURY

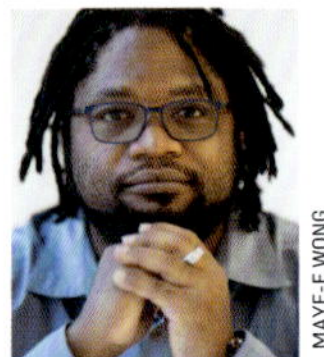

MAYE-E WONG

TSVANGIRAYI MUKWAZHI / CHAIR

—

Tsvangirayi Mukwazhi, Associated Press photojournalist, documents humanity across Africa and beyond. He uplifts emerging photographers through teaching, collaboration, and multiformat storytelling.

—

Zimbabwe
Instagram: @tmukwazhi

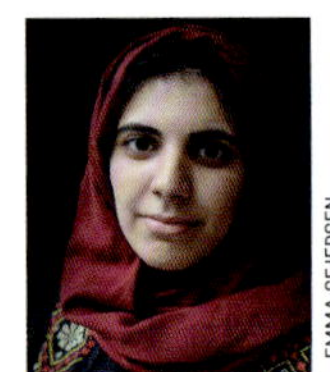

EMMA SEJERSEN

HEBA KHAMIS

—

Heba Khamis is a visual researcher and practitioner. Her work explores the ethics and emotional impact of documenting sensitive social issues through care-centered and participatory image-making.

—

Egypt
Instagram: @heba_khamis

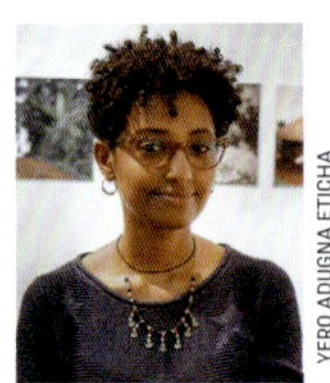

YERO ADUGNA ETICHA

MAHEDER HAILESELASSIE

—

Maheder Haileselassie is a photographer and visual artist based in Addis Ababa. Her work explores themes of history, memory, and urbanization, drawing connections between past archives and imagined futures.

—

Ethiopia
Instagram:
@maheder_haileselassie

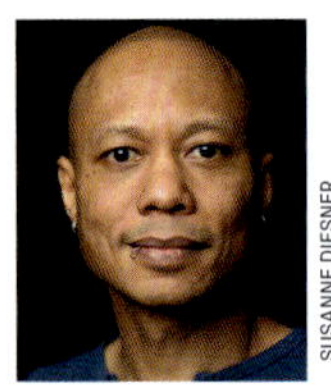

SUSANNE DIESNER

NYANI QUARMYNE

—

Nyani Quarmyne is a free-lance photographer based in Germany. His work centers on global health, social justice, and environmental issues. He is represented by Panos Pictures.

—

Australia
Instagram: @nyaniq

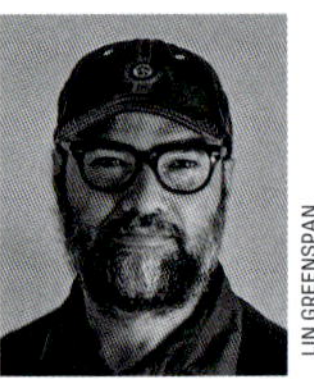

LIN GREENSPAN

PAUL BOTES

—

Paul Botes is the picture editor of *The Continent*. He has over 25 years of experience as a photographer and educator, working across the African continent.

—

South Africa
Instagram: @paulbotes

AFRICA WINNERS

SINGLES

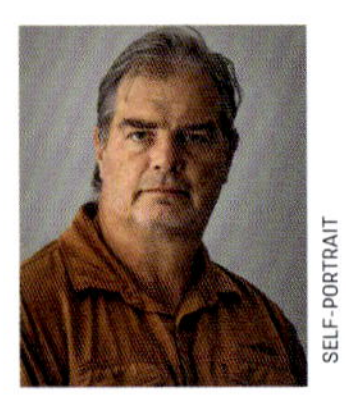

SELF-PORTRAIT

HALDEN KROG

Halden Krog is a freelance photographer based in Cape Town. For the past 27 years, he has covered news, politics, and sporting events nationally and internationally.

—

South Africa
Instagram:
@haldenkrog

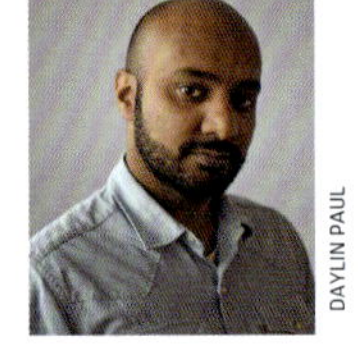

DAYLIN PAUL

IHSAAN HAFFEJEE

Ihsaan Haffejee is a photojournalist based in Johannesburg. He is an independent freelance photographer focusing on social justice issues.

—

South Africa
Instagram:
@ihsaan_haffo

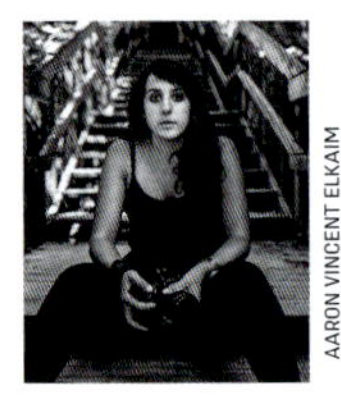

AARON VINCENT ELKAIM

KIANA HAYERI

Kiana Hayeri is a photographer based in Sarajevo. Her work explores complex topics such as migration, adolescence, identity, and sexuality in war-ridden countries.

—

Iran/Canada
Instagram:
@kianahayeri

STORIES

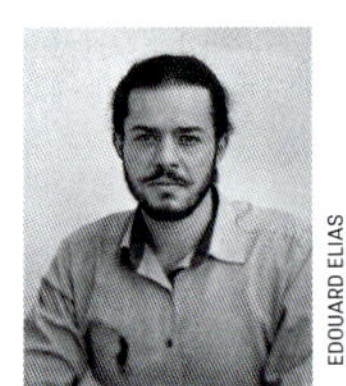

EDOUARD ELIAS

ABDULMONAM EASSA

Abdulmonam Eassa is a photojournalist covering Sudan, Syria and the wider region. His work documents the lives of ordinary people in conflict zones with a focus on dignity, survival, and shared humanity.

—

Syria/France
Instagram:
@abdulmonam_eassa

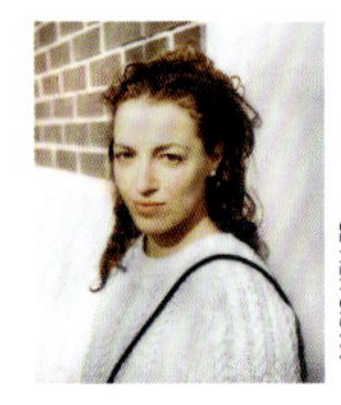

MARIO HELLER

CHANTAL PINZI

Chantal Pinzi is a visual activist based in Berlin. Her photographic work often addresses issues of resilience in fractured and marginalized communities through the voices of women.

—

Italy
Instagram:
@chantalpinzi.
photography

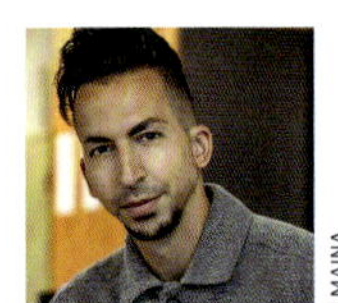

SIMON MAINA

LUIS TATO

Luis Tato is a photojournalist based in Nairobi. He is the chief photographer for East Africa and the Indian Ocean at Agence France-Presse.

—

Spain
Instagram:
@luistatophoto

LONG-TERM PROJECTS

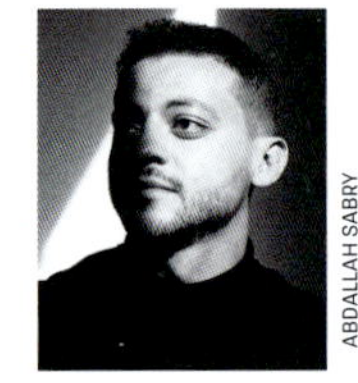

ABDALLAH SABRY

MOHAMED MAHDY

Mohamed Mahdy is a visual storyteller and educator based in Alexandria. He documents marginalized Egyptian communities, exploring impermanence, identity, and resilience.

—

Egypt
Instagram:
@mohamedmahdyph

ASIA-PACIFIC AND OCEANIA JURY

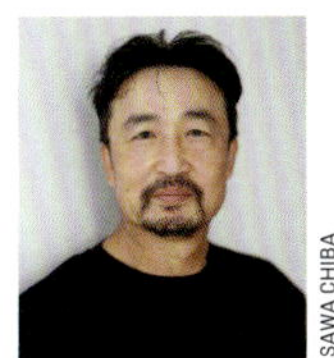

SAWA CHIBA

YASUYOSHI CHIBA / CHAIR

—

Yasuyoshi Chiba is the Agence France-Presse (AFP) chief photographer for Indonesia and East Timor. His work is recognized for his empathetic visual documentation of global realities.

—

Japan
Instagram: @yasuyoshi_chiba

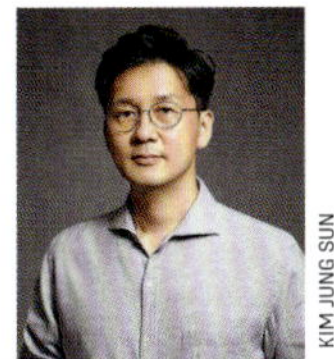

KIM JUNG SUN

KIM KYUNG-HOON

—

Kim Kyung-Hoon is a senior photographer at Reuters, based in Tokyo. He has received the Pulitzer Prize and multiple international awards.

—

South Korea
Instagram:
@kim_reuters_photojournalist

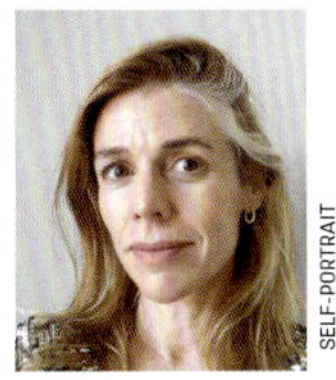

SELF-PORTRAIT

NICKY CATLEY

—

Nicky Catley is one half of the photo editor duo who manage the photography department at *The Sydney Morning Herald*. She also assigns and edits photography for different sections and editions of *The AFR Magazine*.

—

Australia

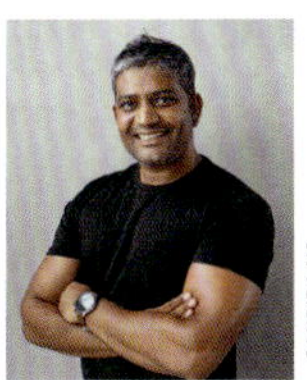

CANDIDA NG

VIVEK PRAKASH

—

Vivek Prakash is Getty Images' managing editor for news for the Asia-Pacific. He has over 20 years of experience as a photographer and editor.

—

Australia
Instagram: @vivpix

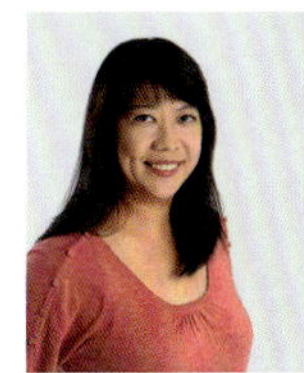

DESMOND WEE

WANG HUI FEN

—

Wang Hui Fen is the photo editor of *The Straits Times*, Singapore's English daily newspaper. A photojournalist since 1999, she has won the SOPA and WAN-IFRA awards for visual storytelling.

—

Singapore

ASIA-PACIFIC AND OCEANIA WINNERS

SINGLES

STORIES

LONG-TERM PROJECTS

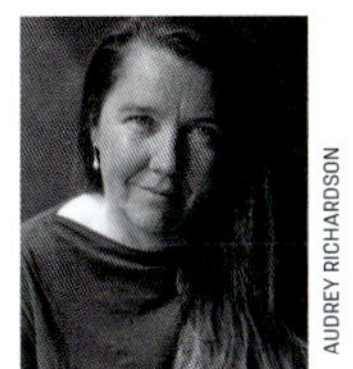

AUDREY RICHARDSON

EDWINA PICKLES

—

Edwina Pickles has been a staff photographer with *The Sydney Morning Herald* since 2000. Her work documents Australian life and humanitarian issues.

—

Australia
Instagram:
@eddiepickles

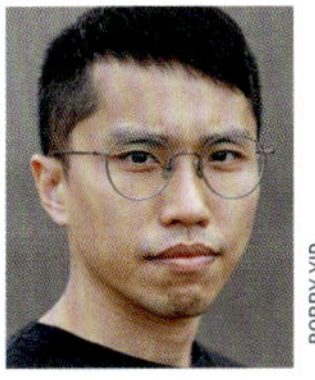

BOBBY YIP

TYRONE SIU

—

Tyrone Siu is a Hong Kong-based photographer for Reuters, covering breaking news, politics, and social issues across Asia.

—

Hong Kong
Instagram:
@tyrone_siu

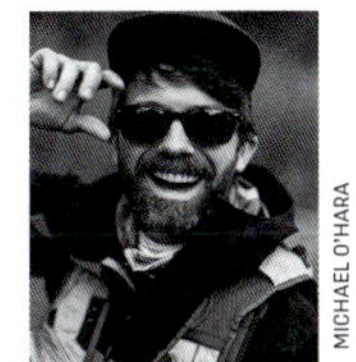

MICHAEL O'HARA

ROB G. GREEN

—

Rob G. Green is a National Geographic Explorer, documentary photographer, and filmmaker based in Montana. Through long-term projects he documents stories about wildlife, wildfire, and wild places.

—

United States
Instagram:
@rob_g_green

AARON FAVILA

—

Aaron Favila is a Manila-based photographer for The Associated Press, covering disasters, conflicts, sports, politics, and daily life.

—

Philippines
Instagram:
@aaronfavila

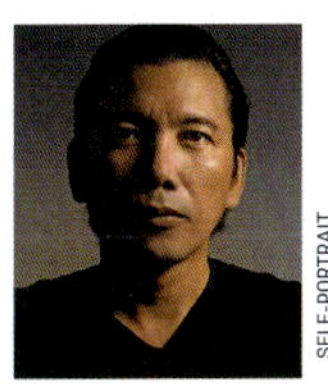

SELF-PORTRAIT

JES AZNAR

—

Jes Aznar is a photojournalist and documentary photographer based in Manila, focusing on Asia and the Pacific.

—

Philippines
Instagram: @jeszmann

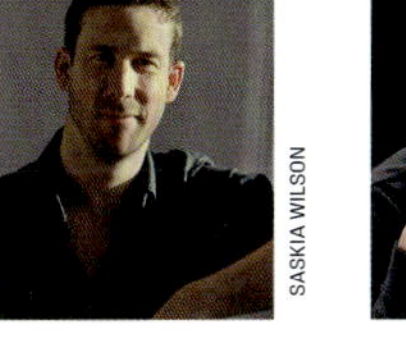

SASKIA WILSON

MATTHEW ABBOTT

—

Matthew Abbott is a Sydney-based documentary photographer specializing in in-depth visual storytelling on social, cultural and environmental issues across Australia and the Pacific.

—

Australia
Instagram:
@mattabbottphoto

LIU XUEWEN

WU FANG

—

Wu Fang is a photographer based in China. Throughout his career he has covered major international events and conflicts, contributing to international agencies and publications.

—

China

EUROPE JURY

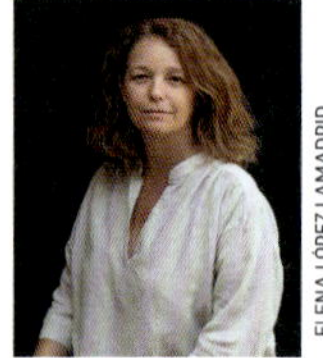

ELENA LÓPEZ LAMADRID

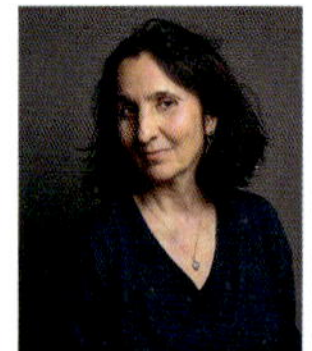

FRANCESCA LEONARDI

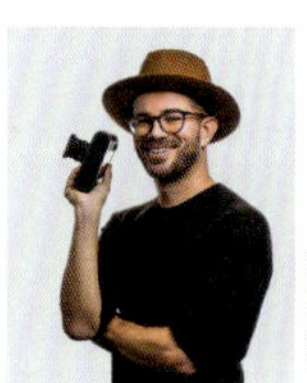

BART BREET

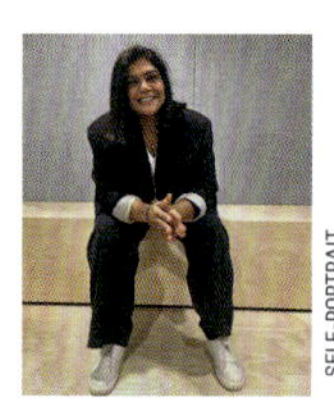

SELF-PORTRAIT

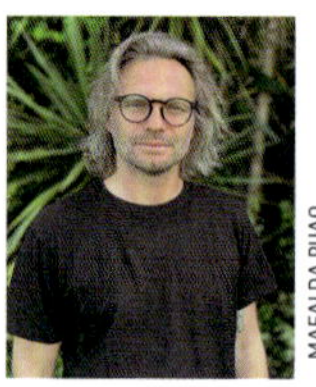

MAFALDA RUAO

SILVIA OMEDES / CHAIR

—

Silvia Omedes is an independent curator, editor, photographers' agent, and cultural manager based in Barcelona. She is the founder and director of the Photographic Social Vision Foundation.

—

Spain
Instagram: @Photographicsv

ELENA BOILLE

—

Elena Boille is deputy editor and photo editor of the Italian weekly magazine *Internazionale*, which she co-founded in 1993. She oversees the photo desk and the science pages.

—

Italy
Instagram: @eboille

JASPER DOEST

—

Jasper Doest is a photojournalist exploring the relationship between humanity and nature, using visual storytelling to inspire empathy, challenge perceptions, and foster meaningful environmental change.

—

Netherlands
Instagram: @jasperdoest

KRISHNA SHETH

—

Krishna Sheth is the director of photography at *The Economist*. She has over 30 years' experience shaping powerful visual storytelling for major publications and international brands.

—

United Kingdom
Instagram: @krishnasheth

KRZYSZTOF CANDROWICZ

—

Krzysztof Candrowicz is an interdisciplinary curator, sociologist, researcher, project facilitator, and activist. He is the co-founder of the Foundation of Visual Education and Fotofestiwal in Lodz.

—

Poland
Instagram: @krisceee

EUROPE WINNERS

SINGLES

STORIES

LONG-TERM PROJECTS

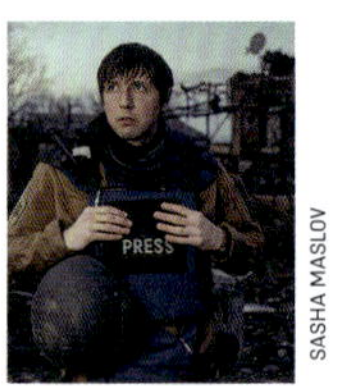

SASHA MASLOV

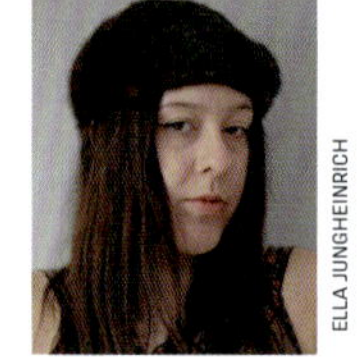

ELLA JUNGHEINRICH

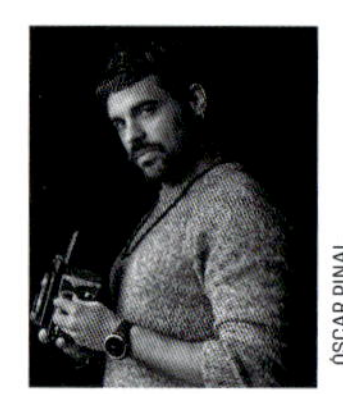

SELF-PORTRAIT

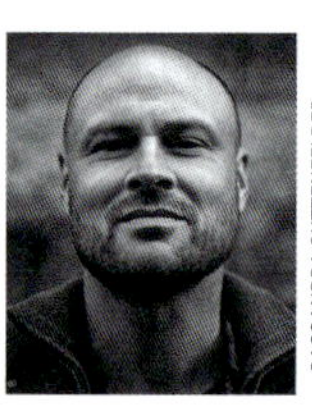

ÓSCAR PINAL

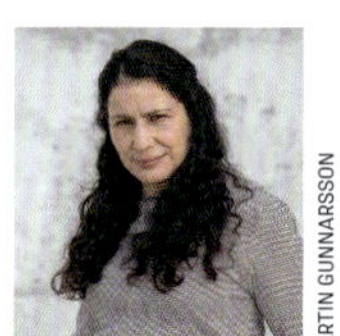

CASSANDRA GUTTENFELDER

MARTIN GUNNARSSON

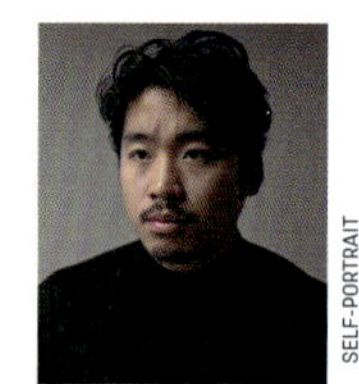

SELF-PORTRAIT

EVGENIY MALOLETKA

Evgeniy Maloletka is a war photographer, journalist and filmmaker based in Kyiv. Working for The Associated Press, he has been covering the war in Ukraine since 2014.

—

Ukraine
Instagram:
@evgenymaloletka

PAULA HORNICKEL

Paula Hornickel is a portrait and documentary photographer based in Dortmund and Berlin. Her work explores future visions, pop culture, and social issues.

—

Germany
Instagram:
@paulahornickel

ROIE GALITZ

Roie Galitz is a wildlife photographer and educator based in Tel Aviv. For over a decade, he has documented wildlife worldwide. He is also the founder of a photography school in Israel and a photo travel company.

—

Israel
Instagram:
@roiegalitz

BRAIS LORENZO

Brais Lorenzo is a photographer based in Ourense whose work focuses on social and environmental issues. He collaborates with national and international press agencies.

—

Spain
Instagram:
@braislorenzo

DAVID GUTTENFELDER

David Guttenfelder is a *New York Times* visual journalist based in Minneapolis, United States, reporting globally on geopolitical conflict, humanitarian crises, environmental challenges, and social injustice.

—

United States
Instagram:
@dguttenfelder

SANNA SJÖSWÄRD

Sanna Sjöswärd is a photographer, author, and visual storyteller based in Stockholm. Her work focuses on identity, memory, and human dignity.

—

Sweden/Iran
Instagram:
@ginosarfatti

WILLIAM KEO

William Keo is a photographer based in Paris. His work covers themes of migration, social exclusion, and inter-community intolerance.

—

France/Cambodia
Instagram:
@william.keo

NORTH AND CENTRAL AMERICA JURY

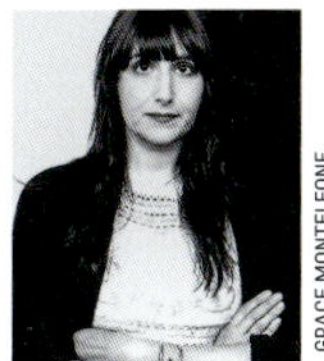

MARIE A. MONTELEONE / CHAIR

—

Marie A. Monteleone is an enterprise senior photo editor at *Bloomberg News*. Her career spans major media organizations and includes ongoing work as a mentor, juror, and speaker.

—

United States
Instagram: @mountainlion6

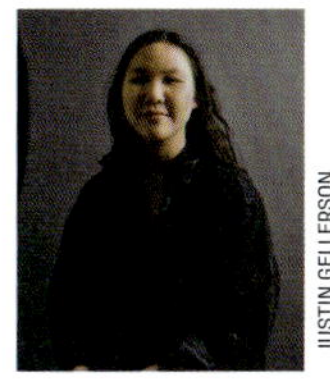

EMILY JAN

—

Emily Jan is the deputy director of Visuals at the *San Francisco Chronicle*, where she helps lead a team of photojournalists and photo editors with the goal of making creative, critical, and moving visuals.

—

United States
Instagram: @emilyjan

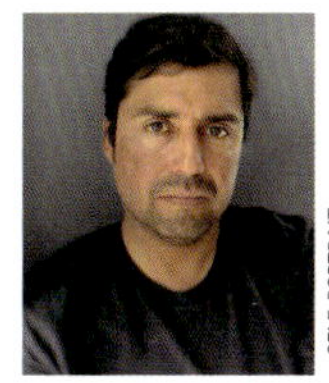

MICHAEL ROBINSON CHÁVEZ

—

Michael Robinson Chávez is a Pulitzer Prize–winning visual journalist who has covered significant events in over 75 countries. He lives with his family in Valencia, Spain.

—

United States
Instagram: @mrobinsonchavez

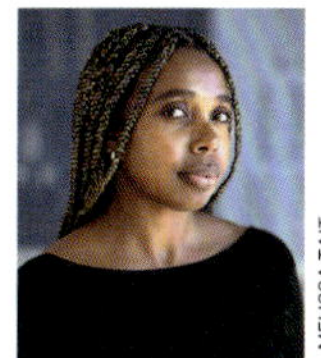

SOLANA CAIN

—

Solana Cain is the senior visuals editor at *The Globe and Mail*. A mentor and educator, she helped establish Room Up Front, mentors emerging photographers, and curates exhibitions.

—

Canada
Instagram: @_solanacain

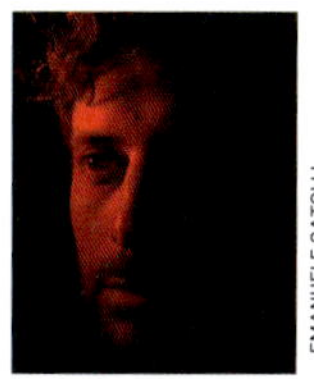

DANIELE VOLPE

—

Daniele Volpe is a documentary photographer based in Guatemala. His work explores issues related to human rights and social justice in Latin American countries.

—

Italy
Instagram: @daniele_volpe

NORTH AND CENTRAL AMERICA WINNERS

SINGLES

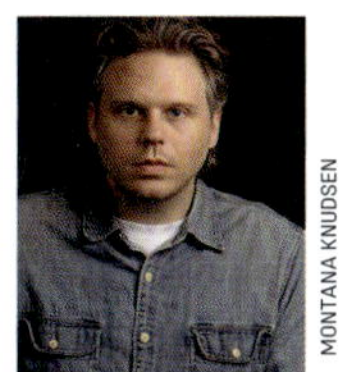

ALEX KENT

—

Alex Kent is a Washington DC–based freelance photojournalist whose work blends documentary and classic photojournalism. His work focuses on justice, power, and lived experience.

—

United States
Instagram:
@not_alex_kent_

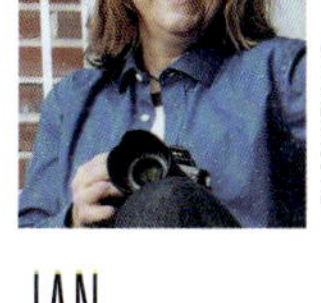

JAN SONNENMAIR

—

Jan Sonnenmair is a photojournalist and filmmaker based in Portland. Her work focuses on intimate human stories and has been published internationally.

—

United States
Instagram:
@antjan

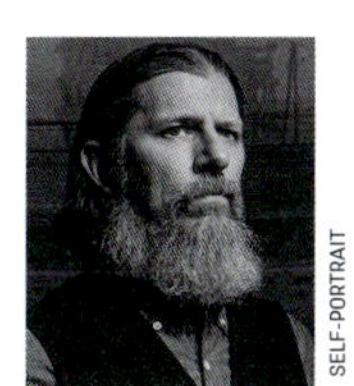

VICTOR J. BLUE

—

Victor J. Blue is a New York-based photojournalist whose work examines the legacy of armed conflict and human rights issues.

—

United States
Instagram:
@victorblue

STORIES

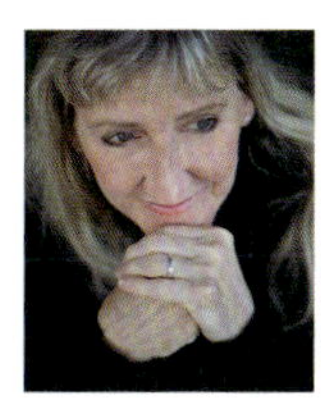

CAROL GUZY

—

Carol Guzy is a photojournalist working on long-form documentary human interest projects, news, and feature stories. She is a contract photographer with ZUMA Press.

—

United States
Instagram:
@carolguzy

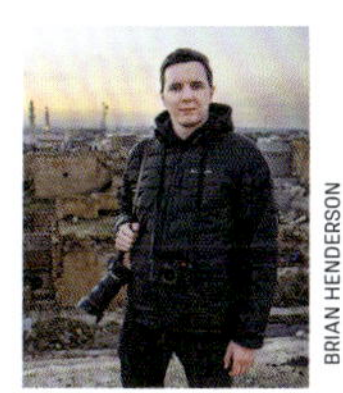

ETHAN SWOPE

—

Ethan Swope is a Los Angeles–based photographer and documentary filmmaker. His work covers California wildfires, the war in Ukraine, and civil unrest in the United States and abroad.

—

United States
Instagram:
@ethanswopephoto

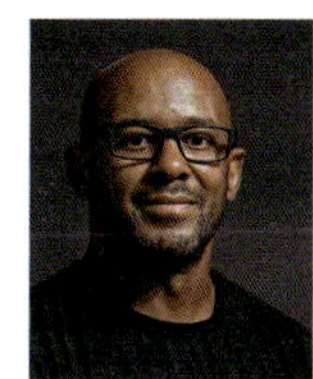

JAHI CHIKWENDIU

—

Jahi Chikwendiu is a photojournalist based in Washington, DC. He worked as a staff photographer at *The Washington Post* for almost 25 years, reporting across dozens of countries on five continents.

—

United States
Instagram:
@jaheezus

LONG-TERM PROJECTS

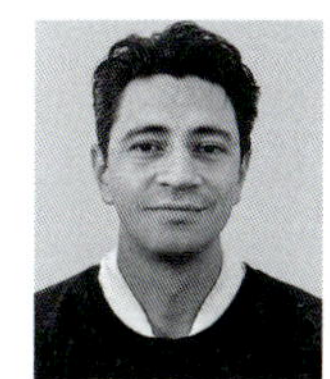

CÉSAR RODRÍGUEZ

—

César Rodríguez is a photographer based in Xalisco. His work focuses on people and their stories about migration, human rights, and climate change.

—

Mexico
Instagram:
@cesar_rodriguezb

SOUTH AMERICA JURY

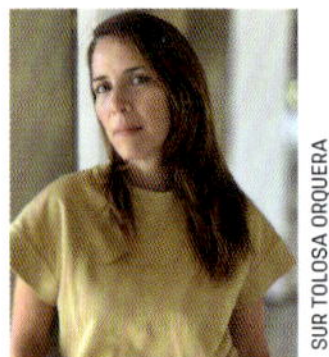
SUR TOLOSA ORQUERA

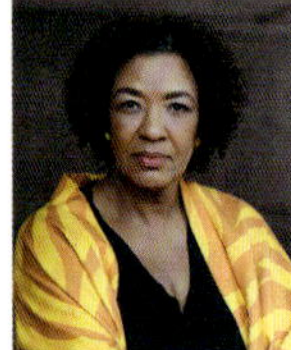
DIEGO BRESANI

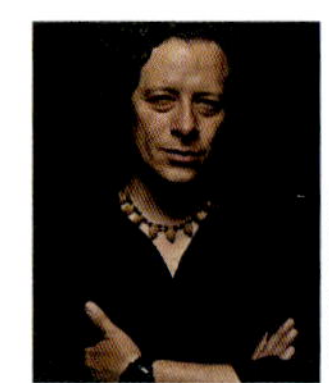
ANDRÉS ANFASSA

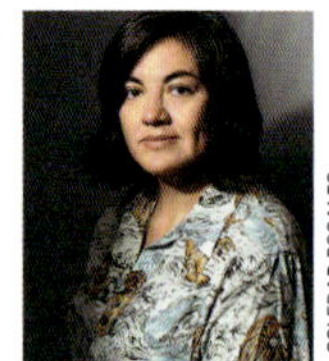
SOLEDAD ROSALES

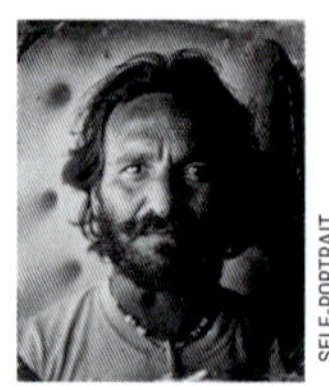
SELF-PORTRAIT

GAEL ALMEIDA / CHAIR

—

Gael Almeida is the executive director for Latin America at the National Geographic Society, where she supports Explorers and generates synergies with different partners in the region.

—

Mexico
Instagram: @galuchis

DENISE CAMARGO

—

Denise Camargo is a photographer with experience in visual arts, teaching, and curating as an artistic practice and method. She focuses on creative processes and the image in Afro-Brazilian matrices.

—

Brazil
Instagram: @camargodenise

FEDERICO RÍOS

—

Federico Ríos is a photojournalist who has extensively covered Latin America, documenting armed conflict, environmental issues, and their impact on society.

—

Colombia
Instagram: @historiassencillas

KARLA GACHET VEGA

—

Karla Gachet Vega is a Los Angeles-based visual storyteller with nearly two decades of experience documenting culture and identity across the Americas, while mentoring collaborative, community-centered storytelling.

—

Ecuador
Instagram: @kchete77

RODRIGO ABD

—

Rodrigo Abd is a staff photographer for The Associated Press. He has been covering news in Latin America and around the world for more than 25 years.

—

Argentina
Instagram: @abdrodrigo

SOUTH AMERICA WINNERS

SINGLES

STORIES

LONG-TERM PROJECTS

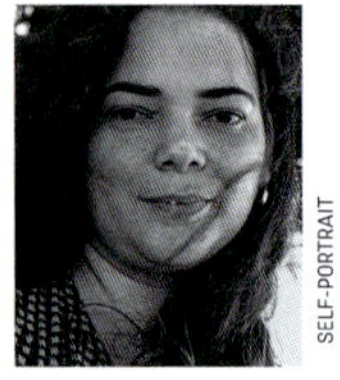
SELF-PORTRAIT

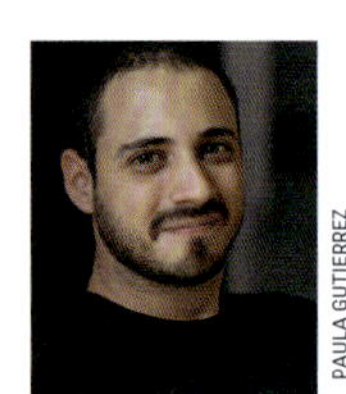
PAULA GUTIERREZ

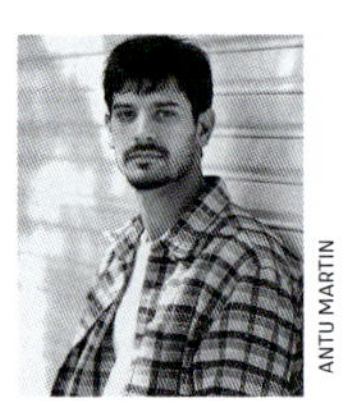
ANTU MARTIN

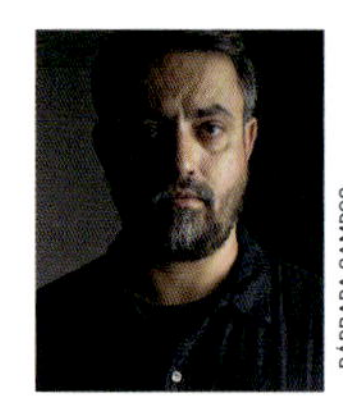
BÁRBARA CAMPOS

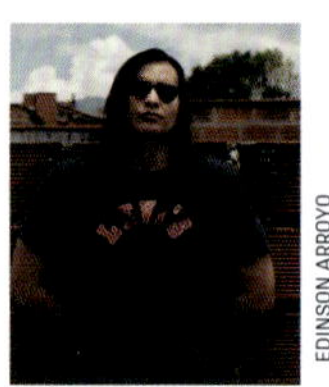
EDINSON ARROYO

CAMILO TRIANA

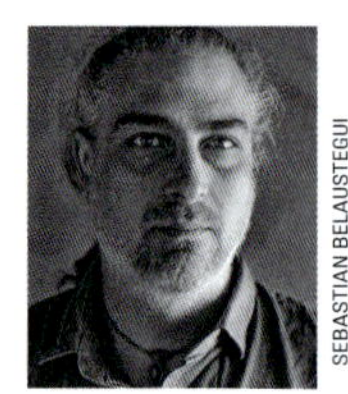
SEBASTIAN BELAUSTEGUI

PRISCILA RIBEIRO

Priscila Ribeiro is a documentary photographer based in Curitiba. Her work focuses on human rights, migration, gender-based violence, and the environment.

—

Brazil
Instagram:
@priscilaribeiroft

SANTIAGO ARCOS

Santiago Arcos is a photographer based in Guayaquil. His documentary and photojournalism work focuses on social and environmental issues.

—

Ecuador
Instagram:
@santiarcosv

TADEO BOURBON

Tadeo Bourbon is a Buenos Aires-based documentary photographer with perspectives oriented toward human rights and the history of Latin America. He is a member of Colectivo Triada.

—

Argentina
Instagram:
@bourbontadeo

EDUARDO ANIZELLI

Eduardo Anizelli is a staff photojournalist at *Folha de S.Paulo*, where he has worked since 2012. His work has been published both nationally and internationally.

—

Brazil
Instagram: @anizelli

FERLEY A. OSPINA

Ferley A. Ospina is a photographer based in Cúcuta. His work explores migration, environmental, and social issues.

—

Colombia
Instagram:
@ferleyospina

EVER ANDRÉS MERCADO PUENTES

—

Ever Andrés Mercado Puentes is a photographer based in Buenaventura. His documentary work centers on human rights, peacebuilding, and ancestral culture.

—

Colombia
Instagram:
@everandresmercado

PABLO E. PIOVANO

Pablo E. Piovano is a documentary photographer based in Buenos Aires. His work investigates human rights, public health, and environmental harm.

—

Argentina
Instagram:
@piovanopablo

WEST, CENTRAL, AND SOUTH ASIA JURY

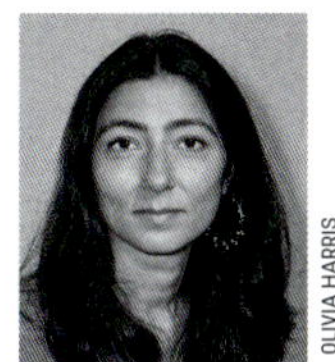

OLIVIA HARRIS

GABRIELLE FONSECA JOHNSON / CHAIR

—

Gabrielle Fonseca Johnson is the South Asia Editor for Reuters, based in New Delhi. Previously, she was the senior editor for Wider Image, the agency's imprint for long-form photojournalism.

—

United Kingdom
Instagram: @gfonsecajohnson

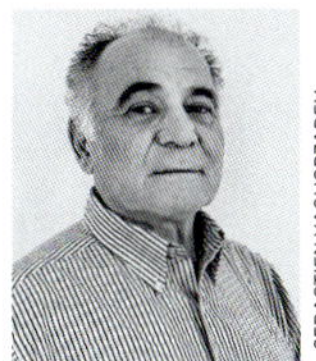

SEBASTIEN YAGHOBZADEH

ALFRED YAGHOBZADEH

—

Alfred Yaghobzadeh is a photojournalist based in France. His extensive career spans breaking news, major conflicts in Asia and Africa, humanitarian crises, fashion, and sport.

—

France/Iran
Instagram:
@alfredyaghobzadehphoto

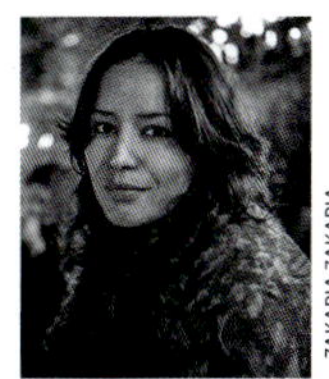

ZAKARIA ZAKARIA

ALICE MARTINS

—

Alice Martins is an independent photojournalist reporting on armed conflict and humanitarian crises since 2012 in Gaza, Syria, Iraq and Ukraine. She is currently based in Damascus.

—

Brazil
Instagram: @martinsalicea

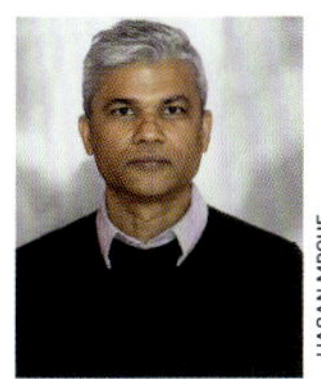

HASAN MROUE

JEWEL SAMAD

—

Jewel Samad is a photojournalist currently serving as photo editor-in-chief Middle East and North Africa for Agence France-Presse (AFP).

—

Bangladesh/United States

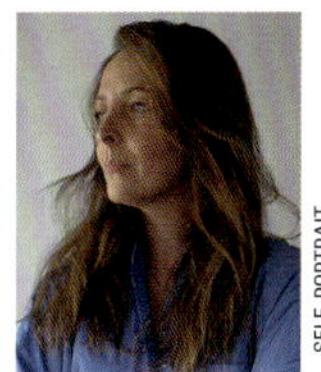

SELF-PORTRAIT

SIMA DIAB

—

Sima Diab is a managing editor for EPA Images, based in Cairo, overseeing photographers and editors across Southwest Asia, North Africa, as well as globally.

—

Syria/United States
Instagram: @sima_diab

WEST, CENTRAL, AND SOUTH ASIA WINNERS

SINGLES

STORIES

LONG-TERM PROJECTS

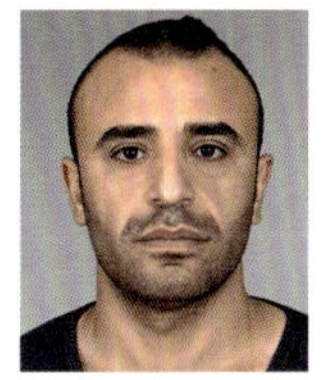

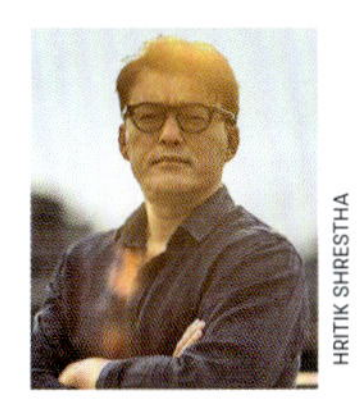

HRITIK SHRESTHA

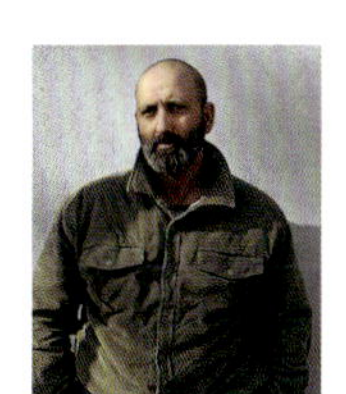

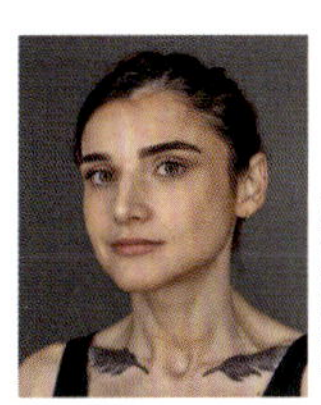

RENAUD BOUCHEZ

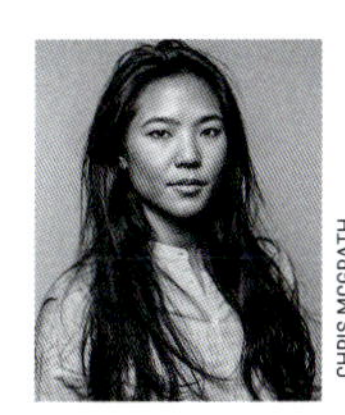

CHRIS MCGRATH

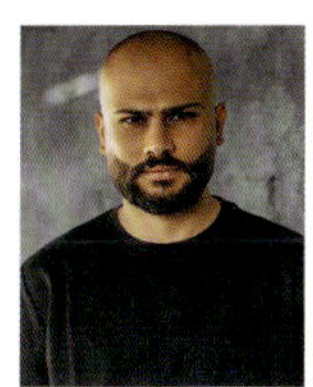

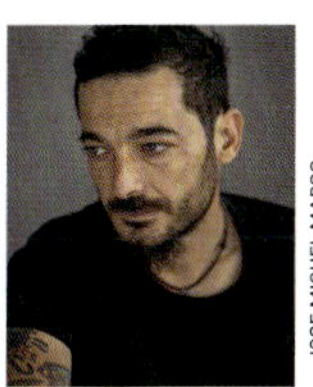

JOSE MIGUEL MARCO

SABER NURALDIN

—

Saber Nuraldin is a photojournalist reporting from the Gaza Strip for EPA Images. His work focuses on the human impact of the Israeli-Palestinian conflict, documenting major events since 1997.

—

Palestine
Instagram:
@saber.nuraldin

NARENDRA SHRESTHA

—

Narendra Shrestha is a photojournalist based in Kathmandu. He began his career in national publications before joining EPA Images in 2003, documenting historic events in Nepal and international assignments.

—

Nepal
Instagram:
@narenphoto

YASIR IQBAL

—

Yasir Iqbal is a photojournalist based in Kashmir. Since beginning his career in 2007, he has worked independently and as a staff photographer for various publications in New Delhi.

—

India
Instagram: @yaasiriqbal

ELISE BLANCHARD

—

Elise Blanchard is an independent photojournalist, based in Afghanistan since 2019. Her work focuses on women and girls under Taliban rule, documenting conflict, humanitarian crises, and maternal healthcare.

—

France
Instagram:
@eliseblchrd

NICOLE TUNG

—

Nicole Tung is a freelance photojournalist based in Istanbul. Her work explores those most affected by conflict and the consequences of war, human rights abuses, and women's rights.

—

Hong Kong/
United States
Instagram:
@nicoletung

SAHER ALGHORRA

—

Saher Alghorra is a photojournalist based in the Gaza Strip, collaborating with international agencies and publications.

—

Palestine
Instagram:
@saher_alghorra

DIEGO IBARRA SÁNCHEZ

—

Diego Ibarra Sánchez is a photographer based in Lebanon. Aiming to inspire critical thinking, his long-term visual storytelling explores conflict, resilience, and education.

—

Spain
Instagram:
@diego.ibarra.sanchez

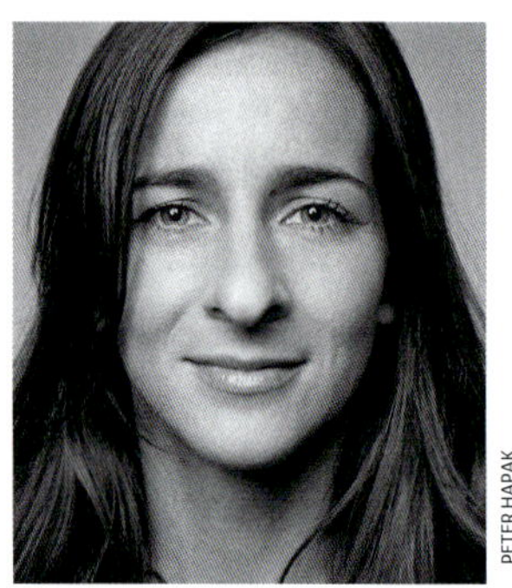

PETER HAPAK

KIRA
POLLACK / CHAIR
—
Kira Pollack is a Harvard
Shorenstein Center fellow
exploring archival innovation
through emerging technologies.
She previously held leadership
roles at *Time*, *Vanity Fair*, and
The New York Times Magazine.
—
United States
Instagram: @kirapollack

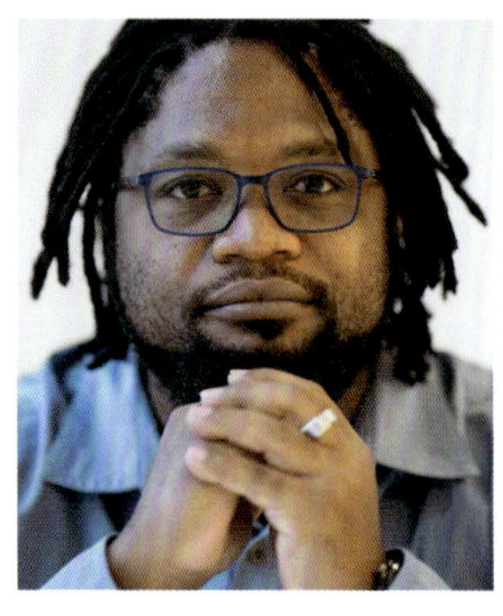

TSVANGIRAYI
MUKWAZHI

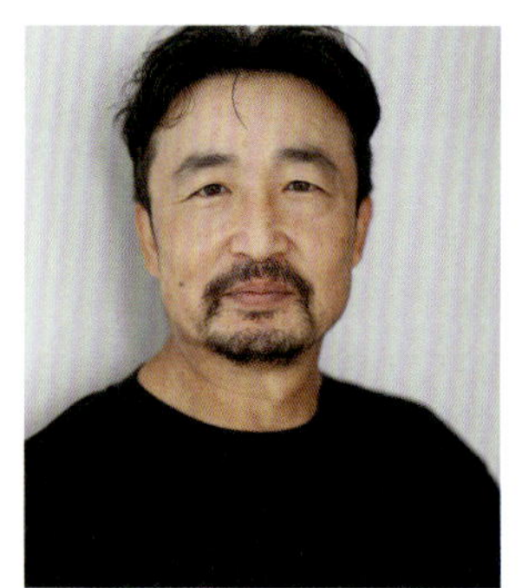

YASUYOSHI
CHIBA

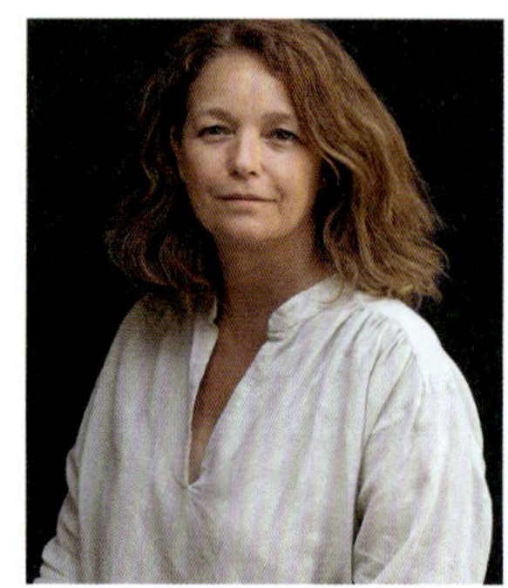

SILVIA
OMEDES

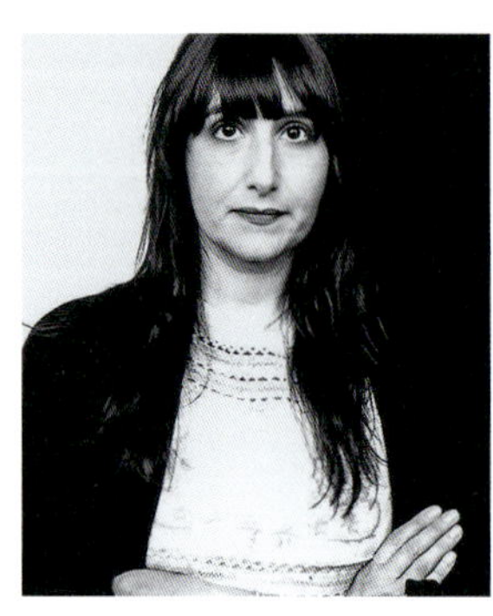

MARIE A.
MONTELEONE

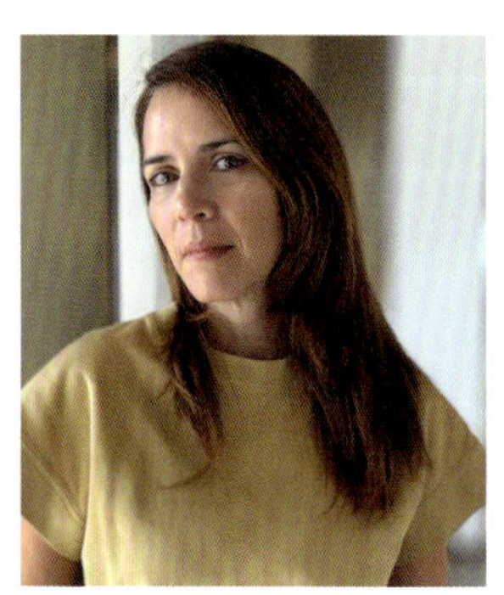

GAEL
ALMEIDA

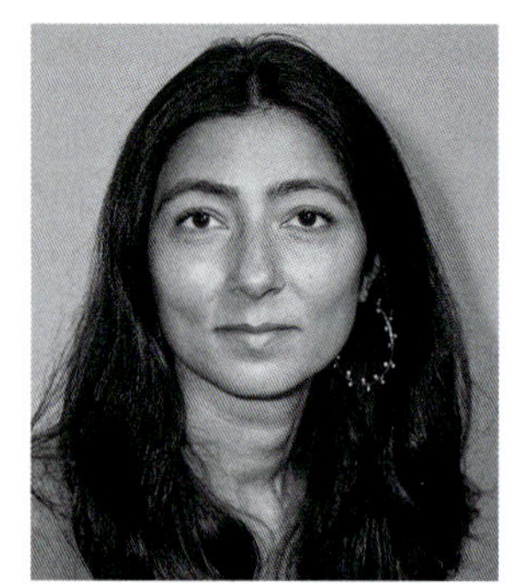

GABRIELLE FONSECA
JOHNSON

HOW WE VERIFY ENTRIES

In an era of misinformation, credibility in photojournalism matters more than ever. To ensure transparency and trust, all work submitted to the contest goes through three rigorous verification stages.

Entry checks

Each submission is carefully reviewed to ensure it meets the contest rules and category requirements. We verify, for example, that photographers work professionally, that entries consist of single-frame images, and that creation and publication dates align with our guidelines. This first step ensures that all entries are assessed on equal and transparent terms.

Forensic analysis

As photographs progress in the competition, they are examined more closely. Those that reach the final rounds undergo forensic analysis. At this stage, photographers are asked to submit their RAW files – the unedited images as captured by the camera. These files allow us to see exactly what was recorded at the moment the photograph was taken and to compare it with the final image that was entered into the contest. An independent verification team carefully examines the files to detect any signs of manipulation. Even subtle changes, such as removing a shadow or altering a small detail, can change how a story is understood.

World Press Photo maintains clear and strict guidelines about image manipulation. Adding or removing content, or making excessive adjustments that alter the original scene, can lead to disqualification. Images may only move forward in the competition if they meet our criteria.

If concerns arise, they are carefully reviewed by the World Press Photo team and the global jury. By verifying every winning image, we aim to ensure that audiences can trust what they see.

Fact-checking and research

Once the winners are selected, an external research team fact-checks the context in which each photograph or story was produced, shared, and published. This includes verifying names, dates, locations, and events, and confirming that captions accurately reflect what is shown in the image. In addition, the research team gathers additional background information to place each photograph within its broader context. While photographers provide the initial captions, these texts are refined and expanded to give audiences a full picture of the story.

World Press Photo is responsible for the texts that accompany the winning images, as they appear in this yearbook, our exhibitions, and on our website. Providing context is essential. By offering carefully researched and factual information, we aim to support visual literacy and invite readers to engage more deeply with the stories behind the images.

During this process, photographers are consulted to provide additional details and to fact-check the final captions and story descriptions. Through this shared process of verification, we work to ensure that the images you see can be trusted – and that the stories they tell are presented with accuracy, respect, and responsibility.

REGIONAL MODEL

Regions

The 2026 World Press Photo Contest worked with six regions worldwide: Africa; Asia-Pacific and Oceania; Europe; North and Central America; South America; and West, Central, and South Asia. Entries were judged and awarded in the region in which the photographs and stories were made.

Categories

Each region has three format-based categories: Singles, Stories, and Long-Term Projects. These categories welcome entries that document news moments, events, and aftermaths, as well as social, political, and environmental issues or solutions. Three winners per region are chosen for the Singles and Stories categories. One Long-Term Project winner is awarded per region.

Singles

Single-frame photographs made in 2025.

Stories

Between four and ten single-frame photographs, made in 2024 or 2025. At least four photographs in a story must have been made in 2025.

Long-Term Projects

Projects on a single theme, containing between 24 and 30 single-frame photographs. An entry must contain photographs from at least three different years, and a minimum of six photographs must have been made in 2025.

World Press Photo of the Year

The global jury chooses the World Press Photo of the Year and two finalists out of photographs made in 2025, from all 42 winning entries.

SUPPORT THE FUTURE OF PHOTOJOURNALISM

We hope you've enjoyed this book and that it has offered you meaningful insight into some of the most important stories shaping our world today. As we continue to amplify these stories and share them globally, we invite you to consider supporting our work.

Your generosity helps us train the next generation of photographers – especially those working in high-risk areas – and safeguards the legacy of independent, trustworthy visual journalism, now and for the future. You can support us with a one-off or recurring donation, or by leaving a gift to World Press Photo in your will, helping ensure that these stories continue to be told for generations to come.

For more information, please contact us at
fundraising@worldpressphoto.org

Editor-in-Chief
Joumana El Zein Khoury

Managing Editor
Mercedes Almagro
Ocaña

Writers
George Zhu
Kirstie Crail

Project Management
Juliane Steinbrecher
Marika Cukrowski
Pia Pol

Captions Coordinator
Beatrice Harbour

Research Coordinator
Catharine Isabelle
Haitzmann

Research
Belén García Aldana
Catharine Isabelle
Haitzmann
Daisy Corbin O'Grady
Kuljit Dhami
Leyla Eminova
Nada Hossam Elbohi
Nadine Joinville
Ryan P.R. Pears

Design
–SYB–
syb-photobooks.com

**Translations
Coordinators**
Juliane Steinbrecher
Michael Konze
Naomi Purswani

Translations
Aurélie Daniel | French
Han van der Vegt | Dutch
Oscar Zoetman | Dutch
Nina Goldt | German
Laura Guidetti | Italian
Cristina Rodríguez
Fischer | Spanish

Proofreading
Aymeric Lorenté | French
Melanie Wesselingh,
Oscar Zoetman, Renate
Schipper, and Simone
Bassie | Dutch
Britta Norris | German
Martina Torrione and
Roberta Curia | Italian
Iris Maher and Rodney
Bolt | English
Juan José Pérez Rubiño
and Paula Melchor Pérez
| Spanish

Typesetting
Juliane Steinbrecher

Reproductions
Marc Gijzen

Printing and Binding
Westermann Druck
Zwickau GmbH

Cover
Carol Guzy, ZUMA Press,
iWitness, for *Miami Herald*

Back cover
Victor J. Blue, for *The
New York Times Magazine*

Published by
Hatje Cantz Verlag
GmbH
Mommsenstraße 27
10629 Berlin / Germany
www.hatjecantz.com
A Ganske Publishing
Group Company

Copyright © 2026
Stichting World Press
Photo, Amsterdam, the
Netherlands
www.worldpressphoto.org
© 2026 Hatje Cantz,
Germany, and the authors

All photography copy-
rights are held by the
photographers.

978-3-7757-6214-4

Printed in Germany

World Press Photo
World Press Photo, foun-
ded in 1955, is an independent, non-profit organization based in Amsterdam,
the Netherlands.

#WPPh2026

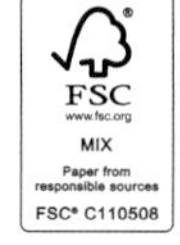

Patron
HRH Prince Constantijn
of the Netherlands

Executive Director
Joumana El Zein Khoury

Communications
Charlotte Zajicek
Emmy Dexel
Mathilde Beck
Mariana Ferro
Olga Karavasili
Rae Alexander

Curatorial Affairs
Beatrice Harbour
Inji Kim
Marika Cukrowski
Noa Wassink
Victoria de Quadros
Zeynep Özçelik

**Exhibitions and
Fundraising**
Alba Noguera
Anouk Jolly
Arthur Sigu
Babette Warendorf
Ben Camus
Bori Bálint
Lennart Bak
Mariana Rettore Baptista
Martha Echevarría
Raphael Dias e Silva

Programs
Anita Huynh
Anna Kućma
Anna Lena Mehr
Csenge Nagy-György
Mercedes Almagro Ocaña
Naomi Purswani
Noor Chehabeddine
Panagiota Dimitrakopoulou
Saba Moshtagh Askary

**Office, Human
Resources, and Finance**
Adrienne Schneider
Erik Jager
Joke Snoek
Marijn Beneder
Milou Scholing
Pieterbas Kist

Supervisory Board
Chair:
Dr Janne E. Nijman
Ilvy Njiokiktjien
Jamila Aanzi
Lara Luten
Marc Diepstraten
Marc Prüst
Yoka Brandt

**International Advisory
Committee**
Chair:
John Fleetwood
Mark Sealy
Newsha Tavakolian
Tanvi Mishra

Supporters
The World Press Photo
Foundation appreciates
the support of all its
partners, funders,
individual donors
and legacy donors.

Strategic Partners
Nationale Postcode Loterij
FUJIFILM

Partners
Stichting Dioraphte
Stichting Democratie &
Media
Rutgers & Posch
Pictoright Fonds
Porticus
Stichting Maanwater
Gieskes Strijbis Fonds

Official Suppliers
EPAM
HDV visual branding
Kleurgamma
VISE Logistics

Media Partners
Alexandra Fanning
Communications
Mirandola Comunicazione
Studio Nicola Jeffs